LIBRARY OF HEBREW BIBLE/
OLD TESTAMENT STUDIES

456

Formerly Journal for the Study of the Old Testament Supplement Series

IMAGINING THE OTHER
AND CONSTRUCTING ISRAELITE IDENTITY
IN THE EARLY SECOND TEMPLE PERIOD

Edited by

Ehud Ben Zvi and Diana V. Edelman

Bloomsbury T&T Clark
An imprint of Bloomsbury Publishing Plc

B L O O M S B U R Y
LONDON · OXFORD · NEW YORK · NEW DELHI · SYDNEY

Bloomsbury T&T Clark

An imprint of Bloomsbury Publishing Plc

50 Bedford Square	1385 Broadway
London	New York
WC1B 3DP	NY 10018
UK	USA

www.bloomsbury.com

Bloomsbury and the Diana logo are trademarks of Bloomsbury Publishing Plc

First published 2014
Paperback edition first published 2016

British Library Cataloguing-in-Publication Data

A catalogue record for this book is available from the British Library.

ISBN: HB: 978-0-56724-872-5
PB: 978-0-56766-752-6
ePDF: 978-0-56765-534-9

Library of Congress Cataloging-in-Publication Data

Imagining the other and constructing Israelite identity in the early Second Temple period /
edited by Ehud Ben Zvi and Diana V. Edelman.
pages cm – (Library of Hebrew Bible / Old Testament studies ; 456)
ISBN 978-0-567-24872-5 (hardback)
1. Ethnicity in the Bible–Congresses.   2. Group identity–Congresses.
3. Ethnoarchaeology–Congresses.   4. Jews–Identity–Congresses.
5. Identity (Philosophical concept)–Congresses   I. Ben Zvi, Ehud, 1951- editor.
II. Edelman, Diana Vikander, 1954- editor.

BS1199.E84143   2014
221.8'3058–dc23

2014031796

Typeset by Forthcoming Publications Ltd (www.forthpub.com)

CONTENTS

Abbreviations   vii
List of Contributors   xi

INTRODUCTION
   Diana V. Edelman   xiii

THE OTHER:
SOCIOLOGICAL PERSPECTIVES IN A POSTCOLONIAL AGE
   Jeremiah W. Cataldo   1

OTHERING, SELFING, 'BOUNDARYING' AND 'CROSS-BOUNDARYING'
AS INTERWOVEN WITH SOCIALLY SHARED MEMORIES:
SOME OBSERVATIONS
   Ehud Ben Zvi   20

YHWH'S OTHERING OF ISRAEL
   Diana V. Edelman   41

CATEGORICAL IDENTITIES:
'ETHNIFIED OTHERNESS AND SAMENESS'—
A TOOL FOR UNDERSTANDING BOUNDARY NEGOTIATION
IN THE PENTATEUCH?
   Kåre Berge   70

NATIVES AND IMMIGRANTS IN THE SOCIAL IMAGINATION
OF THE HOLINESS SCHOOL
   Mark G. Brett   89

GENDER AND IDENTITY IN THE BOOK OF NUMBERS
   Claudia V. Camp   105

WOMEN ON THE EDGE
   Carey Walsh   122

RUTH: A BORN-AGAIN ISRAELITE?
ONE WOMAN'S JOURNEY THROUGH SPACE AND TIME
     Anne-Mareike Wetter   144

OVERCOMING OTHERNESS IN THE BOOK OF RUTH
     Robert L. Cohn   163

IMAGINED AND FORGOTTEN COMMUNITIES:
OTHERING IN THE STORY OF JOSIAH'S REFORM (2 KINGS 23)
     Terje Stordalen   182

JONAH AND THE OTHER:
A DISCOURSE ON INTERPRETATIVE COMPETENCE
     Susanne Gillmayr-Bucher   201

DENIAL, DECEPTION, OR FORCE: HOW TO DEAL
WITH POWERFUL OTHERS IN THE BOOK OF ESTHER
     Jean-Daniel Macchi   219

IMAGINING THE OTHER IN THE CONSTRUCTION
OF JUDAHITE IDENTITY IN EZRA–NEHEMIAH
     Tamara Cohn Eskenazi   230

PHINEHAS AND THE OTHER PRIESTS IN BEN SIRA
AND 1 MACCABEES
     Tobias Funke   257

DISABILITY, IDENTITY, AND OTHERNESS IN PERSIAN-PERIOD
ISRAELITE THOUGHT
     Rebecca Raphael   277

THE OTHER OTHERS:
A QUMRAN PERSPECTIVE ON DISABILITY
     Anke Dorman   297

Index of References   317
Index of Authors   331

ABBREVIATIONS

AB	Anchor Bible
ABiG	Arbeiten zur Bibel und ihrer Geschichte
AnBib	Analecta biblica
ANEM	Ancient Near Eastern Monographs
AOAT	Alter Orient und Altes Testament
AThANT	Abhandlungen zur Theologie des Alten und Neuen Testaments
BAR	*Biblical Archaeology Review*
BASOR	*Bulletin of the American Schools of Oriental Research*
BDB	Francis Brown, S. R. Driver and Charles A. Briggs, *A Hebrew and English Lexicon of the Old Testament* (Oxford: Clarendon Press, 1907)
BETL	Bibliotheca ephemeridum theologicarum lovaniensium
Bib	*Biblica*
BibInt	*Biblical Interpretation*
BKAT	Biblischer Kommentar: Altes Testament
BN	*Biblische Notizen*
BThSt	Biblisch Theologische Studien
BWANT	Beiträge zur Wissenschaft vom Alten und Neuen Testament
BZ	*Biblische Zeitschrift*
BZAR	Beihefte zur *Zeitschrift fur altoreintalische und Biblische Rechtgeschichte*
BZAW	Beihefte zur *Zeitschrift für die alttestamentliche Wissenschaft*
BZNW	Beihefte zur *Zeitschrift fur die neutestamentliche Wissenschaft und die Kunde der alteren Kirche*
CBET	Contributions to Biblical Exegesis and Theology
CBQ	*Catholic Bible Quarterly*
CCRMS	Cross-Cultural Research and Methodology Series
DCH	Clines, D. J. A. (ed.), *The Dictionary of Classical Hebrew* (9 vols.; Sheffield: Sheffield Academic Press and Sheffield Phoenix Press, 1993–2011)
EASA	European Association of Social Anthropology
EHS.T	Europäische Hochschulschriften
ESHM	European Seminar in Historical Methodology
FAT	Forschungen zum Alten Testament
FAT II	Forschungen zum Alten Testament II
FCB	The Feminist Companion to the Bible

FRLANT	Forschungen zur Religion und Literatur des Alten und Neuen Testaments
GCTS	Gender, Culture, and Theory Series
HALOT	Koehler, L., W. Baumgartner, and J. J. Stamm, *The Hebrew and Aramaic Lexicon of the Old Testament* (translated and edited under the supervision of M. E. J. Richardson; 4 vols.; Leiden: Brill, 1994–99)
HBS	Herders biblische Studien
HSM	Harvard Semitic Monographs
HTR	*Harvard Theological Review*
ICC	International Critical Commentary
Int	*Interpretation*
JBL	*Journal of Biblical Literature*
JHS	*Journal of Hebrew Scriptures*
JPS	Jewish Publication Society
JSJSup	*Journal for the Study of Judaism*, Supplement
JSNTSup	*Journal for the Study of the New Testament*, Supplement Series
JSOT	*Journal for the Study of the Old Testament*
JSOTSup	*Journal for the Study of the Old Testament*, Supplement Series
JTS	*Journal of Theological Studies*
KAT	Kommentar zum Alten Testament
LHBOTS	Library of Hebrew Bible/Old Testament Studies
LSJ	Liddell, H. G., R. Scott, H. S. Jones, R. McKenzie, *A Greek–English Lexicon* (9th ed. with revised supplement; Oxford: Oxford University Press, 1996)
LXX	Septuagint
MACO	Monografías sobre el Antiguo Cercano Oriente
OBO	Orbis Biblicus et Orientalis
OENEA	Meyers, E. M. (ed.), *Oxford Encyclopedia of Near Eastern Archaeology* (New York: Oxford University Press, 1996)
OTL	Old Testament Library
OTM	Oxford Theological Monographs
OTS	*Oudtestamentische Studiën*
PTSDSSP	Princeton Theological Seminary Dead Sea Scrolls Project
QD	Questiones Disputatae
RB	*Revue biblique*
RevQ	*Revue de Qumran*
SBL	Society of Biblical Literature
SBLDS	Society of Biblical Literature Dissertation Series
SBLMS	Society of Biblical Literature Monograph Series
SBLSymS	Society of Biblical Literature Symposium Series
SBS	Stuttgarter Bibelstudien
SJOT	*Scandinavian Journal of the Old Testament*
STDJ	Studies on the Texts of the Desert of Judah
ThG	*Theologie der Gegenwart*

UTB	Uni-Taschenbücher
VT	*Vetus Testamentum*
VTSup	*Vetus Testamentum,* Supplements
WBC	Word Biblical Commentary
WUNT	Wissenschaftliche Untersuchungen zum Neuen Testament
ZAR	*Zeitschrift für altorientalische und biblische Rechtgeschichte*
ZAW	*Zeitschrift für die alttestamentliche Wissenschaft*
ZDPV	*Zeitschrift des deutschen Palästina-Vereins*

CONTRIBUTORS

Ehud Ben Zvi
University of Alberta

Kåre Berge,
NLA University College

Mark G. Brett
Whitley College, University of Divinity, Melbourne

Claudia V. Camp
Texas Christian University

Jeremiah W. Cataldo
Grand Valley State University

Robert L. Cohn
Lafayette College

Anke Dorman
University of Zurich

Diana V. Edelman
*Research Associate, Department of Near and Middle Eastern Studies
Trinity College, Dublin*

Tamara Cohn Eskenazi
Hebrew Union College – Jewish Institute of Religion

Tobias Funke
University of Leipzig

Susanne Gillmayr-Bucher
Katholisch-Theologische Privatuniversität Linz (KTU)

Jean-Daniel Macchi
University of Geneva

Rebecca Raphael
Texas State University

Terje Stordalen
Faculty of Theology, University of Oslo

Carey Walsh
Villanova University

Anne-Mareike Wetter
Utrecht University

INTRODUCTION

Diana V. Edelman

The present volume grew out of two sessions of papers and an ensuing substantial discussion dedicated to the theme 'Imagining the Other and Constructing Israelite Identity' that were organized by the research group, 'Israel and the Production and Reception of Authoritative Books in the Persian and Hellenistic Period' (co-chaired by Ehud Ben Zvi and me) that took place at the 2011 meeting of the European Association of Biblical Scholars in Thessaloniki, Greece.

The theme was selected for two reasons. The first was the sense that a conversation involving multiple perspectives, bringing together different types of Othering, and conducted using various methodological approaches, would be particularly helpful within the field. The second was the intrinsic interest of the topic. In the early Second Temple period, imagining the Other was a continual process deeply involved in and crucially facilitating ongoing negotiations and re-negotiations of identity, which, in itself, is a 'problematic' concept. At the same time, such imagining involved negotiating and re-negotiating substantial aspects of social constructions concerning the inner organization of 'normal', at times shaping forms of its hierarchy and associated conceptualizations. As such, Othering was deeply associated with socio-cognitive processes, with social mindscapes, and, often, with mnemonic narratives that served to explore and communicate the former.

Texts are a main, though problematic, 'source' for studying these matters, and we have devoted our sessions and our volume to examples of Othering in texts. As per the mandate of the research group, we have focused on texts that were read and reread as authoritative by the late Persian or early Hellenistic period, but we still have considered it important to include essays that deal with materials from Qumran, Sira, 1 Maccabees, and Esther.

Following our initial discussions, the editors contacted additional colleagues with expertise on these matters, and although neither this volume nor any volume can even attempt to be comprehensive, this collection succeeds in addressing a wide range of Othering processes, including processes involving the social construction of gender and disability. The essays draw on a range of interdisciplinary approaches informed by insights from sociology, anthropology, philosophy, social psychology, social memory, gender studies, post-colonial studies, disability studies, ethnicity studies, and historical and literary studies. Readers will easily notice shared and sometimes unshared threads, dialogues that have opened up between and among the essays, and the multiple ways in which the various contributions inform each other.

One subset of essays within this volume focuses on Otherness within the group, which establishes grades of membership status over against the stranger or foreigner, who is different at a distance (Cataldo, Camp, Stordalen, Brett, Funke, Raphael, and Dorman). A second subset focuses on examples that explore in-group boundary permeability or fuzziness (Ben Zvi, Wetter, Cohn, and Walsh), and a third subset looks at the dynamics of corporate, in-group identity in relation to outside groups (Edelman, Berge, Gillmayr-Bucher, Macchi, and Eskenazi). However, the boundaries between these groups are very permeable, and some essays could be included in more than one subset.

Following traditional genre conventions, this collection opens with the most 'theoretical' essay. It is followed by chapters that deal with examples across a wide range of texts. Since disability studies is a relative newcomer to Biblical Studies and since the editors are convinced that it carries a very strong potential, the two chapters addressing this theme were chosen to conclude the volume, to draw particular attention to them.

To whet the appetite of the reader, a brief abstract of each contribution follows. The collection opens with Jeremiah W. Cataldo, 'The Other: Sociological Perspectives in a Post-Colonial Age'. This essay explores concepts of the Other, human and divine, and Othering among theorists from philosophy, psychology, and sociology, including Slavoj Žižek, Alain Touraine, Gilles Deleuze, Michel Foucault, Emmanuel Lévinas, and Melanie Klein, in addition to drawing on work done in the fields of post-colonial and feminist studies. He uses Ezra–Nehemiah throughout to illustrate various concepts from a biblical perspective.

This contribution is followed by the essay of the co-editor of the volume, Ehud Ben Zvi ('Othering, Selfing, "Boundarying" and "Cross-Boundarying" as Interwoven with Socially Shared Memories: Some Observations'). Ben Zvi explores here important sites of memories and mnemonic narratives that were interwoven to create in-between realms that included both the partial Israelitization of Others and partial Otherization of Israel. Ben Zvi notes that not all biblical systems of categorization are based on a simple, clear-cut Us vs. Them principle and proceeds to examine multiple examples where a generative grammar of reciprocal mirroring that creates discursively contingent rather than categorical Othering has been employed. He notes that Othering can also take place along an axis of gender and of disability in addition to one of a construed ethno-cultural group and provides additional examples. Mirroring strategies cut across boundaries defining insider and outsiders and evoke porousness and 'fuzziness' while maintaining a grammar of rejection.

Ben Zvi's contribution is followed by my own essay ('YHWH's Othering of Israel'). I examine threats attributed to YHWH across the corpus of the Hebrew Bible to Other Israel against a wider perspective of collectivist social psychology. I identify four strategies used by the biblical writers to establish in-group identity that includes YHWH as a corporate member and then note how all four are also used to threaten ostracism or termination of the in-group. A fifth Othering category that derives from the universalization of YHWH is also considered, which has no corresponding form of in-group formation.

Then Kåre Berge ('Categorical Identities: "Ethnified Otherness and Sameness"—A Tool for Understanding Boundary Negotiation in the Pentateuch?') explores the creation in the Pentateuch of a political category of residual minorities, typified as the Canaanites, in relation to 'the people' who constitute the nation of Israel. He notes, like Ben Zvi, the ambivalence toward the Other, especially in Genesis, where such residual minorities can be viewed positively and behave like insiders. In Deuteronomy, the annihilation of the Canaanites is a necessary precursor to a 'sacred beginning' as well as a pedagogical example of the fate awaiting those who fail to follow Torah. He emphasizes that in both Genesis and Deuteronomy, the relation between Israel and the nations does not correspond to 'categorical identity' proposed by the modern social theorist Eric Hobsbawm, even as modified by sociologists Anthony D. Smith and Thomas Scheff and anthropologist Michael M. J. Fischer but rather, to 'relational identity', as described by Craig Calhoun. While modern social theory that tends to emphasize externally oriented 'powering' is not fully applicable to many ancient societies, the current emphasis on the role of sentiment in shaping nationality is and should inform future studies in our field.

Mark G. Brett ('Natives and Immigrants in the Social Imagination of the Holiness School') surmises that the policy on 'native' in the Holiness Code, which introduces a new vocabulary, must stem from a need to articulate a new understanding of the relationship between land and identity that had not been present in earlier, Deuteronomistic theology, due to a new set of problems about the legitimacy of land possession. The phrase 'people of the land' must already have taken on negative connotations that prevented it from expressing a sense of equity between native and immigrant. The H editors of the Persian period were imagining new ways to express religious and economic integration via permeable social boundaries that would allow a reconciliation of the peoples of the land who never went into exile with the 'children of the *golah*', while at the same time opening possibilities for including the surrounding *goyim* as both land-owners and participants in the cult.

Claudia Camp ('Gender and Identity in the Book of Numbers') initiates a gender and identity-critical reading of the book of Numbers and argues that such a reading is crucial for understanding the construction/s of identity and authority in the Second Temple period. She systematically critiques the specific ways that subordination is represented in the book and how gender construction intersects with other identity-construction mechanisms, particularly priestly identity, to inform the limits of, and hierarchy within, 'Israelite' identity.

Carey Walsh ('Women on the Edge') explores how Rahab, Jael, Ruth, Jezebel, Esther, and Vashti are used by male scribes in an open system able to incorporate and instruct on difference to explore the laudatory value of circumventing boundaries and listening to marginalized women. She employs both feminist and post-colonial theory in her quest to analyze how these womanly figures exercise power to gain insight into negotiating within hegemonic systems from places of vulnerability and risk.

The next two contributions deal with Ruth, a book and a mnemonic character of widely acknowledged relevance for the theme of this volume. Anne-Mareike Wetter ('Ruth: A Born-Again Israelite? One Woman's Journey') explores the criteria defining Israelite identity in the book of Ruth and if and how, in the story world, it is possible to change ethnic identity. Drawing on ethnicity theory, she identifies the concept of *ḥesed* and the willingness to leave the safety of one's home in order to build the house of Israel, both of which Ruth enacts with Naomi and Boaz, as specific Israelite markers of solidarity and common culture. This leads the community of Bethlehem to accept her as an insider, providing her with a common proper name, a myth of common ancestry, and shared historical memories. In theory, such an ethnic cross-over must have been conceivable in the world behind the text.

Robert L. Cohn ('Overcoming Otherness in the Book of Ruth') uses literary and anthropological theory to understand how Ruth goes from Moabite Other to an insider Israelite, offering an example of inclusive Israelite identity over against a more exclusive identity in the books of Ezra and Nehemiah. He explores the rhetorical strategy within the narrative centering on interrogations concerning identity and then Ruth's intertextual and exegetical role as a commentary on Torah narrative and law, playing off the stories of Lot's daughters (Gen. 19.30-38) and the birth of Perez, Boaz's forebear (Gen. 38.27-29), as a type scene of the tale of a young woman who seduces an older man in order to preserve the man's family line. Finally, he looks at social processes of identity formation in the real world that take place in liminal space, which he thinks best suits the understanding of the book's author, who charts some of the dynamics of this later rite of passage in the likely absence of a formal rite of conversion.

The next contribution is by Terje Stordalen, who uses social memory as a lens to study 'Imagined and Forgotten Communities: Othering in the Story of Josiah's Reform (2 Kings 23)'. He explores how Josiah's remembered reform in 2 Kings 23 would have been understood and used in the early Persian period to model correct behaviour for current and future members of the community. Those who do not conform to the formalities and beliefs of the newly emerging religion, who continue to engage in ancestor worship in the Kidron and Hinnom valleys, will be considered Other and forgotten, like those in the story world who engaged in what was deemed to be 'illicit' religious practices and who were literarily silenced by and forgotten in the wake of the actual or imagined reforms.

From Jerusalem to the Mediterranean Sea and to Nineveh. Susanne Gillmayr-Bucher ('Jonah and the Other: A Discourse on Interpretative Competence') approaches the character of Jonah as an example of a reluctant 'prophet to the nations' and examines the sense of Other that emerges in the book. In contrast to the 'oracles concerning the nations' in other prophetic books, in Jonah the assimilation of Others takes the form of nations finding salvation without being destroyed or included within a Zion-centred worldview. YHWH cares for all creatures and people; Nineveh repents, changes it behaviour, but does not convert to YHWH.

Jean-Daniel Macchi ('Denial, Deception or Force: How to Deal with Powerful Others') focuses on different strategies of resistance that reflect insider Othering of the imperial power explored in various versions of the book of Esther. Three options for resistance are presented: refusal to comply, the use of cunning and courage, and the use of force. Macchi then notes that divergent textual traditions endorse differing strategies; the earliest Greek Alpha text, probably written in the Ptolemaic period among the Judaean Diaspora in Egypt, omits the massacre of Jewish enemies and the inability to change Persian law. It assumes openness to collaboration with the imperial power. The Hebrew MT text, which includes the final massacre and an inalterable Persian law, would seem to reflect a rewriting in the Hasmonaean period in Jerusalem, where opposition to the foreign imperial power at any cost, including war, was deemed necessary for survival. The LXX presupposes a parent text close to the MT. Thus, the book represents diverse insider responses to dealing with imperial Others within the larger Jewish community in different periods and places.

Tamara Cohn Eskenazi ('Imagining the Other in the Construction of Judahite Identity in Ezra–Nehemiah') explores how the book of Ezra–Nehemiah reconstructs an identity for the community living in the territory of Judah in the Persian period. In a three-part movement from Ezra 1–6 to Ezra 7–10 and then to Nehemiah 1–7, the book 'traces three journeys from exile and Diaspora to Judah'. It begins with an identity for the label יהודים ('Judahites') based on geography, designating any-one associated with the region of the hills of Judah in the present or the past. Then, after an encounter with hostile Others, the further, decisive restriction is added of anyone committed to God and Torah, which requires separation from the people(s) of the land(s). In Nehemiah 1–7 a final necessary marker of the new group identity is asserted: a level of politico-religious self-determination. YHWH's home expands from the temple mount to the entire city, spreading holiness throughout, so that only in completing the building of the temple, the city walls, and the inhabitants of Jerusalem is the new group identity as a holy community committed to YHWH's *torah* and temple finalized.

Tobias Funke ('Phinehas and the Other Priests in Ben Sira and 1 Maccabees') leads us to later communities that considered themselves as standing in continuity with those of the late Persian/early Hellenistic period. He examines strategies used by various priestly lines to legiti-mate the combination of profane and cultic power in the office of high priest in the Hellenistic period and to vie for internal power against other priestly groups. By comparing the use of Aaron, David, and Phinehas in the biblical texts with uses in both the Hebrew and Greek versions of Ben Sira and Maccabees, he is able to analyze the differences and identify the shifts in stress by the later writers. The Hebrew book of Ben Sira probably reflects a pro-Oniad stance, which saw them to be of Aaronide lineage and deliberately distanced them from Levitical traditions and rival priestly lines. The deletion of Phinehas in the Greek version of Ben Sira implies that a pro-Maccabean author suppressed the connection between the Oniads and the Maccabees so Phinehas could represent the Maccabees alone, while the composition also could voice a harsher tone toward Samaria, which traced its priestly ancestry to Phinehas.

The first of the two concluding contributions that draw attention to disability studies and its substantial contribution to the matters discussed here is Rebecca Raphael, 'Disability, Identity, and Otherness in Persian Period Israelite Thought'. She uses insights from disability studies to discuss in particular intersections between the ability/disability axis and religio-cultural identity as articulated in biblical texts set or likely composed in the Persian period. She moves from the central category of 'defect' in P texts to an examination of texts dealing with health, illness, physical impairment, and social disability in 1–2 Chronicles, Proverbs, Job, Zechariah 1–8, Ezekiel, and Second Isaiah. As was common in the wider ancient Near East, deficits of the senses and congenital variations of the body's form that had not resulted from warfare or other violence were thought to derive from divine action. Differences in emphasis for the motivation for such divine impairment are apparent in the range of writings examined, with two predominant pathways of embodiment: a Judaism centred on sacrificial cult and another centred on devotion to verbal performance, oral or textual. Both were imaginative and ideal constructions in response to the loss of the monarchic-era temple but continued in use once the temple was reconstructed.

The final essay in this collection continues the focus on Othering and disability and deals also with a community later than those of the late Persian/early Hellenistic period, but one that is very different from those studied by Tobias Funke. Anke Dorman ('The Other Others: A Qumran Perspective on Disability') seeks to understand the membership status of those with disabilities in the Qumran community as reflected in the Dead Sea Scrolls. She is able to establish levels of membership that allowed those who exhibited various disabilities, including blindness, deafness, deformity, or visible skin disease, to belong to the community and be considered 'holy' but then also be disqualified from attending the assembly and the annual Feast of Weeks because they were not holy or qualified *enough* to mix with the holy angels who were present in the congregation. The community's rules and views are built upon the rules that exclude disabled priests from officiating in Lev. 21.16-23. Texts that attribute a profaning quality to disability are the *Rule of the Congregation* (1QSa), the *Damascus Document* (CD) written by a related group, and the rules in the *Temple Scroll* (11QTᵃ), which likely applied rules against the blind and anyone with ritual impurities to prohibit pilgrims from entering the city of YHWH. The War Scroll excludes the disabled from participation in the final war at the end of time for practical, not ritual reasons, and MMT similarly excludes blind and deaf priests from working due to the limitation in functional capability caused by disability, not because of assumed impurity.

All in all, this is a collection that carries multiple voices and approaches and which addresses a wide variety of texts and contexts, all of which are brought to bear on each other so as to produce a multi-faceted reconstruction of various processes of Othering and their social, ideological, cultural, and mnemonic roles in ancient Israel. No single scholar, no matter how knowledgeable and gifted she or he may be, could have produced this multiplicity and the ensuing conversations, which were the primary goals the editors set out to accomplish in this volume. It is our hope that readers will join the conversation and add to the existing multiple voices, so all of us may increase our understanding of these matters.

THE OTHER:
SOCIOLOGICAL PERSPECTIVES IN A POSTCOLONIAL AGE

Jeremiah W. Cataldo

...because no political act can claim a direct foundation in some transcendent figure of the big Other (of the 'we are just instruments of a higher necessity or will' type) because every act involves the risk of a contingent decision, nobody has the right to impose his choice on others—which means that every collective choice has to be democratically legitimized.[1]

The Other as a Sociological Concept

Who or what is the Other? An object? A category? A role or position? Other? Within sociology, the Other may be considered an object of knowledge, so much so that sociology itself is the study of society as an object of knowledge: 'a set of interdependent mechanisms', writes A. Touraine, 'ensuring the integration or combination of mutually opposed elements: the individualism of actors and the internalization of institutional norms in the service of collective integration'.[2] Of course, Touraine's description presumes a position that stems from a postcolonial rather than colonial approach to knowledge, even though the latter, which includes subjugating the Other through domination over the dominant systems and meanings of knowledge, still bears influence on modern postcolonial scholarship, even if only in the guise of paternalistic notions of protection.[3] After all, the Other is more often spoken for and

1. Slavoj Žižek, 'The Ongoing "Soft Revolution"', *Critical Inquiry* 30.2 (2004), pp. 292-323 (320).

2. Alain Touraine, 'Sociology After Sociology', *European Journal of Social Theory* 10.2 (2007), pp. 184-93 (184).

3. One need only consult Edward Said's impressive work, *Orientalism* (repr., New York: Vintage Books, 1994 [1979]), for a well-informed introduction to the entrenched influences that Orientalism has had upon academic and other cultures. On 'paternalistic notions of protection', see also Uday Chandra, 'Liberalism and Its Other: The Politics of Primitivism in Colonial and Postcolonial Indian Law', *Law & Society Review* 47.1 (2013), pp. 135-68. In addition, see Esther Fuchs, who argues that even neoliberal feminism is guilty of the same fundamental dichotomies that

defined rather than heard. And our readings of the biblical texts can really only hope to reconstruct the Other through interpretations of this Other by authors who assume dominant positions over her. In postcolonial scholarship, the Other—and perhaps it is best that we invoke the noncommittal phrase, 'in theory'—is less the exotic and mysterious colonial Oriental (although, as implied above, artefacts of that view still remain)[4] who necessarily must be subjugated to and civilized by a 'superior' law, but the other side of an *active* relation in which the subject identifies himself, or expresses her identity.[5] In that, the Other still necessitates a corresponding, defined subject against which identification occurs through processes of difference and distinction. Or, in the words of S. Handelman, ' "otherness" is usually accompanied by the notion of a "radical rupture" which subverts closed identities and all-encompassing systems'.[6] In that sense, identities and systems resist closing because they are always engaging, responding, projecting, and rejecting as expressions of themselves. Correspondingly, reading the biblical texts through a postcolonial lens exposes presuppositions of a (closed) dominant position before the Other as 'foreigner', 'sinner', 'woman', and 'gay', or other. It exposes presuppositions that are themselves relics or artefacts of an imperialist-minded culture with a heavy hand in shaping the traditional paradigms of modern biblical scholarship.[7]

characterize paternalistic Orientalism ('Reclaiming the Hebrew Bible for Women: The Neoliberal Turn in Contemporary Feminist Scholarship', *Journal for Feminist Studies in Religion* 24.2 [2008], pp. 45-65 [48-49]). See also Danna N. Fewell, 'Reading the Bible Ideologically: Feminist Criticism', in *To Each Its Own Meaning: An Introduction to Biblical Interpretations and Their Applications* (ed. Steven L. McKenzie and Steven R. Haynes; Louisville: Westminster John Knox, 1993), pp. 268-82 (275). And see also Rasiah S. Sugirtharajah, *Exploring Postcolonial Biblical Criticism: History, Method, Practice* (Chichester/Malden: Wiley-Blackwell, 2012), pp. 41-47. It is also important to note that most uses of the term 'colonialism' in the twentieth century and later often define it as a near synonym to 'imperialism'. For that reason, this chapter, following the decision of the *Stanford Encyclopedia of Philosophy*, will treat 'colonialism' as a broad term that refers to a project of political domination, one of whose direct influences is the European project from the sixteenth to the twentieth centuries CE.

4. See again Chandra, 'Liberalism and Its Other', pp. 135-68.

5. Fuchs offers a similar petition for poststructural feminism (see 'Reclaiming the Hebrew Bible', p. 48).

6. Susan Handelman, 'Facing the Other: Lévinas, Perelman and Rosenzweig', *Religion & Literature* 22.2/3 (1990), pp. 61-84 (61).

7. With an understanding that scholarship typically conflates any distinction between imperialism and colonialism, Sugirtharajah argues 'there has been a remarkable unwillingness to mention imperialism as shaping the contours of biblical scholarship' (*Exploring Postcolonial Criticism*, p. 25).

With that in mind, the following sections of this chapter identify a few of the influences upon perceptions of the Other in sociology as well as in biblical studies that draw upon sociological methods. Recent critical methods in biblical studies, for example, have largely defined the Other in one or more of the manners outlined in the following discussion. This general tendency is due not only to the ideological or cultural agendas of the Western, industrialized, biblical interpreter but also to the ideological agenda of the biblical authors, especially those of the Second Temple period. They (re)wrote a history that supported the political domination of a single community over the land of Palestine.[8] Ezra–Nehemiah's emphasis upon a division between *golah* and עם הארץ, 'the people of the land', embodies this claim; Ezra's redefinition of 'Israel' to mean the *golah* community alone (as can be inferred from 6.19-22) further emphasizes that point. Likewise, the prophetic emphasis upon the 'righteous community' invokes the same emphasis upon a dominant subject, whether real or hoped for (cf. Mic. 4.6-8; Zech. 8.13; 12.1-9). In short, there are parallels between the intent of the biblical author in his pursuit of a dominant position of socio-political authority expressed through processes of identification, categorization, and definition and the traditionally colonial position of the biblical interpreter. Those parallels, which often have resulted in an emphasis upon 'Israelite' as the divinely chosen identity, have offered ready justification for more colonial perspectives on both the Bible and the interpreter's 'authoritative' position before the broader socio-political world. This latter position has been manifest at times, for example, in Zionism, including so-called Christian Zionism, which is a uniquely U.S., Christian variant of the former; both have had an unavoidable influence upon Western biblical scholarship.

The Causality of Difference in Identifying the Other

Otherness necessitates difference. After all, according to G. Deleuze it is the causalities of difference that generate the foundation for society.[9] We are recognizable as ourselves because we recognize that we are different from someone or something else. To be clear, difference is a process, an

---

8. As I have argued in detail in *A Theocratic Yehud? Issues of Government in Yehud* (LHBOTS, 498; London: T&T Clark International, 2009).

9. Claire Colebrook describes Deleuze's work thus: 'From his earliest work in philosophy to his engagements with politics, art and culture, Deleuze insisted on the prehuman problem. What are the forces, differences, processes or (to use his term) "syntheses" which produce recognizable entities such as human beings or political classes?' (*Understanding Deleuze* [Crows Nest: Allen & Unwin, 2002], p. xl).

ongoing process, and not a static thing. Nor is it even a passive process, as though there were creation and then, the moment following the creative act, the original difference was frozen so as to moor all variations of identity to that singular act—a belief that has shaped the overly dichotomized worldview of monotheism. Consequently, recognition of difference (assuming a human society or culture in contrast to other organisms) produces new processes of socio-political engagement. Deleuze refers to this as 'interruptions': 'A machine may be defined as a system of interruptions or breaks. These breaks should in no way be considered as a separation from reality; rather, they operate along lines that vary according to whatever aspect of them we are considering.'[10]

When Ezra–Nehemiah tells of how the *golah* community separated itself from the עם הארץ, and when it *articulated* a seemingly impermeable distinction between the two groups (cf. Ezra 4.5; 9.1-4; 10.30-31), the text both drew upon previously defined categories in identity and produced a new paradigm for socio-political engagement by interrupting previous relations of engagement. Along these lines, Nehemiah's rejection of Tobiah, Sanballat, et al. (Neh. 2.19-20) *makes sense* only within a new paradigm framed by Ezra's so-called Mosaic Law—one presuming the identification of a new social-political body. As Deleuze argues, the production of difference is the very process upon which the uniformity of a society is based. The forces that produce social cohesion are the same as those that preserve difference so that a single group is identifiable in its distinction from others. But—and here is where Ezra–Nehemiah is caught—as part of this distinction necessary in identity, differences must be preserved or canonized within the collective memory of the group. It is only through a slowing down of the production of difference, according to Deleuze, that we perceive things.[11] We see, interpret, and understand in relation to ourselves, and we often assume a preserved, codified, legitimated system of categorical knowledge. This assumption has resulted in the 'freezing' of the 'other' as an objective, categorizable, subjugatable role or position.

Deleuze maintains that individual and social consciousness is a product of the recognition of an original difference. 'Difference is this state in which determination takes the form of unilateral distinction'.[12] Prior to that distinction, however, the indeterminate univocality of Being must

10. Gilles Deleuze and Félix Guattari, *Anti-Oedipus: Capitalism and Schizophrenia* (Minneapolis: University of Minnesota Press, 2005), p. 36.

11. As described by Colebrook (*Understanding Deleuze*, p. 34).

12. Gilles Deleuze, *Difference and Repetition* (New York: Columbia University Press, 1994), p. 28.

generate difference from within itself.[13] There is no recognition of self, no concept of I (or We) without difference. Or, in terms closer to our intent here, the self-aware subject necessitates the Other as a contrasting foil. That, in any case, is the monotheistic assumption that overshadows the face of biblical studies: the emphasis upon existence (and being) generated by a fundamental difference between Creator and created.[14] Where difference was seen traditionally as derivative of identity, Deleuze inverts the paradigm and argues that identities are effects and affects of perceived differences. 'It is said', Deleuze observes, 'that difference is negativity, that it extends or must extend to the point of contradiction once it is taken to the limit. This is true only to the extent that difference is already placed on a path or along a thread laid out by identity.'[15] Given the natural tendency toward distinction and repetition of differences, Deleuze argues that being is necessarily self-creating and always differentiating. 'All life is constant becoming, including inorganic, organic and even virtual life. We need to do away with the idea that nature merely *is* while man *decides* his being.'[16] Ontologically, the Other manifests itself through repetition of Being;[17] the Other represents 'centres of envelopment which testify to the presence of individuating factors'.[18] The Other is individual, different, expressive of a distinction from the Self or the I of the subject.[19] 'The Other cannot be separated from the expressivity which constitutes it. Even when we consider the body of another as an object, its ears and eyes as anatomical pieces, we do not remove all expressivity from them even though we simplify in the extreme the world they express...'[20] The Other, then, does not fit within the dominant–normative (hetero- or otherwise) system. It represents possibility outside the dominant structure while still being very much dependent upon the

13. Deleuze, *Difference and Repetition*, pp. 35-42. Note also, 'The essence of univocal Being is to include individuating differences, while these differences do not have the same essence and do not change the essence of being—just as white includes various intensities, while remaining essentially the same white... Being is said in a single and same sense of everything of which it is said, but that of which it is said differs: it is said of difference itself' (p. 36).

14. Cf. Jacques Berlinerblau, '"Poor Bird, Not Knowing Which Way to Fly": Biblical Scholarship's Marginality, Secular Humanism, and the Laudable Occident', *BibInt* 10 (2002), pp. 267-304.

15. Deleuze, *Difference and Repetition*, pp. 49-50.

16. Colebrook, *Understanding Deleuze*, p. xlii.

17. Deleuze, *Difference and Repetition*, p. 24.

18. Ibid., pp. 259-60.

19. Ibid., p. 260.

20. Ibid.

structure that defined it as external to the system itself.[21] 'The I and the Self, by contrast, are immediately characterized by functions of development or explication: not only do they experience qualities in general as already developed in the extensity of their system, but they tend to explicate or develop the world expressed by the other, either in order to participate in it or to deny it'.[22] The structure of the Other is an interiorization of difference—I am 'black', 'female', and 'gay' because I am not 'white', 'male', and 'straight'.[23] It is, to employ a biblical example, the עם הארץ actively and self-referentially defining itself as distinct, different, or foreign based on the qualities projected upon them by the *golah* community (cf. Ezra 4.1-4). Or, it is Judaean women interiorizing within their own identities 'not male' qualities (I am 'xx' because I am 'not xy'), which are qualities found in the margins of power, projected upon them in glorious phallic display by their male counterparts (cf. Ezra 10.44).[24]

It is this interiorization of difference that marks the Deleuzian approach to the Other. In contrast to the traditional colonial perspective of the Other as something exotic, barbarian, uncivilized, or lacking in civilized sophistication and intrinsically different, Deleuze appreciates difference as positive and productive. It is true that conflicts occur due to differences, and oppressions are seemingly legitimated due to differences: 'And I contended with them and cursed them and beat some of them and pulled out their hair; and I made them take an oath in the name of God, saying…' (Neh. 13.25). But those actions are attempts to *homogenize* difference, which is a tendency we see also within the monotheistic concept of the 'restoration' of a 'polluted' world.[25] But these attempts to resolve difference would simultaneously dismantle the basis of the Self/I/Subject, which cannot exist without a corresponding production of difference. Or, as Deleuze puts it, '[I]t is the Other-structure that ensures individuation within the perceptual world. It is not the I, nor the self: on the contrary, these need this structure in order to be perceived as individualities.'[26]

---

21. Deleuze, *Difference and Repetition*, p. 261.
22. Ibid., p. 260.
23. Ibid., p. 261.
24. See also Fuchs, who argues that women cannot be studied outside male power and hegemony ('Reclaiming the Hebrew Bible', pp. 51-52).
25. Compare the discussion of the necessity of a homogenous, categorical Other for monotheistic identity and its attendant dependence upon restoration in Jeremiah W. Cataldo, *Breaking Monotheism: Yehud and the Material Formation of Monotheistic Identity* (LHBOTS, 565; London: Bloomsbury T&T Clark, 2012), pp. 186-94.
26. Deleuze, *Difference and Repetition*, p. 281.

Deleuze's theory has not received a great deal of direct attention in Second Temple studies. In part, this is likely due to his dense prose[27] as well as his resistance to committing to a unified statement regarding difference and the Other. Moreover, a positivistic approach to difference often runs contrary to a prevailing emphasis upon the negativity of difference in biblical studies, which tends to focus on the Other and its consequent, perpetuated oppressions, whether ideological or physical. In addition, rather than an emphasis on the productive potential of difference, biblical studies retains a positivistic, to use the same word in a different context, emphasis on the correlation between the social world and the biblical text, which treats the text's silence on minorities as an artefact of the cultural world, leading readers to identify the Other through applications of inverted or negative analyses of the biblical texts.[28] Perhaps the biggest hurdle is the biblical text itself, the primary source of evidence, which was largely written with a homogenizing tendency and an overly critical and negative view of difference and the Other.[29] This has encouraged scholars to follow theories directly from or influenced by Hegel and Lacan, who focus on the negativity of difference.[30]

To be fair, it is difficult to view subjugation, oppression, marginalization, and any modern justification of such actions based on the biblical texts as productive. But perhaps what Deleuze can help us do is to see Other not as a reducible category of difference of the externalized, sometimes forcibly non-normative, even though it can include that. Instead, we might begin treating difference and Other less as presumed facticities, cultural or otherwise, and more as processes that are productive not only of desire, but that are also foundational parameters in *every* social relationship,[31] which makes possible a more comprehensive perception

27. There is an entire sub-discipline in philosophy devoted to deciphering Deleuze's theories.

28. Cf. John A. Coleman, 'Bible and Sociology', *Sociology of Religion* 60.2 (1999), pp. 125-48 (125-26).

29. Take, for example, Ezra–Nehemiah's treatment of the distinctions between the *golah* community and the *'am ha'aretz*. Regarding the status of women in the Bible, Carol Meyers writes, 'To begin with, the Bible as a whole is androcentric, or male-centered, in its subject matter, its authorship, and its perspectives' ('Everyday Life: Women in the Period of the Hebrew Bible', in *Women's Bible Commentary* [ed. Carol A. Newsom and Sharon H. Ringe; Louisville: Westminster John Knox, exp. edn, 1998], pp. 251-59 [251]).

30. See Colebook's discussion of the influence of Hegel and Lacan within Academia generally (*Understanding Deleuze*, p. 17).

31. Deleuze and Guattari work from a presupposition that desire is the foremost motivator in all living organisms (*Anti-Oedipus*, p. 269). In that, they are not far from Freud. Note also, for many feminist theorists, desire remains identified as a

of both cause and effect, of identity, of the Self, and of the qualities that make a social world and its agents unique. In short, it is treating Other as an active relationship within its social world that generates change and difference, whether positive or negative, within the normative of that world. It is this active relationship that shapes the parameters of the forces and means of production and, subsequently, power.[32] And let it be said here, if we were to follow Deleuze's prompting, we would lose the very concept of Other as a byproduct of hegemonic power or structure. Perhaps there would be some benefit to seeing ourselves as defined by a complex network of relations and reactions and of differences and distinctions.

The Other as the Body Upon Which Power Relations Are Written

For Foucault, Othering has everything to do with knowledge, or rather, with power acting through knowledge.[33] What facilitates the expression of power is the formation of objects in discourse, which is itself a complex system of relations.[34] In this sense, the Other is less an objective facticity in terms of preconceived, epistemological categories and more a permeable or even pliable object, a subjective body upon which discourses are written for the benefit of an author.[35] Foucault's emphasis

tool, an object, for use in the male hegemony of power (e.g. Harold Washington, 'Violence and the Construction of Gender in the Hebrew Bible: A New Historicist Approach', *BibInt* 5.4 [1997], pp. 324-63 [326]; Mieke Bal, *Loving Yusuf: Conceptual Travels From Present to Past* [Chicago: University of Chicago Press, 2008], p. 203).

32. Cf. Deleuze and Guattari, *Anti-Oedipus*, p. 263. Eve K. Sedgwick's discussion of shame as a process of individuation through relationality supports the assertion that production is shaped by relational actions (*Touching Feeling: Affect, Pedagogy, Performativity* [Series Q; Durham: Duke University Press, 2003], pp. 36-37).

33. Michel Foucault, *Discipline and Punish: The Birth of the Prison* (trans. A. M. Sheridan-Smith; New York: Vintage Books, 1995), p. 194.

34. Michel Foucault, *The Archaeology of Knowledge and the Discourse on Language* (trans. A. M. Sheridan-Smith; New York: Pantheon Books, 1972), pp. 43-44. Note also Stephen Moore, who writes, 'Foucault, for his part, shows how textual relations are imbricated with power relations; texts link up, not just with other texts, but with institutions, professions, systems of oppression, and so on' (*Poststructuralism and the New Testament: Derrida and Foucault At the Foot of the Cross* [Minneapolis: Fortress, 1994], p. 130).

35. One may be reminded of the feminist position that 'the personal is political', as quoted in Athalya Brenner, 'Who's Afraid of Feminist Criticism? Who's Afraid of Biblical Humour? The Case of the Obtuse Foreign Ruler in the Hebrew Bible', *JSOT* 19.3 (1994), pp. 38-55 (54).

on power as being not an object in itself but the consequence of discourses among interrelated individuals or bodies has largely permitted the dismantling of the preconceptions of a hegemonic power that have characterized, for our intent here, classical biblical studies, which took their lead from twentieth-century German Higher Criticism. Feminist studies, for example, have appreciated Foucault's emphasis upon the discursive nature of power and political economy as a way to liberate women by rewriting modern perceptions and presuppositions regarding discourses and relations of power. Power must not be understood as a negative thing or force but in terms of the relations and positions of social-political agents. The latter, according to Foucault, provides the basis for socio-political identity. For instance,

> [T]he body is also directly involved in a political field; power relations have an immediate hold upon it; they invest it, mark it, train it, torture it, force it to carry out tasks, to perform ceremonies, to emit signs. This political investment of the body is bound up, in accordance with complex reciprocal relations, with its economic use; it is largely as a force of production that the body is invested with relations of power and domination...[36]

The possibilities and the delimitations of a statement, idea, expression, or relation of power are determined by what Foucault identifies as the 'referential of the statement'.[37] There is an inference there that can be clarified by C. W. Mills: 'By justifying the arrangement of power and the ascendancy of the powerful, images and ideas transform power into authority'.[38] With specific reference to the Other, it is the referential space between the subject and the Other—either of which may be a person, institution, or other—that both defines them as subject and as Other and also determines the limits of possibility that identifies the relevant power relation. Foucault's theory permits a 'dismantling' of concepts of power from hegemonic, patriarchal structures that assume an inherent objectivity in power. Power, in this dismantled sense, can no longer be considered an objective facticity,[39] as though an object or idea that can be obtained and used for ulterior purposes. Instead, it is a process of regulation of behaviour and otherwise, based on referential positions between social-political agents.

36. Foucault, *Discipline and Punish*, pp. 25-26.
37. Foucault, *Archaeology of Knowledge*, p. 91.
38. Charles Wright Mills, *The Sociological Imagination* (Oxford: Oxford University Press, 2000), pp. 80-81.
39. By 'objective facticity' we mean that which is perceived to be objective within a given socio-cultural viewpoint.

Scholarly use of Foucault's theory has often emphasized the body of the victim in contrast to the victimizer, which betrays the colonial structure that remains a relic in academic discourse.[40] In such theoretical applications, the Other is that which has been victimized, subordinated for the purpose of emphasizing the dominant 'self' via distributed relations of power, such as women in a patriarchal society who exist only in relation to a man. In this case, biblical texts like Ruth and Esther offer easy and fruitful subjects for such Foucaultian analysis due to their focus on women succeeding in a hegemonic 'man's world', which the biblical authors considered to be the normal and intended state of affairs. Perhaps more importantly, Foucault's theory provides theoretical avenues out of the traditional tendency to identify gender, especially, in an essentialist fashion.[41] It reveals perceptions (and structures) that previously had been taken for granted by emphasizing the positionality of the other before the subject.[42] Second-Temple period texts such as Ezra–Nehemiah, however, offer more of a challenge because they present a patriarchal context so effectively that minorities are almost entirely removed from the texts.[43] Moreover, in its silencing of the Other, Ezra–Nehemiah 'denigrates and shames' the culture, history, and faith of the 'conquered', which is a tendency that would later become quite characteristic of colonialism.[44]

---

40. As Sugirtharajah points out, this emphasis identifies a strong corollary with liberation hermeneutics, though the latter locked itself into a narrow economic agenda with its focus (*Exploring Postcolonial Criticism*, p. 46).

41. Cf. Christiana de Groot, who argues that one of the biggest transitions for feminist biblical scholarship was away from treating gender as essentialist, which perpetuated the dominant patriarchal ideology of biblical scholarship and biblical interpretation ('Contextualizing the Woman's Bible', *Studies in Religion/Sciences Religieuses* 41.4 [2012], pp. 564-77 [565-66]).

42. As a comparative example, Simone de Beauvoir argued that the Other represented the opposite of what was 'positive and neutral', which was male. As Margaret Simons says of de Beauvoir, 'Woman is never considered a subject, because she is defended as the essence of absolute alterity. The affinity between Otherness and negativity runs throughout *The Second Sex* from history, myths, and lifestyle. Consequently, I read Beauvoir's constant references to woman as Other as strongly enmeshed in an understanding of woman as the absolute negative of man's positive assertion of self' (*The Philosophy of Simone de Beauvoir: Critical Essays* [Bloomington: Indiana University Press, 2006], p. 286).

43. Ezra–Nehemiah's attention to the Other regarding intermarriage (Neh. 13.23-31), for example, has nearly nothing to do with the Other as an active socio-political agent and everything to do with denigrating socio-political institutions that characterize the *golah* community.

44. On this characteristic of colonial rhetoric, see Sugirtharajah, *Exploring Postcolonial Criticism*, p. 38.

Postcolonial concerns, however, forget, overwrite, or bury their colonial heritage. As Touraine writes:

> We are coming out of several decades characterized by the idea that the dominated are mere victims, subject to manipulation and surveillance or punishment, when in fact no actor may exist if we are not able to do more than denounce the powers that be. As brilliant as such thinking was, it has proved self-destructive, since the reduction of the dominated to the status of victims is the position that best serves the interests of the dominators.[45]

Even employing categories such as victim and Other, asserts Touraine, maintains the very structures of domination (and oppression) they were intended to lay bare and offer a corrective for. It is an intellectual transgression that cannot be fixed by mere redefinition of the concepts. Without changing the fundamental structures of knowledge, redefining such categories merely legitimates and perpetuates the structure they reflect. This is where Foucault's theories on power and knowledge have proven helpful in dismantling modern assumptions about power structures.[46] For the purpose of sociological study then, as Touraine argues, one should focus on the 'conversations' that occur between sociopolitical agents. Moreover, one should not view the positionalities of those agents in a dichotomized sense of subject–other or victimizer–victim but more in the way of Pierre Bourdieu's *habitus*, a 'playing field' of infinite possibilities, relations, and conversations.[47]

What Touraine describes is certainly a notable development. Within biblical scholarship, however, the tendency to view power relations primarily in an overly dichotomized way is largely preserved by our tendency to cling to traditional modes of interpretation and overlook the growing polyvalence of methodological interpretations.[48] Even feminism has been guilty here.

---

45. Touraine, 'Sociology After Sociology', p. 189.

46. See also Lorna Burns and Birgit Mara Kaiser, 'Introduction: Navigating Differential Futures, (Un)Making Colonial Pasts', in *Postcolonial Literatures and Deleuze: Colonial Pasts, Differential Futures* (ed. Lorna Burns and Birgit M. Kaiser; New York: Palgrave Macmillan, 2012), pp. 1-17 (6).

47. Pierre Bourdieu, *In Other Words: Essays Toward a Reflexive Sociology* (trans. M. Adamson; Stanford: Stanford University Press, 1990), p. 11.

48. Note, for example, Brenner, who writes, '[F]eminist Bible criticism is not a good name. It hardly conveys the fact that, after twenty years of intensive work, feminists have evolved a polyvalence of approaches to the Bible' ('Who's Afraid of Feminist Criticism', p. 39). Similar things could be said of other types of criticism that have made the 'other' their main (starting) enterprise.

Othering via Projection

In both the 'colonial' and the 'postcolonial' senses, Other is less a moral subject that moves and acts independently of a corresponding subject and more an object of translation that politicizes cultural expectations and differential relations of power.[49] Othering creates distinctions; rather, it generates distinctions based on a preconception of self as the logical and moral subject. In generating distinctions, it enforces boundaries and thus, also, the spaces and their parameters that define objects upon which projections of self, as the embodiment of perception and experience, may be cast.[50] What this means is that Othering may be considered a type of obtuse, solipsistic singularity, because in identifying an Other we are more accurately identifying ourselves and our experiences in negative terms, identifying what we are not or do not perceive ourselves to be.[51] Nevertheless, we engage the Other as an external object through which we validate our own hegemonic power systems. This 'objectifying' of the Other does not produce a pattern of relationship between two self-aware and self-referential individuals but between the individual and his object.

According to Melanie Klein, an early champion of object-relations theory, organisms, individual and collective, define themselves by categorizing their experiences. On the one hand, we internalize that which is pleasing. On the other hand, we externalize and project that which is disturbing, uncomfortable, and threatening. That which is 'pleasing', Klein argues, is that which does not create within us anxieties over death or which alleviates already present anxieties.[52] From the very

49. Graham Huggan, *The Postcolonial Exotic: Marketing the Margins* (New York: Routledge, 2001), p. ix.

50. The concern that women are the objects upon which male concerns are cast has largely been the argument of feminist biblical scholarship. Brenner, for example, writes, 'Discrimination and subjectivity, two important issues on the feminist agenda, are at the foreground of contemporary scholarship in the humanities and social sciences. It is therefore clear to feminists and their supporters that looking at the world, reading and studying it as a woman recreate [*sic*] it, as a different and exciting place—and this must be true for theology and biblical studies too' ('Who's Afraid of Feminist Criticism', pp. 39-40).

51. For further reference, see the discussion of singularity in postcolonial thought that is combined with Deleuzian theory in Burns and Kaiser, 'Introduction', pp. 1-17.

52. Melanie Klein, *Envy and Gratitude, and Other Works, 1946–1963* (New York: Vintage Digital, 2011), p. 5. Release of anxieties is also achieved in the form of humor. Brenner, for example, argues that sexual and toilet humor are some of the strongest forms of this type of release in the Bible ('Who's Afraid of Feminist Criticism', pp. 42-43, 51).

beginning, our anxieties are brought on by the need to survive, to eat. Thus, for Klein, the 'good breast'—her psychoanalytic symbol, provided some meaning through Freud's Oedipal theory—represents the foundational 'good object'; it provides food and eases discomfort and anxiety brought on by hunger. The 'bad breast' does not provide sustenance or any alleviation of discomfort and only heightens anxiety because the object that should provide comfort does not.[53] 'Projection, as Freud described', writes Klein, 'originates from the deflection of the death instinct outwards and in my view it helps the ego overcome anxiety by ridding it of danger and badness. Introjection of the good object is also used by the ego as a defense against anxiety.'[54]

With Kleinian object-relations theory, the Other is distinguished through what the subject, or individual self, perceives self-referentially as bad.[55] What is bad for me, I project upon an external object. But that object was first created through my externalizing of what was displeasing. In turn, I internalize that which I perceive to be good for me. It is in this way that individuals began the process of constructing their individual consciousness within the framework of society.[56] As individuals and societies become more 'complex', perceptions of 'good' and 'bad' objects become more complex as well. 'Objects' may cease to be directly related to material survival and more associated with ideas, values, social truths, or other. In Ezra–Nehemiah, for example, while the text's emphasis upon the insider–outsider distinction can be linked to the material land, it is also the result of a complex development of interpretation of and blame for the exiles.[57] The 'foreigner', who could also have been a Judaean who had remained in the land during the Babylonian Exile, became the object upon which the radical consequences of exile were cast: permanent dissociation from Yahweh, homelessness, and perpetual subjugation. Where Ezra–Nehemiah blames the remnant for transgressions

53. Klein, *Envy and Gratitude*, pp. 49-50.

54. Ibid., p. 6. The debated status of the ego is not under discussion here. Whether or not it is the ego or some aspect of the self, individual, identity, or other, Klein's theory still works, with its emphasis upon object relations.

55. Bal offers a similar argument without drawing upon Klein directly (*Loving Yusuf*, pp. 77-78).

56. In fact, for Klein, affirmation of the individual self also entails a denial of others: 'The frustrating and persecuting object is kept widely apart from the idealized object. However, the bad object is not only kept apart from the good one but its very existence is denied, as is the whole situation of frustration and the bad feelings (pain) to which frustration gives rise' (*Envy and Gratitude*, p. 7).

57. For a more sustained argument on this point, see Cataldo, *Breaking Monotheism*, pp. 149-85.

that brought about the 'bad experience' of the Exile, the Exile was explained as a consequence of the actions of all previous generations (that included members of the עם הארץ). In that way, the Exile as a punishment for transgression was externalized from the *golah* community, even though the community might once again embody those actions, which required the need for the so-called National Confession [cf. Neh. 9.1-37] to serve as a reminder. This example from Ezra–Nehemiah also reveals a tendency toward what Klein terms as 'splitting' or the separation of the self/ego from sources of anxiety.[58] It occurs because the *golah* community cannot rid itself fully of internal 'bad objects' that are its history or of the possibility of transgression.[59] Nehemiah's rejection of foreign marriages and the concomitant process of driving the 'foreigner' out from the community is but one example (cf. Neh. 13.1-9, 23-31) in which splitting physically manifested in the form of the *golah* community's separation from the עם הארץ. Ezra–Nehemiah identifies the עם הארץ as representative of all that is threatening to and creates anxiety within the community (cf. Ezra 4.4; Neh. 10.28).

The Other as a Source, or Product, of Conflict

The first duty of the sociologist is to refuse the discourses of rejection that poorly mask the defense of privileges and the negation of the other as at once different and equal.[60]

The sociologist, in other words, must reclaim Other from its colonial moorings as a term denoting a class-based power relation in which the Other is defined by what the subject is not—or as according to the previous discussion, the summation of the projected 'bad experiences', where doing so supports and legitimates the dominant power relations and corresponding social-political normative.[61]

---

58. Klein, *Envy and Gratitude*, p. 56.

59. Klein writes, for example, 'There is therefore a constant fluctuation between the fear of internal and external bad objects, between the death instinct acting within and deflected outwards. Here we see one important aspect of the interaction—from the beginning of life—between projection and introjection. External dangers are experienced in the light of internal dangers and are therefore intensified; on the other hand, any danger threatening from outside intensifies the perpetual inner danger-situation' (ibid., p. 31).

60. Touraine, 'Sociology After Sociology', p. 189.

61. See also Burns and Kaiser, 'Introduction', p. 6.

In this sense, Touraine is not so far from Žižek, who has made a career out of arguing that the politically imposed limitations on current discourses and modes of production results in a conflict between an ordered structure of society and those without a place in it. For him, the Other is always in conflict with society because the Other's productive activities are limited by social regulations that have been preserved within the dominant normative as those things beneficial to society. In this sense, the Other has no place in society because she has been dis/placed and identified as an object external to the dominant order. But that, according to Žižek, is a 'screen'.[62] The Other or 'neighbour', to use Žižek's term, must exist for me to do so. The subject, the self, the I, exists in relation to the object or individual who is simultaneously rejected *and* a necessary component of the subject's self. There is thus an emphasis upon an *inhuman* dimension of the other: the Other acts only in reference to the subject in order to sustain the sort of ethical universality that characterizes something as monolithic and regulating as monotheism (from the Second Temple period onward); she is not herself a self-referential subject.[63] According to Žižek, this emphasis is a consequence of the performative dimension of acting in relation to a fundamental relationship upon which self-referentiality is based: the relationship between the subject and the Other.

In truth, however, it is the ongoing performance of distinction, of repeating differences, that continually defines and redefines the category of Other. The Other is not a static or permanent category but the 'cause' of our response. Moreover, the Other must always exist as an object against which to measure our responses.[64] Even the big Other, as the universal Other, must exist, according to Žižek, for the sake of society. Yet, while some have identified this Other as the monotheistic God, it is more correctly a form of sociality that transcends individuals but binds them together in relation.[65] Even in that, we have moved beyond the concept of a big Other that is prevalent within Lacan's *doxa*. For Žižek, the Other 'is disintegrating into particular "worlds" (or lifestyles) whose coordination is regulated by purely formal rules'.[66] Society and

62. Slavoj Žižek, *In Defense of Lost Causes* (London: Verso, 2008), p. 12.
63. Regarding this need to emphasize an inhuman dimension in the Other, see ibid., pp. 365-74.
64. Ibid., p. 31.
65. Ibid., p. 34.
66. Ibid. Note further, 'What…is missing in today's social bond, if it is not the big Other? The answer is clear: a small other which would embody, stand in for, the big Other—a person who is not simply "like the others", but who directly embodies authority' (p. 35).

community, and the rules legitimated therein, have become the so-called big Other against which we define ourselves. There is no longer any consideration of an objective, transcendent Other. When it comes to an analysis of the Other in the traditional sense, in the sense of the marginalized non-member, the minority, or the 'foreigner', it is not the Other as an object that we analyze. We analyze the negative or inverse of our own identity that is legitimated within the rules of our social worlds. In other words, the Other is not an object in the essentialist sense but an intersection wherein our performances as social-political agents step outside the formalized rules of our communities or 'worlds'.[67] Performance, for Žižek, produces conflict through its articulation of identity by resisting the subject of the Other. Thus, the Other, or even big Other, is simultaneously a source and product of conflict. We produce the Other as a set of formalized rules that governs and identifies society, and we also subject ourselves to its 'draconian' restrictions leveraged upon us. It produces conflict by symbolizing what we are not, by reminding us of the restricted nature of our identities, of the finite limitations of the social-political order upon which those identities are based. This conflict is a consequence of the Other's form and content: the Other is something that we perceive through our performance as social-political agents, but its very essence is a product of our own aspirations, actions, and positional arrangements in the socio-political hierarchy.[68] Consequently, the Other as a necessary component in the subject's identity represents the failure of closure between what is included and what is excluded. It represents the permeability within the boundaries of our social-political identities. It is this failure of closure, where 'closure' is what preserves in perpetuity the existence of the other, which necessitates the authoritative performance of ideology: '[A]n ideology always admits the failure of closure, and then goes on to regulate the permeability of the exchange with its outside'.[69]

In biblical studies generally, there has been acknowledgment of the relationship between the Other and conflict. Yet it has been more in the

---

67. In this sense, the law can also be Other.

68. The Other as a restriction upon reaching full potentiality frames Žižek's criticism of Derrida: 'Or, to put it in yet another way, in a kind of inverted phenomenological epoch, Derrida reduces Otherness to the "to come" of a pure potentiality, thoroughly deontologizing it, bracketing its positive content, so that all that remains is the specter of a promise; and what if the next step is to drop this minimal specter of Otherness itself, so that all that remains is the rupture, the gap as such that prevents entities from reaching their self-identity?' (Slavoj Žižek, 'Return to Différence [with a Minor Pro Domo Sua]', *Critical Inquiry* 32.2 [2006], pp. 226-49 [232]).

69. Žižek, *In Defense of Lost Causes*, p. 29.

vein of the Other as an oppressed object rather than the intersection of performance. The Other has been read as a victim of conflict and thus, as a socially objective category, where conflict represented the material and ideological contests for power itself as an object that is attainable.[70] That, at least, has been a traditional tendency. A more recent tendency is to view power not as a static object, material, or idea but as a discursive process. The latter is necessarily obligated to take into account socio-political actors in mutually referential positions, in *relation*. Žižek reminds us that being in relation is, foremost, self-referential, that there exists a narcissistic egocentrism behind our actions.[71] Since the Bible is a cultural artifact, what this means for studies of the biblical text and, specifically, of the Other in the Bible, is that there is no factual Other in the biblical text.[72] Any attempts to reconstruct the objective identity of the Other are entirely fantastical. Given the understandable limitations of any ancient historical text, what can be determined is the author's self-referencing in his engagement with the decentering permeability of the boundary between insider and outsider. The Other is no longer a person but the formalized rules that the biblical authors either embraced or resisted as they projected their own perceptions upon cultural artefact.

There remains an important limitation to Žižek's emphasis upon Othering as performance: its blurring over polarities that are in some ways essential to their related objects. We perceive others, for example, without our necessarily having engaged them in any exchange of relations. Certainly that perception, or the ability to make it, is a basic reality of consciousness and self-referentiality and is itself a product of social and political processes that shape our self-awareness; never-theless, there is still something, essential or innate, in being aware of myself. I am also aware that you are not me in ways that will always

70. So Brenner, 'Who's Afraid of Feminist Criticism', pp. 44-46; Joseph Blenkinsopp, 'Bethel in the Neo-Babylonian Period', in *Judah and the Judeans in the Neo-Babylonian Period* (ed. Oded Lipschits and Joseph Blenkinsopp; Winona Lake, IN: Eisenbrauns, 2003), pp. 93-107 (104).

71. For example, Žižek writes, '[C]ivility is not simply obligation-feigned-as-free-act; it is rather its exact opposite: *a free act feigned as an obligation*' (*In Defense of Lost Causes*, p. 20).

72. Note also, 'In short, whereas the inherited historical criticism emphasized the time, place, and circumstances that elicited the writing of the text, this current approach emphasizes the political interests of the writers, users, and canonizers, who relied on the biblical texts to suppress alternatives that threatened their own hegemony' (Leander E. Keck, 'The Premodern Bible in the Postmodern World', *Int* 50.2 [1996], pp. 130-41 [130]).

remain unique to you. That said, perhaps Žižek's theory is most helpful in its forcing us to recognize the processes that shape interrelationships between subjects and others or between social agents generally.

Some Final Thoughts

In postcolonial thought, Otherness tends to lose its ethical binding.[73] This is due in part to the loss of the individual as identifiably other, a loss to which E. Lévinas reacts when he identifies 'ethics' as the irreducible obligation to the other that must be primary to any relation or ontology.[74] Lévinas, like Lacan, defined the Other as *radically Other*. But whereas Lacan associated the Other with the symbolic order and language, Lévinas did so with the monotheistic, traditional God, whom he presumes is *infinitely* Other and so unsusceptible to change in the same way a symbolic order is. For Lévinas, 'ethics' is 'the irreducible obligation to the other'.[75] The Other, he argues, necessitates religion: 'Religion is the relation with a being as a being. It does not consist in *conceiving* it as such, which would be an act where the *being* is already assimilated, even if this assimilation were to succeed in disengaging it as a *being*, in *letting it be*.'[76] The 'other' is an encounter toward which one must turn and come face to face (Hebrew פנים אל פנים), and in turning, there is the creation (better, *repair*) of relationship. 'To be in relation with the Other face to face is to be unable to kill. It is also the situation of discourse.'[77] As Handelman describes it, 'The other faces my own separate and narcissistic ego, interrupts, and shames it—a calling into question which is the call of conscience as both an appeal and an order'.[78] In facing the

---

73. Handelman, 'Facing the Other', p. 61.

74. As Handelman describes it (ibid., p. 62). Miroslav Volf, a theologian whose work has focused on social tendencies toward exclusion, takes a similar position when he writes, 'The human self is formed not through a simple rejection of other—through a binary logic of opposition and negation—but through a complex process of "taking in" and "keeping out". We are who we are not because we separate from the others who are next to us, but because we are both separate and connected, both distinct and related; the boundaries that mark identities are both barriers and bridges' (*Exclusion and Embrace: A Theological Exploration of Identity, Otherness, and Reconciliation* [Nashville: Abingdon, 1996], p. 66).

75. Handelman, 'Facing the Other', p. 62.

76. Emmanuel Lévinas, 'Is Ontology Fundamental?', *Philosophy Today* 33.2 (1989), pp. 121-29 (126).

77. Ibid., pp. 127-28.

78. Handelman, 'Facing the Other', p. 63.

Other we are judged by her, called into an ethical relationship by her. It is through this position before the Other that our own identities may be known.[79]

Lévinas prioritizes the ethical dimension of Otherness as a performative responsibility, because other forms of relationship, of philosophical thought, turn into forms of violence and tyranny.[80] Žižek has devoted much of his work to this same argument. By denying the alterity and singularity of Otherness, which is the essence of the ethical relation, politics, as that which regulates reference and position, becomes its own autonomous realm among other modes of thought and relation.[81] This is precisely what Žižek argues to *be* the case: that the formalized rules of a society *are* Other. The Other, therefore, is known on account of our responsibility and response to the Other and our judgment by the Other, through which we become responsible to the Other. As Handelman, referring to Lévinas, puts it, 'The aim of Lévinas' work is to show that reason and freedom are not autonomous but are founded on prior structures, and that freedom is justified not of itself, but *by and for the other*'.[82] All said, if theorists such as Deleuze, Foucault, Klein, and Žižek are correct, then our responsibilities are not to an objective, self-referential Other or even a big, absolute Other. Our responsibilities lay not in any objective ethics but in preserving our own referentialities to and before others, and to do that in such a way that we remain approachable through and for the purpose of discourse.

79. Ibid., p. 64.
80. See, for example, Lévinas, 'Is Ontology Fundamental?'
81. Handelman, 'Facing the Other', p. 70.
82. Ibid., p. 71.

Othering, Selfing, 'Boundarying' and 'Cross-Boundarying' as Interwoven with Socially Shared Memories: Some Observations

Ehud Ben Zvi

There is a vast corpus of literature on matters of Othering as a discursive strategy of exclusion, as one of dialectical selfing, on whether Othering necessarily involves exaggerations of differences, essentialization of differences and of self, on Othering as a manifestation and/or sharp instrument in power (hierarchical) relations, on Othering as a delegiti-mizing tool, on the contingent character of Othering, on Othering as a common or even 'natural' cognitive tool, and on various social grammars of Othering. Discussions about self, constructions of sameness, 'strong' or 'weak' concepts of identity, and about processes of social identity formation or categorization and identification are often deeply inter-twined with those about Othering.[1]

Being a historian of ancient Israel, my intention is not to contribute to the discussion of disciplinary or cross/inter-disciplinary, explicit or implicit theoretical understandings of Othering evidenced in today's critical literature. Nor is it to discuss the use of constructions of, and social memories about, biblical Israel that served to frame, conceptualize,

---

1. The literature on these issues, whether discussed directly or indirectly, whether theoretical or based on case-studies, is beyond massive. Moreover, it cuts across multiple disciplines and areas. It plays important roles, for instance, in anthropology, a field that began as an exercise in Othering, social-anthropology, sociology, cognitive studies, history, political science, cultural and postcolonial studies, gender studies, disability studies, contemporary European (and EU) studies, and genocide studies. Against common perception, it should be stressed that, although 'processes of negative "othering" clearly are common aspects of many societies and social groups,...they are by no means universal and are not built into all theoretical under-standings of identity processes' (Hector Grad and Luisa Martín Rojo, 'Identities in Discourse: An Integrative View', in *Analysing Identities in Discourse* [ed. Rosana Dolón and Júlia Todolí; Philadelphia: J. Benjamins, 2008], pp. 3-28 [13]).

and justify the Othering of various groups by a wide range of communities, across time and space to the present, that each were strongly influenced by their own Bible and, as they saw it, by 'The Bible'. There can be no doubt that a wide variety of historical instances of oppression, domination, persecution, marginalization, and the like were justified and partially conceptualized in these ways. Such studies, as important as they are, are unlikely to contribute to our knowledge of the discourse of ancient Israel in the early Second Temple period, which is my own area of research.

Instead, I will focus on an array of important sites of memories and mnemonic narratives that were shared at least among the community's literati within early Second Temple Israel and which were interwoven in one way or another in processes involving the (partial) Israelitization of Others and (partial) Otherization of Israel. As a whole, these sites and narratives shaped a discursively significant series of 'in-between' realms that communicated and socialized the community in terms of ternary systems rather than simple, clear-cut Us vs. Them systems of categorization.[2]

One may claim that ternary categorizations are ubiquitous in human societies,[3] but the particular features and contours of the 'in-between' realms and the underlying discursive grammar generating them provide significant information about the ideological discourse of the community in question, about what it considered and remembered as being 'Israelite', its rules of classification, and indirectly, its take on matters of 'sameness' and 'identity'.[4] Moreover, since the array of cases discussed

2. For additional examples of ternary systems reflected in texts in the Hebrew Bible, see the contribution in this volume by Kåre Berge, 'Categorical Identities: "Ethnified Otherness and Sameness"—A Tool for Understanding Boundary Negotiation in the Pentateuch?', pp. 70-88.

3. See Gerd Baumann, 'Grammars of Identity/Alterity: A Structural Approach', in *Grammars of Identity/Alterity: A Structural Approach* (ed. Gerd Baumann and André Gingrich; EASA Series, 3; New York: Berghahn, 2006), pp. 18-50.

4. The texts to be discussed below do not really construct a 'thirdspace' as the latter is usually understood, because they did not construct a contact zone characterized by concrete intercultural or transcultural encounters involving more than one partner. These texts were written in Hebrew, by and for a very narrow group. They were not primarily aimed at facilitating negotiations with contemporary Others, even if they may have reflected such negotiations in some way. These texts were aimed above all at constructing a sense of self-understanding within the inner group through the partial development of a shared social memory. As was usual in these cases, the endeavour required a discursive, imaginative act of creation of Others. Whether the in-between categories discussed here eventually facilitated the creation

here involved cutting across diverse Othering boundaries and binaries like 'ethnic' origin, gender, and 'normal' bodiedness, it seems that the construction of significant 'in-between' areas and the concomitant construction of boundaries as porous, flexible, and even contingent and contextual were not minor 'accidents' but a reflection of some substantial aspect of the social mindscape of the community, or at least its literati. This shared aspect, in turn, came to be reflected in a tendency to shape and prefer certain types of memories.

The memories discussed here suggest quite complex grammars of constructing 'others' that were far more advanced than a simplistic, binary of Us = good, male, able-bodied, righteous, and pure that included a Them = bad, female, not fully able-bodied, unrighteous, and impure. They suggest multiple grammars were involved in appropriations of the Other; *inter alia*, reciprocal mirroring and discursively contingent rather than categorical Othering. To be sure, the cases discussed here are selective. Certainly, there were other memories that reflected and emerged out of other discursive and ideological needs of the community,[5] which seem to be in clear tension with the patterns observed in and underlying those selected for discussion here. Moreover, the community was well aware that mnemonic narratives were not the only way to explore matters of Otherness. Various 'legal' texts concerning multiple Others and the divine Other existed in the community as well.[6] None of this, however,

---

of historical thirdspaces or failed to do so in the late Hellenistic or Roman periods is a completely different matter. Had this essay been focused on northern Israel/ Samaria, the main historical counterpart and inner-group Other of Yehud, a discussion using 'thirdspace' approaches might have been in order. But all the cases discussed here involve Others who were not categorized as 'Samarians'. On 'thirdspace' in general, see, inter alia, Karin Ikas and Gerhard Wagner (eds.), *Communicating in the Third Space* (Routledge Research in Cultural and Media Studies, 18; New York: Routledge, 2009) and the now 'classical' work, Homi K. Bhabha, *The Location of Culture* (New York: Routledge, 1994).

5. See, for instance, Num. 31; Ezra 10; Neh. 13. Interestingly, most of these memories were balanced by other memories that also existed in the community. The case of the Midianites was offset by the memory of Jethro, the priest of Midian. In the case of the foreign wives, remembering that a significant number of central characters in Israel's formative past wedded 'foreign' wives (e.g. Moses, Joseph, Judah, Boaz, David, Solomon) and remembering that those 'who separated themselves from the pollutions of the nations of the land to worship YHWH, the God of Israel' were fully accepted in the midst of the (early) Second Temple community as encoded and communicated by Ezra 6.21 provide balance to claims about a 'holy seed' and its purity implications advanced in other sections of Ezra–Nehemiah.

6. See, for instance, the recent collection of essays in Reinhard Achenbach, Rainer Albertz, and Jacob Wöhrle (eds.), *The Foreigner and the Law: Perspectives*

takes away from the importance of the set of memories discussed and its implications for the study of Othering, Selfing, 'boundarying', and 'cross-boundarying' within the general social mindscape of the remembering community/ies. To the contrary, the explorations advanced provide an important stepping stone for a more integrated approach to the study of the Otherness embodied in the Others who were imagined, remembered, and above all, vicariously encountered by the literati of the early Second Temple period when they read all the texts that served to construe their own past.

Shifting our attention to the cases to be discussed here, one of the most memorable narratives about David that serves as a turning point in the narrative about him involved a central character, Uriah the Hittite. His very name, Uriah, 'YHWH is my light/fire',[7] asked the community to remember him as an embodiment of a worshiper of YHWH. What they remembered about him only supported this portrayal. He was remembered as a righteous foil against which an unrighteous David was found extremely lacking. He represents what an Israelite male, never mind an Israelite king, was supposed to be and how he was supposed to behave. Even as he carries his deadly letter,[8] likely aware or at least suspicious of

from the Hebrew Bible and the Ancient Near East (BZAR, 16; Wiesbaden: Harrassowitz, 2011). See also Mark A. Christian, 'Openness to the Other Inside and Outside of Numbers', in *The Books of Leviticus and Numbers* (ed. Thomas Römer; BETL, 215; Leuven: Peeters, 2008), pp. 579-608; Christiana van Houten, *The Alien in Israelite Law* (JSOTSup, 107; Sheffield: Sheffield Academic Press, 1991); Jacob Milgrom, 'Religions Conversion and the Revolt Model for the Formation of Israel', *JBL* 101 (1982), pp. 169-76; and Rainer Albertz and Jakob Wöhrle (eds.), *Between Cooperation and Hostility: Multiple Identities in Ancient Judaism and the Interaction with Foreign Powers* (Journal of Ancient Judaism Supplements; Göttingen: Vandenhoeck & Ruprecht, 2013).

7. It has been proposed that the name Uriah was originally derived from Hurrian. Whether this is the case or not is clearly irrelevant to the matters discussed here, because the mnemonic community in the early Second Temple period would not have recognized it as a Hurrian name, even if those advancing such a position in contemporary scholarship were right. The remembering community would have understood Uriah as carrying the meaning, 'YHWH is my light/fire'.

8. The literary/folkloristic topos of the person carrying the 'deadly letter' to his putative executioner is well known. In this case, the bearer dies, unlike the case in the Sargon story. On this motif, see Bendt Alster, 'A Note on the Uriah Letter in the Sumerian Sargon Legend', *Zeitschrift für Assyriologie* 77 (1987), pp. 169-73; idem, 'Lugalbanda and the Early Epic Tradition in Mesopotamia', in *Lingering Over Words: Studies in Ancient Near Eastern Literature in Honor of William L. Moran* (ed. Tzvi Abusch, John Huehnergard, and Piotr Steinkeller; Atlanta: Scholars Press, 1990), pp. 59-72 (70-71); and William W. Hallo, 'Introduction: Ancient Near Eastern

its significance, he faithfully carries out his duty to the king, who fails to carry his own. By doing so, he not only highlights the fault of David but also the illegitimacy of human rebellion against a Davidic king and, by extension, the Davidic dynasty, even when their rulers grievously sin. In addition, he is remembered as faithful to YHWH, not only by being faithful to the unfaithful David but also by following YHWH's laws of purity (cf. 1 Sam. 21.5-6; see also Exod. 19.15; Deut. 23.11). His fate, like Bathsheba's, was sealed by a proper observance of purity laws (see 2 Sam. 11.4).[9] In all this, Uriah is remembered as an exemplary Israelite man, wrongfully oppressed and persecuted, and yet, or perhaps because of that, one with whom the male remembering community was supposed to identify and aspire to imitate. In fact, in the parable of Nathan, Uriah stands for any proper male in Israel who is good.[10] Thus, within this episode, Uriah stands for male Israel and David for the male Other;[11] Uriah stands for the pious and dispossessed and David for the powerful oppressor and dispossessor, a type of Oriental despot. David/Israel may remain alive only because he undergoes a retributive and punitive process that turns him into a quasi-Uriah (2 Sam. 11.12-13).[12]

Given that Uriah stands for any proper male in Israel, and thus, for Israel itself, the existence of a very strong preference to remember him

---

Texts and Their Relevance for Biblical Exegesis', in *The Context of Scripture* (ed. William W. Hallo and K. Lawson Younger; Leiden: Brill, 1997), p. xxvii and bibliography cited there.

9.   This is another site of memory communicating to the remembering community that at times proper behaviour, piety, and faithfulness led to premature death/execution. The individuals were remembered despite or perhaps because their fates were considered positive examples for behaviour. For other examples, see 2 Chron. 24.19-22; cf. 2 Chron. 16.10. For the general lack of anticipated coherence between behaviour and fate, see Qohelet, passim, but also Psalms, passim. In both cases, the conclusion is similar to that expressed in Qoh. 12.13.

10.   The characterization of Uriah as both a military hero and the 'owner' of the ewe-lamb is clearly gendered.

11.   Who is significantly, within the gendered discourse of the period, feminized when he prefers to remain in his city and 'house' instead of joining his warriors in battle. On shared concepts of masculinity in the ancient Near East, see Timothy M. Lemos, '"They Have Become Women": Judean Diaspora and Postcolonial Theories of Gender and Migration', in *Social Theory and the Study of Israelite Religion: Essays in Retrospect and Prospect* (ed. Saul M. Olyan; Resources for Biblical Study, 71; Atlanta: SBL, 2012), pp. 81-109 (99-101).

12.   Cf. from a different perspective, Regina M. Schwartz, 'Adultery in the House of David: "Nation" in the Bible and Biblical Scholarship', in *Shadow of Spirit: Postmodernism and Religion* (ed. Philippa Berry and Andrew Wernick; New York: Routledge, 1992), pp. 181-97.

in terms of Uriah the Hittite is particularly noteworthy (2 Sam. 11.3, 6, 17, 21, 24; 12.9, 10; 23.29; 1 Kgs 15.5; 1 Chron. 11.41). It repeatedly evokes a memory of a notable character who was Us and, at the same time, explicitly and saliently, a Hittite Other.[13]

Uriah is not a unique case. One may note the explicit salience of constructions of Otherness in characters like Doeg the Edomite (1 Sam. 21.8; 22.9, 18; Ps. 52.2). Doeg was remembered as the head of Saul's entire administration, a loyal servant of the king, and a much stronger defender of his master and his household than Abner. Significantly, Saul, who is chastised elsewhere for not following YHWH, is never censured for having given Doeg such an influential position of leadership over Israel. He was both a faithful and zealous (perhaps overzealous) Saulide Israelite, a zealous (perhaps overzealous) worshiper of Israel's deity, and saliently, an Edomite as well.[14]

Beyond the memories explicitly evoked by book of Samuel, Ruth is the most obvious figure of the past that is similarly imagined. She is both integral to Israel (see Ruth 1.16b) and serves as a 'mother' for David, for the Davidic, royal/messianic line, and even for Israel itself, because David was identified by the remembering community with Israel and vice versa.[15] At the same time, Ruth is saliently and repeatedly Othered

13. I am not interested here in the question of the 'historical' Uriah. The point is that he is a site of memory that embodies both Israel and the Other. A comparable salient association of ethnic Otherness is present in the case of Ruth, the Moabite, who is constantly remembered as a Moabite and as a mother in Israel, who became one of Us (see Ruth).

14. As an aside, one may mention that, among the constructions of Doeg that were reflected and shaped in rabbinic literature, one finds Doeg, the 'ethnic boundary maker', who claims that David was unworthy of even entering the community of Israel, never mind being king over it, because he comes from a Moabite woman. The partners in that imagined 'halachic' discussion were Abner and Saul. On Doeg, Uriah, and a few other cases of zealous worshipers of YHWH, see Jacob Milgrom, *Leviticus 17–22* (AB, 3A; Garden City: Doubleday, 2000), p. 1417. Milgrom considers them all *gērim*, because he reads the stories about them in a way informed by (his reading) of Leviticus and related texts and in light of his claim that 'religious conversion' was not an option in 'biblical times' (p. 1417). But significantly, none of these characters is ever called a *gēr* in the narratives themselves or in references to them elsewhere in the Hebrew Bible. It is likely that they were not imagined as *gērim* by the readers.

15. See, for instance, Isa. 55.3 and the increased identification of Israel (the communal I) with David (and vice versa) in the Psalms (e.g. Ps. 89.50-51). Note the common exchange between David's house/kingdom and YHWH's house/kingdom in Chronicles (e.g. 1 Chron. 17.14; 28.5; 29.23; 2 Chron. 13.5, 8).

by the repeated attachment of the Othering gentilic, the Moabite (Ruth 1.22; 2.2, 21; 4.5; cf. 1.4).[16]

Significantly, one may note that whereas the Othered is remembered as an Israelite and even a mother in and of David/Israel, within the world evoked by readings of the Ruth's narrative, Elimelech's sons were remembered as Israelites Othering themselves when they married Moabite women, in Moab, which was not part of Israel at that time nor worshiped its deity. So, too, was their father Elimelech, indirectly, due to his role as the head of his household.

'Foreignness' could be evoked by explicit 'foreign' gentilics, as in the case of Ruth, or by the identification of 'foreign' places.[17] But ethnocultural Otherness could be evoked in other ways as well. For instance, a personal name could fulfill that role and, at times, might even add to the texture of the memory/narrative and facilitate its role in communal memorability and socialization. A good example is the story involving Obed-Edom and Amaziah, king of Judah, in 2 Chronicles 25. This text raises multiple images and a plethora of issues,[18] but for present purposes it suffices to highlight two points. According to 2 Chron. 25.24: (a) the treasures of (the house of) YHWH were under the care of an officer bearing the name Obed-*Edom*, meaning 'servant of Edom', and (b) Amaziah, whose name evokes the sense, 'YHWH is strong', a Davidic king of Judah, worshiped *Edomite* gods and thus caused YHWH's treasures, those kept by Obed-Edom, to be lost. Who is theologically characterized here as 'servant of Edom', but Amaziah? Who is characterized as YHWH's servant, but Obed-Edom?

Moreover, this positive image of YHWH's servant associated with Obed-Edom is reinforced among the readership of the book by the fact that the readers approach the text in a way informed by their image of a second Obed-Edom present in Chronicles. This second Obed-Edom is imagined and remembered by these readers as not only a person whose name communicates the meaning, 'servant of Edom', but also as both a

16. For an analysis of Ruth using feminist and postcolonial theories in this volume, see Carey Walsh, 'Women on the Edge', pp. 122-43; for one using ethnic theory, see Anne-Mareike Wetter, 'Ruth: A Born-Again Israelite? One Woman's Journey Through Space and Time', pp. 144-62; and for a literary and anthropological analysis, see Robert L. Cohn, 'Overcoming Otherness in the Book of Ruth', pp. 163-81.

17. See the case of the widow of Zarephath in Sidon. On this example, see below.

18. I have expanded on the matter elsewhere; see Ehud Ben Zvi, 'A House of Treasures: The Account of Amaziah in 2 Chronicles 25—Observations and Implications', *SJOT* 22 (2008), pp. 63-85.

Gittite and a pious Levite (see esp. 1 Chron. 13.13-14; 16.5; 26.4-8).[19] Both characters converge and shape together a site of memory, 'Obed-Edom', within readers of Chronicles. This site of memory, or cipher, if one prefers, embodied and communicated a sense of fuzziness, of images and memories of apparent Others who were part of Israel even though they bore and communicated explicit Otherness and, conversely, memories of central Israelites who Otherized themselves.[20] Once again, Otherization has been used here to explore what being Israel and thus a faithful servant of YHWH might entail, but, significantly, through the construction of 'in-between' areas and of Others who are or become Us and of Us who become Others.

It is worth stressing that the Other did not have to be imagined within the remembering community as one of Us to be construed and remembered as a substantially 'Israelitized' individual and thus able to facilitate the kind of 'mirroring' that generates the 'in-between' realms that serve as grounds for exploring, negotiating and constantly reformulating and undermining boundaries. For instance, the gap between 'proper' Israel and Otherized Israel construed by the story of Elijah carried an interesting mirror gap within the Other. Whereas Jezebel, the Sidonian woman (see 1 Kgs 17.31) who was queen over the Northern Kingdom, persecutes YHWH's prophets, another Sidonian woman, the widow of Zarephath, supports the prophet. Jezebel and the elite of the kingdom of Israel follow Sidonian gods; the widow acknowledges YHWH and YHWH's true prophet. The Israelite elite is Otherized and a non-elite Other woman is 'Israelitized'. Moreover, given that the prophet stands

---

19. Cf. 2 Sam. 6.10-12. He is associated here with Edom and with Gath, but, in addition, the readers are asked to imagine him as a proper Israelite. Moreover, readers who would approach 2 Sam. 6.10-12 in light of their readings of Chronicles would imagine their Obed-Edom as a Levite. It is possible (and even likely) that the association of Obed-Edom with the Levites in Chronicles does not represent an 'innovation', but rather, was a common reading of the story in Samuel that existed among the literati of the late Persian or early Hellenistic period. On readings of Samuel and memories evoked by reading Samuel that were influenced by readings of and memories evoked by reading Chronicles in the late Persian or early Hellenistic period, see my 'Chronicles and Samuel–Kings: Two Interacting Aspects of One Memory System in the Late Persian/Early Hellenistic Period', in *Rereading the Relecture? The Question of (Post)chronistic Influence in the Latest Redactions of the Books of Samuel* (ed. Uwe Becker and Hannes Bezzel; FAT II, 66; Tübingen: Mohr Siebeck, 2014), pp. 41-56.

On Obed-Edom in Chronicles see also Nancy Tan, 'The Chronicler's "Obed-edom": A Foreigner and/or a Levite?', *JSOT* 32 (2007), pp. 217-30.

20. See also 2 Sam. 6.2-12.

in this story for, and as a representative of, YHWH, the proper relation between YHWH and Israel is partially explored through an Israelite prophet and a Sidonian woman who, like Jezebel, is twice Othered as a foreigner and a woman.[21] A system of double mirroring is clearly at work here.

Nebuzaradan, the person who burned the temple and Jerusalem and deported Israel and the temple vessels (2 Kgs 25.8-11; Jer. 39.9; 52.12-27), was also remembered as someone who thought and talked like a godly disciple of the prophet Jeremiah,[22] unlike most of Israel at the time. Significantly, Nebuzaradan is not the only case of an enemy military leader who is partially 'Israelitized'. Naaman was remembered as the head of the army of Aram and as a military leader who defeated Israel and took captives from it but also as one who came to acknowledge YHWH and wished to worship YHWH alone (2 Kgs 5.17).

21.   The preference for a story in ancient Israel's social memory in which Jezebel is imagined as the daughter of a Sidonian rather than a Tyrian king, as one might have expected historically, is consistent with, and reinforces the construed anti-pair, Other 'Israelitized' Jezebel and still Other Israel, which, by implication, also deals with proper yet Otherized Israel. This preference is at work even in Josephus. He harmonizes his understanding of the biblical story with his reliance on Menander when he refers to Jezebel as the daughter of the king of Tyre and Sidon (see *Ant.* 8.371; for Ethbaal as king of Tyre, see *Ant.* 8.324 and cf. 8.318). Most significantly for our purposes here, he shifts the description of Zarephath from 'belonging to Sidon' (1 Kgs 17.9) to 'a city not far from Sidon and Tyre, for it lay between them' (*Ant.* 8.320), closing the circle again.

The tendency to conceptualize one's group optimally by constructing and embodying oneself in the remembered figure of someone who is also the Other, along with all the mirroring and crossing of boundaries in multiple directions that is involved, is more common in societies with a low sense of existential anxiety (see below). It is not by chance that in later tradition, the widow of Zarephath becomes a full Israelite and the mother of Jonah (e.g. *y. Sukk.* 5.1; 22b; *Gen. Rab.* 98.11) or even of the Messiah-son-of-Joseph (e.g. *Seder Eliahu Rabba*, ch. 18, *siman* 19); she is eventually included among the twenty-two 'women of valour'.

On Jezebel and the widow as 'analogous' characters see Dagmar Pruin, 'What Is in a Text?—Searching for Jezebel', in *Ahab Agonistes: The Rise and Fall of the Omri Dynasty* (ed. Lester L. Grabbe; LHBOTS, 421/ESHM, 6; New York: T&T Clark International, 2007), pp. 208-35 (213-14).

22.   'The author wants to persuade us that Nebuzaradan was a pupil of Jeremiah (40:2–3)', Klaus A. D. Smelik, 'The Function of Jeremiah 50 and 51 in the Book of Jeremiah', in *Reading the Book of Jeremiah: A Search for Coherence* (ed. Martin Kessler; Winona Lake, IN: Eisenbrauns, 2004), pp. 87-98 (97). Compare also Jer. 40.2 with Jer. 32.23.

Naaman was doubly Othered by being made an Aramean and a 'leper'. Particularly relevant to the argument here, whereas Naaman's Otherness is largely overcome in the narrative because he becomes partially 'Israelitized' and also is cured of his leprosy, the latter disease becomes associated subsequently with Gehazi (2 Kgs 5.27), the most central 'insider' aside from the prophet. The community imagined Gehazi as the servant of the servant of YHWH. Otherness was shifted, as it were, from Naaman to Gehazi. The outsider became an insider, even if a crypto-insider in some ways (2 Kgs 5.18), whereas the insider became the certainly non-cryptic outsider, now and for generations (2 Kgs 5.27).

Moreover, whereas Naaman was remembered as partially 'Israelitized' after he inflicted blows on Israel, Pharaoh Necho was remembered as partially 'Israelitized', fulfilling the role of an Israelite prophet (2 Chron. 35.22), *before* he inflicted a severe blow on Israel. He killed Josiah, a pious Israelite who, however, rejected YHWH's word and thus was construed as a kind of Other. It is not by chance that the memories Chronicles evoked about Josiah's death were partially evocative of those the community had about Ahab's death.[23] To remember Necho as partially 'Israelitized' and as a temporary prophet went hand in hand with remembering Josiah as partially 'Ahabized' and partially Otherized.[24]

Foreign rulers like Hiram of Tyre, the Queen of Sheba, and Cyrus of Persia are all remembered as non-Israelite but also as individuals who, to a substantial extent, understood and were able to participate in the discourse of well-educated Israelites, even able to talk like one of them.[25] Whereas the Queen of Sheba was remembered as going to Jerusalem to hear and learn from Solomon's wisdom, Jethro, the priest of Midian, was remembered as going to Moses to provide him with necessary practical wisdom (Exod. 18). In addition, Jethro the Midianite evoked the image

---

23. See, among others, Christine Mitchell, 'The Ironic Death of Josiah in 2 Chronicles', *CBQ* 68 (2006), pp. 421-35; Ralph W. Klein, *2 Chronicles: A Commentary* (Hermeneia; Minneapolis: Fortress, 2012), pp. 526-27; Paul K. Hooker, *First and Second Chronicles* (Westminster Bible Companion; Louisville: Westminster John Knox, 2001), p. 285.

24. It is worth noting that, just as in the case of the widow mentioned above, there was an attempt to remove the 'foreign prophet' from the mnemonic narrative and replace him with Jeremiah in the story remembered by the community (compare 2 Chron. 35.22 with 1 Esd. 1.26).

25. I discussed some of these cases elsewhere; see 'When a Foreign Monarch Speaks', in *The Chronicler as Author: Studies in Text and Texture* (ed. M. Patrick Graham and Steven L. McKenzie; JSOTSup, 263, Sheffield: Sheffield Academic Press, 1999), pp. 209-28.

of a father figure to Moses, while Cyrus was remembered as YHWH's anointed king, Hiram as Solomon's brother, and the Queen of Sheba as a female quasi-counterpart to the wise Israelite king.

Most significantly, it was not necessary for the Other to be in direct contact with Israelite territory, its main sites, or even its main heroes to be construed in such a manner, as the case of Job demonstrates. Job was remembered as a man from the land of Uz, a non-Israelite who engaged in direct dialogue with YHWH and whose discourse and the discourse of all his friends were part and parcel of Israelite discourse.

Of course, there were some limits to these processes of 'Israelitization' of the Other; Cyrus does not know YHWH (Isa. 45.5), and Jethro is not present at the revelation at Sinai. Even so, it is obvious that it is not by chance that all these characters are construed and remembered the way they are. Moreover, memories of this type are encoded in works belonging to multiple literary corpora, across genre and collection. In addition, these memories are not associated with any particular remembered/construed period but cut across temporal lines. They are part and parcel of the entire mnemonic landscape of the community and reflect systemic preferences in terms of both mnemonic narratives and ways of Othering and cross-Othering, which existed in the early Second Temple period.

The above examples demonstrate that, at times, remembering the Other as partially Us was associated with partial Othering of some of Us or even Us.[26] But memories of Israelites who remain Israel but who are partially Othered were certainly not limited to these types of cases. They include the obvious case of Zimri (Num. 25), the motif of Israel asking for a king 'like all the other nations' (1 Sam. 8; significantly, a request that was remembered as tantamount to rejecting YHWH and YHWH's kingship), ubiquitous deuteronomistic memories about Israel following the ways of the other nations and about repeated warnings not to do so, memories of Israel's kings worshiping other gods or their symbols and the like, or even attaching some Othering attributes to some of the more central and pious figures of Israel's constructed past (e.g. Moses, Joseph, David, Solomon). At times, however, the process is far subtler, as when 'Qohelet's king (mnemonically, Solomon) is rendered as one of the Eastern monsters [i.e., monster monarchs] of popular history'.[27] At times,

26. E.g. Solomon is both implicitly and explicitly compared and contrasted to either the kings or wise people of the other nations (cf. 1 Kgs 5.1-8, 9-14; 10.23; 11.1-3).

27. See Jennifer Barbour, *The Story of Israel in the Book of Qohelet: Ecclesiastes as Cultural Memory* (OTM; Oxford: Oxford University Press, 2012), citation from p. 34.

the process involves mirroring characters and groups in substantially different temporal circumstances, evoking long-term narratives in which mirroring serves as a main tool to remember and 'experience' manifestations of Us vicariously.[28]

Perhaps one of the most interesting and sophisticated cases of mirror Othering is present in the book of Esther.[29] There are numerous kinds of Othering in the book,[30] but a particularly salient case of Otherness that demands attention involves Israel/Esther/Mordecai vs. Haman/Amalek. As is well known, the memory of this conflict encoded in the book/s of Esther reflected and evoked an ideological discourse in which Israel and Amalek were construed as mutually genocidal (cf. Exod. 17.14-16; Deut. 25.17-19; 1 Sam. 15; 28.18). Each of the two was remembered as trying to exterminate the other. Thus, when readers were asked to remember that Haman wanted to destroy all the Jews/Judahites,[31] this would have

---

28. E.g. Deborah sitting under the tree; Siserah's mother inside a palace; or victorious 'judges' as Us and defeated royal courts as They. But as the remembering community knows all too well, 'royal courts' became We and We were defeated. Compare Judg. 5.28 and 2 Kgs 9.30 and notice the similar language. Multiple forms of mirroring were reflected in and evoked by the memory of the mother of Sisera. A serious examination of them and the ways they complement each other requires a separate discussion that cannot be undertaken here. Beth Hayes is currently working on this and related matters. For another case of mirroring across time, see the Deuteronomistic comparison between social memories about the 'nations that YHWH disinherited' and memories of late monarchic Israel.

29. This chapter is not the proper place to address the various proposals for dating of the books of Esther (e.g. MT Esther, proto-AT Esther, LXX Esther and their forerunners or textual successors) critically and their underlying mnemonic stories. The favoured date between 400 and 300 BCE may be in range, but even a date of several decades after 300 BCE will have no substantial bearing on the arguments advanced here. For the 400–300 BCE range, see, among others, Adele Berlin, *Esther* (JPS Bible Commentary; Philadelphia: JPS, 2001), pp. xli-xliii, and Jon Levenson, *Esther: A Commentary* (OTL; Louisville: Westminster John Knox, 1997), pp. 26-27.

30. For an analysis in this volume of Othering due to power dynamics deriving from minority status in an imperial system, see Jean-Daniel Macchi, 'Denial, Deception or Force: How to Deal with Powerful Others', pp. 219-29.

31. I prefer the term 'Judahites' over 'Judaeans', because it reflects the self-understanding of the readers better and the role of their ideological identification with the kingdom of Judah and its traditions, as they understood them to be, in their inner discourse. Within that discourse there was a substantial level of overlap between 'Judahite' and 'Israelite' that involved and effected the appropriation and encompassing of 'Israel' under and for Judah/Yehud/the reading community. This process is at work in the case discussed here as well; notice how mnemonic Amalek (i.e. Amalek as a site of memory) was construed around its desire/attempt to exterminate Israel/(all of the) Judahites/Jews.

been a familiar narrative/mnemonic motif. This realization explains the seeming enigma presented by the conceptual rarity in Esther of a political plan to exterminate an entire *ethnie* from the face of the earth in the ancient Near East.[32] What is more telling, however, is the way in which Haman is portrayed as constructing his Other (i.e. Israel) as 'a certain people scattered and separated among the peoples in all the provinces of your kingdom; their laws are different from those of every other people, and they do not keep the king's laws' (Est. 3.8, NRSV). For present purposes, the issue is not that the book, written within the inner group for the use of the inner group, characterized Israel as keeping the king's laws and bringing benefit to him and the like—which it does—but that Haman was remembered as construing his Other, Israel, in terms of its own laws. Moreover, the issue is not that their laws are characterized as different *per se*; every group had somewhat different laws. What stand out is that the Otherness of the laws of the Jews/Judahites was presented as essentially different from that of all Others. Amalek/Haman construed his Other according to Israel's social norms, thus reflecting/refracting self-identities among Yehudites/Judahites/Israel in the Persian and Hellenistic period as a *torah*-centred group. Even more importantly, Mordecai/Israel construed those doomed to destruction in an analogous way. His/Their Other was not necessarily constructed in terms restricted to lineage, even if it included an element of that, because his/their Other consisted of those who wished calamity on Israel, that is, the enemies of the Jews or Judahites, whatever their (original) lineage might be. In other words, Haman's people (the counterpart of Mordecai's people) also were construed as a norm-centered group.[33] Those imagining and remembering this world were involved in mirror Othering at multiple and connected levels.[34]

All the previous sets of examples have dealt primarily and often exclusively with one common axis of Othering: a construed ethnocultural group with which the in-group identifies itself and then distinguishes

32. This is not to deny that there were some negative constructions of Jews/ Judahites in the early Hellenistic period. See Peter Schäfer, *Judeophobia: Attitudes Toward the Jews in the Ancient World* (Cambridge: Harvard University Press, 1997).

33. For a different perspective on Israel vs. Amalek in Esther, see André LaCocque, *Esther Regina: A Bakhtinian Reading* (Evanston: Northwestern University Press, 2008), pp. 65-80.

34. The potential mnemonic significance of the 'Jewishization'/'Judahitization' of many Others is likely related to these issues (see Est. 8.17 and note its possible narrative continuation in 9.1). But an analysis of this verse demands a substantial, separate study that cannot be carried out within the scope of this essay. The variegated set of examples brought to bear in this discussion suffices for present purposes.

outside groups by shaping them as Other in its conceptual world. But this is not the only possible axis for Othering. A very common, transcultural axis is based on gender constructions. In patriarchal societies, it is the inner group that would tend to identify with the hierarchically superior pole, masculinity, and would relegate Others to the socially construed pole of 'femininity'.[35] There are memories of future and past events that clearly reflect this common type of Othering (e.g. 1 Sam. 4.9; 8.7; 2 Sam. 13.28; Isa. 19.16).[36] It also is easy to comprehend why constructions of 'exilic'/defeated Israel would at times feminize Israel.[37]

Nor is it difficult to understand that Israel could identify with both female Esther and male Mordecai in a 'diasporic tale' such as Esther. A fundamental assumption on the narratival level is that the welfare and life of the Israelite/Israel depends, at least on the surface, on the protection and support of a powerful non-Israelite male, the foreign king. Thus, in the narrative world, just as the fate of female Esther is in the hands of her husband, so, too, Israel's future is in the hands of the king of Persia. Both are interwoven; Esther is Israel.

But matters are not so simple. For one, within the ideological discourse of the time, it is not only Israel who is imagined as dependent on the heroic male king for protection, but everyone in the empire. Only the presence of the genocidal Other Amalek makes Israel's dependence more vivid and unique.[38] Particularly interesting for the present discussion of Othering within the axis of gender is the fact that the Persian king is not portrayed heroically at all in Esther. While he is de-masculinized in the story, Mordecai becomes more and more masculine as the story progresses, culminating in Est. 10.2-3, and more kingly, even he cannot become the king without breaching the world of the story. Since both Mordecai and Esther stand for Israel, toward the end of the story Esther also begins to be portrayed as fulfilling roles commonly associated with male leaders (Est. 9.29-32).[39] Othering through gendered categories proves

---

35. E.g. Cynthia R. Chapman, *The Gendered Language of Warfare in the Israelite–Assyrian Encounter* (HSM, 62; Winona Lake, IN: Eisenbrauns, 2004). Cf. 'They Have Become Women'.

36. The motif of the woman in birth can be used in more than one way, though. See Isa. 13.8; Jer. 30.5-6; Mic. 4.9-10; but also and significantly, Isa. 42.13-15.

37. See, for instance, Lemos, 'They Have Become Women'.

38. Thus, in that sense, Israel has a 'unique' existence because of Amalek's Othering of Israel, and vice versa (see above).

39. See the shift from an Esther who achieves influence through 'feminine wiles' and female beauty to that of a leader who sets up ordinances (Est. 9.32; cf. 9.29 and notice the order of the names).

in this case to be a relatively fluid business; Israel is both Mordecai and Esther, both at the beginning of the narrative and at its conclusion.

Other cases of Othering seem to be even more remarkable. Two come to mind. The first involves discursive negotiations of Otherization by males who construct themselves using obvious female characteristics, thereby shaping their identity and Israel's identity through a construction of qualified, seeming alterity. The second includes cases in which masculinity itself has to be and actually is reshaped to include a realm that allows the Israelite literati to construct themselves as males who are hierarchically superior to Others.

Turning to the first category, Israel was imagined as YHWH's bride/wife (Jer. 2.2; 31.32; Hos. 2.16-25; Isa. 54.5-8; 62.3-5). There is nothing strange in the conceptualization of a hierarchical relationship in gendered terms; moreover, the marital imagery is helpful and preferred discursively and mnemonically because it is an easy and fruitful means to characterize Israel negatively. Less obvious features of this metaphorical realm are, however, equally important. For instance, in ancient Israel there was an 'assumption that a virgin woman can be altered like clothing. Once she has sex, however, she becomes unalterable, marked or branded by her husband's "personness"... His [the husband's] person and hers become interwoven through sexual contact.'[40] Israel was certainly imagined as unalterably 'branded' by her husband YHWH, and to some extent their 'personhood' becomes intertwined. The noted assumption raises at least two important issues.

First, Israel could not be remembered as branded by anyone before YHWH. She had to be a virgin when meeting YHWH (cf. Jer. 2.2; Hos. 2.16). The male literati, then, had to imagine their ancestors in the distant past in terms equivalent not only to women but virgin women, and unborn generations in the distant future as 're-virginized' Israel for whom the ba'als will be erased (Hos. 2.19), who will return to the wilderness to be allured by YHWH once again (cf. Hos. 2.16). They also know that bride Israel concerns only a transformative but still fleeting moment in their narrative about their future. The final and permanent state will be Israel as the eternally good wife of YHWH. Other 'female' characters, each with her own husband, lover/s, or their dead counterparts, are necessary within this discourse to make full sense of the marriage between YHWH and Israel.[41] Thus, the Othering and hierarchies

40. Susan Niditch, *War in the Hebrew Bible: A Study in the Ethics of Violence* (New York: Oxford University Press, 1993), p. 85.

41. Even 'I love you' is meaningless if the 'unloved' are not excluded as correctly stressed in Baumann, 'Grammars of Identity/Alterity', p. 36.

involved in this process of shaping a sense of self-understanding and boundaries move away from differences shaped around dichotomies of male/female toward a binary consisting of virgin bride/non-virgin bride. The latter then contrasts a wife with the most masculine, powerful husband with wives/lovers or widows of less masculine husbands, which is how nations other than Israel are conceptualized. Within this patriarchal system of hierarchical classification and Othering, the lowest rung is occupied by the whore and cheating wife. Significantly, this was exactly how Israel also remembered itself. Boundaries are not only porous but can be crossed by all at more than one point.

YHWH was the husband of Israel but also 'the king' among all the gods. The self-understanding of Israel construed and remembered YHWH as a male who took no wives in addition to Israel,[42] and yet, since kings were among the relatively few males in society who took multiple wives as a way to broadcast, as it were, their great masculine power, a contradiction arose requiring resolution. To maintain YHWH's conceptualization as the top, most masculine king required the renegotiation of socially constructed norms of masculinity. A conceptual realm was required in which YHWH remained the hierarchically top man who, at the same time, was completely monogynistic.[43]

Re-negotiations of masculinity involved not only YHWH but a self-understanding of Israel and its literati as the top 'man' in the world in the late Persian and early Hellenistic period. Because YHWH was the top 'man', faithfully serving him made the literati and their Israel, who were powerless in worldly terms, the top 'men' of the world and hierarchically superior to the seemingly masculinized, mighty warriors of the other nations, whose fate was and would be eventual defeat. Israel was masculinized and the Other feminized, but mirroring and the reconceptualization of categories had to take place. As a result, the 'great warrior' aspect of main biblical military heroes like David and Joshua has been strongly tempered by remembering them as learners and conveyors of divine knowledge and de-emphasizing their warrior-like personal achievements. A similar tendency shapes the way in which founding

---

42. See Ehud Ben Zvi, 'Monogynistic and Monogamous Tendencies, Memories and Imagination in Late Persian/Early Hellenistic Yehud', *ZAW* 125.2 (2013), pp. 263-77.

43. Perhaps some play among various manifestations of transtemporal/ideological 'Israel', i.e., as northern and southern, as Jerusalem and the like, may have provided room for a safe acceptance of the monogynistic character of YHWH, but the room for play was minor and ultimately irrelevant. YHWH could never marry Edom, Assyria, Egypt, or the like; none of the 'women' of the world except transtemporal/ideological Israel.

figures like Moses and Abraham tended to be remembered in the community. Even a future ideal king was imagined in one case as riding on a donkey rather than in a war chariot or on a horse (Zech. 9.9).

This being said, blurring, in-between, overlapping realms were still necessary for the process to work. YHWH still remained a top warrior, not only a teacher; and wisdom, although belonging to YHWH and partially to Israel's literati, was also female. As much as Israel identified with the wife/wives of YHWH in Hosea, it still identified itself with husband YHWH/Hosea; as much as it identified with Jerusalem as YHWH's wife, it also identified itself as the male children of that union (e.g. Isa. 62.4-5).[44]

I will round off this exploration with a brief discussion of another axis that was employed to Other in the biblical texts and continues in use today: bodily ableness and the lack thereof (e.g. Lev. 21–22; Deut. 15.21 or 17.1). One would assume Israel was supposed to construct itself as bodily able/whole/תם, since this is the normally preferred status, and even more so, given the tendency toward viewing Israel as a nation of priests (e.g. Exod. 19.6).[45] Yet, the community remembered Isaac as blind, Moses having a speech impediment, and Jeremiah's rescue by a double Othered individual, Ebed-Melech, a Cushite and a eunuch (Jer. 38.7-13). Moreover, it remembered Israel as embodied in a (future) servant of YHWH who was emphatically imagined as far from possessing 'body normalness'.

Although one may claim that, at times, the construction of exilic (though not necessarily exiled) Israel took the form of the Other whose body was not 'normal', even so, YHWH's servant and, indirectly, the Others, point at a *positive Israel in the future* that was characterized at least temporarily as not being whole or able-bodied. Here again is a case of mirrored construction of otherness in which positive images of Israel are associated with the lack of physical wholeness.

These images are also informed and balanced by more usual images. Non-Israelite can be described as not having a complete body (e.g. for the Philistines see Judg. 14.3; 1 Sam. 14.6, passim), enemy bodies can be maimed (e.g. Judg. 1.6 and see also v. 7), and good Israelites who sin

44. Cf. Ehud Ben Zvi, 'Exploring Jerusalem as a Site of Memory in the Late Persian and Early Hellenistic Period', in *Memory and the City in Ancient Israel* (ed. Diana V. Edelman and Ehud Ben Zvi; Winona Lake, IN: Eisenbrauns, forthcoming).

45. Cf. Isa. 61.6 and notice the presence of a generative grammar in which 'Israelitization' is associated with 'priestization'. The entire issue of the partial 'priestization' and partial 'kingization' of the ideological concept of 'Israel' in the late Persian/early Hellenistic period (and later) demands a separate discussion.

may be remembered as symbolically and physically 'othered' (e.g. Uzziah in Chronicles or Miriam).[46] The lack of a complete body is associated with impurity and with social marginalization. These two seemingly contradictory ways of Othering along the body-wholeness axis actually complement one other and together create additional realms of blurring, of in-between and double-edgeness in which the direction of the Othering is basically contextual and contingent rather than categorical.

Examples can be multiplied, additional axes for Othering may be explored (see, for instance, Isa. 2.3-4), and each example already given could be analysed further. Nevertheless, the cumulative weight of the evidence from these three different axes of Othering indicates that, while Othering was a main tool for shaping constructions of self and corresponding memories of Israel, those Othered or the Othering features used point at the inner group and vice-versa. Boundaries not only were porous but also could be crossed in multiple directions. In-between realms could be expanded and crucial attributes were shifting, contingent, and constantly balanced in terms of the ways in which they served to construct Otherness. Deliberate fuzziness also was a key strategy.

Even when it takes place primarily as internal discourse without involving direct engagement with living 'ethnic' Others,[47] socially shared Othering is enmeshed in processes of identify formation and socialization. Significantly, the literati of the period discussed here were involved, *inter alia*, in imagining and developing memories of a future world empire of YHWH experienced only through acts of shared readings and imagination.[48] Thus, it is not surprising that a relatively common, cross-cultural, imperial attitude was also at work in their Otherizing. After all, good Israelites or a good 'Israelitized' non-Israelite, like Jethro, Hiram, or the Queen of Sheba, all had to be imagined as complying with what the literati considered to be in line with YHWH's teachings. In other words, these texts and memories reflect and socialize the Othering community into a variant of a cross-cultural, relatively imperial attitude, where foreigners can be like Us or even Us, provided they think or

46. On Gehazi, see p. 29 above. Gehazi is not construed as a 'good Israelite' who sinned.

47. The texts were written in Hebrew and accessible only to a few literati who knew Hebrew.

48. I expand on this topic in 'The Yehudite Collection of Prophetic Books and Imperial Contexts: Some Observations', in *Divination, Politics and Ancient Near Eastern Empires* (ed. Jonathan Stökl and Alan Lenzi; ANEM/MACO; Atlanta: SBL, 2014), pp. 145-69.

behave like Us. Yet, this is also a reminder that Us and the Other can and do share an in-between area; the kind of area evoked by memories like those of Moses and Jethro, of Solomon and the Queen of Sheba, or of Solomon and Hiram, of Elijah and the widow, of a Job with whom Israelites can easily identify, of foreigners and eunuchs who are not separate from YHWH's people (Isa. 56.3), and of imagining a glorious future Israel embodied in an impaired body or as both male and female.

The other side of an encompassing grammar of Otherness,[49] where some of Us may (temporarily?) become some of Them if they fail to behave and think like Us, is also a common, cross-cultural topos of Otherization that serves obvious roles in socialization processes. Yet, it also shapes and evokes memories of in-between areas, mirroring, and even double mirroring, which, by necessity, imply a reconceptualization of boundaries as very porous. The Other is often potentially Us and We are often potentially the Other in this type of grammar of Otherization.

The imperial, encompassing grammar of Othering mentioned above cuts across seemingly important boundaries and evokes fuzziness and porous boundaries; at the same time, however, it could not but involve a grammar of rejection. Boundaries still remain and exclude others, like the sinful Israelite and the nations that do not acknowledge or even scorn YHWH. Such preferences in the boundaries used in 'othering' have prioritized following YHWH and YHWH's ways as understood by the community, which one would expect among literati whose Israel was *torah-* (and text-) centred and who explained calamities of the past in terms of forsaking YHWH and YHWH's *torah*. Othering, memories, and systemic mnemonic preferences are all contingent and are an integral component of a larger discourse.

The paragraphs above have stressed encompassing grammars of Othering. But, as is often the case, they were complemented by other grammars at work simultaneously. Segmentation grammars of Othering were clearly at work among the literati who shaped their memories by reading the literature that eventually became the Hebrew Bible. From their perspective, various groups were Us and not Us or Us or not Us, depending on the context in which the We talked about, imagined and construed the Us. Among the most obvious examples of this grammar of Othering are the Northern tribes, Samaria, the generation of the 'wanderings', and even the far more tricky case of Benjamin, which was part not only of Israel but also of a Judah that stood in direct mnemonic continuity with Yehud and yet was, at same time and in the same general

49. On generative grammars of alterity, see in particular Baumann, 'Grammars of Identity/Alterity'.

discourse, clearly non-Judah, depending on the context.[50] Segmentation grammars, like the others already explored, could not but evoke in-between areas and fuzziness, since the very same sites of memory embodied both Us and the Other at the same time within the general memory-scape of the community.

As shown above, there was much use of reverse mirror Othering, which is another generative grammar for Otherness and for memories that construe and evoke Otherness. Mirroring involves, by its very nature, constructions of Others who were both rejected and emulated. They were rejected when they embodied and helped Us to formulate in our own discourse what was wrong with Us now, in the past, or in the future, and emulated when they embodied and helped Us to formulate in our own discourse what was or could be right with Us, like the sailors and the repentant Ninevites.[51] Mirror grammars of Othering were ubiquitous in the period. Significantly, the extended use of mirrors and mirrors of mirrors as a means to explore and formulate ways of thinking about Us reflects a sense of comfort with fuzziness. Social preferences for fuzziness and openness, even within limits, are historical, contingent features. They are far more likely to be present in groups that do not face perceived existential threats to their existence and which are relatively secure and 'at ease' in their circumstances.[52] This observation suggests

50. See my 'Total Exile, Empty Land and the General Intellectual Discourse in Yehud', in *The Concept of Exile in Ancient Israel and its Historical Contexts* (ed. Ehud Ben Zvi and Christoph Levin; BZAW, 404; New York: de Gruyter, 2010), pp. 155-68, and 'The Concept of Prophetic Books and Its Historical Setting', in *The Production of Prophecy: Constructing Prophecy and Prophets in Yehud* (ed. Diana V. Edelman and Ehud Ben Zvi; BibleWorld; London: Equinox, 2009), pp. 73-95 (83-85).

51. For a discussion of the Ninevites 'Israelitizing' their behaviour in response to Jonah's delivery of YHWH's word yet remaining fully Other rather than readjusting or undermining the boundaries of Israel, see the essay in this volume by Susanne Gillmayr-Bucher, 'Jonah and the Other: A Discourse on Interpretative Competence', pp. 201-18.

52. I have discussed these matters elsewhere; see Ehud Ben Zvi, 'On Social Memory and Identity Formation in Late Persian Yehud: A Historian's Viewpoint with a Focus on Prophetic Literature, Chronicles and the Dtr. Historical Collection', in *Texts, Contexts and Readings in Postexilic Literature: Explorations into Historiography and Identity Negotiation in Hebrew Bible and Related Texts* (ed. Louis Jonker; FAT, II/53; Tübingen: Mohr–Siebeck, 2011), pp. 95-148, esp. 141-43; 'Exploring the Memory of Moses "The Prophet" in Late Persian/Early Hellenistic Yehud/Judah', in *Remembering Biblical Figures in the Late Persian and Early Hellenistic Periods: Social Memory and Imagination* (ed. Diana V. Edelman and Ehud Ben Zvi; Oxford: Oxford University Press, 2013), pp. 335-64, esp. 362-64.

that in later periods, groups in Israel who were not as 'at ease' may have had different Othering tendencies, but a discussion of these matters is beyond the scope of this essay.[53]

53.   The same holds true for the issue of YHWH as the Other, which requires an entire monograph. Here, it suffices to note the strong presence in the world of ideas and the imagination of the community of a binary. On the one hand is the principle of *imitatio Dei* (e.g. Lev. 19.2), of *imago Dei* and the fact that the ideal/future Israel/Jerusalem is often imagined with godly attributes (e.g. Hos. 2.21; Isa. 60.3) and, on the other hand, multiple sites of memory that time and again assign human attributes to YHWH, anthropomorphizing the divine. Multiple levels of negotiating, partially bridging, and leaving open the gap between human and divine or some humans and the divine through explorations of potential 'in-between' areas of attributes shared by both are all at work as well. The considerations advanced above all seem, at the very least, heuristically relevant to the study of the divine as the Other within the imagination and historical discourse of the literati of the early Second Temple period, and probably not to them only. This said, a significant differ-ence between this case of Othering and the other cases discussed above should be noted: trends that enhance a measure of 'fuzziness' in this case are less common in societies that are 'at ease' and more common in those that are not, but his matter demands a separate study. For some strategies used to make the divine one of Us and also for the Divine to assert its Otherness, see the Diana Edelman's contribution to the present volume, 'YHWH's Othering of Israel', pp. 41-69.

YHWH'S OTHERING OF ISRAEL[*]

Diana V. Edelman

Introduction

Othering is a psychological strategy for establishing and reinforcing individual or group identity through separation and the establishment of boundaries of difference.[1] It is part of human nature to want to feel unique or special in some way, and Othering is a necessary process to use to set oneself or one's group apart from the rest of humanity so that the individual or the group can be assigned one or more unique characteristics. It is a strategy widely used in the Hebrew Bible to establish the traits that set the religious community of Israel apart from surrounding nations and groups in the larger ancient Near East. It is also used, however, to argue that YHWH will reject or has rejected or Othered Israel, his otherwise treasured, selected people, making them an outside group rather than an inside one. The subject of this essay is strategies used by various biblical writers to depict or threaten YHWH's Othering of Israel in the texts that came to form an authoritative collection being read and reread[2] by and to those with ties to the former kingdom of Judah by the late Persian or early Hellenistic period.

---

[*] I am grateful to Ehud Ben Zvi, Philip Davies, Philippe Guillaume, and Kåre Berge for reading various versions of this paper and providing helpful feedback.

1. For an interdisciplinary study that includes Othering as understood in the social sciences and in theology, see Lisa Isherwood and David Harris, *Radical Otherness: Sociological and Theological Approaches* (Gender, Theology and Spirituality; Durham: Acumen, 2013).

2. While reading often appears to have been aloud, there is now some thought challenging the former arguments that it was always done vocally, even by individuals reading to themselves. See, e.g., Ehud Ben Zvi, 'Introduction: Writing, Speeches, and the Prophetic Books—Setting an Agenda', in *Writings and Speech in Israelite and Ancient Near Eastern Prophecy* (ed. E. Ben Zvi and M. H. Floyd; SBLSymS, 10; Atlanta: SBL, 2000), pp. 1-29, esp. 16-18, 21-24.

Cultures include both individualist and collectivist elements that people utilize in different degrees in varying circumstances. If more collectivist elements are typically drawn upon by most members, a culture can be classified as collectivist and if more individualist elements dominate actions and attitudes, the culture can be considered individualist. Social behaviour in a collectivist culture is characterized by association, super-ordination, intimacy, overtness, cooperation, inequality, informality, security, restricted conformity, traditionalism, and benevolence. In an individualist culture, by contrast, social behaviour takes the form of disassociation, subordination, formality, covertness, competition, equality, self-direction, stimulation, hedonism, and achievement.[3] On the basis of attitudes and behavioural norms advocated in the biblical texts and material cultural remains recovered through archaeology, Israel and Judah can be classified as predominantly collectivist cultures. This means the self was defined in terms of in-group relationships and that self-linked memories were few in comparison with group-linked memories; achievement was supposed to be for the sake of the group, and in-group needs and goals took precedence over personal needs and goals, with cooperation, endurance, order, and self-control valued personal attributes. Group-endorsed memories of individual figures from the collective past that belonged to the in-group or to outsider groups would shape the attitudes of the individual group member. The individual actions of these remembered figures would provide both positive and negative reflections of insider values, norms, and ideals. Membership in the in-group tended to be defined by ascribed attributes like kinship, caste, race, village, or tribe vs. achieved ones.[4]

The family or clan, and with it, values like filial piety, numerous offspring, the importance of ancestors, and family or blood-line, constitutes the core of collectivism.[5] There is little cognitive dissonance. Emotionally, members focus on other group members, displaying empathy; they value modesty and favour embeddedness in in-groups and beliefs that reflect interdependence. They accept hierarchy, viewing vertical

3. Harry C. Triandis, 'Theoretical and Methodological Approaches to the Study of Collectivism and Individualism', in *Individualism and Collectivism: Theory, Method, and Applications* (ed. Uichol Kim et al.; CCRMS, 18; London: Sage, 1994), pp. 41-51 (45).

4. Ibid., pp. 47-48.

5. Jae-Ho Cha, 'Aspects of Individualism and Collectivism in Korea', in Kim et al. (eds.), *Individualism and Collectivism*, pp. 157-74 (161). This correlates with Geert Hofstede's findings ('National Cultures Revisited', *Behavior Science Research* 18 [1983], pp. 285-305).

relationships as more important than horizontal ones. They value obedience, duty, and in-group harmony and accept the deep influence the in-group's norms have on many individual behaviours. Relationship to the in-group is close, and it is perceived to be more homogenous than to out-groups; concern for the integrity of the in-group is a high priority.[6]

Social behaviour is very different toward in-group members than out-group members. There is more rejection of out-groups and more difficulty in communicating with strangers in collectivist cultures than in individualist ones.[7] Interaction with out-group members tends toward competition instead of cooperation, exploitation in the place of sacrifice, manipulation rather than help, and fighting instead of accommodation.[8]

This brief look at social psychology helps us understand the larger cultural attitudes that would have prevailed in ancient Yehud when the books that now form the Hebrew Bible collection were serving as written embodiments of social values and encapsulations of a selected common past deemed meaningful for the present and useful also in shaping the future. The books gave definition to and voiced the shared values of a group that no longer shared territorial or political integrity but wanted to preserve a sense of peoplehood and unique identity as a community bound to the deity YHWH Elohim and the god's favoured territory and city, the hill-country of Judah and Jerusalem.[9] Undoubtedly created by a small group of literate scribes who considered themselves guardians of social memory, customs, values, and identity, and read within these circles initially, they eventually served as a basis to enculturate Judaean youth who sought an education by the mid-Hellenistic period, as indicated by

6. Triandis, 'Theoretical Approaches', pp. 47-48, 50. For similar values in Indian social groups, see Jai B. P. Sinha, 'Collectivism, Social Energy and Development in India', in *From a Different Perspective: Studies of Behavior Across Cultures* (ed. Isabel Reyes Labunes and Ype H. Poortinga: Lisse: Swets & Zeitlinger, 1985), pp. 109-19.

7. Triandis, 'Theoretical Approaches', p. 50.

8. So Durghanda Sinha and Rama Charan Tripathi, 'Collectivism in Collectivist Culture: A Case of Coexistence of Opposites', in Kim et al. (eds.), *Individualism and Collectivism*, pp. 123-36 (129). The comments refer specifically to Indian culture but could apply in other collectivist cultures.

9. The primary target audience of the collection of books in the Hebrew Bible was descendants of former citizens of the kingdom of Judah. However, the target audience of the first five books alone included descendants of former citizens of the kingdom of Israel as well, so in those books, the god's favoured territory included the hill country of Ephraim and Manasseh, the Galilee, and the Transjordanian highlands as well—all the territory associated with the eponymous twelve tribes of Israel, with an unspecified favourite city.

Ben Sira. How much earlier that occurred is open to debate, as is the question whether the books were compiled with such a goal in mind.[10]

In order to understand how values and behaviours expressed in the biblical texts would have been perceived, reinforced, or discouraged in the collectivist culture of Yehud in the Persian and Hellenistic periods, we need to understand the underlying motivations that would have been at play in society. Threats to the group's cohesion, existence, and beliefs would have been taken seriously and should have served as rallying points to defend the *status quo* and its defining principles and behaviours actively. In a collectivist society particularly, the threat of ostracism from the in-group or the elimination of the in-group would have been particularly stressful and a strong motivator to change behaviour to conform.[11] While there are examples of the use of reverse psychology in the collected texts comprising the Hebrew Bible, where a person tries to get a desired result by suggesting another do the opposite of what is really wanted, this strategy tends to be used on the individual level by those who know the other's personality well rather than as a strategy to

10. For discussions of when the wider educational use that went beyond strict scribal training and alphabetic competency developed, see, for example, Philip R. Davies, *Scribes and Schools: The Canonization of the Hebrew Scriptures* (Library of Ancient Israel; Louisville: Westminster John Knox, 1998); David M. Carr, *Writing on the Tablet of the Heart: Origins of Scripture and Literature* (Oxford: Oxford University Press, 2005); Thomas M. Bolin, '1–2 Samuel and Jewish Paideia in the Persian and Hellenistic Periods', in *Deuteronomy–Kings as Emerging Authoritative Books: A Conversation* (ed. Diana V. Edelman; ANEM; Atlanta: SBL, 2014), pp. 111-32.

11. Because Israel was a collectivist society, it is likely that YHWH's threatened dis-election of Israel was not a deliberate use of reverse psychology, where the deity was attributed the espousal of the opposite of what was desired to happen, in order to get the audience to follow the prescribed divine path and remain part of the chosen in-group. Such an approach is used when the recipient is reactant, feeling his or her personal freedom under threat, which would be more likely in an individualist society. For the same reason, the related technique called paradoxical intervention in psychotherapy is not likely to be in mind. For the latter, see Gerald R. Weeks, *Paradoxical Psychotherapy: Theory and Practice with Individuals, Couples, and Families* (New York: Brunner/Mazel, 1982); Leon F. Seltzer, *Paradoxical Strategies in Psychotherapy: A Comprehensive Overview and Guidebook* (Wiley Series on Personality Processes; Chichester, UK: Wiley, 1986); David M. Foreman, 'The Ethical Use of Paradoxical Interventions in Psychotherapy', *Journal of Medical Ethics* 16 (1990), pp. 200-205. Israel's unique relationship with YHWH has been encoded as central group norm so that members will have internalized the idea as a non-negotiable core value on the individual as well as the collective level.

motivate collective behaviour.[12] By first understanding the ways in which Israel's election by YHWH are expressed in various books, we can then see how threats by this deity to reject its chosen family or to destroy its special people by reversing these forms of election are primary mechanisms used to prompt group members to reaffirm and ensure adhesion to core group values, principles, and history.

1. *Divine Strategies for Creating and Defining the In-Group*

1.1. *Israel as YHWH's People, Nation, and Treasure*

Israel's having a special relationship with YHWH, out of all the peoples and nations of the earth, is emphasized in many ways throughout the books in the Hebrew Bible collection. The most direct expressions involve use of the root 'to choose' (בחר)[13] and often describe Israel as YHWH's 'chosen' people[14] or, in one case, chosen nation (Ps. 33.12). A synonymous root that conveys a similar sense of a special relationship between YHWH and Israel is ידע, 'to know'.[15] Amos 3.2 provides perhaps the strongest illustration—'You only have I known among all the clans (משפחות) of the cultivated soil (אדמה)'—which, if reading the current collection of books in the Hebrew Bible, constitutes an allusion to the divine promise in Gen. 12.3.[16] The verb euphemistically can refer to

12. The following examples were pointed out to me by Ehud Ben Zvi in feedback: Gen. 3.1-5 (serpent to Eve); 1 Kgs 22.13 (the messenger to Micaiah ben Imlah, assuming he represents the view of King Jehoshaphat in v. 8); Job 2.9 (Job's wife to Job); Isa. 6.10 (YHWH to Isaiah); and Ezek. 20.39 (YHWH to each individual member of the house of Israel).

13. So, for example, Deut. 4.37; 7.6-7; 10.15; 14.2; Pss. 33.12; 135.4; Isa. 14.1; 41.8-9; 44.1-2; 45.4; Jer. 33.24; Ezek. 20.5.

14. So, for example, Deut. 7.6-7; 10.15; 14.2; Ps. 33.12; Isa. 43.20.

15. So, for example, Gen. 18.19; Exod. 2.25; Deut. 9.24; 34.10; Ps. 36.11 [36.10]; Hos. 2.20; 5.3; 8.2; 13.5; Amos 3.2.

16. It is seen to continue v. 1 and so allude to the Exodus and election (covenant at Sinai), with Gen. 18.19 cited as an example of a similar use of the root ידע by Alfons Deissler and Mathias Delcor, *La Sainte Bible, Tome 8 (1re partie): Les petits prophètes* (Paris: Letouzey & Ané, 1961–64), p. 200. In a subsequent commentary, Alfonse Deissler adds Gen. 4.19 as another example of the use of ידע alongside Jer. 1.5 and then cites Gen. 12.3 and 28.14 as parallels for the phrase 'out of all tribes of the earth' (*Zwolf Propheten: Hosea–Joël–Amos* [Die neue Echter Bible; Würzburg: Echter, 1981], p. 103). The recollection of Gen. 12.3 and also 28.14 has specifically been noted by, for example, Wilhelm Rudolph, *Joel–Amos–Obadja–Jona* (KAT, 13/2; Gütersloh: Gerd Mohn, 1971), p. 153; James Limburg, *Hosea–Micah* (Interpretation; Atlanta: John Knox, 1988), p. 95; Douglas Stuart, *Hosea–Jonah* (WBC, 31; Waco, TX: Word, 1989), p. 322. I find an intentional allusion to Gen. 28.14 secondary at best.

sexual intercourse but more commonly expresses acknowledgment and understanding, acquisition of knowledge, proclamation in a causative sense, and revelation in a passive sense. In a few instances, it expresses intimacy and understanding that arises from personal closeness in the context of friendship (e.g. Ps. 55.14 [55.13]) or family kinship.[17] It also was a technical term used in treaties.[18]

Additional memorable expressions that emphasize the special relationship between Israel and YHWH include, on the one hand, Israel's characterization as the god's 'treasure' (סגלה)[19] or as YHWH's treasured people (עם סגלה)[20] and, on the other, Israel's status as a holy nation (גוי קדוש; Exod. 19.6) or a holy people (עם קדוש, Deut. 7.6) due to its 'separation' (Hiphil of בדל) from other nations to be YHWH's (Lev. 20.24, 26). Israel's conceptualization as YHWH's chosen nation can be expressed contrastively in statements about other nations not being special to or known by YHWH or so treated by him (e.g. Ps. 147.20; Isa. 40.17; Amos 3.2).

With the foregoing strategies for expressing Israel's special status vis à vis YHWH in mind, it is logical to assume that descriptions of Israel as YHWH's 'people' (עם) or 'nation' (גוי), usually with no additional qualifiers except possessive suffixes, are meant to express the same, special status and relationship that forms an 'in-group' belonging to YHWH. What is stated explicitly in Amos 3.1 is implicit elsewhere; the people of Israel constitute 'the whole family (משפחה) that I brought out of the land of Egypt'. Examples of Israel as a עם[21] are more numerous than those as a גוי,[22] but even rarer are descriptions of Israel as a לאום, a national group (Gen. 25.23; Isa. 51.14).

17. For a helpful discussion of the nuances of this term, see Meir Malul, *Knowledge, Control and Sex: Studies in Biblical Thought, Culture and Worldview* (Tel Aviv-Jaffa: Archaeological Center, 2002), pp. 216-29 and passim.

18. As pointed out, for example, by Herbert Huffmon, 'The Treaty Background of Hebrew *YĀDAʿ*', *BASOR* 181 (1966), pp. 31-37.

19. Exod. 19.5; Ps. 135.4; Mal. 3.17.

20. Deut. 7.6; 14.2; 26.18; thus, an expression peculiar to this biblical book.

21. So, for example, Deut. 26.19; 32.43-44; 2 Sam. 7.23; Pss. 3.9 [3.8]; 14.7; 33.12; 44.13 [44.12]; 50.7; 68.8 [68.7]; 72.2; 79.13; 81.9 [81.8]; 81.12, 14 [81.11, 13]; 85.3, 7, 9 [85.2, 6, 8]; 89.16 [89.15]; 95.7, 10; 100.3; 106.40; 110.3; 111.6, 9; 135.12, 14; 144.15; 149.4; Isa. 43.21; 51.4, 22; 52.4-6, 9; 57.14; 58.1; 64.9; 65.19, 22; Jer. 31.1; Hos. 4.6, 8, 12; 11.7; Joel 2.17-19, 26-27; 4.2-3 [3.2-3]; 4.16 [3.16]; Amos 3.1; 4.5; 7.8; 8.2; 9.14; Mic. 1.9; 2.8-9; 3.3, 5; 6.2, 3, 5; 7.14; Hab. 3.13; Zeph. 2.9-10; Hag. 2.14; Zech. 8.7-8; 13.9.

22. Examples of Israel as a גוי include: Gen. 12.2; 18.18; 25.23; 35.11; 46.3; 48.19; Exod. 19.6; 33.13; Num. 14.12; Deut. 4.6, 7, 34, 38; 7.1, 17; 9.1, 14; 11.23; 26.5, 19; 28.1; 32.28; Josh. 3.17; 4.1; 5.6, 8; 10.13; Judg. 2.20; 1 Sam. 8.5 implied;

Arguably, descriptions of YHWH's loving Israel is part of this complex of thought in which Israel is embraced as an 'in-group' member by the god.[23] Two sources for the idea are apparent. The first is the family unit; Israel constitutes YHWH's family; sometimes his child or children,[24] sometimes his wife,[25] and at other times, his clan (משפחה).[26] The concept of YHWH 'knowing' Israel might fit this larger complex of thought, implying the idea that Israel is the wife of YHWH with whom he has mated or enjoyed conjugal intimacy. As noted in the introduction, kinship and values like filial piety, numerous offspring, the importance of ancestors, and family or blood-line constitute the core of collectivism, so the use of family imagery and language would resonate with an audience that espoused a collective worldview.[27]

The second is drawn from technical language used in vassal treaties; love is the duty owed by the lesser party, the 'son', to the superior one, the 'father', and optionally can describe any duties the superior party commits to undertake on behalf of the lesser party.[28] Here, 'father'

2 Sam. 7.23 implied; 2 Kgs 18.33 implied; 19.12 implied; 2 Chron. 32.14-15, 17 implied; Pss. 33.12; 83.4; Isa. 1.4; 9.2 [9.3]; 10.6; 26.2, 15; 36.18 implied; 37.12 implied; 51.4; 58.2; 60.22; 65.1; 66.8; Jer. 2.11 implied; 5.9, 29; 7.28; 9.8 [9.9]; 31.36; Ezek. 2.3; 37.22; Zeph. 2.1, 9; Hag. 2.14; Mal. 3.9.

23. Israel: Deut. 23.6 [23.5]; Jer. 31.1-3; Hos. 3.1; 11.1; 14.1, 4; Israel's forefathers: Deut. 4.37; 10.15.

24. Deut. 32.6; Pss. 27.10; 68.6 [of orphans]; 103.13 [of those who fear YHWH]; Prov. 3.12 [of the one YHWH loves]; Isa. 1.2-3; 41.13; 43.1, 4; 45.11; 46.3; 50.1; 63.16; 64.8; Jer. 3.4, 14, 19; 31.9; Hos. 11.1, 3; 13.12-13 of Ephraim; Mal. 2.10; 3.17.

25. So, for example, Isa. 54.5-6; Hos. 3.1. For what might underlie the interesting situation that YHWH can have many children besides Israel but only one wife—be that Israel (Jer. 2.2; Hos. 2.16-25; Jer. 31.32), Jerusalem, or Samaria (Jer. 3.6-13; Ezek. 23)—see Ehud Ben Zvi, 'Monogynistic and Monogamous Tendencies, Memory, and Imagination in Late Persian/Early Hellenistic Yehud', *ZAW* 125.2 (2013), pp. 263-77 (272-76).

26. So, for example, Jer. 8.3; 33.24; Amos 3.1-2; Mic. 2.3.

27. Another discussion of this familial relationship, which explores different aspects, can be found in Ehud Ben Zvi's contribution to the present volume, 'Othering, Selfing, "Boundarying" and "Crossing-Boundarying" as Interwoven with Socially Shared Memories: Some Observations', pp. 20-40.

28. For the recognition of the familial nature created by treaties, see, for example, William L. Moran, 'A Note on the Treaty Terminology of the Sefire Stelas', *JNES* 22 (1963), pp. 173-76; Delbert R. Hillers, 'A Note on Some Treaty Terminology in the Old Testament', *BASOR* 176 (1964), pp. 46-47; F. Charles Fensham, 'Father and Son as Terminology for Treaty and Covenant', in *Near Eastern Studies in Honor of William Foxwell Albright* (ed. Hans Goedicke; Baltimore: Johns Hopkins University Press, 1971), pp. 121-35; Dennis J. McCarthy,

YHWH loves Israel, whom he made his 'son' during the covenant at Mt. Sinai/Horeb (Deut. 7.12-13). The pact also draws on family imagery, creating a fictive kinship unit of the contracting partners so that, ultimately, the concept of love derives from blood kinship within a family.

1.2. *Israel as YHWH's Flock*

Another means of expressing the relationship between YHWH and Israel is shepherd-flock imagery.[29] This metaphor avoids the kinship implications of the family metaphor in favour of legal ownership; Israel is YHWH's movable property; his possession. Yet, while this analogy dehumanizes Israel, it still assigns it life and does not move it totally to the status of an object, which is implied by the term 'treasure' (סגלה), for example. It is a living entity that will die without proper tending by its owner/shepherd.

1.3. *Israel as YHWH's Garden*

A third expression of the relationship is agricultural in origin: Israel is a grape vine or, occasionally, a tree that YHWH plants and tends on his estate, the Promised Land. Like the shepherd-flock symbolism, this metaphor emphasizes Israel as YHWH's personal property. As gardener and owner, the deity plants (verb נטע)[30] or transplants (שתל)[31] Israel and is responsible for watering it and nourishing it so that it grows and produces fruit. As an extension of this agricultural metaphor, Israel is sometimes described as YHWH's נחלה ('inalienable property'), becoming the agricultural land in which plants take root instead of the plants themselves.[32] In this latter usage, there may be an intentional equation of Israel with the Promised Land, which, in turn, might be linked to the

Old Testament Covenant: A Survey of Current Opinions (Growing Points in Theology; Richmond: John Knox, 1972), p. 66; Paul Kalluveettil, *Declaration and Covenant: A Comprehensive Review of Covenant Formulae from the Old Testament and the Ancient Near East* (AnBib, 88; Rome: Pontifical Biblical Institute, 1982), pp. 91, 98-101; Noel Weeks, *Admonition and Curse: The Ancient Near Eastern Treaty/Covenant Form as a Problem in Inter-Cultural Relationships* (JSOTSup, 407; New York: T&T Clark International, 2004), p. 103.

29. So, for example, Pss. 44.12 [44.11]; 74.1; 77.21 [77.20]; 78.52; 79.13; 80.2 [80.1]; 95.7; 100.3; Isa. 40.11; Mic. 2.12; 7.14.

30. Exod. 15.17; 2 Sam. 7.10; 1 Chron. 17.9; Pss. 44.2; 80.8; Isa. 5.2, 7; Jer. 2.21; 11.17; 12.2; 17.8; 24.6; 32.41; 42.10; 45.4; Ezek. 36.36; Amos 9.15. For Israel as grain, see Isa. 40.24.

31. Pss. 1.3; 92.14 [92.13]; Ezek. 17.8, 10; 19.10, 13; Hos. 9.13.

32. See, e.g. 1 Kgs 8.51, 53; 2 Kgs 21.14; Pss. 33.12; 78.71; 94.5, 14; 106.40; Isa. 19.25; 47.6; 63.17; Joel 2.17; 4.2 [3.2]; Mic. 7.18.

covenant tradition. Though the land is initially promised to the patri-archs, its possession becomes a condition of obedience to the stipulations of the Sinai/Horeb covenant. The concept of divine gardeners was part of the worldview of the ancient Near East more widely.[33]

1.4. *Israel as* YHWH's *Covenanted People*

The covenant tradition by which YHWH formally made Israel and its descendants his own people bound to him by stipulations that were to be fulfilled is perhaps the central expression of the special, in-group relationship between these two parties, as opposed to other peoples and nations who never experienced a similar covenant with this particular deity.[34] The presence of two accounts of the covenant-making, one set at Mt. Sinai in Exodus and the other at Mt. Horeb in Deuteronomy, high-lights the importance of this concept in the Pentateuch, the core books of what would become the collection comprising the Hebrew Bible. The repetition makes the covenant the key moment within the biography of Moses that spans the books of Exodus, Leviticus, Numbers, and Deuter-onomy. Hosea 8.1 invokes it as the basis of Israel's claim, 'My God, we Israel know you' (8.2), and later in the same book, YHWH proclaims, 'I am YHWH your god from the land of Egypt; you know no God but me' (13.4). References to the covenant appear outside Exodus and Deuteron-omy in, for example, Pss. 44.18-20 [44.17-19]; 74.20; 81.8 [81.7]; 103.7; 111.5, 9; Zech. 9.11; and Mal. 3.22 [4.4].[35]

---

33. See Bernhard Lang, who cites texts and iconography concerning weather-gods particularly but also gods associated with springs and rivers (*The Hebrew God: Portrait of an Ancient Deity* [New Haven: Yale University Press, 2002], pp. 139-69). For a cautionary analysis of commonly cited examples of divine gardens in ancient Near Eastern mythical texts that does not find support for a commonly shared 'garden of God' theme, see Terje Stordalen, *Echoes of Eden: Genesis 2–3 and Symbolism of the Eden Garden in Biblical Hebrew Literature* (CBET, 25; Leuven: Peeters, 2000), pp. 139-61.

34. In feedback, Ehud Ben Zvi has pointed out that ברית stands for, evokes, and can even *embody* a single particular group or entity—the covenanted. See, e.g., Prov. 2.17, Isa. 42.6, and Mal. 3.1, especially the parallelism in the former two. Compare also Dan. 11.22, 28, 30; 1QM 33 14.4; 1QS 5.11, 18.

35. For studies on the theology associated with the covenant idea, see, e.g., William Dumbrell, *Covenant and Creation: An Old Testament Covenantal Theology* (Exeter: Paternoster, 1984); Ernest W. Nicholson, *God and His People: Covenant and Theology in the Old Testament* (Clarendon: Clarendon, 1986); Rolf Rendtorff, *The Covenant Formulary* (trans. M. Knohl; Old Testament Studies; Edinburgh: T. & T. Clark, 1998); Andrew D. H. Mayes and R. B. Salters (eds.), *Covenant as Context: Essays in Honour of E. W. Nicholson* (Oxford: Oxford University Press,

For a community with current or former ties to the region of Judah in the Persian or Hellenistic period, which read and reread in the late Persian or Hellenistic period at least what became the first five books, YHWH's covenant with Abram in Gen. 17.1-21 would foreshadow the covenant tradition at Mt. Sinai/Horeb.[36] Here, YHWH enters a formal agreement in v. 7 to establish an eternal relationship (ברית עולם) with Abraham and his descendants to be their god. Both Abraham and his descendants are also deeded the land of Canaan as a perpetual holding (אחזת עולם, v. 8). The conditions of the covenant are (1) walking before YHWH (Hitpael of הלך) and being without fault (תמים, v. 1) and (2) the circumcision of native-born males and slaves that are associated with the household (vv. 9-14). Any uncircumcised male will be cut off from his people because he has broken (Hiphil of פרר l) the covenant. In vv. 19 and 21 YHWH specifies that his eternal covenant will be with the descendants of Isaac, not Ishmael (repeated in 21.12).

Subsequently, in 18.19, the two aspects of the first condition are paraphrased as keeping/observing the way of YHWH to do righteousness and justice, and for the first time the verb ידע is used to describe Abraham's status: YHWH has 'known' him or singled him out for special treatment. It is interesting that in this verse, the covenant seems to be conditioned on the performance of righteousness and justice, even though no consequence for the failure to do so is specified, as it is with the second stipulation. In the ongoing story line, the reader learns that Abraham personally fulfils these stipulations (26.5), which then leads to YHWH's affirmation with Isaac of the terms of the covenant agreement

2003); Stephen L. Cook, *The Social Roots of Biblical Yahwism* (SBL Studies in Biblical Literature, 8; Boston: Brill, 2004).

36. The prior formal covenant in 15.18-21 is a deeding of the land from the Euphrates to the Nile to Abram's descendants, which builds on two promises announced in Gen. 12.1-2: the promise of land and of Abraham fathering a great nation. Neither element, however, explicitly establishes a special, chosen relationship between YHWH and the forefather of Israel. It is never stated explicitly that the land of Canaan is YHWH's special domain (Gen. 12.1, 7; 13.14-15, 17; 15.7; 17.8; 22.18; 24.7, 60; 26.4; 28.4, 14-15; 31.3, 13; 32.9; 35.12), so that Abraham's descendants who will live there will logically constitute his special people. There is no emphasis here yet on an adoptive family relationship either; Israel is to be a גוי, not an עם (Gen. 12.2; the remaining references are to numerous offspring: 3.16; 15.5; 16.10; 22.17; 26.4; 28.3, 14; 32.12; 35.11; 48.4; 50.20), through whom other nations will gain blessing (12.2; 18.18; 22.18; 26.4; 28.14). These two key themes read as introductions to the meta-story that runs from Genesis through the book of Kings, where Israel does eventually gain a land, taking possession of the enemies' gates (22.18; 24.60), and exists as a great nation under David and Solomon.

made with Abraham. It remains unclear if such fulfilment is required of
each succeeding generation in order for the covenant to continue in effect
to the next generation or if Abraham's exemplary behaviour alone is
enough to secure the eternal status of the unique relationship between
YHWH and Israel.

The use of the phrases, 'YHWH, the deity of Israel' (יהוה אלהי ישראל),[37]
'God of Israel' or 'the deity of Israel' (אלהי ישראל),[38] 'YHWH your
god/deity' (יהוה אלהיך),[39] 'YHWH our god/deity' (יהוה אלהינו),[40] 'YHWH
my god/deity' (יהוה אלהי),[41] 'YHWH their god/deity' (יהוה אלהיהם),[42]
'YHWH his god/deity' (יהוה אלהיו),[43] '(my) lord, YHWH' (אדני יהוה),[44]
'YHWH our lord' (יהוה אדנינו),[45] and 'YHWH, king of Israel' (יהוה מלך
ישראל)[46] reinforces the in-group identity of Israel as YHWH's people.
Images or claims of YHWH being or going 'with' Israel (preposition עם,[47]
עמדי,[48] or את[49]) or 'in their midst' (preposition בתוך[50] or בקרב[51]) similarly
imply a special closeness, where the deity's physical presence makes him
'one of them', conveying the sense of solidarity as well as safety and
protection, given his otherwise superhuman, Other nature. Since he is
not described as behaving in this way with other peoples or nations, it
highlights the special relationship he has with Israel vis-à-vis other

---

37. Pss. 41.14 [41.13]; 106.48; Isa. 45.3; Mal. 2.16.

38. Pss. 59.6 [59.5]; 68.9 [68.8]; 68.36 [68.35]; 69.7 [69.6]; 72.18; Isa. 41.17;
48.1; 52.12; Zeph. 2.9.

39. So, for example, Pss. 81.11 [81.10]; 94.23; Isa. 41.13; 43.3; 48.17; 51.15;
55.5; 60.9; Hos. 3.5; 7.10; 12.9; 13.4; 14.1; Joel 1.13-14; 2.13-14, 26-27; Amos
9.15; Mic. 7.10; Zeph. 3.17; Zech. 6.25.

40. So, for example, Pss. 20.8 [20.7]; 99.5, 8-9; 105.7; 106.47; 113.5; 122.9;
Mic. 4.5; 7.17.

41. Pss. 7.2 [7.1]; 7.4 [7.3]; 18.29 [18.28]; 30.3 [30.2]; 30.13 [30.12]; 31.15
[31.14]; 35.24; 40.6 [40.5]; 104.1; 109.26; 140.7 [140.6]; Hab. 1.12; Zech. 11.4;
13.9; 14.5.

42. Zeph. 2.7; Hag. 1.12; Zech. 9.16; 10.6.

43. Pss. 144.15; 146.5.

44. Pss. 68.21 [68.20] (order reversed); 140.8 [140.7] (order reversed); Amos
3.7-8, 11; 4.2, 5; 5.3; 6.8; 8.1, 3, 9, 11; Obad. 1-2; Hab. 3.19 (order reversed); Zech.
9.14.

45. Pss. 8.2 [8.1]; 8.10 [8.9].

46. Isa. 43.15 (variation); 44.6; Zeph. 3.15.

47. So, for example, Gen. 23.26; 28.15; 31.3; 48.21; Exod. 33.16; Ezek. 34.30.

48. So, for example, Gen. 28.20; 31.5; 35.3.

49. So for example, Gen. 26.24.

50. So, for example, Josh. 22.31; Zech. 2.14 [2.10].

51. So, for example, Exod. 33.5; Num. 11.20; Josh. 3.10; Joel 2.27; Mic. 3.11;
Zeph. 3.15.

nations he also controls. Finally, it can be noted that uses of the root 'to reject, spurn' (מאס) to describe YHWH's actions or frame of mind toward Israel or to claim on his behalf that Israel has rejected him in some fashion can be understood to presume a more normal situation where Israel enjoys divine selection and special favour or status (e.g. Isa. 41.9).[52] 'To choose' (בחר) is used as the antonym of 'to reject' (מאס) in Jer. 33.24, 26 and Ps. 78.67. As noted in the first section, the concept of YHWH's (chosen) people or nation may also in some instances relate to the larger complex of thought involved in the covenant relationship. The fluidity between these two sets of ideas should be acknowledged without any attempt to draw firm distinctions.

2. Divine Othering Strategies

2.1. Rejecting the People of Israel

There are a number of threats made by YHWH to Israel to reject them, to disinherit them from their land and scatter them among the nations, or simply, to destroy them. These usually are presented as tactics designed to get the people to change their behaviour to avert the threatened situation, where failure to comply could result in the loss of special status as YHWH's people should the deity deliver on his threat. In a collectivist society like Judah/Yehud, the thought of being cut off from the group or the elimination of the group altogether would have been a terrifying prospect whose avoidance would have been a top priority.[53] As noted above, the root מאס is used primarily to portray these potential forms of dis-election, along with the root נטש.

Jeremiah 6 contains threats by YHWH to destroy Daughter Zion (vv. 1-2) and to make Jerusalem a wasteland and uninhabited land (v. 8), and v. 30 claims that YHWH has rejected them=his people (Niphal of מאס). In 7.29 it is then proclaimed, 'YHWH has rejected (מאס) and forsaken the generation of his wrath'. Here, the capture and destruction of Jerusalem by the Neo-Babylonians in 586 BCE is interpreted in terms of Othering. Amos similarly warns northern Israel that his god will reject them because they have not listened to YHWH; they will become wanderers

---

52. Lev. 26.44; 1 Sam. 8.7; 10.19; 2 Kgs 17.15, 20; Ps. 78.59; Isa. 41.9; 54.6; Jer. 6.19, 30; 7.29 (only a single generation); 14.19 (of Judah and Zion); 31.37 (as an impossible proposition); 33.24; Lam. 5.22; Ezek. 20.13; Hos. 9.17.

53. For another study in this volume that sees the same psychology at work in trying to get members of the in-group to accept one segment's understanding of proper behaviour as a group norm, see Terje Stordalen, 'Imagined and Forgotten Communities: Othering in the Story of Josiah's Reform (2 Kings 23)', pp. 182-200.

(נדדים) among the nations (9.17). The passage in Amos reflects a bit of family squabbling where one sibling is predicting the permanent rejection and ostracism of the other by the 'father'. It is treating a rival sibling as though he were Other rather than family, which then allows the normal range of behaviours towards outsiders to come into play temporarily. Instead of empathy, cooperation, sacrifice, help, and accommodation, there is competition, exploitation, manipulation, and fighting. The same idea of favouritism in the family, where one branch can be disinherited in favour of another, is found in Ps. 78.67-70. It is claimed that YHWH rejected (מאס) the tent of Joseph and the tribe of Ephraim and chose instead the tribe of Judah, Mt. Zion for his sanctuary, and his servant David.

A variation on the Othering theme is found in Lev. 26.44 and Jer. 31.35-37, where YHWH affirms he will not reject his people or break his covenant with them, and has no future plans to have the descendants of Israel cease from being a nation before him forever or to cast off all the descendants of Israel for all they have done. The underlying assumption is that such a situation has been contemplated earlier either by the deity or has been assumed by the people. Similarly, in Jer. 33.23-26 YHWH denies any validity to the claims made by others that he has rejected the two families (משפחות) he had chosen so they no longer need to be viewed as a nation. In Isa. 41.8-10, YHWH likewise states that he has chosen his servant Israel, the offspring of Abraham, his friend, whom he has called from the ends of the earth, implying an address to Diasporic Jews; he specifies he has not rejected him, implying this has been claimed, but falsely. Two other passages express uncertainty on the part of Israel as to whether their deity has rejected them or not (Jer. 14.19; Lam. 5.22), which presumes the possibility that YHWH could Other them.

The root נטש is used in a number of contexts to describe how YHWH has or will 'leave unheeded', 'not bother with further', 'cast off', or even 'leave fallow or uncultivated' his people Israel. This intentional neglect implies a reversal of a situation where he cared for them, saw to their needs, and tended them so they would flourish. In addition to Jer. 7.29 already quoted, examples include Judg. 6.13, where Gideon asks, 'If YHWH is with us, why then has all this happened to us? And where are all his wonderful deeds that our ancestors recounted to us, saying, "Did not YHWH bring us up from Egypt"? But now YHWH has not bothered with us further/cast us off and has given us into the hand of Midian.' In a similar vein, in 2 Kgs 21.14 YHWH proclaims:

> I will stretch over Jerusalem the measuring line for Samaria, and the
> plummet for the house of Ahab... I will not bother further with the rem-
> nant of my heritage but will give them into the hand of their enemies;
> they shall become a prey and a spoil to all their enemies, because they
> have done what is evil in my sight and have provoked me to anger, since
> the day their ancestors came out of Egypt, even to this day.

YHWH is no longer 'with' all-Israel but instead, has cast them off/left
them unheeded, allowing them to be preyed upon by Midian. Just as he
Othered the kingdom of Samaria, he plans to do the same to the kingdom
of Judah. In 1 Sam. 12.20-25, Samuel reassures the people that in spite of
their evil request for a king, 'YHWH will not cast away his people, for his
great name's sake, because it has pleased YHWH to make you a people
for himself'. Solomon prays that YHWH will be with 'us' (Israel) as he
was with our ancestors and will not abandon us or 'leave us unheeded'
(1 Kgs 8.57). Jeremiah is instructed to tell inquirers who ask about
YHWH's oracle that it is, 'I will leave you unheeded/cast you off'
(23.33), 'I will surely lift you up and "cast you away" from my presence,
you and the city that I gave to you and your ancestors' (23.39).

Drawing either on the image of Israel as YHWH's firstborn son or as
his special people bound to him by covenant, in Num. 14.12 the deity
says to Moses, 'I will disinherit (Hiphil ירש) them and make of you a
nation, גוי, greater and mightier than they'. Those who are family
members can lose their anticipated heritable portion of the Promised
Land if they rebel against their father's authority, just as members of the
covenant community can lose their anticipated heritable portion of the
Promised Land if they fail to observe a stipulation of the agreement
made at Sinai/Horeb. Threatened Othering, which opens up the possibility of replacement by others who might gain the group's privileges, is
meant to be a strong, anxiety-producing deterrent to disobedience.

The book of Hosea is unique among the Hebrew Bible collection in
having YHWH announce that Israel is no longer his people. The assertion
occurs three times in the first two chapters of the book: in Hos. 1.9; 2.1,
and 2.25. In Hos. 1.9, YHWH instructs the prophet to name his third child
'Lo-Ammi, because you are not my people and I myself will not be
yours'. Yet, immediately, the next verse (2.1 [1.10]) indicates that the
rejection is a temporary situation; Israel will be as numerous as the sand
of the sea, and in the place (or temple?) where it had been announced,
'You are not my people', it will now be said to them, 'Children of a
living god' (בני אל חי).

Then, after the children's mother has been divorced and shamed by
YHWH for crediting other lords/husbands (בעלים) for providing her with
food and shelter and for whoring after them, he will take her into the

wilderness and give her vineyards so that she will respond[54] as in her youth, making the Valley of Achor a door of hope, and replying as she did at the time she came out of Egypt. She will take him again as husband and he will take her as wife forever, having made a (new?) covenant with the living things on the earth. By means of righteousness, justice, steadfast love and faithfulness, all covenantal traits, he will betroth her, so that she will 'know' him [only], and he will also then provide her with grain, wine and oil and plant her personally in the land (2.1-25a [2.1-23a]). Then he will say to Lo-Ammi, 'You are my people', and he will respond, 'My divinity' (אלהי; 2.25 [2.23a]). These verses envision a new covenant to be made between YHWH and Israel in addition to the new covenant to be made with the animal and bird inhabitants of the earth, where Israel will become YHWH's faithful wife for eternity; the grain, wine, and oil are the normal divine gifts Israel could have expected from its suzerain YHWH for loyalty to the former Sinai/Horeb covenant (Deut. 28.1-14).

This story or lesson in chs. 1–2 presumes that Israel was the people of YHWH at some prior point in time. It refers to taking Lo-Ammi's mother, who also is portrayed here as YHWH's wife, back to the wilderness, where she will answer (וענתה, 2.17 [2.15]) as she did at the time of her going up from the land of Egypt (Exod. 19.8; 24.3, 7). Knowledge of the Exodus tradition is implied, with the reference to 'responding' seeming to be an allusion to the events at Sinai, where Israel responded and accepted the terms of the covenant that defined them as YHWH's chosen people. Elsewhere in Hos. 13.4-5, the tradition is found that YHWH is 'your god from the land of Egypt… [I]t was I who knew you in the wilderness, in the land of drought.'

The mention of the Valley of Achor as a door of hope is only made intelligible by reading Hosea in the context of the larger collection of the Hebrew Bible. Then, it becomes a reversal of the story in Joshua 7 of the sin of Achan and his punishment by stoning, with a heap of stones placed over his grave memorializing the event. The location of the valley is south or east of Debir according to Josh. 15.7, and the geography of Joshua 7 suggests it is close to Jericho, which also would be consistent with Josh. 15.7. Debir is known alternatively as Kiriath-sepher (Josh. 15.15; Judg. 1.11) or Kiriath-Sannah (Josh. 15.47). In addition, a location

---

54. For the various translational options for the root ענן, see conveniently, Francis I. Anderson and David N. Freedman, *Hosea: A New Translation with Introduction and Commentary* (AB, 24; Garden City, NY: Doubleday, 1980), pp. 276-77; Andrew A. Macintosh, *A Critical and Exegetical Commentary on Hosea* (ICC; Edinburgh: T. & T. Clark, 1997), pp. 72-73.

in the Jordan Valley rift east of the central highlands would balance the reference in Isa. 65.10 to the Valley of Sharon, on the western side of the highlands.[55]

In Joshua 7, the Valley of Achor recalls the failure to take the Promised Land from those already there due to a transgression of sacred things owed to YHWH. Thus, the author of Hosea is saying that with a return to the wilderness, Israel need not repeat the mistake it made the first time; the valley is one of hope for successful occupation this time ('I will sow her/them myself in the land', 2.23). There will be no snags if the people obey the terms of the Sinai covenant that made their ancestors YHWH's elected people, his 'in-group'. The stipulations are still binding.

In Hos. 2.16-23 [2.14-21], it can be noted that future Israel, YHWH's remarried bride, functions as a paradigmatic, positive Other for the reading community. It is specifically contrasted with disobedient Israel of the past monarchic era and the reading community's present experience as Israel, where it has not yet attained or realized this perfected status. The envisioned future Israel will be able to be a loyal covenantal partner and metaphorical spouse because of the divine engagement gifts of righteousness, justice, steadfast love, and faithfulness. The gifts effectively will give her a 'new heart', as in Jer. 31.31-34, that will allow her to remain a devoted spouse who will build up her husband's reputation actively while overseeing the needs of her family and household (Prov. 31) by following the covenant stipulations. This image of a 'perfect' future Israel is crucial for the group's self-identity and expression of values, presenting what is to be striven toward by the entire community.[56]

2.2. *Scattering the Flock of Israel*

There are only four passages where YHWH is said personally to scatter his flock, Israel, or strike it with plague (1 Chron. 21.17; Pss. 44.11, 22; 74.1; Zech. 13.7). Poetry regularly uses metaphors and similes to express thoughts and feelings, so the two psalmic occurrences are not surprising. In Zech. 13.7, YHWH calls on his sword to awake and strike the shepherd who is his associate so that the sheep will scatter. There follows a

---

55. It was equated with the modern Buqēʻah leading from the Jordanian plain southwest of Jericho by Frank M. Cross and Jósef T. Milik, 'Explorations in the Judean Buqēʻah', *BASOR* 142 (1956), pp. 5-17. This location is adopted, for example by James L. Mays, *Hosea: A Commentary* (OTL; Philadelphia: Westminster, 1969), p. 45.

56. I wish to thank Ehud Ben Zvi for encouraging me to develop this aspect of future covenanted Israel and not commenting solely on the negative aspect of Israel as temporary Other in the book of Amos.

declaration that the deity will also turn against the little ones, presumably of the scattered flock.[57] Here, then, God is portrayed as intending to scatter his flock by killing their earthly shepherd/leader and then personally killing the vulnerable, unprotected young who get separated in the dispersion. In the fourth passage, it is noteworthy that while YHWH actively strikes his flock with plague in 1 Chron. 21.17, in the corresponding passage in 2 Sam. 24.17 the angel of YHWH does the smiting on behalf of the deity and not the god directly. In these four instances, YHWH acknowledges Israel as his personal flock and as their divine shepherd, with or without an appointed human overseer, decides to disperse or kill off his private property when he becomes angry over their failure to obey.

In Deutero-Isaiah, the people acknowledge they are sheep who have strayed and followed 'their own path', implicitly rejecting the one specified by YHWH, their shepherd (Isa. 53.6). Such disobedience triggers direct divine intervention to chastise the wayward flock, as in Ps. 44.11, 22 and Ps. 74.1. In this case, the sheep themselves must bear responsibility for straying; there is no shepherd who has been lax or inattentive to be punished in their stead.

Interestingly, in another four passages the scattering of YHWH's flock is done either by foreign kings or by native kingly shepherds who have been entrusted with their care, feeding, and protection but who have not carried out their appointed tasks (1 Kgs 22.17=2 Chron. 18.16;

57. The reference to 'the little ones' is seen to be taken from Jer. 49.20 and 50.45 by e.g. Hinckley G. Mitchell in Hinckley G. Mitchell, John M. P. Smith and Julius A. Brewer, *Haggai, Zechariah, Malachi and Jonah* (ICC; New York: Charles Scribner's Sons, 1912], p. 317; Carol L. Meyers and Eric C. Meyers, *Zechariah 9–14: A New Translation with Introduction and Commentary* (AB, 25C; New York: Doubleday, 1993), p. 388; and Raymond Person, *Second Zechariah and the Deuteronomic School* (JSOTSup, 167; Sheffield: Sheffield Academic Press, 1993), p. 134. The suggestion the shepherd is a foreign king and the little ones his lower ranked bureaucrats who will be dispersed one day as punishment for oppressing the people of Judah has no clear basis in the present wording of the text (e.g. Abraham Cohen [ed.], *The Twelve Prophets: Hebrew Text, English Translation and Commentary* [Soncino Books of the Bible, 5; Bournemouth: Soncino, 1948], p. 325). It is seen to be a reverse echo of Jer. 30.19 and Job 14.21 by Magne Sæbø, *Sacharja 9–14: Untersuchungen von Text und Form* (Wissenschaftliche Monographien zum Alten und Neuen Testament, 34; Neukirchen–Vluyn: Neukirchener Verlag, 1969), p. 280. Meyers and Meyers see the shepherd imagery to link up with that used in Jer. 23.1-6 and Ezek. 34.1-23 to condemn kings, which sets it apart from Zech. 11.17, where it represents prophets (*Zechariah 9–14*, p. 385). They also highlight the claim here that the refined remnant that will become YHWH's people will stem from those who remain in the land and do not experience Exile (pp. 389, 391, 404-405).

Jer. 13.20; Ezek. 34.1-34). Ineffectual native kings who fail to shepherd
Israel often are removed from power through the agency of foreign kings
in war. All of these passages presume that YHWH is the real owner of
Israel and so ultimately controls its fate as well as the fate of those
appointed to shepherd it on earth.

Two universalizing visions concerning the day of YHWH emphasize
the unhappy future for the collective flocks of the earth and their
shepherds. In Isa. 13.13-14, on the day of YHWH, all of humanity will be
like sheep without tenders and each will turn to their own people and will
flee their own land. In Jer. 25.34-37, on the other hand, destruction of the
lords of the flocks, the shepherd kings, who flee in vain, leaving their
flocks unprotected, is announced. Israel will suffer the same fate as other
groups, all of which constitute YHWH's flocks that have cowardly
appointed overseers who fail to defend the animals entrusted to their care
when their own lives are jeopardized. There is no escaping the fierce
anger of YHWH.

2.3. *Uprooting or Destroying Planted Israel and Casting Off Israel Conceived of as Landed Property*

Building on the metaphor of a divine gardener, in certain passages
YHWH threatens to uproot (נתשׁ)[58] Israel as he sees fit, be it a vine or a
tree. Such imagery reverses the normal created order, returning things to
a wild, uncultivated state. It is a threatened act of the wilful undoing of
the established order by the deity, designed to instil submission by fear
and anxiety. It could also be seen to imitate the deliberate destruction
of crops and sources of livelihood that foreign troops practiced when
they captured or besieged an enemy territory, which also likely was a
psychological tactic designed to instil fear and surrender or cooperation
and show who now controlled the land.[59] From this vantage point, YHWH

---

58. Deut. 29.28; 1 Kgs 14.15; 2 Chron. 7.20; Jer. 12.14-15; 24.6; 31.28, 40;
42.10; 45.4; Ezek. 19.12; Amos 9.15. It is perhaps worth noting that the homonym,
נתשׁ, means 'to leave the earth fallow or uncultivated' in Exod. 23.11 and possibly in
Zech. 10.32 as well.

59. See. e.g. the boast of Sargon II in the Annals: 'I let my army eat [the fruit] of
their orchards; the date palms, their mainstay, the orchards, the wealth of their
province, I cut down' (Daniel David Luckenbill *Ancient Records of Assyria and
Babylonia*. Vol. 2, *Historical Records of Assyria from Sargon to the End* [Chicago:
University of Chicago Press, 1927], §32, p. 16); he also claims to have cut down the
trees surrounding the palace at Ulhu and the fortress at Shardurihudra in Mt. Kishte
in the land of Sangibutu and to have uprooted the crops (§161, pp. 87-88) and to
have done the same to seven cities in the regions of Armarili (§165, pp. 90-91) of

could be acting toward his rejected people like a conquering foreign king rather than a divine gardener who is free to change the design of his garden or the types of crops he chooses to plant at will.

Another tactic of Othering that draws on the same set of agricultural imagery is found in Jer. 12.7, where YHWH announces that he has abandoned his house and 'cast off', 'given up', or 'left neglected' his landed inheritance (נחלתו), in spite of the reassurance given in Ps. 94.14 that he will not forsake his people; he will not נתש his heritage (נחלתו). Here, Israel seems to be envisioned as the Promised Land itself rather than a planting of that land, but even so, its divine owner and gardener can do with it as he pleases. He can cultivate it, leave it fallow, or uproot its plantings, leaving it an unplanted, neglected wild place.

Finally, Hos. 9.16-17 suggests that YHWH has dried up Ephraim's root so they shall bear no fruit. He has implicitly deprived the corporate plant of water so that it withers because its people have not listened to him. In a similar fashion, those among the people of Judah who are wise in their own eyes, who reject the instruction of YHWH, will develop rotten roots and their blossom will rise like dust (Isa. 5.21, 24). Since the deity is considered the source of all forms of water, disease, and pests, there is an unspoken assumption that YHWH is directly responsible for the rottenness. These two passages indicate that YHWH need not only uproot plants to destroy them but can kill them in place by under-watering or over-watering them or infecting them with disease or through attack by pests.

Aiadî (§166, pp. 91-92) and of Uaiais (§167, p. 92). Sennacherib boasts to have cut down the orchards and poured out misery over the fertile (?) fields of Ellipi in his second campaign (§279, pp. 135-35). Earlier, Tukulti-[Nin]Urta II states that he had done something to the crops of the fields of Pîru in the land of Mushki after burning the cities of the region. The text is broken but the implication is he destroyed the crops (Daniel David Luckenbill, *Ancient Records of Assyria and Babylonia*. Vol. 1, *Historical Records of Assyria from the Earliest Times to Sargon* [Chicago: University of Chicago Press, 1926], §413, p. 132). Shalmaneser III states he shut up Ahuni, son of Adini, in his city, carried off the crops of his fields and cut down his orchards (§620, p. 229); he did the same to Marduk-bêl-usâte, king of Gannanâte (§622, pp. 229-30). He cut down the orchards of Hazael of Aram, who was shut up in his royal city of Damascus (§672, p. 243). These were siege tactics. Subsequently, Tiglath-Pileser III recounts how he shut up a king whose name has not survived 'like a bird in a cage in his city and cut down his gardens...plantations without number' (§774, pp. 278-79). It is likely that generic references to the laying waste, destruction, or devastation of a land in war routinely includes destruction of crops and in some instances, the cutting down of fruit trees.

2.4. *Suspending the Covenant*

Given the amount of space devoted to the covenant at Mt. Sinai/Mt. Horeb in the Hebrew Bible, it should not be surprising to see some biblical writers use it as the basis of an Othering strategy by claiming that the Sinai/Horeb covenant has been terminated due to the people's disobedience. The construction of the in-group can be reversed; YHWH can reject the people who enjoyed a special relationship with the deity and they can lose their status as his special people. The stipulations of the covenant make it clear that obedience to divine *torah* is paramount for its continued validity.

The termination of the kingdom of Israel in 721 BCE and of the kingdom of Judah in 586 BCE, with both population groups subjected to forced relocation and the lands converted into provinces, was interpreted by many to signal divine punishment by YHWH. This prompted a reflection over the status of the relationship between the territorial deity and the people who had lived in its land. The date of the idea of the formal covenant at Sinai/Horeb is debated; it might well have been developed relatively late, after the loss of Judahite independence, as a concretization of the common understanding that the people who lived in the territory of a given deity were under its special care and belonged to it.[60] The god's blessings were normally mediated through his earthly vice-regent,

---

60. In his survey of regional types of treaties and formal agreements sealed by oaths, Weeks notes a distinction between Assyrian and Hittite treaty forms. Assyrian treaties highlight the power of the central ruler by not appealing to a vassal's loyalty via historical precedent, but instead emphasizing a fear factor by invoking curses for disobedience. Hittite treaties, on the other hand, appeal to a vassal or peer's loyalty in the past in a historical prologue and do not invoke curses for failure to observe stipulations. Weeks concludes that the appeal to history to secure loyalty is a tactic used in situations of relative political decentralization. While he then suggests this would likely point to an early phase in the history of Israel for the formulation of the biblical covenantal tradition, he also clarifies in a footnote that what is crucial in his observation is the implausibility of the concept of religious covenant developing in a centralized environment, which would allow for a post-monarchic situation under imperial control where a sense of identity is being forged for those of Samarian and Judaean descent scattered across the Empire primarily based on religion (*Admonition and Curse*, pp. 53-45, 123, 176-80, 180 n. 2). This author's search for determining when treaty ideas would have entered Israel (p. 170) in order to be able to date their use in biblical texts is somewhat misguided; formal contracts and treaties would have been used regularly during the kingdom of Judah. As an established genre whose possible components could be drawn on and tailored to suit the specific circumstances of a given situation, legal or literary, clues to the date of composition of the covenants in Exodus and Deuteronomy are unlikely to lie in comparisons with known ancient Near Eastern documents.

the king, who enacted his deity's wishes on earth. But if a god became angry, it could reject its land and people.[61] The possible late date for the development of the Sinai/Horeb pericopes is suggested by the relatively few explicit mentions of either mountain, the scenes of constitutive covenant-making, in other biblical books.

No other ancient Near Eastern society or polity expressed the bond between a god and its followers in terms of a formal covenant. The decision to do so among the people of Israel may well have been the result of the loss of native kingship and political independence, where the usual channel for blessing, the king who served as the god's earthly vice-regent, was eliminated, and there was concern that the Empire ruler could not fulfil this role adequately. In addition, since many people were resettled far from their original homeland, there logically would have arisen reflection over whether their former national god had any further relevance in their lives when they no longer were under its jurisdiction in its territory. The covenant at Mt. Sinai/Mt. Horeb creates a social memory set in the commonly shared, distant past of an agreement made between YHWH and the forefathers outside the Promised Land that involved no human king as mediator and was not conditioned on the occupation of a single territory. Rather, it was conditioned on following a path of ethical behaviour laid out in a series of legally framed stipulations. It would remain in effect regardless of one's physical location or the political system in power, unless the stipulations were not fulfilled. Then YHWH had to decide how to deal with transgressors.[62]

---

61. For this motif in the five Sumerian city-laments over Ur, Uruk, Nippur, Erech, and Sumer and Ur, for example, where the angered deity rejects the city housing its temple and the people living in the city, see for example Mark E. Cohen, *The Canonical Laments of Ancient Mesopotamia I* (Potomac, MD: CDL, 1988).

62. For additional arguments for a postmonarchic date, see Philip R. Davies, 'The Authority of Deuteronomy', in *Deuteronomy–Kings as Emerging Authoritative Books: A Conversation* (ed. Diana V. Edelman; ANEM, 6; Atlanta: SBL, 2014), pp. 27-47. Suggestions to date the Sinai/Horeb covenant tradition to the late monarchy, with direct modelling after and borrowing from the succession loyalty oaths imposed by Esarhaddon on his Median bodyguards and vassals, have found many supporters—too many to cite here. Initial work traced Deut. 28.23 to ll. 528-33 of the treaties (Donald J. Wiseman, 'The Vassal Treaties of Esarhaddon', *Iraq* 20 [1958], pp. 1-99 [88]; Riekele Borger, 'Zu den Asarhaddon-Verträgen aus Nimrud', *Zeitschrift für Assyriologie* NF 20 [1961], §§63,73-96, pp. 191-92) then Deut. 28.26-35 to ll. 419-30 (Moshe Weinfeld, 'Traces of Assyrian Treaty Formulae in Deuteronomy', *Bib* 46 [1965], pp. 417-27). Rintje Frankena, on the other hand, pointed out how expressions within these vassal treaties resonated with a range of biblical texts, including Deut. 4.29; 5.32; 6.5, 7, 20-25; 10.12; 11.13; 17.11, 20; 28.14, 20-57; 32.46, with Deut. 28.20-57 exhibiting a material dependence' on an Assyrian

Most biblical writers suggest that the termination of the kingdoms of Israel and Judah and the forced relocations of large portions of their populations were punishments by YHWH for multi-generational disobedience but suggest that the covenant remains in effect. The punishment will end and a remnant will be restored to their former homeland, YHWH's favourite domain, where they will follow his ethical demands

'Vorlage' ('The Vassal-Treaties of Esarhaddon and the Dating of Deuteronomy', *OTS* 14 [1965], pp. 122-54, esp. 140-50, with quote from p. 150). Hans Ulrich Steymans expanded Weinfeld's proposed influence to cover Deut. 28.20-44 based on an Aramaic translation of sections 39, 40, 42, 56, 63, and 64, coming closer to Frankena's observation but providing a means of transmission that did not require Judahite scribes to know Akkadian (*Deuteronomium 28 und die adê zur Thronfolgeregelung Asarhaddons: Segen und Fluch im Alten Orient und in Israel* [OBO, 145; Fribourg, Switzerland: University Press, 1995], pp. 284-312). Subsequent work found additional dependencies in Deut. 13; see, e.g., Paul E. Dion, 'Deuteronomy 13: The Suppression of Alien Religious Propaganda in Israel during the Late Monarchical Era', in *Law and Ideology in Monarchic Israel* (ed. Baruch Halpern and Deborah W. Hobson; JSOTSup, 124; Sheffield: JSOT Press, 1991), pp. 147-216 (198-205), though he emphasizes there is no 'mechanical calque of some foreign archetype' (p. 196) and even considers Exod. 22.19 as a possible source for Deut. 13 (p. 197 n. 1); Bernard M. Levinson, '"But You Shall Surely Kill Him!": The Text-Critical and Neo-Assyrian Evidence for MT Deut. 13:10', in *Bundesdokument und Gesetz: Studien zum Deuteronomium* (ed. Georg Braulik; HBS, 4; New York: Herder, 1995), pp. 37-63; idem, 'Esarhaddon's Succession Treaty as the Source for the Canon Formula in Deuteronomy 13:1', *Journal of the American Oriental Society* 130.3 (2010), pp. 337-47. For a general discussion of various possible dependencies, see, e.g., Eckart Otto, 'Treueid und Gesetz: Die Ursprünge des Deuteronomiums im Horizont neuassyrischen Vertragsrechts', *ZAR* 2 (1996), pp. 1-52. For the possible influence of a west-Semitic treaty tradition exemplified by the Sefire treaty, which was not purely Aramaic in origin but an amalgam of different traditions that included direct influence from the dominant neo-Assyrian culture, see, e.g., William S. Morrow, 'The Sefire Treaty Stipulations and the Mesopotamian Treaty Tradition', in *The World of the Aramaeans III: Studies in Language and Literature in Honour of Paul-Eugène Dion* (ed. P. M. Michèle Daviau, John W. Wevers, and Michael Weigl; JSOTSup, 326; Sheffield: Sheffield Academic Press, 2001), pp. 83-99. He does not argue for direct influence, but a case could be made based on his understanding of this treaty. For many debated issues and various proposed solutions concerning possible genres and their particular sub-regional formats that might have influenced the formulation of the covenant tradition in Deuteronomy, see relevant contributions in the collection of articles in Markus Witte et al. (eds.), *Die deuteronomistischen Geschichtswerke: Redaktions- und religionsgeschichtliche Perspektiven zur "Deuteronomismus"-Diskussion in Tora und Vorderen Propheten* (BZAW, 365; Berlin: de Gruyter, 2006), especially those by Udo Rüterswörten (pp. 229-38), Gary Beckman (pp. 279-301), Lorenzo d'Alfonzo (pp. 303-29), Hans Ulrich Steymans (pp. 331-49), Karen Radner (pp. 351-78), and Christoph Koch (pp. 379-406).

without further rebellion. This is the view that predominates in the final form of most prophetic books, for example. Thus, for some, the covenant remains in effect, with punishment meted out for transgression (e.g. Lev. 26.44; Ezek. 20.33-44; Zech. 9.11-16). In Deuteronomy, the exile is anticipated for failure to obey the covenant, but it is not stated that Israel will cease to be YHWH's nation or people at that point.

It is likely that the authors of Isa. 14.1-2 and Ezek. 16.59-63 also assume the covenant has not been completely overturned but that it has been suspended, which means at some future point it can be reinstated. In Isa. 14.1, the adverb עוד is used in conjunction with בחר; it can mean YHWH will 'choose again' or 'still choose' Israel. In light of the ensuing claim that YHWH will set Israel in its own land, the latter option makes better sense; the return to the Promised Land recalls the Sinai/Horeb covenant, which made occupation of that territory contingent on obedience to the covenantal stipulations. There is an implication that rejection will end and YHWH will resume the former covenant with his people Israel.

In Ezek. 16.58-63, YHWH similarly states that after he has punished Israel, who despised the oath, breaking the covenant, he will remember the covenant with her in the days of her youth and will establish an everlasting covenant (ברית עולם) with her, and she, in turn, will 'know' YHWH. The second passage goes further than the first in changing the nature of the resumed covenant from one that can be and has been suspended to one that will never be interrupted again. This, in turn, allows for the possibility that the old covenant will be terminated in the future in favour of a new one. But if so, the writer does not seem to be contemplating the termination of the first covenant at the time of the destruction of Jerusalem when Judah was converted into the neo-Babylonian province of Yehud and the issuing of a new covenant at some future point, with a period when no covenant existed. Instead, he seems to envision the suspension of the first covenant and then its resumption, either as before, which subsequently will be changed to an unconditional covenant, or resumed in a new, unconditional form.

The author of Jeremiah also foresees a new future covenant (ברית חדשה, 31.31), this time with the surviving descendants of both houses of the old Israel (31.31; 50.5), whose forefathers had broken the old covenant. He states it will not be like the old covenant made with the ancestors when YHWH took them by the hand to bring them out of Egypt. Instead, YHWH will put his *torah* within them and engrave it directly upon the hearts of the members of Israel, which will then establish YHWH as Israel's God and Israel as YHWH's people (31.32-33). It will be an unconditional covenant (ברית אולם, 32.40; 50.5) in which YHWH will

never turn back from doing good to them (32.40) because they will have
'one heart' and 'one path' to fear YHWH always, for their own good and
for the good of their children after them (32.39). They shall be his people
and he their God (32.38) and they shall not forget the (new), unconditional covenant (50.5).

The explicit mention of a new, unconditional covenant that will
replace the Sinai/Horeb covenant raises the same question as Ezek.
16.58-63 did: Has there been a termination of the old covenant already,
or will this only happen at the time the new covenant is enacted? The
forefathers broke the old covenant, but did that lead to its suspension
while YHWH, in his anger, wrath, and indignation, destroyed some people in Jerusalem with sword, pestilence, and famine and drove others
away to various lands (Jer. 32.36-37), or to its rupture? The new covenant
will be made with the descendants of those who were the beneficiaries of
the old covenant. It seems likely that temporary suspension rather than
actual termination is being envisioned.

For a member of the community that considered this book to encode
vital aspects of its collective memory, it may well have been conceivable
that YHWH could have temporarily ruptured his covenant with his people
and punished them for repeated infractions of his *torah* by destroying
Jerusalem and exiling many Judahites in 586 BCE, but it certainly would
have been a 'minority report' in comparison to the explanation that the
covenant was suspended. The holocaust has similarly led some Jews to
question the status of God's covenant and protection of his chosen
people. But, as seen from the vision of the new covenant, even one who
might voice such a minority report about the possible termination of the
old covenant could not contemplate Israel's permanent loss of special
status and relationship with the deity.

A clear example of the permanent exclusion of part of Israel from the
covenant for repeated disobedience to the covenantal stipulations is
provided by the Judaean author of the book of Kings. He claims that
YHWH rejected the people of the kingdom of Israel, after the Assyrians
conquered it, forcibly relocated much of its population, resettled other
population groups in its territory, and made it the Assyrian province of
Samerina (2 Kgs 17.20). However, as noted earlier, this view reflects
'insider' rivalry and debate over membership entitlement in the chosen
people. From such a perspective, even if the former Northern Kingdom
and its descendants have been rejected, the Southern Kingdom or its
descendants still constitute Israel; a sibling may have been rejected, but
not the entire collective family. The concept of covenantal election that
gave Israel its self-conceived, unique status as a community became such
a core, in-group definitional element that it would have become both an

individual and a collective belief capable of testing, bending, and even of temporary suspension but not of permanent rejection or dissolution. Within the group, eternal Othering was inconceivable.

2.5. *Changing the Status of the Nations and Peoples of Earth as a Universal God*

The final Othering strategy that will be considered relates to universalizing theology applied to YHWH. This has no direct counterpart among election strategies; however, it impacts on all of them to some degree when other people groups or nations now also are seen to belong to YHWH, affording them a measure of insider status. Israel's special status as YHWH's nation or people that sets it apart from other nations and people collapses when all become his children. In Amos 9.7, YHWH claims to have brought Israel from Egypt, the Philistines from Caphtor, the Arameans from Kir, and states rhetorically that the people of Israel are like the Ethiopians to him. This is a clear assertion that this deity controls the histories of all people/nations and Israel is not even a first among equals.[63]

Two passages in Deutero-Zechariah reflect different understandings of Israel's status vis-à-vis the universal deity, YHWH: Zech. 2.11 and 11.10. On the one hand, Zech. 11.10 refers to YHWH annulling the בריתי אשר כרתי את־כל־העמים, 'my covenant which I made with all the peoples', which might be an allusion to the covenant with Noah in Gen. 9.9-17 but is not clear. Whatever it is referencing, it asserts some sort of equal treatment in which all people groups belong to YHWH and have a formal relationship with him, which then tends to cancel the separate election of Israel.

The reference to Zech. 2.11, on the other hand, claims that on the day YHWH will dwell in the midst of Zion, many nations shall join themselves to YHWH and shall become his people. The singular form of people is used here, not the plural, suggesting that members of separate political groups will now become members of the single people of YHWH.[64] It is unclear if existing insiders would feel threatened by this vision of the expansion of their group to include former outsiders. As indicated in the introduction, in collectivist societies, membership in the

---

63. Such a view is countered by Ezek. 25.8, where Moab wrongly claims the house of Judah is like all the other nations and YHWH vows to execute judgments against the offending nation so they will come to know who he is.

64. This claim seems to be consistent with the view expressed in e.g. Deut. 23.3-8, which denies entry to the congregation forever to Ammonites and Moabites but allows Edomites to join after the third generation (cf. Lam. 1.10).

in-group tends to be defined by ascribed attributes like kinship, race, village, or tribe vs. achieved ones, but one also is to accept the decisions of the head of household without question. In any event, there will remain non-Yahwistic nations, which will allow this expanded, elected Israel to maintain its special relationship with its deity, unlike in Zech. 11.10. Thus, Zech. 2.11 is a more tempered view that maintains the older covenantal election theology in contrast to Zech. 11.10 or Amos 9.7, where Israel's specialness appears to be denied.[65]

It should be noted that universalizing texts that ascribe control over all the people groups and nations of the earth to YHWH generally maintain a distinction between Israel and these other families or leave open the possibility that Israel has the status of first among equals or firstborn, which sets it apart in some way. The oracles against the foreign nations in prophetic books, for example, while demonstrating YHWH's control over the histories of various nations other than Israel or Judah, still occasionally situate his punitive actions against other ancient Near Eastern nations as retribution for their hostile attacks against the chosen in-group, gloating over their exile, or as a means of distinguishing the ultimate saving of the remnant of the in-group while some or all the other nations will be totally destroyed.[66] And in passages primarily about the latter days when the peoples and nations shall flow to Mt. Zion to seek YHWH, to worship the King, or to learn the *torah* of YHWH, there is no overt claim that Israel has lost its special status among the nations or people groups, even if the other ones now acknowledge YHWH as their god or divine *torah* as binding (e.g. Isa. 2.2-4; 45.22-23; 56.3-8;[67] Jer. 3.17; Mic. 4.1-5; Zech. 8.22-23; 14.16-19).

65. For other passages that recognize Israel's uniqueness while asserting when it acts like other nations it must be punished, or when it disobeys it will be scattered and will adopt the practices of nations in which survivors are found, see, e.g., Lev. 18.24-30; Deut. 28.58-68. The latter reverses the situation envisioned in Gen. 12.3; 22.18; Isa. 61.9, and possibly Mic. 5.6 [5.7]. In LXX Isa. 19.24, Israel, YHWH's heritage, will be one of three with Egypt, YHWH's people, and Assyria, the work of his hands. It is open to debate whether Israel's status as YHWH's 'heritage' preserves a privileged position over the other two in this passage or if this is an example that belongs with Amos 9.7 and Zech. 11.10.

66. E.g. Isa. 17.13-14; 19.16; 47.4, 6-9; Jer. 46.27-28; 50.11, 15, 17-19, 33-34; 51.35-36, 49; Ezek. 25.3-5, 12-14; 26.1-4; 28.24-25; 29.6-9, 16; Obad. 9-10, 15; Zeph. 2.5-10. For another discussion of this genre, which emphasizes different aspects, and the novel approach to YHWH's dealing with the Other nations in the book of Jonah, see the contribution in this volume by Susanne Gillmayr-Bucher, 'Jonah and the Other: A Discourse on Interpretative Competence', pp. 201-18.

67. The reference in v. 6 to the children of the foreigner who bind themselves to YHWH to serve him, to love the name of YHWH, and to become his servants has been

3. *Conclusion*

All human groups define themselves as unique in some respect as a means of establishing boundaries that separate them from others who might otherwise share a number of common traits, beliefs, and customs. Their individual members accept these definitions in order to belong to the group. The collective memory encoded in the books that came to be included in the Hebrew Bible have framed the uniqueness of the community of Israel in terms of a special relationship with the deity YHWH/YHWH Elohim. At the same time, it has acknowledged that the

construed by some to refer to foreign priests who will offer burnt offerings and sacrifices on the altar in the temple in Jerusalem that YHWH will accept (v. 7). See, for example, John D. W. Watts, *Isaiah 34–66* (WBC, 25; Waco, TX: Word, 1987), p. 249; Roy D. Wells, ' "Isaiah" as an Exponent of Torah: Isaiah 56.1-8', in *New Visions of Isaiah* (ed. Roy F. Melugin and Marvin Sweeney; JSOTSup, 214; Sheffield: Sheffield Academic Press, 1996), pp. 140-55 (147-48); and Joseph Blenkinsopp, *Isaiah 56–66* (AB, 19B; New York: Doubleday, 2003), p. 140. Watts and Blenkinsopp link it with the reference in 66.21 to some from the gathered gentile nations whom YHWH will take to become priests [and] Levites. However, such an understanding in ch. 56 is not patent, even if the reference in 66.21 is more so. First, it is unclear if the group in question is the offspring of 'mixed marriages' where one parent is foreign but the other a member of the community, or if both parents are foreign, without any blood ties to the community of Israel and its deity. It is also unclear if the ensuing description of 'each who observes the Sabbath and does not profane it, and who hold to my covenant' in v. 6 refers back to the children of the foreigner or introduces a new group beside the first. The root שרת, 'to serve', can be used of both secular and cultic service, so it is not a conclusive indicator that the first group consists of priests. Nor does the wording in v. 7 about the burnt offerings and sacrifices specify that the foreigners will be officiating as priests but rather, suggests that such sacrifices, when brought to the temple by non-Israelites who have voluntarily bound themselves to the community of YHWH, will be accepted on the altar. So e.g. Claus Westermann, *Isaiah 40–66: A Commentary* (trans. D. M. G. Stalker; OTL; Philadelphia: Westminster, 1969), p. 315; R. Norman Whybray, *Isaiah 40–66* (New Century Bible Commentary; Grand Rapids, MI: Eerdmans, 1981), p. 198-99; and Jan L. Koole, *Isaiah. Part 3*, vol. 3, *Isaiah Chapters 56–66* (Historical Commentary on the Old Testament; Leuven: Peeters, 2001), pp. 20, 23. Even if it were meant to refer to the inclusion of foreign converts as priests, it would represent a 'minority report' by an author who might have been developing the concept of Israel as 'a nation of priests' to its logical extension in a universalizing context. Or, he might have been upset with some members or aspects of the contemporary priesthood of his day, like the author of Mal. 1.6–2.17, and envisioned their replacement by more loyal priests of foreign pedigree, to make his point sting. In any event, whether vv. 6-7 refer to one or two groups and includes foreign-born priests or not, they do not conflict with other passages where members of other nations will embrace YHWH as their personal god or follow his *torah* as binding.

relationship was suspended by the deity as a form of punishment for disobedience, as a means to contextualize the termination of the kingdom of Israel in 721 BCE and the termination of the kingdom of Judah in 586 BCE. The biblical writers have chosen to formulate the group memory of these events in terms of YHWH's threats to Other his selected in-group, his actual temporary Othering of both groups, but also, his promise not to do so again in the future, which reaffirms for readers both a return to favour and unique status in the present as well as a reassurance of the irreversible nature of that status no matter what, in the future. They accept that temporary rejection and Othering by their deity has occurred but will never do so again in the future, modeling the kind of behaviour and attitudes that will ensure future success so that Israel can become the perfect wife, mother, son, and covenantal partner and maintain its unique status as YHWH's special treasure, people, and kingdom of priests.

Four strategies for expressing Israel's enjoyment of a unique, in-group relationship with the deity YHWH/YHWH Elohim in comparison to other people groups and nations on the earth have been explored: Israel as YHWH's people, nation, or treasure that has been chosen, set apart, or known by the deity; Israel as YHWH's flock; Israel as YHWH's garden or, metaphorically, the Promised Land itself; and Israel as YHWH's covenantal vassal/son. All of these strategies assert and reassure that Israel constitutes a unique in-group that includes the former territorial deity of Cisjordan. The first and fourth approaches tend to use family imagery to express this conception, making YHWH the head of the family (*paterfamilias*) and Israel the wife or firstborn child, children, or clan. Both reflect the principles of a collectivist society, especially association, intimacy, cooperation, inequality, membership based on kinship or tribe, embeddedness in the in-group with shared beliefs that reflect interdependence, acceptance of hierarchy, valuing of obedience, duty, and in-group harmony and norms to regulate many individual behaviours, and a high concern for the integrity of the in-group. The second and third approaches conceive of Israel as a living personal possession of the deity, who has complete control over its collective life and well-being. YHWH can treat Israel in any way he chooses, with the only negative repercussion being potential damage to his reputation or name (שם) for mistreatment or undeserved harshness (e.g. 1 Sam. 12.20-25; 2 Sam. 7.23 = 1 Chron. 17.21; 1 Kgs 8.41-43; Pss. 72.17; 105.1; 106.8; Isa. 63.12; Ezek. 20.9, 14, 22; 36.20-23; Dan. 9.19; 39.7; Mal. 1.11, 14). This is consistent with the collectivist value of accepting hierarchy and following the decisions of the leader without questioning them.

It has then been observed that all four of the strategies for creating an in-group identity have been reversed in various books as a means to threaten or bring about YHWH's Othering of Israel. The special in-group can be rejected for its failure to behave according to the stipulated and agreed norms, for failing to value obedience, duty, or to cooperate with and respect the in-group's hierarchy and integrity. In a collectivist society, such a threat of ostracism from the group or, even worse, dissolution of the group would be terrifying and would provide a strong motivational incentive to do whatever was necessary to maintain group integrity in the present and future.

While many biblical writers have interpreted the incorporation of Judah into the Neo-Babylonian Empire in 586 BCE as the deserved punishment for Israel's failure to adhere to the covenantal stipulations, they have tended to assume the covenantal relationship remained intact, if perhaps temporarily suspended (e.g. Lev. 26.44; Ps. 111.9; Isa. 41.8-10; Jer. 31.35-37; 33.23-26; Hos. 1–2). In their view, YHWH's justified anger and wrath resulted in Israel's temporary rejection and loss of status as YHWH's chosen, special people and treasure. No biblical writer was able to contemplate the permanent Othering of Israel, however; there is always a remnant saved, and those who might think the Sinai/Horeb covenant was broken envision YHWH's creation of a new, everlasting covenant in the future with Israel (e.g. Jer. 31.31-34; 32.36-41; 50.5). There also is no view entertained that another nation or people could replace Israel as YHWH's special treasure or new covenantal son. Even the threat to make a new Israel from Moses' offspring in Num. 14.12 keeps the source of the bloodline within former Israel, as it were.

A fifth and final Othering strategy notes that, as a universal deity who has created and controls the earth and all its inhabitants, YHWH's family circle has necessarily expanded to include other peoples and nations. Two passages, Amos 9.7 and Zech. 11.10, assert that Israel has lost any special status and is just like the other nations or people; all belong to YHWH, with no hint it is considered the first-born with extra privileges or a first among equals. Yet even here, no other group assumes the place of Israel; instead, all family 'siblings' get equal treatment. These two passages represent a minority view among the passages that express a universalistic attitude. The majority maintains Israel's special status by leaving some nations out of YHWH's expanded family or clan, which then upholds Israel's uniqueness against others who have not been treated in this favorable way. In addition, as in the case of Zech. 2.11, members of other nations and people become part of YHWH's family by being 'adopted' or incorporated into Israel, the single, privileged, recognized offspring. They do not become younger siblings.

CATEGORICAL IDENTITIES:
'ETHNIFIED OTHERNESS AND SAMENESS'—
A TOOL FOR UNDERSTANDING BOUNDARY NEGOTIATION
IN THE PENTATEUCH?

Kåre Berge

Building a nation means constructing a new narrative about who belongs and who does not belong to this entity. National identity-building is primarily a discursive formation, which, according to the anthropologist M. Gullestad in reference to the creation of national identity in Europe since the eighteenth century CE, not only requires the suppression of internal difference but also the creation of various minorities and turning them into a residual political category in relation to 'the people' who constitute the nation.[1]

In biblical tradition, this creation of minorities especially applies to the Canaanites who, according to the texts, were living inside the Land of Israel and were generally to be banned and excommunicated from Israel. In some regards, this is seen as a problem that needs special explanation.[2] A 'living' relationship involves peoples and groups with which one makes transactions, and while the Other may be regarded with suspicion or derision, they cannot be banned totally. Therefore, in most scholarship,

---

1. Marianne Gullestad, 'Imagined Sameness: Shifting Notions of "Us" and "Them" in Norway', in *Forestillingen om 'Den Andre': Images of Otherness* (ed. Line Alice Ytrehus; Kristiansand: Norwegian Academic Press, 2001), pp. 33-50 (33).

2. Markus Zehnder, for instance, writes that the rigorous declarations against the original Canaanite population, are, in cultural regards, a curious phenomenon, as one normally keeps a positive relation to the sojourners as opposed to the strangers outside the land (*Umgang mit Fremden in Israel und Assyrie. Ein Beitrag zur Anthropologie des 'Fremden' im Licht antiker Quellen* [BWANT, 168; Stuttgart: Kohlhammer, 2005], p. 400). However, his citation from John Gilissen is significant and is somewhat similar to Gullestad's observations, which attest to the fact that, to a certain extent, national minorities are allowed to keep their institutions and identity markers. In addition, inside strangers serve the function of ethnic or national identity-formation by the ruling group. This is what concerns me in this article.

this unambiguous condemnation of the Canaanites has been explained by asserting that at the time of the composition of the actual texts, there were no more Canaanites, Girgashites, Perizzites, and so on. For instance, the injunctions in Deuteronomy 7 are regarded as utopian; the implementation of חרם, 'ban', against the Canaanites is wishful thinking and an adjustment of reality to the ideal norm. It is unhistorical, a vehicle with which to transmit ideas contemporary with the Deuteronomist.

There is, of course, a 'national' idea in the entire Pentateuch: Israel against the Egyptians, Israel against the different nations Edom, Moab, and so on. But in Genesis in particular, this is embedded in a strong focus on individuals. The encounter between nations is largely narrated as a face-to-face encounter between persons: Abraham and Lot, Abraham and Abimelech, Isaac and Ishmael, Jacob/Israel and Esau, Jacob and Laban, even Joseph and Pharaoh. Furthermore, the patriarchal story's ambivalent picture of the Other must be noted, which even includes some positive allusions.[3] In Genesis 16, 21, and 27, narrative analysis cannot determine where the sympathy lies. Isaac's cry (ויצעק צעקה גדלה ומרה עד־מאד) and his weeping (וישא עשׂו קלו ויבך) in 27.34 and 38 do not 'silence' him; in fact, he speaks in the narrative with his own voice. The same applies to Hagar; and the angel's comforting words to Hagar (כי־שׁמע יהוה אל־עניך) in 16.11, which resemble the words to Israel in Exodus 3, and her own reply, indicate at least a positive relationship between God and Hagar. The same could be said about Genesis 21. Even Abimelech, in the narrative in ch. 20 that is probably very late, speaks and acts as an ethically responsible king; God even admits that he is innocent, acting with integrity (בתם־לבבך עשׂית זאת, v. 6) like the king (Ps. 78.72) and the wise in Israel. Abimelech regards himself as צדיק, even though Abraham thought there was no fear of God (יראת אלהים) in Gerar. Abimelech's answer may be read as his rejection of this opinion about him and his people, and the narrator does not contradict him. I will discuss the term 'categorical identity' later; but one cannot say that these persons are presented with a 'categorical identity'; they are allowed to speak, to present their feelings (Isaac), self-estimations (Abimelech), and experiences (Hagar). Of course, the perspective is from the national viewpoint of the Israelite nation, but we hear the voice of the Other to a certain degree as well. Hence, Israel's self-understanding as a nation in Genesis is deeply embedded in a positive picture of the nations, at least

---

3. This phenomenon is explored in detail elsewhere in this volume in the contribution by Ehud Ben Zvi, 'Othering, Selfing, "Boundarying" and "Cross-Boundarying" as Interwoven with Socially Shared Memories: Some Observations', pp. 20-40.

in some texts. True, there are texts that go in the opposite direction, notably Gen. 9.25; and the promises presuppose that 'the Canaanites' will be driven out of the country (Gen. 12.6; 15.18-21); but the latter, as well as Exod. 3.8, 23.23 (also vv. 31-33), 34.11, are now usually regarded as Deuteronomic redactions stemming either from the exilic or post-exilic period.[4] The Canaanites are not mentioned in the Priestly land promise in Gen. 17.8; they do not occur in the P-material at all in the negative sense. In Numbers 13–14, which appear as secondary, 'Priestly' additions belonging to the Second Temple period, their fight against Israel is a means by which God punishes Israel. But even the very late story of Abraham's dealings with Melchizedek in Genesis 14 and his negotiations for Sarah's burial place with the 'Hittites' in Genesis 23 express no explicitly negative bias. The story of Shechem and Dinah in Genesis 34 fits into a picture of changing, ambivalent attitudes toward close neighbours.[5] Accordingly, except for the strange condemnation of Canaan in Genesis 9 and with the possible exception of Gen. 12.6, which some scholars argue is late in its entirety, or at least that the second half of the verse is late, the summary references to the Canaanites as enemies to be driven out from the Land belong to very late redactional stages of the Pentateuch (including Deut. 7.1). If it is correct that there were no Canaanites in the land during the Second Temple period, the common anthropological picture is confirmed: one does not indiscriminately ban or 'annihilate' groups with which one has living relations.

Scholarly discussion of the Canaanites has concentrated on their identification, dating, and function. Although there seems to be con-sensus about dating the 'Canaanite' texts to the exilic or post-exilic period, there are different opinions about the meaning of the term.[6] As

---

4. See, for instance, Reinhard G. Kratz, *Die Komposition der erzählenden Bücher des Alten Testament* (UTB, 2157; Göttingen: Vandenhoeck & Ruprecht, 2000), pp. 141, 148.

5. Robert L. Cohn states, somewhat simplistically, that 'in the narratively earlier tales of Israel's ancestors in Genesis, the natives of Canaan appear as decent hosts, sometimes even sympathetic individuals' ('Before Israel: The Canaanites as Other in Biblical Tradition', in *The Other in Jewish Thought and History: Constructions of Jewish Culture and Identity* [ed. Lawrence J. Silberstein and Robert L. Cohn; New York: New York University Press, 1995], pp. 74-90 [75]).

6. See, for example, the presentation of scholars' comments on this matter in Zehnder, *Umgang mit Fremden*, pp. 390-91; Kenton L. Sparks, *Ethnicity and Identity in Ancient Israel: Prolegomena to the Study of Ethnic Sentiments and their Expression in the Hebrew Bible* (Winona Lake, IN: Eisenbrauns, 1998), p. 258 and passim distinguishes between 'objective others' (Ammonites, Moabites, Edomites, and Egyptians) and 'rhetorical others', the primeval populations within the land (Deut. 7.1-5), who were to be completely destroyed.

M. Zehnder has demonstrated,[7] the Canaanites have been seen to represent the past history of Israel before the exile, which has to be vindicated and suppressed; they have been regarded as an ideological consolidation against the Assyrian practice of forcing their cult on their vassal states; and the declarations in Deuteronomy 7 and elsewhere have been interpreted as an attempt by the post-exilic returnees to equate the people remaining in the land with the (idea of) Canaanites in the time of the conquest.

The notion of Othering has mostly been explained in terms of power relations. This presupposes that the Others are part of the society's struggle for power (normally the marginalized). Speaking of the Canaanites as former, no longer existing Others changes the entire concept. This is probably a major reason why some scholars think that 'the Canaanites' stand for other social constellations. M. Weinfeld and others have drawn attention to the 'genre' of founding tales in which the founding father settles down in a new country. Such stories cannot easily be explained by the modern, power-related understanding of Othering.[8] From this perspective, Deuteronomy's ethical identity formation happens as a discursive practice through definitions of boundaries but without elements of externally oriented 'powering'. One should also note that in Deuteronomy, space appears as a more important ethical and identity-shaping entity than do border-lines between Israel and other nations.[9]

More sustainable explanations have explicated the pedagogical function. K. L. Sparks, referring to Deut. 8.19-20, regards the inhabitants as pedagogical models for the fate awaiting unfaithful Israelites.[10] In 7.25-26, the peoples who will be destroyed completely represent religious practices that were 'an abomination' (תועבה): production of divine images, illegal intermediation, unclean foodstuffs, transvestism, and cult prostitution. This pedagogical function seems clear from the multiple threats of destruction and annihilation linked to the Israelite admonitions. It also corresponds to the possibly late redactional 'didactic level' in the

---

7. See previous note.

8. For references, see Peter Machinist, 'Outsiders or Insiders', in Silberstein and Cohn (eds.), *The Other in Jewish Thought and History*, pp. 35-60 (50).

9. In a more recent book, Lawrence J. Silberstein has pointed just to the importance of space in modern thought about identity formation, see Lawrence J. Silberstein (ed.), *Mapping Jewish Identities* (New York: New York University Press, 2000), especially pp. 11, 16. See also the small book by J. Gordon McConville and J. Gary Millar, *Time and Place in Deuteronomy* (JSOTSup, 179; Sheffield: Sheffield Academic Press, 1994). Silberstein thus understands identity in terms of spatialization, location, and mapping more than as an essence.

10. Sparks, *Ethnicity and Identity in Ancient Israel*, p. 261.

Exodus story (1–15), which presents Pharaoh and 'the sicknesses in Egypt' as pedagogical tools.[11] Drawing on a comprehensive overview of recent research on Deuteronomy, including her own studies, K. Finsterbusch finds the subject of the exilic (and also the original) Deuteronomic composition to be a combination of the theme of Exile as the threatening background in the constitution of Israel and a community learning the Deuteronomic laws (Deut. 4.1-40). She identifies the main theme to be securing the community's identity by linking it to the new law (Torah).[12] This conclusion is easy to accept. The 'polity' that appears in Deuteronomy is, however, a utopian scribal community of people studying the Torah.[13]

Representative of modern research is a 1995 article by R. L. Cohn.[14] Asserting that the texts preserve no historical memories of the actual Canaanites, he holds that they are constructions of the Other, which serve as signifiers of Israel's cultural identity and its boundary. Cohn explains the Canaanites 'within' Israel by referring to the insecurity of former 'outside' people who become insiders; they are never quite secure in their land. The Canaanites 'as the insiders who became outsiders serve as the symbol of that insecurity': 'The group defining the Other has projected its insecurities concerning its potential loss of power onto the world in the shape of that Other through which it imagines itself threatened'.[15]

This corresponds in a way to J. Kristeva's view, based on psychoanalysis, as presented by L. J. Silberstein, the editor of the volume where Cohn's article appears: 'The Other within is the foreigner, the uncanny within ourselves'.[16] Following this line of thought, the Canaanites in

---

11. For this interpretation, see my earlier article, Kåre Berge, 'Didacticism in Exodus: Elements of Didactic Genre in Exodus 1–15', *SJOT* 22.1 (2008), pp. 3-28.

12. Karin Finsterbusch, *Weisung für Israel. Studien zu religiösem Lehren und Lernen im Deuteronomium und in seinem Umfeld* (FAT, 44; Tübingen: Mohr Siebeck, 2005), pp. 37-38.

13. For arguments, see my article, Kåre Berge, 'Literacy, Utopia and Memory: Is There a Public Teaching in Deuteronomy?', *JHS* 12.3 (2012), pp. 1-19.

14. Cohn, 'Before Israel', pp. 74-90. The recent interest in 'the other' in biblical research is documented, e.g. by Daniel C. Harlow et al. (eds.), *The 'Other' in Second Temple Judaism: Essays in Honor of John J. Collins* (Grand Rapids. MI: Eerdmans, 2011).

15. Cohn, 'Before Israel', p. 77; cf. Sander Gilman, *Jewish Self-Hatred: Anti-Semitism and the Hidden Language of the Jews* (Baltimore: The Johns Hopkins University Press, 1986), p. 3.

16. Lawrence J. Silberstein, 'Others Within and Others Without: Rethinking Jewish Identity and Culture', in Silberstein and Cohn (eds.), *The Other in Jewish Thought and History*, pp. 1-34 (8).

Deuteronomy, including the Dtr additions, are the visualization and symbols of the elite's utopia of a people consisting of Torah-pious scribes.[17] To realize this utopia, one needs to fight the uncanny 'within'.

The insecurity to which Cohn refers usually has been explained as a consequence of the idea of the conditional covenant and its relation to monotheism.[18] Some scholars link this concept to the 'Yahweh-Alone-Movement' in the Northern Kingdom.[19] This altogether 'textual', religious, and 'ideational' explanation omits any consideration of the social location and function of such ways of Othering the Canaanites, as well as the societal conditions under which such Othering would take place. It only focuses on the concept, not the question about which group(s) within 'Israelite' society could possibly have produced this concept and for what purpose, which should be included in explanations that refer to circumstances in the 'Israelite'-Yehudite society. To be convincing, such explanations should be integrated into a theory of society and changing social forms that can account for the difference between the narratives in Genesis and the Deuteronomic text. The problem with and challenge to the societal explanations listed above is that, for the most part, they fail to discuss such theoretical models. I will address this oversight.

Accordingly, in the rest of this article, I will: (1) clarify the conceptual relation between the texts referred to above and the concept of 'categorical identity' and related notions. Is the ban on the Canaanites an instance of the essentializing Othering that scholars normally connect with identity formation?[20] If so, how is this included in the broader picture of the Other in the Pentateuch? (2) I will suggest how the presentation of the Other in Genesis vis-à-vis Deuteronomy, including the Dtr additions mentioned above, can be theorized in terms of different social formations.

17. See again, Berge, 'Didacticism in Exodus'.
18. See, e.g., Cohn, 'Before Israel', pp. 76-79; Zehnder, *Umgang mit Fremden*, p. 168. He says the ban (Deut. 7.2) is religiously motivated as an expression of the exclusive covenant between Israel and Yahweh against foreign cultic practices and mixed marriages.
19. See Sparks, *Ethnicity and Identity in Ancient Israel*, pp. 234-36, 257-58, 265; Zehnder, *Umgang mit Fremden*, p. 389. Idiomatic to him is the understanding that the prohibition against a covenant (לא־תכרת להם ברית) with the Canaanites is a prohibition against making them subject to vassalship and subjugated to corvée labour (pp. 392, 497).
20. For this concept, see also Silberstein, 'Others Within and Others Without', pp. 1-34.

After the seminal work by E. Said,[21] the anti-essentialistic view of ethnic and national identity as something that constantly is 'in becoming' and basically understood as a discursive process has been combined with the concept of the Other. As stated by Silberstein, '[t]he concept of the Other is basic to the revised interpretation of cultural identity. According to these theories, we form our sense of self, our identity, in relation to Others over and against whom we define ourselves.'[22] He holds that the concept of the Other as a part of identity formation is particularly prominent among so-called postmodern thinkers.

At least since Said's work, the notion of Othering as a part of ethnic-national identity formation has commonly been regarded as something negative. It consists of exclusion, silencing, and even acts of violence. Resting on complex theoretical presuppositions, its most central foundation is the constructionist model of national identity formation as presented, for example, by E. Hobsbawm and others. The concept has been applied and explored in biblical studies in a volume of essays from a 1999 NOSTER conference.[23]

In spite of many references to Foucault and other 'hermeneutical' intellectual thinkers, this picture of identity and nationality as discourse is solidly anchored in social-scientifically oriented research on culture that focuses on objectivity, institutions, social structures, and individuals rather than on persons, subjectivity, and subjective experience, at least within the functionalistic and structuralist branches.[24] A. Giddens holds that this difference is not only epistemological but also ontological, which probably means that it is socially grounding (defining modes of being and appearing in structures and inter-relations). In this research on nationality and ethnicity, ethnic and national myths have been regarded as the primary *means* by which nationality was created. National and ethnic traditions were invented by the mythmaking elites. According to the reading of Hobsbawm by A. D. Smith, these invented traditions were deliberate creations of cultural engineers who forged symbols, rituals, myths, and histories to meet the needs of the modern masses. In other words, they were deliberate instruments of control by the ruling elite.[25]

21. Edward Said, *Orientalism* (New York: Random House, 1994).

22. Silberstein, 'Others Within and Others Without', p. 5.

23. Jan W. van Henten and Anton Houtepen (eds.), *Religious Identity and the Invention of Tradition: Papers Read at a NOSTER Conference in Soesterberg, January 4–6, 1999* (Studies in Theology and Religion, 3; Assen: Van Gorcum, 2001).

24. Here I follow the categorization by Anthony Giddens, *The Constitution of Society* (Cambridge: Polity Press, 1984), pp. 1-2.

25. Anthony D. Smith, *Nationalism: Theory, Ideology, History* (Cambridge: Polity Press, 2001), pp. 80-81.

One should be careful, however, not to equate this with 'fabricated' or 'false'.

The problem here is not the idea of elites but the priority that is given to the myths. In reaction to this, the sociologist T. Scheff holds that ethnic formation and ethnic nationalism arise out of a *sentiment*. In his presentation, this sentiment comes from a sense of alienation and resentment against unfair exclusion. Without going into his specific model of alienation as the motor of nationalism, the point is that sentiment and feeling come before myth.[26] In a similar vein, the anthropologist M. M. J. Fischer holds, 'a deeply rooted emotional component of identity, it [ethnicity] is often transmitted less through cognitive language or learn-

26. Thomas Scheff, 'Emotions and Identity: A Theory of Ethnic Nationalism', in *Social Theory and the Politics of Identity* (ed. Craig Calhoun; Oxford: Blackwell, 1994), pp. 277-303. The notion of sacrifice and willingness to die for the nation is regarded as a central part of the national sentiment by Ernest Renan ('What Is a Nation?', in *Becoming National: A Reader* [ed. Geoff Eley and Ronald G. Suny; Oxford: Oxford University Press, 1996), pp. 41-55) and recently, by Benedict Anderson (*Imagined Communities: Reflections on the Origin and Spread of Nationalism* [London: Verso, rev. edn, 2006]). See also Paul James, *Nation Formation* (London: Sage, 1996), p. 8: 'The idea of nationalism never *in itself* moved anyone'. At this point he cites Miroslav Hroch, who argued that nation-building was never a mere project of ambitious or narcissistic intellectuals. Intellectuals can invent national communities only if certain objective preconditions for the formation of a nation already exists. Even Anthony Giddens, who defines nation-*states* in terms of administrative power and institutional form, defines nationalism as a psychological phenomenon with primordial sentiments (kin connection) (see the presentation by James in *Nation Formation*, p. 67). This, of course, refers to modern nationality. However, if there were some kind of national engagement in the society that produced the biblical books, even if restricted to intellectuals, and if this process resembled our ideas of nationality, we would expect to find something similar in antiquity. In any case, we should note that *we* use terminology and concepts from modern time even when talking about the 'Israelite'-Yehudite society as nation and *ethnie* (the term from A. D. Smith). This leaves us with an entire set of modern concepts whose relevance for understanding ancient material we at least need to discuss. We should also note that the Vulgate uses *gentes, populous, nationes* for the nations of the Bible and that the term appears at the universities in Paris, Bologna, and Oxford in the thirteenth century CE (see James, *Nation Formation*, p. 11). James also notes that nation/ nations was used in the Vulgate with reference to the Gentiles, which corresponds to the frequent use of גוים to denote 'pagan' peoples in the Hebrew Bible, while the chosen people was the populous. A little later, it came to refer to all classes of people with a common 'ethnic' background (*Nation Formation*, p. 11). So, we should be careful not to read modern models of nation formation, including constructivism and the negative 'other', directly into ancient 'national' ideas.

ing (to which sociology has almost entirely restricted itself) than through processes analogous to the dreaming and transference of psychoanalytic encounters'.[27] He even applies Freud's *id* to this 'it-ness' of experience: 'The recognition of something about one's essential being thus seems to stem from outside one's immediate consciousness and control, and yet requires an effort of self-definition'.[28] With reference to today's ethnicity and to autobiographical writing of African Americans, he speaks of ethnic anxiety and fear as a 'feeling welling up out of mysterious depths'; of the soul engaged in memory and recollections; and of what is hidden in language, containing sedimented layers of emotionally resonant metaphors, knowledge, and associations. Turning to ethnography, he stresses 'bifocality': seeing others against a background of ourselves and ourselves against a background of others. But this should not lead into the trap of simplistic better–worse judgments; cultures and ethnicities should be seen as sets more like families of resemblances than simple typological trees.[29] It needs to be added, however, that this is not the same as claims to real national primordiality.

The same modern perspectives should be applied to studies of how ethnicity and nationality were formed, understood, and expressed in history.[30] One should not simply presume that the shaping of nationality, even by an elite, took the form of negative expressions of the ethnic Other. One should presuppose, rather, that there was a 'national' sentiment, a *feeling* of primordiality and ethnic commonality that changed focus and perspective over the years. People frequently shift their ethnic identities in order to maximize their advantage in different situations. As C. Calhoun states:

> Ethnicity occupies something of an intermediary position between kinship and nationality. Ethnic identities have become important historically wherever multiple groups have dealings with each other in a common territory. Ethnicity is thus not simply an extension of kinship, but the way in which collective identity gets constituted when kinship loyalties,

27. Michael M. J. Fischer, 'Ethnicity and the Post-Modern Arts of Memory', in *Writing Culture: The Poetics and Politics of Ethnography* (ed. James Clifford and George E. Marcus; Berkeley: University of California Press, 1986), pp. 194-233 (195-96).

28. Ibid., p. 196.

29. Ibid.

30. For a comprehensive discussion of modern perspectives on the state, see Bruce E. Routledge, *Moab in the Iron Age* (Philadelphia: University of Pennsylvania Press, 2004). Space does not permit me to go discuss Steven Grosby's analysis of Israelite nationality that he bases on the concepts by Anthony D. Smith (*Biblical Ideas of Nationality: Ancient and Modern* [Winona Lake, IN: Eisenbrauns, 2002]).

traditions...confront a broader arena in which most interaction is not organized by the same kinship and culture as within the group. Internally, an 'ethnic group' may be organized in terms of kinship and descent. Externally, vis-à-vis other ethnic groups or the state, it appears as a category of equivalently 'ethnic' members.[31]

The non-deuteronomic 'national' stories in Genesis depict Israel's ethnicity in terms of a differentiated relation to the fathers of the other nations. This continued into post-exilic time (e.g. Gen. 20) but seemed to predominate in narratives that were likely pre-exilic in date. The Deuteronomists do not seem to have been interested in kinship relations within Israel, which appears 'as a category of equivalently "ethnic" members'.[32] If Calhoun's distinction holds also for the society that created those texts, it is possible to conclude that the authors of Deuteronomy found pressure from outside the society to be much stronger than the first group of differentially authored texts did. For the Deuteronomists, there seem to have been social forces that demanded a clearer vision of 'the Israelites', which also resulted in a focus on the teaching of 'national' values.

There is another aspect in this theoretical presentation that relates to how the researcher envisions her/his material or to the hermeneutical problems of (re)presentation of cultures in writings. As J. Clifford writes, anthropology no longer speaks with automatic authority for Others defined as unable to speak for themselves, drawing attention to the poetical character of ethnographic writing and to the ethnographical presentation's polyvocality.[33] In fact, ethnographic writing is (true) fiction in the sense of something made up, *invented*, even by subversion, exclusion, and the silencing of other voices. He also challenges the notion of *vision* in ethnographic understanding, replacing it with the idea of *discourse*, which involves dialogues, incongruent voices, and even partiality. In another article in the same volume, he discusses the presentation of the Other in ethnographic writing.[34] Ethnographic interpreters constantly construct themselves through the others they study. Accordingly, any ethnographic, intercultural encounter and dialogue with the Other includes the moral implications of the encounter.

31. Craig Calhoun, *Nationalism* (Concepts in the Social Sciences; Buckingham: Open University Press, 1997), p. 40.

32. Ibid., p. 40.

33. James Clifford, 'Introduction: Partial Truths', in Clifford and Marcus (eds.), *Writing Culture*, pp. 1-26. The book was re-published with a new foreword in 2009.

34. Clifford, 'On Ethnographic Allegory', in Clifford and Marcus (eds.), *Writing Culture*, pp. 98-121.

The consequences of Clifford's argument for social studies of the Bible should not be under-estimated. As the scholars above remark, there was a *literary* turn in cultural analysis, but there was also a *cultural* turn, not only in social science but in biblical studies as well. Asking about the formation of national and ethnic identity in the Bible or looking for the work of literate elites in its textualization or seeking to understand the relation between the elite and the public are all issues of cultural relevance. They are questions that go far beyond literary critical reading and which lead to cultural (re)presentation, even when the majority of the material we have is textual.

It has been demonstrated by scholars like P. R. Davies and N. P. Lemche that we need to anchor our picture of biblical societies in societal theories. But we also need to be aware of the subjectivity in and the constructional aspect of the pictures we create. Hence, the way cultural anthropologists configure and question their representation of culture also affects questions like those mentioned above within biblical studies. For instance, it is one thing to state that the notion of ban and extinction (Deut. 7.2-3) was a common cultural phenomenon in ancient times, citing the Mesha stone as a non-Judahite example. It is quite another matter to see how this played a part as an artefact in biblical cultural identity-building. We simply do not know what role the vision of the Other found in the biblical texts played in ethnic and national identity formation in, for example, Yehud; the entire question is determined by modern social-scientific and cultural models and theories.

Clifford and others remind us, by implication, that the picture we make of 'Israelite'-Yehudite depicting of the Other is *our narrative*. This is, to use a term from Clifford, a palimpsest. It interprets the textual world as a theater of multiple and divergent stories woven together. Clifford speaks of the ethnographic narrative's different registers, one of which is an allegory in which *our* story, *our* esthetic and moral concerns, and even *our* diagnosis and therapeutic treatment of contemporary situations are involved in our representations of cultures.[35] Consequently, I will hold that there is in the cultural interpretation of biblical texts 'a hierarchical structure of powerful stories that translate, encounter, and recontextualize other powerful stories'.[36]

The Bible is, in itself, an interpretation or rather a creative effort of ethnic, national identity; but the most basic difference between this and

35. For the notion of therapy in ethnography, see Steven Taylor, 'Post-modern Ethnography: From Document of the Occult to Occult Document', in Clifford and Marcus (eds.), *Writing Culture*, pp. 121-40 (134).

36. Clifford, 'On Ethnographic Allegory', p. 121.

an ethnographic encounter is oral versus literary, which makes a great difference but not with regard to the arguments presented here that the biblical text always has a fictional character. Even the native informants of ethnography construct, combine, and create interpretations.

There is a moral obligation on scholars who treat the presentations of the Other in the biblical texts as expressions of national ethnicity. Modern models of nationalism are more or less based on the idea that the ethnified Other presents the negative framework for the national Us, the moral backside. If biblical scholars base their work on this assumption, they will look for negative presentations of the Other, especially focusing on the Canaanites, and in case of the other nations, one will highlight features in the texts that present them at least in an ambivalent light. One needs to look for 'our story' or 'our therapy' when reading biblical texts as 'ethnographic material' for their ethnic identity.

Turning now to 'categorical identity', I follow C. Calhoun in using the term to denote large-scale identification, for instance, nations and ethnic units, 'by similarity of attributes as a member of a set of equivalent members'.[37] This term appears in his distinction between the reproduction of identity groups through standardized mediating agencies and through interpersonal interactions, which also is a distinction between categorical identities and relational ones. It appeals to 'cohesion based more on the similarity of individuals than on their concrete webs of relationship'.[38] Hence, 'categorical identity' stands in opposition to the kind of relationship based on personal relations and interchange. Calhoun explicates this by referring to the difference between a nationalistic appeal to peoples' loyalty to their 'brothers', that is, describing the nation as a family, and a small-scale, segmentary lineage society. In the first case, one would recognize the moral force of the rhetoric of the people as 'brothers' in describing the national bond, but this is not the template for the entire social order. In the second case, the members of a segmentary lineage society would see a sliding scale of loyalties, depending on where in the lineage system the actual relation or interchange takes place. There is the nuclear family of parents and children, a minimal lineage of two or more nuclear families, lineages of various intermediate scales, all the way up to maximal lineages defined by common ancestors.

Once again, segmentary lineage society contrasts with nationality as a categorical identity. The latter posits whole categories of people without reference to their internal differentiation; one is a member of a nation directly as an individual; and the individuality of the individuals alone is

37. Calhoun, *Nationalism*, p. 42.
38. Ibid., p. 43.

the point. The rhetoric of kinship and descent, however, constitutes society as 'a conglomeration of multiple and overlapping memberships of different segments none of which is a trump card against the others'.[39] Put another way, and in more negative terms, individuals are regarded as *units* grouped together into categorical identities, or even *tokens* of one specific type.

Hence, according to Calhoun, nations are organized primarily as categories of individual members, identified on the basis of various cultural attributes. He then states the following concerning the traits of the 'individual': 'In the main modern Western view, individuals exist in and of themselves; the basic source of identity is neither webs of relationships nor encompassing hierarchy…'[40] By hierarchy, Calhoun refers to a hierarchy of specific relationships with reciprocal obligations.

Now, it is clear that in real life one always negotiates identity on a number of levels. While people act at some levels in ways closer to the kinship/ethnicity model, at other levels their consciousness was mobilized by reference to nationality or larger religious groupings, like Christians vs. Muslims.

Genesis presents a picture of the nation of Israel as a lineage of families.[41] In Calhoun's vocabulary, the narratives present a relational Israelite identity. There is face-to-face contact, even when the ancestors conclude a covenant with their neighbours (Gen. 21 and 31.45-47). In Deuteronomy, the various levels at which loyalty typically operates are not expressed. As K. L. Sparks has noted, Deuteronomy's preoccupation is more religious than ethnic. For instance, 'brotherhood' is connected with all Israelites; it is not an internal, distinguishing trait.[42] There is a

39. Ibid, p. 40. On p. 78, in reference to the US civil war, Calhoun distinguishes between the country 'conceived from the immediate family and community outward (and largely through a hierarchy of gentry and aristocratic connections, not laterally)', 'as a web of relationships to land and specific other people', and on the other hand, 'not conceived primarily as a categorical identity, coterminous with a single polity and culture'. It was the civil war itself that 'reinforced the idea of the categorical commonality of Confederate citizens (as it reinforced American nationalism for the United States as a whole', he says (p. 79). And, it is 'the very scale' that makes Calhoun write about the nations (and their networks) as categorical identities, even when nationalists may rely on a rhetoric of 'community' and 'family' (*Nationalism*, p. 93).

40. Ibid., p. 44.

41. For a more extensive presentation of this, see my article, 'National Identity and Popular Sentiment in Genesis and Exodus', in *Enigmas and Images: Studies in Honor of Tryggve N. D. Mettinger* (ed. Göran Eidevall and Blaženka Scheuer; Winona Lake, IN: Eisenbrauns, 2011), pp. 37-52.

42. Sparks, *Ethnicity and Identity in Ancient Israel*, p. 264.

priority of religious relationship with Yahweh, which exceeds any ethnic requirement, says Sparks, referring to the opportunity of a *gēr* to be accepted into the community. This does not invalidate ethnic origins, but it is not a distinguishing criterion within the community itself.

What kinds of 'nationality' do we find in the Pentateuch? It depends on which typology we use. Traditional biblical scholarship distinguished between עַם as a multitude of ethnically related individuals, and גּוֹי as an organized political and military entity with central government and land.[43] Israel was an עַם in Egypt, but it is presented as a גּוֹי in, for example, Gen 12.2, which anticipates its future status as a kingdom. As a social category, this no longer suffices.

The social theorist P. James has introduced a typology of social formation by focusing on levels of abstraction, claiming that the interchange between such levels constitutes the forms of social formation, such as the nation-state. Central issues are modes (levels) of integration and what he calls the ontological, commonsensical categories that are possible to generalize, such as tribalism, traditionalism, and so on, which are linked to time (origins), space (delimination), and the body.[44] This is an attempt to overcome the objectivity–subjectivity dilemma in social science, referred to above. The main focus is on the levels of integration, 'understood as modes of structured practices of association (and differentiation) between people'.[45] The levels are: face-to-face integration, agency-extended integration, and disembodied integration. The first level emphasizes immediacy of interaction and co-presence, resembling Calhoun's description of the small-scale, segmentary, lineage society. Its main characteristics are the modalities of co-presence.[46] In agency-extended integration, social integration is based on institutions or agencies like church, state, guild, corporation, merchants, traders, and so on, and binds people across larger expanses of space; new formations

43. E.g. Aelred Cody, 'When Is the Chosen People Called a Goy?', *VT* 14 (1964), pp. 1-6; Ephraim A. Speiser, 'People and Nation of Israel', *JBL* 79 (1960), pp. 157-63. See also *HALOT*, under גּוֹי.

44. James, *Nation Formation*, p. 22.

45. Ibid.

46. Ibid., p.24: 'In a setting marked by the dominance of face-to-face integration, such as a tribal or peasant society, the limitations and possibilities of fully embodied interaction constitute the boundaries of social existence and thus of social subjectivity. It conditions the way in which people live such apparently pre-given but already abstracted "natural" categories as the body, space and time. It binds the abstracting practices of myth-telling, long-distance gift exchange and even cross-tribal partnership with unseen others, within the modalities of co-presence. It binds them within the modalities of reciprocity, continuity and concrete otherness.'

become possible. Central notions are *agency* as an institution or the office of an agent exerting power, and *mediation*. James includes 'traditional empires', like the Assyrian and the Roman, under this category:

> The power of the early empires over their dominions was effected by military coercion, and though it was often religiously sanctioned it was dependent on the beginnings of an agency-regulated exaction of surplus production from subservient, often ethnically differentiated, populations... At the same time, relations between the ruling factions still were based commonly upon face-to-face modalities such as extended-kinship or reciprocal loyalties. In other words, ruling power was still substantially founded upon patrimonial or traditional authority as opposed to the more abstract, bureaucratic and relatively impersonal power of legal authority.[47]

In the case of disembodied integration, '...the social relation transcends time and space quite apart from any personal intermediation'.[48] Written communication and appeal to abstract 'rules' listed in written code are pointed out as typical to this level, which also includes an abstract relationship between a person and their unseen, unheard, 'massified' national fellows. James expresses a common formulation when noting that the national community is replete with strangers.

Applying this theory to the Pentateuch material, we may conclude that it is the difference in abstraction that structurally and theoretically explains the difference between the subtle, multi-dimensional relation between Israel's forefathers and the other peoples of the land (and of bordering lands) in Genesis and the Deuteronom(ist)ic presentation. The stories in Genesis present both a particularity of space and time. In Gen. 13.14, Abraham is promised the land he can see from his standpoint in Bethel. He is told to 'walk up' the land, and he furnishes it with altars. The particularity of time is visible through the genealogical kinship relations.

In Deuteronomy, as already mentioned, Israel as an entity is presented as 'brothers'. It is this abstraction that enables the authors to speak of the king as a scribe who sits reading a copy of the Torah scroll, the original of which is in the care of the Levite priests. It is clear that the injunctions to kill even the genealogical brother, son, or wife, if they entice the addressed 'you' to go to other gods (Deut. 13.6), stem historically and generically from the treaty tradition.[49] However, typologically, this also

---

47. Ibid., p. 27.
48. Ibid., p. 31.
49. For this, see Eckart Otto, 'Die Ursprünge der Bundestheologie im Alten Testament und im Alten Orient', *ZAR* 4 (1998), pp. 1-84, and a number of later publications.

belongs to the homeland ('*pro patria mori*').[50] Its context is the abstract notion of the covenant with God, not the practice of 'honour-killing' or revenge (Gen. 34).

The notion of the Other is intimately linked to the imminent entrance into the Promised Land, the injunction to keep the covenant, and the threat of extinction from the land if they do not (Deut. 7.4; 8.19-20; 11.28). But the land is not presented in a concrete and visible way, like in Genesis (13.14-18); even the law to establish asylum cities (Deut. 19) does not specify which cities will function in this capacity. There is no play on names and geography as in Genesis. Three examples should suffice as illustrations. At his birth, Esau is described as 'red, ruddy' (אדמוני) and like a 'a hairy garment' (אדרת שׂער) (Gen. 25.25; cf. 27.11; 36.1, 53). The first term evokes the toponym Edom and the second Mt. Seir. In contrast to 'hairy' Esau, in Gen. 27.11 Jacob is described to be חלק, 'smooth', which evokes the site of Mt. Halak near Mt. Seir in the southern part of the Promised Land (Josh. 11.17). Finally, Laban, the uncle of the twins, evokes the region of Lebanon, which adjoins the northern boundary of the Promised Land in Josh. 11.17. With the exception of the land east of Jordan, the borders are not mentioned. The land is only mentioned by its qualities and the primordial peoples.

Hence, Deuteronomy goes far beyond embodied interactions dependent on kinship and face-to-face relationship; these are subordinated to the territorial concept, the land. However, it is presented in very general terms and is dependent on a more abstract, decontextualized, and disembodied extension of social interaction linked to the medium of literacy. This lack of connectedness to actually lived relationships in the land would perhaps suggest that the Deuteronom(ist)ic authors were writing from outside the country, possibly Babylon. However, even more important is the structural conclusion.

In its present form, Deuteronomy is first and foremost a narrative about how Israel—whatever social group that might be—received the scroll of the Torah of Moses. This scroll should be studied, recited, and taught by the priests to all the people. There is an enormous focus on the literary aspect, of Israel as more or less narrowed down to a scribal community (the king, who was the family's father, and the Levitical priests) studying the Torah scroll that was in the custody and safe-keeping of the scribal, Levitical priests, who also served as its interpreters. They were to gather the entire people at a special occasion to listen to the

---

50. James, *Nation Formation*, p. 29, referring to Roman law, from which 'jurists drew antecedents to assert that a person acting in the name of the *patria* could legitimately kill his (or her) *pater*'.

Torah being read out and explained through a sermon. This presupposes both a level of abstraction and particularization and traditionalism (see below). Let us turn to the issue of literacy.

According to James, intellectual practice, by definition, works to transcend the limitations of embodied interaction:

> [A]t a time when the intersection of face-to-face and agency-extended relations provided the constitutive setting for philosophical debates over the meaning of sovereignty and the office of the king, writing provided a medium of disembodied interchange held in place, by, but abstracting from, those dominant forms of social relations. In short…there are groupings of people who by virtue of the form of their practice work at a level more abstract than the dominant mode(s) of integration. It is this capacity that makes intellectuals and the intellectually trained…important to any discussion of abstract communities.[51]

This understanding corresponds to J. Goody's view of literacy in primarily oral societies.[52] Competence in writing tends to depersonalize interaction between the bureaucracy, in this case the religious elite, and the rest of the people.

Indirect contact via written communication is demonstrated, paradoxically, in the claim to centralize the festivals. In Exodus, the Pesah was to be celebrated in the homes of the individuals but in Deuteronomy, it was to be held in the one city where Yahweh would place his name, which implies that it would be under the control of the scribal and priestly elites. Depersonalized contact is also reflected in the prescription to assemble the people only every seventh year to hear the Torah scroll being read and explained by the scribal priests (Deut. 31). However, this corresponds to James's thesis of the ambiguous place of intellectuals, between intellectual abstraction and an increased focus on the particular, traditionalism, and individualism.[53] This view of modern society seems relevant also to the Deuteronomists' society. B. Ego has demonstrated how the festivals and celebrations were necessary means by which the scribes secured their authority as custodians of the written Torah.[54]

51. Ibid., p. 43.
52. Jack Goody, *The Logic of Writing and the Organization of Society* (Cambridge: Cambridge University Press, 1986), pp. 16, 19: 'Religious literates often think that, ideally, God's reign should come to pass on earth and the priesthood should administer His estate'. In Deuteronomy, a clear utopian picture appears of the whole of Israel as a scribal society, the whole of Israel like the community of the scribes.
53. James, *Nation Formation*, p. 43.
54. Beate Ego, '"In der Schriftrolle ist für mich geschrieben" (Ps 40.8)', in *Die Textualisierung der Religion* (ed. Joachim Schaper; FAT II/62; Tübingen: Mohr

Let me proceed by stating the obvious. Deuteronomy tells a story about the past. More precisely, it is a narrative that creates a normative universe. The late professor of Law at Yale Law School, R. Cover, states that law is a bridge linking a concept of a reality to an imagined alternative, or put differently in his own words:

> Law...is a bridge in normative space connecting [our understanding of] the 'world-that-is'...with our projections of alternative 'worlds-that-might-be'... In this theory, law is neither to be wholly identified with the understanding of the present state of affairs nor with the imagined alternatives. It *is* the bridge—the committed social behavior which constitutes the way a group of people will attempt to get from here to there.[55]

He also puts it this way: 'A *nomos* is a present world constituted by a system of tension between reality and vision'.[56] In his presentation, this understanding is connected with the view that a *nomos*—a normative universe—includes not only a *corpus juris* but also a mythos, myths that establish the paradigms for behaviour.[57] He may also call this narrative the codes that relate our normative system to our social construction of reality and to our visions of what the world might be.[58]

Deuteronomy is the narrative about how Israel received the scroll of the Torah of Moses and how the scroll should be studied, recited, and taught by the priests to the entire people. Cover also states that every legal order must somehow conceive of itself as emerging from some kind of discontinuity, from a 'sacred beginning' represented by a theophany, a revolution, a migration, and so on. To illustrate, he refers to the Pilgrim Fathers, the conquest of Canaan, or Mount Sinai. Cover states it this way: 'Every legal order must conceive of itself in one way or another as emerging out of that which is in itself unlawful'.[59] Now, to rephrase this with regard to Deuteronomy: The annihilation of the Canaanites belongs to the 'sacred beginning' of the Torah of Moses, not to present reality.

Siebeck, 2009), pp. 82-104. There is a comprehensive discussion on the relation between the written Torah and teaching in Deuteronomy that cannot be rehearsed in this article. See the references in this book.

55. Robert Cover, 'Nomos and Narrative', in *Narrative, Violence, and the Law: The Essays of Robert Cover* (ed. Martha Minow, Michael Ryan, and Austin Sarat; Ann Arbor: The University of Michigan Press, 1995, 2004), pp. 175-93 (176).

56. Ibid.

57. Ibid., p. 101.

58. Ibid., p. 102.

59. Ibid., p. 118.

They are there no more. But, as Cover also says, 'The return to foundational acts can never be prevented or entirely domesticated'.[60] There is a danger that there be a new legal beginning, which also might include an annihilation of the Canaanites, whatever that means.

I will conclude this essay with the following observation. The Pentateuch's presentation of the relation between the Israelites and the other nations can hardly be seen as a practice of 'categorical identities'. The implication of this term and cognate formulations, as described by certain modern social theorists, does not cover the function of the other nations in Genesis nor the Canaanites in Deuteronomy. In the latter book, the confrontation with the Canaanites and their annihilation serves as a stage for the 'sacred beginning' and as a pedagogical tool in the teaching of the Torah. When discussing the Pentateuch and social identity formation in Yehud, one should note that the authors who wrote about the Canaanites were very much aware that this group of people belonged to the ancient past, not to the present. One should also keep in mind that these late redactors and authors included the previous narrative layers of the Pentateuch, which tell about a very complex and 'living' relationship between the Israelite ancestors and the Other peoples, including those in the Land, in some instances also letting their representatives, as individual subjects, speak for themselves. As interpreters and commentators on the biblical view of the Others and its ethical implications, we are morally required to present this full and complex picture.

60. Ibid., p. 119.

Natives and Immigrants in the Social Imagination of the Holiness School

Mark G. Brett

Introduction

The broader issues that surround this essay concern the constitution of Israel in the late Persian period, the discourse of insiders and outsiders, and the evidence for permeability of social boundaries. Anthropologists usually take the view that traditional societies are populated by ethnic primordialists, for whom the congruencies of language, custom, and cult are so overwhelming that incorporation of strangers often needs to happen 'behind the back' of explicit native discourse, for example, in the plasticity of genealogies that present themselves as traditional, unchanging, and having been derived from a distant past.[1] Perhaps the narrative of Ruth can be read as departing only minimally from a primordial view in that this biblical book presents a complex narrative defense of an anomalous foreign woman whose presence, on closer investigation, is seen not to be anomalous at all.[2] But my focus in this essay is on a group of texts within which the inclusion of strangers is not so much anomalous as a legally explicit and regular feature of Israel's life.

A suggestion of regularity appears even in the narrative of Ezra 6.21, where it is simply stated without further explanation that the Passover was joined by 'all who separated themselves (הנבדל) from the impurities of the nations of the land',[3] that is, these newly purified people were

---

1. See, e.g., Frank Crüsemann's discussion in 'Human Solidarity and Ethnic Identity: Israel's Self-Definition in the Genealogical System of Genesis', in *Ethnicity and the Bible* (ed. Mark G. Brett; *BibInt* Series, 19; Leiden: Brill, 1996), pp. 57-76.

2. The approach taken by Neil Glover, 'Your People, My People: An Exploration of Ethnicity in Ruth', *JSOT* 33 (2009), pp. 293-313.

3. Similar formulations are found in Neh. 9.2 ('the seed of Israel separated themselves *from the foreigners*') and 10.29 ('and all who separated themselves *from the peoples* of the lands'), except that Ezra 6.21 seems to add an extra nuance by suggesting that it is the *abominations*, rather than the persons, that are the source of

added to the core community of Israel, who are designated 'children of
Israel who had returned from the *golah*'. This evidence of inclusiveness
contrasts strongly with the notorious standards of impermeable genealogical purity articulated in Ezra 9.1-3, which, at least on its linguistic
surface, envisages a sharp distinction between the *golah* returnees and
the 'peoples of the lands'. It is perhaps possible that the linguistic surface
of Ezra 9.1-3 is to be taken as nothing more than a primordialist exterior
behind which individual Moabite women like Ruth might be smuggled—
on the condition that their religious and cultural convictions exhibit very
little difference from the dominant culture of Israel. But the very lack of
explanation provided in Ezra 6.21 warrants further comment. At the very
least, we need to have some understanding of why it stands prominently
'against the more broadly exclusionary policy found in Ezra 9 and
Nehemiah 13'.[4]

My hypothesis here is that the discourse of inclusion in Ezra 6.21 is
indebted to the Holiness School, whose convictions subsist in the 'background knowledge' of the audience of Ezra 6.21 and which, therefore,
require no further explanation.[5] This hypothesis may amount, in some
respects, to an 'allusion' to H, although there are only isolated terms in
Ezra 6.21, notably 'separate' (בדל) and 'abominations' (sg. טֻמְאָה), that
might form the particular points of linguistic contact with the earlier
texts. For example, the call to be *separate* from the peoples is shared
with the discourse in the Holiness Code's in Lev. 20.24-26. One might

offence. Cf. Rainer Albertz, 'Purity Strategies and Political Interests in the Policy of
Nehemiah', in *Confronting the Past: Archaeological and Historical Essays on
Ancient Israel in Honor of William G. Dever* (ed. Seymour Gitin, J. Edward Wright,
and J. P. Dessel; Winona Lake, IN: Eisenbrauns, 2006), pp. 199-206. Cf. the uses of
בדל (Hiphil) in Ezra 8.24; 9.1; 10.8, 11, 16; Neh. 13.3.

4. Alan Cooper and Bernard Goldstein, 'The Development of the Priestly
Calendars (I): The Daily Sacrifice and the Sabbath', *Hebrew Union College Annual*
74 (2003), pp. 1-20 (20).

5. In the more technical jargon of linguistics, the procedures for inclusion
established by the Holiness School form part of the inexplicit 'conversational impli-
catures' that belong to ordinary communication. For a classic discussion of implica-
tures, see Stephen C. Levinson, *Pragmatics* (Cambridge Textbooks in Linguistics;
Cambridge: Cambridge University Press, 1983), pp. 97-225. Cf. Yan Huang,
Pragmatics (Oxford Textbooks in Linguistics; Oxford: Oxford University Press,
2007); Alan Cruse, *Meaning in Language: An Introduction to Semantics and Pragmatics* (Oxford Textbooks in Linguistics; Oxford: Oxford University Press, 3rd edn,
2011); Siobhan Chapman, *Pragmatics* (Modern Linguistics Series; Basingstoke:
Palgrave Macmillan, 2011).

imagine that there is an innovation in Ezra 6.21 to the extent that this is conceived as a separating from *impurities*, rather than from *persons*, but I would argue that this is not actually an innovation, since it is clearly implied already in other H texts, notably in Exod. 12.43-49, as we shall see.[6]

Of course, the dating of both Ezra 6.21 and the H materials are much disputed, but there is, nevertheless, a broad consensus that H would chronologically precede Ezra 6.21. This would be self-evidently the case for scholars who date the Holiness Code to the late monarchic or exilic periods. However, the discussion below recognizes that a good deal of H may have been written 'after Nehemiah',[7] so a problem of chronology might arise if Ezra 1–6 were taken to be a straightforward historical narrative composed early in the Persian period. But this is very unlikely to be the case; there are a number of significant arguments for dating the bulk of Ezra 1–6 to the late Persian or early Hellenistic period, so there is still no substantial reason to doubt that H *precedes* Ezra 6.21 and so could inform the background assumptions of this verse.[8]

It should be noted at this point that I do not see the opposition to strangers in the earlier Ezra–Nehemiah texts as evidence of the organic unfolding of Priestly tradition. On the contrary, the most influential tradi-

---

6. A number of scholars have now converged on the conclusion that Exod. 12.43-49 belongs to H; e.g. Christophe Nihan, *From Priestly Torah to Pentateuch: A Study in the Composition of the Book of Leviticus* (FAT, II/25; Tübingen: Mohr Siebeck, 2007), pp. 566-67; Saul Olyan, *Rites and Rank: Hierarchy in Biblical Representations of Cult* (Princeton: Princeton University Press, 2000), pp. 69-70; Jakob Wöhrle, 'The Integrative Function of the Law of Circumcision', in *The Foreigner and the Law: Perspectives from the Hebrew Bible and the Ancient Near East* (ed. Reinhart Achenbach, Rainer Albertz, and Jakob Wöhrle; BZAR, 16; Wiesbaden: Harrassowitz, 2011), pp. 71-87 (81-84).

7. Nihan, *From Priestly Torah*, pp. 559-62.

8. See, for example, the range of arguments advanced by H. G. M. Williamson, 'The Composition of Ezra 1–6', *JTS* 34.1 (1983), pp. 1-30, reprinted in *Studies in Persian Period Historiography* (FAT, 38; Tübingen: Mohr Siebeck, 2004), pp. 244-70 (269); Jacob Wright, 'Writing the Restoration: Compositional Agenda and the Role of Ezra in Nehemiah 8', *JHS* 7 (2009), Art. 10, pp. 19-29; idem, *Rebuilding Identity: The Nehemiah Memoir and Its Earliest Readers* (BZAW, 348; Berlin: de Gruyter, 2004), pp. 338-39; Juha Pakkala, *Ezra the Scribe The Development of Ezra 7–10 and Nehemiah 8* (BZAW, 347; Berlin: de Gruyter, 2004), pp. 69-73; Diana Edelman, 'Ezra 1–6 as Idealized Past', in *A Palimpsest: Rhetoric, Ideology, Stylistics, and Language Relating to Persian Israel* (ed. Ehud Ben Zvi, Diana V. Edelman, and Frank Polak; Perspectives on Hebrew Scriptures and Its Contexts, 5; Piscataway, NJ: Gorgias, 2009), pp. 47-59.

tion is Deuteronomic.[9] Some complexity arises when Ezra–Nehemiah appears to be taking up distinctive vocabulary from P and H. However, the scholarly habit of inventing a separate layer of redaction wherever purity discourse appears in Ezra–Nehemiah is an overly mechanical methodology; a discourse might be borrowed and adapted from another tradition for quite different reasons. In order to support the hypothesis of a separate layer of redaction, one needs to establish a much broader range of factors than simply vocabulary, as has been amply demonstrated in the case of Ezra 1–6. The appearance of בדל in Neh. 9.2, 10.29, or 13.3, for example, might well reflect a *knowledge* of priestly tradition without thereby amounting to the advocacy of P's or H's own view of things. The discourse of 'natives and immigrants' in material of the Holiness School may serve as one illustration of how H's convictions actually stand in opposition to the exclusionary perspectives in the core Ezra–Nehemiah traditions.[10]

The Advent of the Native in H

Having sketched the preliminary issues that form the outer framework of our discussion, we can now examine H's distinctive use of the term 'native' (אזרח). Of the seventeen uses of this term in the Hebrew Bible, its use in Ps. 37.34-35 is the only one that is usually dismissed as of no direct relevance to its meaning in H, although one should note that even in this case, the text raises the issue of land rights:

> Wait for YHWH, and observe his way,
> and he will exalt you to take possession (ירש) of the land;
> you will see when the wicked are cut off (כרת).
> I have seen the ruthlessly wicked,
> flourishing like a luxuriant native tree (אזרח).

The simile in v. 35b suggests that the grasp of the אזרח on the land is only ostensibly secure, and in due course it will be shown to be tenuous. In Ezek. 47.22, on the other hand, there is an assured presumption that the native holds the land by right. As part of Ezekiel's vision for return and restoration after the Babylonian exile, we hear that:

9. Sara Japhet, 'Periodization Between History and Ideology II: Chronology and Ideology in Ezra–Nehemiah', in *Judah and the Judeans in the Persian Period* (ed. Oded Lipschits and Manfred Oeming; Winona Lake, IN: Eisenbrauns, 2006), pp. 491-508.

10. This proposal might be read as a further development of Rolf Rendtorff's tentative suggestion in 'The *Ger* in the Priestly laws of the Pentateuch', in Brett (ed.), *Ethnicity and the Bible*, pp. 77-87 (86-87).

You shall allot it as an inheritance for yourselves and for the immigrants
(גרים) who reside among you and have begotten children among you.
They shall be regarded as natives (כאזרח) among the children of Israel;
with you they shall be allotted an inheritance among the tribes of Israel.

While the linguistic evidence for the meaning of אזרח is relatively
meagre, there is no real dispute that it can be rendered as 'one arising
from the land' or 'native'.[11] But as soon as one moves from the domain
of semantics to pragmatics, the debates become more complex: which
groups were denoted by אזרח and which by גר? The term גר has a large
number of uses in the prior legal traditions of the Covenant Code and
Deuteronomy, along with a common underlying assumption that these
'strangers' or 'immigrants' are people who have been displaced from
their country of origin for reasons such as famine or war and who are,
therefore, dependent on assistance. Yet the language of אזרח has no place
at all in the earlier legal tradition. Based on the distribution of its usage,
it is evident that—leaving aside the two cases in Ezek. 47.22 and Ps.
37.35 already discussed—we are dealing with a linguistic innovation of
the Holiness School that seeks to establish the equality of immigrants
and indigenes.[12] Notwithstanding some variations in legal terminology,
H's view that there should be 'one law' for natives and immigrants is
almost identically expressed in Lev. 24.22, Exod. 12.49, and Num.
15.15-16, 29, although Numbers presents a separable set of questions
that will not be dealt with here.[13] J. G. McConville puts this point quite
well, if slightly paradoxically: 'the concept of אזרח exists in the interests
of elucidating the nature of Israel, precisely by pointing to the alien's

11.   Christoph Bultmann, *Der Fremde im antiken Juda. Eine Untersuchung zum
sozialen Typenbegriff 'ger' und seinem Bedeutungswandel in der alttestamentlichen
Gesetzgebung* (FRLANT, 153; Göttingen: Vandenhoeck & Ruprecht, 1992), p. 204;
Jan Joosten, *People and Land in the Holiness Code: An Exegetical Study of the
Ideational Framework of the Law in Leviticus 17–26* (VTSup, 67; Leiden: Brill,
1996), p. 35.

12.   See, e.g., Nihan, *From Priestly Torah*, p. 570. In another study, Nihan notes
that the pairing of גר and אזרח in Josh. 8.30-35 (MT) is probably a later scribal
insertion that builds on Deut. 27.4-8 while borrowing H vocabulary to form a
preface to the inclusion of the Gibeonites in Joshua 9 ('The Torah between Samaria
and Judah: Shechem and Gerizim in Deuteronomy and Joshua', in *The Pentateuch
as Torah: New Models for Understanding Its Promulgation and Acceptance* [ed.
Gary N. Knoppers and Bernard M. Levinson; Winona Lake, IN: Eisenbrauns, 2007],
pp. 187-223 [217-22]).

13.   Cf. Num. 15.15 and 26, where גר is paired with 'the assembly', rather than
with אזרח.

integration'.[14] The question remains: To whom is H referring in this pairing of stranger and native, and why?

There is no shortage of hypotheses in the history of research on this question, even if the positioning of the Holiness materials *after* P has emerged as the most probable perspective only in recent years. Adopting perhaps an overly literal approach, H. Cazelles suggested some time ago that if the גרים at issue were indeed immigrants, then we could conclude that the customary referent of this term in late priestly literature would be the returning Judaeans, while the natives ('the ones arising from the land') would be Samaritans.[15] This proposal was swiftly adjusted by P. Grelot, who suggested that both the Judaeans and Samaritans would be natives, and Jews from the dispersion would, therefore, be strangers. J. G. Vink observed that the returnees could ill afford to compromise their interests in relation to both land rights and the cult by self-identifying as גרים, so he followed Grelot's solution in part by identifying the *golah* returnees as natives, while suggesting that the only group in the historical record that actually ask for participation in the Judean cult were the Samaritans; hence, they must be the גרים.[16] One might be forgiven for thinking that this history of research resembles a game of musical chairs, which moves too quickly to the referential functions of the language, leaving the social implications of the discourse without sufficient explanation.

The first point to make, however, is that there is a considerable convergence now on the view that the returning *golah* community would have seen themselves as natives, as Ezek. 47.22 already suggests. C. Bultmann rightly observes that what is implied here is participation in a line of *tradition*, not actual residence and birth in the land at the time of Ezekiel's vision.[17] Notably, the wording in Ezek. 47.22 suggests that these immigrants can be 'regarded as natives among the children of Israel' rather than 'natives of the land'. C. Van Houten puts considerable weight on Ezek. 47.22 as a key indicator that the *golah* community

---

14. J. Gordon McConville, '"Fellow Citizens": Israel and Humanity in Leviticus', in *Reading the Law: Studies in Honour of Gordon J. Wenham* (ed. J. Gordon McConville and Karl Mölle; LHBOTS, 461; London: T&T Clark International, 2007), pp. 10-32 (24).

15. Henri Cazelles, 'La mission d'Esdras', *VT* 4 (1954), pp. 113-40.

16. Jacobus G. Vink, 'The Date and Origin of the Priestly Code in the Old Testament', *OTS* 15 (1969), pp. 1-144 (47-48); Pierre Grelot, 'La dernière étape de la rédaction sacerdotale', *VT* 6 (1956), pp. 174-89.

17. Bultmann, *Fremde*, p. 204.

configured themselves as natives. In addition, she lists a number of texts in Ezekiel that belong to the 'empty land' paradigm,[18] including Ezek. 33.23-24, 27-28, and concludes that the vision of land restoration in Ezek. 47.22 'completely disregards the people who would have been living in Palestine during the time of the exile'.[19]

Van Houten then contrasts this perspective in Ezekiel with the late priestly laws that seek to establish the equality of natives and immigrants. She sees these laws as usually 'secondary additions' that, unlike Ezekiel, seem to be dealing precisely with the remainees. These people are seen in this legal paradigm as impure, yet capable of being purified.

Following a number of earlier studies, Van Houten concludes that 'the laws stipulating equal treatment in cultic matters are later than laws requiring charity and civil justice for the alien'.[20] Although her discussion has no clear account of these later laws as the work of the Holiness School, her argument may be read as largely congruent with my hypothesis that it is indeed the Holiness School that is responsible for these 'secondary additions' and that stands quietly in the background of Ezra 6.21 and its accommodation of purified, non-*golah* Judaeans.

There is, however, a residual difficulty with Van Houten's view of Ezek. 47.22 in that she provides no account of who the גרים might be in that verse, if the remainees are nowhere in view. It may be that, in effect, she is reiterating the view of Vink that the גרים must be the Samaritans who are the explicit focus of the material in Ezra 4–6. Van Houten's discussion is not clear on this issue, and it leaves a number of other questions unanswered, including the date of Ezra 1–6 and of the 'late' priestly materials that seek to establish cultic equity.

Some of the perceived gaps in Van Houten's discussion in 1991 may be attributed to the fact that I. Knohl's work on H had not yet taken hold outside of Israeli scholarship. There is one particularly significant aspect of Knohl's work that will concern us here: although his argument that H is subsequent to P has enjoyed increasing popularity, his pre-exilic date for P was associated with a view of the Holiness School that saw its

---

18. See now the useful overview of the literature in John Kessler, 'Images of Exile: Representations of the "Exile" and "Empty Land" in Sixth to Fourth Century BCE Yehudite Literature', in *The Concept of Exile in Ancient Israel and its Historical Contexts* (ed. Ehud Ben Zvi and Christoph Levin; BZAW, 404; Berlin: de Gruyter, 2010), pp. 309-51.

19. Christiana Van Houten, *The Alien in Israelite Law* (JSOTSup, 107; Sheffield: Sheffield Academic Press, 1991), p. 152.

20. Ibid., pp. 154-55, with literature. On p.155 n. 1 there is a typographical error where the reference to Ezra 4.19-22 can only refer to Ezra 6.19-22.

editorial activities extending over a very long period—from pre-exilic times down to the fifth century.[21] One of the consequences of this view is that although the concern with גרים was determined by Knohl to be a distinctive contribution of the Holiness School rather than P, it was unclear whether this contribution could be seen as a response to any particular set of circumstances. Thus, for example, one might reasonably see the beginnings of social concern for strangers in Deuteronomy as a response to the arrival of refugees from the Northern Kingdom,[22] but is it possible to see H's approach to גרים as arising from such specific historical circumstances?

This question is enmeshed in complex debates about the dating of H materials outside of Leviticus,[23] and in spite of the confident epistemological tones adopted in some historical reconstructions, these debates will always be a matter of hypothesis and probability. I want to suggest, however, that the discourse of the native can contribute to these debates in ways that, to my knowledge, have been largely overlooked. While it is clear that the characterization of Israel as native is a novelty without precedence in the earlier legal traditions, there has been insufficient attention to the motives for this novelty.[24]

It might appear obvious to assert, as C. Bultmann does, that a native's identity is orientated around the land,[25] yet why this point would need to be made by adopting an entirely new, non-Deuteronomistic vocabulary is not at all obvious. Apparently something new had to be said about the relationship between land and identity that had not been articulated before in earlier theologies of land tenure. We can also surmise, by way of hypothesis, that a new vocabulary was needed to address a new set of problems about the legitimacy of land possession.

21. Israel Knohl, *The Sanctuary of Silence: The Priestly Torah and the Holiness School* (Minneapolis: Fortress, 1995), pp. 21, 53, 93, 100-103, 201.

22. E.g. Frank Crüsemann, *The Torah: Theology and Social History of Old Testament Law* (trans. A. W. Mahnke; Edinburgh: T. & T. Clark, 1996), pp. 182-85; cf. Israel Finkelstein, 'The Settlement History of Jerusalem in the Eighth and Seventh Centuries BCE', *RB* 115 (2008), pp. 499-515.

23. See, e.g., Nihan, *From Priestly Torah*, pp. 562-72; Jacob Milgrom, 'The Case for the Pre-exilic and Exilic Provenance of the Books of Exodus, Leviticus and Numbers', in *Reading the Law: Studies in Honour of Gordon J. Wenham* (ed. J. Gordon McConville and Karl Mölle; LHBOTS, 461; London: T&T Clark International, 2007), pp. 48-56.

24. Perhaps it is worth noting here that D could hardly have represented Israel as a settler colonial society *and* as indigenous at the same time.

25. Bultmann, *Fremde*, p. 204.

A recent account of the priestly tradition in Genesis offers some highly relevant considerations in any attempt to address these problems. J. Wöhrle takes up the recent suggestion that P has been deliberately shaped in order to present Abraham as the ideal *golah* immigrant of the Persian period, beginning his journey from 'Ur of Chaldeans', that is, from a residential area of the Babylonian exilic community. The ancestor arrives to find that the land is inhabited, and P's approach to this problem departs significantly from the Deuteronomistic conquest discourse that is adopted in Ezra 9.1-3.

> According to P, the existence of the people who already lived in the land before the ancestors came to it is not presented as being a temporary fact that has to be overcome. The land is given to the ancestors, not instead of the people of the land, but in addition to these people.[26]

The encounter between Abraham and the 'people of the land' in Genesis 23 is apparently paradigmatic of P's approach: the land is acquired peacefully and via purchase, rather than via any violent confrontation or act of dispossession.

Yet there is a deep ambivalence in the P tradition since, although the ancestors are characterized as גרים, they are also said to be 'gathered to their kin' in death, which implicitly establishes the kind of connection to land that could be understood as in some sense indigenous.[27] This may be considered one among a range of factors that leads some scholars to suggest a diachronic explanation of the tension: the bearers of the earlier ancestral narratives may be identified as Judah's pre-exilic citizenry, עם הארץ, terminology that is still being used in a neutral sense as 'land holders' in Hag. 2.4 and Zech. 7.5.[28] In this scenario, the earlier ancestral

---

26.   Jakob Wöhrle, 'The Un-Empty Land: The Concept of Exile and Land in P', in Ben Zvi and Levin (eds.), *The Concept of Exile in Ancient Israel*, pp. 189-206 (204). Nihan suggests that the Abrahamic traditions probably circulated first among non-exiles, whereas by contrast, D's Exodus and conquest traditions were favoured by 'segregationist circles' among the exiles. By re-framing Abraham as an ideal immigrant, P promotes the 'cohabitation between returning exiles and non-exiles' (*From Priestly Torah*, p. 387). For an earlier account of Abraham as the ideal immigrant, see Norman Habel, *The Land Is Mine: Six Biblical Land Ideologies* (Minneapolis: Fortress, 1995), pp. 115-33.

27.   See P's characteristic description of death as being 'gathered (אסף) to one's kin (עמם)' in Gen. 25.8, 17; 35.29; 49.33; cf. Num. 20.24; 27.13; 31.2 (Elizabeth Bloch-Smith, *Judahite Burial Practices and Beliefs about the Dead* [JSOTSup, 123; Sheffield: JSOT Press, 1992], pp. 110-12).

28.   See, e.g., Konrad Schmid, *Genesis and the Moses Story: Israel's Dual Origins in the Hebrew Bible* (Winona Lake, IN: Eisenbrauns, 2010), pp. 106-10. Similarly, for Schmid, the ancestors were in pre-Priestly tradition 'not foreigners in

traditions carried by עם הארץ (are reflected in Ezek. 33.24, where the remainees lay claim to Abraham) have apparently been overlaid with the representation of Abraham as the ideal *golah* immigrant.

Whether this reconstruction of P is plausible or not, it provides an interesting analogy with a similar linguistic ambivalence in the Holiness Code. On the one hand, Israelites are to be understood as immigrants on land that is ultimately owned by YHWH (Lev. 25.23), yet on the other hand, we also find a positive reference to the 'people of the land' (עם הארץ) who are exhorted to take on juridical responsibilities that would be inconceivable in the Ezra tradition:

> 2 Any man from among the children of Israel, or any of the immigrants (גרים) who reside in Israel, who give of their seed to Molech shall be put to death; the people of the land (עם הארץ) shall stone them to death. 3 I myself will set my face against that man, and will cut him off from his people, because he gave his seed to Molech, defiling my sanctuary and profaning my holy name. 4 And if the people of the land (עם הארץ) close their eyes to that man, when he gives of his seed to Molech, and do not put him to death, 5 I myself will set my face against that man and against his clan, and will cut him off from his kin (עמם), both him and all who follow him in prostituting themselves to Molech. (Lev. 20.2-5)

The narrative setting in the wilderness has been dropped here, and the real audience is directly addressed, including the immigrants.[29] The 'children of Israel' are, at the same time, 'people of the land' (i.e. land-owners). Once again, a diachronic hypothesis invites itself: this text comes from a period when the phrase 'people of the land' had not yet taken on the pejorative connotations that it does in the Ezra traditions; thus, we may justifiably conclude that an edition of the Holiness Code already existed in the early Persian period, if not in late pre-exilic times.[30]

That being said, it does not follow that this earlier version of the Holiness Code is identical with the one that we have in the received texts of Leviticus, whether the MT or LXX versions. Among other considerations, the classic problem in Nehemiah 8 is relevant to our understanding of the compositional history of the Holiness Code: this chapter shows no awareness of the requirement in Leviticus 23 that the Day of Purgation is to be celebrated 'on the tenth day of the seventh month'. Rising above

Canaan' (p. 84). Cf. Lisbeth Fried, 'The *'am ha'ares* in Ezra 4:4 and Persian Imperial Administration', in Lipschits and Oeming (eds.), *Judah and Judeans in the Persian Period*, pp. 123-45.

29. Joosten, *People and Land*, pp. 42-47; cf. p. 113 and the use of the term ראשנים in Lev. 26.45 to refer anachronistically to the Exodus generation.

30. Jacob Milgrom, *Leviticus 17–22* (AB, 3A; New York: Doubleday, 2000), p. 731.

several of the implausible suggestions for resolving this problem, C. Nihan argues that Nehemiah 8 does not know this particular element in the liturgical calendar of the Holiness Code because it was only added 'after Nehemiah'.[31] One does not need to follow the suggestion that the bulk of the Holiness Code comes after Nehemiah to see the value of his proposal regarding the addition of the Day of Purgation to the liturgical calendar on 'the tenth day of the seventh month'.

More important for our present purposes, however, is Nihan's associated proposal that H has also added the equity principle (the equal standing of גר and אזרח) to the prescriptions for the Day of Purgation in Lev. 16.29-34a.[32]

> This shall be a statute to you forever: In the seventh month, on the tenth day of the month, you shall deny yourselves, and shall do no work, neither the native nor the immigrant who resides among you. (Lev. 16.29)

Perhaps in contrast with the vast majority of theories about intricate redactional additions to the Holiness Code, this proposal from Nihan has far-reaching implications for our topic. It suggests, for example, not only that the equity of the גר and אזרח was an idea that arose 'post-Nehemiah', here in conjunction with the calendrical innovation, but also that it arose *in response to* Nehemiah's more exclusivist account of Israel's identity in Yehud.

It appears that this more inclusive social vision was forged in conscious opposition to Nehemiah's reforms, probably *before* the exclusively negative view of the 'people(s) of the land(s)' was articulated in Ezra 9.1-3.[33] Given that the Holiness Code was still open to editorial

---

31. Cf. my discussion in *Decolonizing God: The Bible in the Tides of Empire* (The Bible in the Modern World Series, 16; Sheffield: Sheffield Phoenix, 2008), pp. 114-19, which does not, however, address the attractive suggestion in Nihan, *From Priestly Torah*, p. 569, outlined here. Jacob Wright has linked both Neh. 5 and 8 to the seventh-year reading of the law during the festival of Sukkot required in Deut. 31.9-13 (cf. 31.10, שנת השמטה בחג הסכו). His argument points again to the primary influence of D on the EN traditions, with the notable exception of the pro-priestly responses in the later material in Ezra 1–6. The striking contrasts between the Sukkot celebration in Ezra 3 and the Sukkot in Neh. 8 are well described by Wright in 'Writing the Restoration'.

32. Nihan, *From Priestly Torah*, pp. 569-70, 613.

33. Among the recent diachronic hypotheses regarding Ezra 9 that require further debate, see especially Pakkala, *Ezra the Scribe* and Christian Frevel and Benedikt J. Conczorowski, 'Deepening the Water: First Steps to a Diachronic Approach on Intermarriage in the Hebrew Bible', in *Mixed Marriages: Intermarriage and Group Identity in the Second Temple Period* (ed. Christian Frevel; LHBOTS, 547; New York: T&T Clark International, 2011), pp. 15-45.

additions, including those relating to the Day of Purgation, it is remarkable that later editors did not choose to remove the positive reference to
עם הארץ in Lev. 20.2-5. Nevertheless, we have seen that there are good
reasons to think that the Holiness School inserted at key points, even
outside of Leviticus, the principle of equity between גר and אזרח. This is
most notably the case in Exod. 12.43-49, where circumcision is offered
to the גר who wishes to participate in the Passover on the grounds that
there should be 'one law' for natives and immigrants. Exodus 12.43-44
excludes the בן נכר from this offer, the most distant 'other' known to H,
but then immediately states the exception to this exclusion: the slave who
has been purchased with money—no doubt purchased from foreigners, as
Lev. 25.44 requires—is to be circumcised.[34] One might surmise that the
commonality between foreign slaves and immigrants is, regardless of
their ethnicity, their long-term residence within the community of Israel.

While it cannot be proven beyond doubt that the statements of equity
between גר and אזרח were all added around the same time in the late
Persian period in response to Nehemiah's policies, this is nevertheless a
very plausible scenario. The usage of the phrase עם הארץ in Lev. 20.2-5
might perhaps be seen as the 'exception that proves the rule': while
עם הארץ belongs in the same semantic field as אזרח, it is evident that H
clearly preferred אזרח when attempting to articulate a principle of equity,
and this might well have been because עם הארץ was no longer available
as a neutral lexical choice when referring to the landed assembly of
Israel.

It might also be argued that the innovations of H did not depart from
the spirit of the earlier Priestly material, which regarded the ancestors as
גרים who share the usufruct rights of the land.[35] Yet perhaps beyond even
P's social imagination, the Holiness Code in Lev. 18.28-29 equalizes the
general conditions of occupancy of the land, so that Israelites and even
the prior occupants of Canaan are bound by essentially the same ethical

---

34. The same exception is found in Gen. 17.12, 23. For this and other reasons,
Wöhrle convincingly argues that Gen. 17.9-14, 23-27 and Exod. 12.43-49 can be
attributed to the redactional activity of H ('Integrative Function of the Law of
Circumcision').

35. See especially Michaela Bauks, 'Die Begriffe מורשה und אחזה in Pg. Über-
legungen zur Landkonzeption der Priestergrundschrift', *ZAW* 116 (2004), pp. 171-
88; Manfred Köckert, 'Das Land in der priesterlichen Komposition des Pentateuch',
in *Von Gott reden: Beiträge zur Theologie und Exegese des Alten Testaments.
Festschrift für Siegfried Wagner zum 65. Geburtstag* (ed. Dieter Viewege and Ernst-
Joachim Waschke; Neukirchen–Vluyn: Neukirchener Verlag, 1995), pp. 147-62;
Philippe Guillaume, *Land and Calendar: The Priestly Document from Genesis 1 to
Joshua 18* (LHBOTS, 391; London: T&T Clark International, 2009), pp. 102-22.

code, lest the land 'vomit' them out.[36] Again regardless of ethnicity, Lev. 18.29 concludes: 'whoever commits any of these abominations shall be cut off from their kin'. Whether indigenous or non-indigenous, the basic rights and obligations of those who live in the land are, at this point at least, collected under a single legal framework. The H editors of the Persian period were thereby imagining ways to express religious and economic integration via permeable social boundaries, implicitly proposing reconciliation between the 'children of the *golah*' and the peoples of the land who never went into exile, as well as possibilities for including the surrounding *goyim* who troubled Nehemiah.

If one were to construe this scenario in less charitable terms, a hermeneutic of suspicion might perhaps propose that the contradictory oscillations in *golah* identity between גר and אזרח point to an ideological obfuscation of the fragility of returnees' land claims.[37] If a claim to native rights on the part of *golah* Judaeans was exposed as an assertion without adequate foundations, then a theological suggestion that everyone shares the גר identity in any case could have the effect of undermining the possessory rights of עם הארץ. Similarly, if the discourse of equity between גר and אזרח implies that neither the *golah* Judaeans nor the remainee community could lay claim to a superior set of rights, then the group that stood to lose the most would arguably be those with current rights of possession, that is, עם הארץ.

As already noted, however, the sharp opposition between עם הארץ and 'holy seed' was probably not to be found in the early Persian period; this polarity appears, on the contrary, to have gathered momentum only in the second half of the Persian period. Accordingly, the Jubilee legislation in H, a 'purgation in the economic realm', as P. Guillaume aptly describes it, is not concerned with the rights of recent returnees but with a general defence of tribal land tenure.[38] This is one element in H's agreement with the pan-Israelite tribal imagination, or 'retribalization', which was

36. Baruch J. Schwartz, 'Reexamining the Fate of the "Canaanites" in the Torah Traditions', in *Sefer Moshe: The Moshe Weinfeld Jubilee Volume: Studies in the Bible and the Ancient Near East, Qumran, and Post-Biblical Judaism* (ed. Chaim Cohen, Avi Hurvitz, and Shalom M. Paul; Winona Lake, IN: Eisenbrauns, 2004), pp. 151-70.

37. Given the low population levels in the early Persian period, the key issues apparently turned not so much on the scarcity of land resources as on disputes about social identity and legitimacy.

38. Guillaume, *Land and Calendar*, p. 141. See further my essay, 'Unequal Terms: A Postcolonial Approach to Isaiah 61', in *Biblical Interpretation and Method: Essays in Honour of Professor John Barton* (ed. Katherine Dell and Paul Joyce; Oxford: Oxford University Press, 2013), pp. 243-56.

asserted over against the narrowing of Israelite identity in Nehemiah essentially to the Judeans.[39] It seems that the narrower Judean option was enveloped over the course of time in the *golah* discourse, which reflects not just the actual experience of a generation who returned from Babylon but, rather, an intergenerational project of ethnic fission.[40]

Standing in opposition to this Judaean project, the Holiness School went a step further than the pan-Israelite vision to propose that under certain conditions, even uncircumcised foreigners might be candidates for partial assimilation, although the rendering of גר as 'proselyte' in the LXX suggests a stronger degree of integration than may be warranted. גרים still had choices in relation to the cult that Israelites did not enjoy, even if all residents shared the obligations to protect the purity of land and sanctuary.[41] While Ezek. 47.22 proposed land rights for the גרים, the possibilities for social accommodation are seen by the Holiness editors in Exod. 12.48-49 to have consequences also for participation in the cult. The verbal similarities between these two texts are striking:

> You shall allot it [land] as an inheritance for yourselves and for *the immigrants who reside among you* and have begotten children among you. They shall be *regarded as natives among the children of Israel*; with you they shall be allotted an inheritance among the tribes of Israel. (Ezek. 47.22)

> If an *immigrant who resides with you* wants to celebrate the Passover to the Lord, all his males shall be circumcised; then he may draw near to celebrate it; he shall be *regarded as a native of the land*. But no uncircumcised person shall eat of it; there shall be one law for the native and for *the immigrant who resides among you*. (Exod. 12.48-49).

---

39. Gary N. Knoppers, 'Nehemiah and Sanballat: The Enemy Without or Within?', in *Judah and the Judeans in the Fourth Century BCE* (ed. Oded Lipschits, Gary N. Knoppers, and Rainer Albertz; Winona Lake, IN: Eisenbrauns, 2007), pp. 305-31 (331); cf. pp. 325-26 for the argument that Sanballat 'likely viewed himself as an Ephraimite'.

40. Katherine Southwood, 'An Ethnic Affair? Ezra's Intermarriage Crisis against a Context of "Self-Ascription" and "Ascription of Others"', in Frevel (ed.), *Mixed Marriages*, pp. 46-59 (51-54), drawing on Thomas H. Eriksen's theory of ethnic fission (*Ethnicity and Nationalism: Anthropological Perspectives* [Anthropology, Culture and Society; London: Pluto, 1993], esp. pp. 67-69).

41. See further, Joosten, *People and Land*, pp. 63-73; Nihan, 'Resident Aliens and Natives in the Holiness Legislation', in *The Foreigner and the Law: Perspectives from the Hebrew Bible and the Ancient Near East* (ed. Reinhart Achenbach, Rainer Albertz, and Jakob Wöhrle; BZAR, 16; Wiesbaden: Harrassowitz, 2011), pp. 111-34 (127-28).

This intertextuality suggests that, unlike the earlier legal traditions, H would have had no difficulty conceiving of a scenario in which גרים are landholders.[42] The גרים of the Persian period are seen by H as obligated to preserve the purity of land and sanctuary, and given the explicit invitation to cultic participation, there is no sufficient reason to suppose that H opposed intermarriage with גרים either.[43] Accordingly, the practices of 'separation' that are required by H are more a matter of separating from impurities than from persons—the distinction that is assumed in Ezra 6.21 without argument.

Conclusion

The innovations of the Holiness School propose degrees of alterity[44] rather than binary oppositions, and the beginnings of an equitable social imagination. This is not yet social constructivism in any modern sense,[45] but the strategies of inclusion have become explicit rather than subtly hidden away. Ironically, the use of the term אזרח in H turns out to be

42. If these strangers are in a position to own Israelite slaves, as indicated in Lev. 25.47-54, the possibility that slaveholders are also landholders becomes difficult to resist. The vision of ancestral land holdings in the Jubilee legislation seems to propose a pan-Israelite tribal imagination, but this does not imply a comprehensive denial of all other forms of land tenure, as Nihan appears to suggest ('Resident Aliens and Natives', pp. 123-24, 129). The practicalities of life in a Persian colony would suggest that H knew of alternative land tenures, but nevertheless proposed that all those who lived in Yehud were obligated to maintain the land's purity.

43. See further my discussion, 'Politics of Marriage in Genesis', in *Making a Difference: Essays on the Bible and Judaism in Honor of Tamara Cohn Eskenazi* (ed. David J. A. Clines, Kent H. Richards, and Jacob L. Wright; Sheffield: Sheffield Phoenix, 2012), pp. 49-59; Joosten, *People and Land*, p. 85; Milgrom, *Leviticus 17–22*, pp. 1584-85: 'The Priestly sources (H and P), on the contrary, express neither opposition to nor prohibition of intermarriage. Endogamy is not a prerequisite for holiness.' Nihan has observed that the גרים are not themselves exhorted to be holy, but his inference that H opposes intermarriage does not follow ('Resident Aliens and Natives', pp. 128-29, 132 n.73; idem, *From Priestly Torah*, pp. 384-85).

44. See also the discussions of תושב as an overlapping but distinct social category in Joosten, *People and Land*, pp. 73-74; José E. Ramírez Kidd, *Alterity and Identity in Israel: The Ger in the Old Testament* (BZAW, 283; Berlin: de Gruyter, 1999), pp. 99-101; Jean-François Lefebvre, *Le jubilé biblique: Lv 25 — Exégèse et Théologie* (OBO, 194; Göttingen: Vandenhoeck & Ruprecht, 2003), pp. 237-44; Joram Mayshar, 'Who was the Toshav?', *JBL* 133 (2014), pp. 225-46

45. See my analysis of constructivist identities in 'National Identity as Commentary and as Metacommentary', in *Historiography and Identity [Re]formulation in Second Temple Literature* (ed. Louis Jonker; London: Continuum, 2010), pp. 29-40.

less 'nativist' than the discourse of the 'holy seed'. That is, if nativism proposes an exclusively authentic indigenous tradition, which character-istically excludes hybrid alternatives,[46] then the Holiness School pro-vided a more complex and more accommodating social imagination in which it was possible to claim—no doubt with rhetorical excess—that the rights of strangers should not be substantially different from those enjoyed by native citizens.

46. Brett, *Decolonizing God*, pp. 112-31 (129-31).

GENDER AND IDENTITY IN THE BOOK OF NUMBERS

Claudia V. Camp

My aim in this essay is to begin a feminist and gender-critical analysis of the book of Numbers as a whole, a perspective that I believe is not just crucial to understanding this book but to any proposal regarding the construction of identity or authority in the Second Temple period. In this regard, this essay is itself but a case study in the importance of feminist and gender criticism of the textual artefacts of this period. Now, when I say 'feminist criticism' I do not mean simply paying attention to texts in which women play key roles, or even taking up an advocacy stance that disavows the textual subordination of women. I mean rather a systematic critique. Such a critique involves, first, analysis of the specific ways that subordination is textually engineered in any given body of literature (paradoxically, in some texts, even in the very act of acknowledging women's status and contributions). Second, and more importantly in this context, is a critique of the ways in which the textual construction of gender intersects with other identity-constructing mechanisms to produce 'Israelite identity' and, in the case of Numbers, priestly identity as well. It is my thesis that the construction of gender is fundamental in this book to both these corporate identities and that it proceeds in a way that is peculiarly priestly.

I take as my main conversation partner the very fine 2008 book by A. Leveen, *Memory and Tradition in the Book of Numbers*,[1] which I admire in almost every way except for its lack of feminist and gender analysis, which I will argue both complements and complicates her argument. Leveen's productive use of theories of memory, though, provides a key point of linkage to my concerns. Let me then begin with a summary of her work. In Leveen's view, the book of Numbers in its present form is the work of priestly editors, who carefully designed it from both pre-existing and newly created material for two main purposes: first, to promote the political authority of the Aaronite priests over against their

1. Adriane Leveen, *Memory and Tradition in the Book of Numbers* (Cambridge: Cambridge University Press, 2008).

Levite opponents and, second, to persuade the editors' own, and all future, generations of 'Israelites' to accept the hierarchical order they envision—from the top down: God, Aaronites, Levites, congregation—as fundamental to obedient and abundant life in the promised land. The key element in this agenda of persuasion is the control of memory; specifically, the presentation of one version of the Egypt and the Exodus experiences as the correct version. No dummies, though, the priestly editors are aware of other memories about this period and therefore choose a rhetoric, indeed a structure for the entire book, that controls these countermemories by acknowledging rather than trying to suppress them and then narrating the disastrous consequences for those who adopted them.

So far, so good! But let me press a little harder on the matter of memory. Though Leveen includes attention to subversive countermemories, her method operates almost entirely at the level of the intentional, even with respect to these. That is, as she argues it, the final priestly editors *consciously* choose a memory they wish to repudiate and *consciously* construct a text to accomplish that goal. This analysis is effective in the parsing of priestly authority, by definition a conscious goal. But, while memory may be used as a vehicle of control, it also operates at a level subtler and less controllable than our conscious intention can access, a fact that Leveen alludes to from time to time but does not exploit. The memories I am interested in are the suppressed ones that leave unintended traces in cultural texts.

This subtlety is especially important when we shift our question from one of establishing authority to one of constructing identity. It is, I think, pretty much a truism by now that an important component in constructing collective identity is the construction of an Other as the not-Us, over against whom We know ourselves *as* Us. This process requires the suppression of certain awarenesses, which often take the form of memories: one must ignore, or forget, the ways in which We and the Other are alike; one must also internalize our assumed difference as natural, repressing any awareness that it is a construction. In androcentric societies—and most have been!—identity is created at a fundamental level as male and female or, better put, as male and not-male: women are the most basic and thus most fully naturalized Other. 'Woman' is thus available as an icon of Otherness; on the one hand, a cipher into which other strands of Otherness may be threaded, but also existentially powerful because embodied, known in the powerfully materialized ways—from suckling to sex—through and against which men come to know themselves as men. The question, then, is: How does Woman figure, both consciously and unconsciously, in Numbers' construction of identity, including its suppression of the act of construction itself? In this essay I continue an argument that I set out in my book *Wise, Strange and Holy*, namely, that the priests responsible for Numbers take the Othering of women to an impossible extreme, attempting to create an all male identity that excludes women altogether.[2] But 'impossible' is the key term, for the Other cannot finally be eliminated if one's own identity is to stand. Women repeatedly re-emerge in Numbers as subverters of priestly memory and identity.

With these thoughts in mind, let me return to Leveen's argument about how memory plays out in the three-part structure of Numbers. Part 1, chs. 1–10, presents a literarily earlier priestly vision of an orderly social utopia, with the tribes numbered and arranged around the ark, an order connected to and validated by the 'proper' memory of Egypt as a land of Israelite slavery from which Yahweh had brought them out (1.1; 3.12-13, 40-45; 8.17; 9.1). The sequence of rebellions in Part 2, chs. 11–25, gives expression to the contrasting countermemory of Egypt as a land of delicacies, indeed, in the words of the rebels Dathan and Abiram, a land 'flowing with milk and honey', a memory whose deadly consequence is repeatedly narrated in these chapters in an effort to induce obedience to Yahweh and his appointed priests. With rebels vanquished and lessons learned in this middle section, Part 3, chs. 26–36, turns to the future, envisioning in hopeful and more practical terms a range of realities Israel will encounter in the promised land. In what follows, I shall consider the presentation of women, men, and memory in each section in turn, generating in the process a less stable, more deconstructive reading of Numbers as a whole.

Part 1, Numbers 1–10

The utopian vision of the first four of these chapters sets forth a social and political hierarchy, cast in religious terms and roles: the Levites serve the tabernacle, and in particular, the Aaronites (1.48-53; 3.6-9). The Levites, in turn, separate the rest of the people from dangerously drawing near to what is holy (1.52-53). They stand between priests and people, the latter persistently referred to as זר(ה) (1.51; 3.10, 38; 18.4) or איש זר, 'the stranger' or 'the outsider' (17.5; 18.7). An ideology of identity built on Othering—priest vs. outsider—undergirds the claim to

---

2. Claudia V. Camp, *Wise, Strange and Holy: The Strange Woman and the Making of the Bible* (JSOTSup, 320; Gender, Culture, and Theory Studies, 9; Sheffield: Sheffield Academic Press, 2000), pp. 191-278.

priestly authority. The Levites live uncomfortably on and as the line between, not merely separating the holy from the strange, but even styled as a substitute for the required offering of the firstborn of the Israelites—of the זר ('outsider') Israelites, that is to say (3.34)! Yet the Levites are in danger themselves of dying like any other זר, should they approach the holy things too closely (4.17-20).[3]

Numbers 1–10 may be seen as a chiastically structured, utopian whole,[4] but it also shows signs of tension. The first four chapters are indeed utopic, but it is notably an all male utopia. The laws in chs. 5–6, on the other hand—the center of Milgrom's chiasm—stand out from those preceding by introducing women, along with impurity and wrongdoing, into the picture. Chapters 7–10 for the most part return to a more static male reality, but not entirely so. Let us look more closely at the interplay of gender, identity, and authority in these chapters.

The gendered quality of the utopian vision of Numbers 1–4 is signaled by the repetitious instructions for the census. 'Every male', כל זכר, is to be counted, according to fathers' houses. But זכר of course is the root for words relating memory as well. Given Leveen's vigorous emphasis on Numbers' concern for memory and use of mnemonics, what might we make of the fact that זכר, 'male', is used no less than ten times in these chapters, before any use of the root זכר in the sense of 'remember'? While I am conscious of the problem involved in indiscriminate appeal to the interpretive relevance of homonyms, I think that the density of זכר's usage in the one meaning (male), coupled with the overt significance of the other meaning (memory), lends it credence in this case. Remembering *maleness* seems to be the point of it all, at least within the ideal world of the priests.

As if to make the point, the series of four ritual laws dealing with *congregational* matters in chs. 5–6 all mention explicitly men *and* women.[5] While the priestly utopia is coded as all male, the people's

---

3. See ibid., pp. 198-215, for a fuller exposition of this paragraph's analysis of Aaronites, Levites, and *zar*-Israelites.

4. Leveen, *Memory and Tradition*, pp. 77-78, following J. Milgrom, *Numbers: The Traditional Hebrew Text with the New JPS Translation* (Philadelphia: Jewish Publication Society, 1990), pp. xxii-xxviii.

5. In the first instance (5.3), the word pair is זכר/נקבה, male/female, the masculine term thus repeating the ten uses of זכר in chs. 1–4. Thereafter we find instead איש/אשה 'man/woman' (in the second law, 5.6; in the fourth, 6.2, and throughout the third, 5.11-31). The change in terms may be due to the shift from an issue related to physical embodiment in the first law to social matters in the next three (Amy Kalmanofsky, 'Naso [Numbers 4.21–7.89]', in *The Torah: A Women's Commentary* [ed. Tamara Cohn Eskenazi and Andrea L. Weiss; New York: Union of Reform Judaism, 2008], pp. 815-35 [820]).

reality is male and female, certainly, where impurity and wrong-doing are involved (the first three laws), but also in those fraught moments when those who are not holy approach and withdraw from that state (the fourth law on the Nazirites). But even when Numbers acknowledges women within the congregation, it also highlights their dangerous strangeness, especially in the third of these laws, which deals with the suspected adulteress (5.11-31). I shall focus on that text, but let me first comment briefly on its context in chs. 5–7.

The focus of the whole appears to be to preserve the holiness represented by the priests by establishing priestly authority over different aspects of the lives of the men and women of the congregation. To a greater or lesser degree, however, all four laws deploy gender difference to do so. The first law, 5.1-4, instructs that a man or woman who becomes unclean, whether by skin disease, discharge, or corpse contamination, be put outside the camp. Despite the gender neutrality of the law itself, the foreshadowing of Miriam's rebellion, which results in her being put outside the camp because of skin disease and to her death and burial in a situation where water for purification from corpse contamination is lacking, seems transparent. The second law (5.5-10), dealing with restitution for one individual's offence against another, is the least obviously gendered of the four, but it does legislate a sacrifice, as well as make 'the priest' the recipient of the repayment if the wronged person has no next of kin. A priestly presence is thus interjected into what would seem to have been secular contractual affairs. Likewise, the fourth of the laws (6.1-21), dealing with the Nazirite vow, is not put forth to initiate or even explain the practice. Its effect, rather, is to bring under Aaronite control what might have been a means to special religious status for non-priests, by focusing on the ritual requirements to repair an unintentionally broken vow and to conclude the time of Nazirite separation, both of which result in bounty for, as well as an assertion of authority by, the priests. Further, while both men and women may take the vow (6.2) and would presumably be equally bound by the restriction on eating products of the vine (6.3-4), by far the greatest part of the law, in addition to the specifications for the sacrificial offerings, deals with the restriction on hair-cutting (6.5-12, 18-19), which would hardly be relevant for those who did not usually cut theirs anyway. And again, as was true of the first law, this one also adumbrates a later passage, Numbers 30, where women's right to make such vows could be limited by the veto of their husbands or fathers.

With this brief analysis of these laws I have tried to draw attention to four important points: first, to the difference between the all male priestly utopia of chs. 1–4 and the real (or at least more real) world of the laws of chs. 5–6, which is composed of both women and men; second, to the fact that it is only in the world where women are that uncleanness and sin against others appear; third, to the hints of gender difference and female subordination even in laws that appear on the surface to be gender neutral; and, fourth, to the insertion of priestly authority into contexts that might well have been, and perhaps once were, managed without them.[6] These points appear relatively subtly in the first, second, and fourth of the laws. The third one, however, puts them in stark relief, making it arguably the lens through which all of them should be read.

For the female Other repressed in chs. 1–4 returns with a vengeance in ch. 5's law on the Sotah (vv. 11-31), the woman suspected of adultery, or 'turning aside'. Sex, of course, is the elephant in the room if the perfect arrangement of father's houses envisioned by the priests is to persist over time, with sons to inherit the land that Yahweh will allot in ch. 26. But sex means women, and women can go strange: the most obvious threat to the patrilineage is a wife who might be pregnant with another man's child. Unlike Deuteronomy, however, which simply legislates execution for offending women, Numbers exudes anxiety about patrilineal identity. The husband suspects his wife of adultery, but he does not know for sure, and she may or may not be guilty in any case. His 'spirit of jealousy' is foregrounded at both the onset and conclusion of the ritual (5.14, 29-30).

The law, however, does not merely *offer* him a ritual remedy, but in fact *requires* that he avail himself of it: if the condition of jealousy exists, 'he shall bring her to the priest' (5.15). So all this is not really, or not simply, 'about the husband'; the law ignores, for example, the shame that would inevitably accompany public confirmation of his having been cuckolded. The larger purpose of the law, rather, is to assert priestly authority over the identity-defining patrilineal system. It establishes the priest, rather than the husband, as master of the workings of patrilineage, pre-empting the husband's right to make decisions about sexual matters in his own household.[7] More subtly, by ordering husband and wife to the

---

6. This fourth point possibly provides some leverage for distinguishing women's actual social roles and sources of authority from the biblical ideology that sometimes seeks to constrain them. The fact that women could be nazirites may well indicate a fairly important religious role, with its incumbent authority, that women shared with men. The text of Numbers, however, tells us nothing of the significance of this role or its meaning to the community; rather, the only concerns here are to identify the restrictions involved and to make sure, by means of sacrifices, that transitions into and out of the role, whether planned or accidental, are handled properly, that is, by the priests.

7. This reading contrasts with those of, e.g. Alice Bach ('Good to the Last Drop: Viewing the Sotah [Numbers 5.11-31] as the Glass Half Empty and Wondering How to View It as Half Full', in *Women in the Hebrew Bible: A Reader* [ed. Alice Bach;

altar on the basis of the feeling of jealousy alone, the priest not only adjudicates a possible lineage aberration, but attempts to control the anxiety itself, thus averting any lack of confidence in the system's perfect functioning. Part of Leveen's argument regarding the goal of the Numbers editors was that they attempted not simply to establish Aaronite authority but also to naturalize it in the lived experience of the people. I would suggest that the Sotah text contributes to this process of internalizing acquiescence to external authority, insofar as its bald assertion of priestly political authority is communicated in and through its portrayal of the priest as the sole means for resolving anxiety associated with male control in the domestic sphere.

Not incidentally, the first use of the root זכר in its meaning 'remember' occurs in the Sotah passage. The ritual offering required is twice, and uniquely, called 'a grain offering of jealousy (מנחת קנאת), which is a grain offering of remembrance (מנחת זכרון), causing iniquity to be remembered' (5.15; cf. 5.18).[8] The naming of the offering, with jealousy and remembrance in paratactic juxtaposition, does not highlight the

New York: Routledge, 1999], pp. 503-22; reprinted from J. Cheryl Exum and David J. A. Clines [eds.], *The New Literary Criticism and the Hebrew Bible* (JSOTSup, 143; Sheffield: JSOT Press, 1993], pp. 26-54) and Tikva Frymer-Kensky ('The Strange Case of the Suspected Sotah [Numbers v. 11–31]', in Bach [ed.], *Women in the Hebrew Bible*, pp. 463–74; reprinted from *VT* 34 [1984], pp. 11-26). For Bach, the ritual's purpose is the restoration of the husband's authority, but limiting the power analysis to the issue of gender alone misses the more complex dynamic that also involves (priest) male vs. (זר) male. Frymer-Kensky argues that the priest is himself subjugated to God by the ritual, but this point is far from explicit in the text itself. Bonna D. Haberman goes further than most scholars in highlighting the priestly authority in this text, with reference to the words of the curse written down and washed into the bitter water: 'The priest emerges potent; he who controls the text'. Yet she, too, immediately pulls the punch, insisting that she 'must emphasize that even the authority of the priest is subject to God's will', since it is God's name that is the 'significant ingredient in the potion' ('The Suspected Adulteress: A Study of Textual Embodiment', *Prooftexts* 20 [2000], pp. 12-42 [33-34]). Again, however, while the rabbis make this point about the special efficacy of God's name, it does not appear in the biblical text. I would argue in any case, even if the text could be read as implying priestly subjugation to God, that the piety expressed in a divine 'subjugation' of the highest earthly authority has its own authority-enhancing effect, insofar as the priest remains the single, necessary, and sufficient mediator of the divine will.

8. The terms 'jealousy' and 'remembrance' are in reverse order in v. 18, and 'remembrance' (זכרון) has the definite article: there the priest is instructed to 'place in the woman's hands the offering of remembrance, which is an offering of jealousy'. The elaborative phrase 'causing iniquity to be remembered' is only in v. 15.

clarity the ritual will produce, but rather, the anxiety that initiates it, the jealousy the husband feels and, perhaps, his fear that it has a cause—iniquity (עון)—that will indeed be remembered, to his ongoing shame.[9] The creating of commemorative ritual objects, also called 'remembrance' (זכרון), will be important in the second part of Numbers, as we shall see. In the Sotah ritual, however, the 'remembrance' is more ephemeral, merely grain, of which a token, or memorial, portion is burned (5.26). The word for 'memorial portion'—אזכרה—is another nominal form of זכר, here with a feminine possessive suffix. The offering is thus divided: most of the זכרון, the material commemoration of the husband's jealousy, is left on the altar; the *woman's* memorial (אַזְכָּרָתָה), though, is turned to smoke.[10]

There remains, though, the trace of anxiety, the snake in the priestly garden, that the law cannot repress: the conclusion of the ritual is famously ambiguous regarding the fate of the woman found guilty and, indeed, of her husband. Her uterus will swell and discharge—is this a 'spontaneous' abortion? She will be forever childless, that much is clear, but then what about heirs for her husband? Will he divorce her? Will she die at God's hand or society's, as per Deuteronomy?[11] She will become an אלה and a שבעה, we are told, that is, an execration and an oath, among her people (5.21; cf. אלה alone in v. 27), but that suggests that her

---

9. Leveen asserts without argument that what is remembered is 'the humiliating procedure itself' (*Memory and Tradition*, p. 75), but this suggestion seems to run counter to the explicit focus of the text on jealousy and iniquity.

10. Both NRSV and JPS translate the possessive as referring to the grain offering, thus '*its* token (or memorial) portion' is burned, which certainly would be in line with the several similar usages in Leviticus. In Numbers, however, with its dense and meaningful references to memory, there may be a double entendre. Whether the suggestion of a literary burning of the woman's (or, at least, a feminine) memory is the product of priestly intention or an artefact of the priestly subconscious, it is of a piece with the vision of an all-male utopia in Num. 1–4. Although I have less confidence in the interpretative force of this word play than I do in the זכר homonym, I cannot help but note that in eight out of the nine occurrence of אַזְכָּרָה (memorial portion) in Leviticus (always, save once in 24.7, with the feminine possessive suffix), its 'turning to smoke' is specified with אִשֶּׁה, 'by fire'. In the Sotah ritual, has an implicit אִשָּׁה (woman) been substituted for אִשֶּׁה? With vowels!!

11. Milgrom asserts that the purpose of the ritual is to protect the woman from a worse fate at the hands of her husband or the crowd ('The Case of the Suspected Adulteress, Numbers 5.11-31: Redaction and Meaning', in Bach [ed.], *Women in the Hebrew Bible*, pp. 475-82 [481]; reprinted from Richard Friedman [ed.], *The Creation of Sacred Literature* [Near Eastern Studies, 22; Berkeley: University of California Press, 1981], pp. 69-75). This seems like special pleading on behalf of an otherwise very troubling text.

memory will indeed persist! Whatever else may be involved, though, the Sotah ritual has served a critical, even if ultimately deconstructable function in the priests' program for constructing authority and identity. For here they show their full ideological hand. It involves, first, the assertion of their authority, at one and the same time, over the most intimate of human interactions—the sexual relations of husband and wife—*and* over the most fundamental identity-creating mechanism of ancient society—the patrilineal kinship system. Thus, the priestly claim to authority is undergirded by the implicit claim of special identity, namely, as men who control the manhood of Other men, men rightly called זר. This implicit special claim is, on the other hand, supported by one more explicit and likely more easily embraced, the claim of gender difference and male privilege. For in the Sotah law, unlike in the other three laws in chs. 5–6, men and women are sundered from one another, a sundering that receives no resolution, while all women are tarred with the brush of strangeness: even the innocent wife suffers the ritual, unlikely ever to escape her shame.

Though Numbers 7–10 largely returns to the orderly, fully male, world of chs. 1–4, this ideal is disrupted by strangeness once more, at its very end, with the sudden appearance of Hobab son of Reuel, the priest of Midian and Moses' father-in-law (10.29-32).[12] Somewhat shockingly, given that the immediately preceding passage has just described the stylized marching and camping of the people at Yahweh's command (9.17-23), always arranged by tribes around the ark, Moses invites Hobab not only to join them but to serve as their guide through the wilderness. Over Hobab's protests that he should really go back to his own land, Moses presses: 'Do not forsake us, for you know where we should camp in the wilderness, and you can be our eyes' (10.31). That Moses would encourage Hobab, a foreigner, to take on, in effect, the role of Yahweh introduces a crack in the orderly, homogeneously Israelite façade presented by chs. 7–10 up to that point. Like the Sotah law, this brief passage ends without resolution—will Hobab come along or will he go home?—and without narratorial judgment on Moses' invitation to him. However, without actually mentioning, much less naming a woman, the mention of Moses' father-in-law brings Moses' Midianite marriage before our eyes, foreshadowing his own woman-problems in ch. 12, along with the brutally terminated marriage of another Israelite man and Midianite woman in ch. 25 and the massacre of the Midianite women in

12. Or, perhaps, his brother-in-law, depending on how one reads the appositives and also on which textual tradition regarding Moses' marriage one associates with this text (compare Exod. 2.18 with Judg. 1.16 and 4.11).

ch. 31.[13] Hobab, in other words—a foreign man who in multiple ways signals the dangers of strange women—prepares us for the decidedly non-utopic disruptions to come.

Part 2, Numbers 11–25

In Leveen's discussion of the countermemories of Numbers 11–25, she beautifully illustrates the priests' overt manipulation of memory through stories of the creation of three commemorative objects—each called a זכרון—in the aftermath of terrible divine punishments. These are to be ritually deployed in the future as wards against such disasters. A gender-critical analysis of each of the זכרון narratives reveals once again the reliance of the priestly authors on gender ideology in crafting their identity and establishing their authority over against זר-Israelites.

Numbers 15.38-41 describes the tassels or fringe to be worn on the edge of men's garments that will remind them in a daily, embodied way of their salvation by God from the land of Egypt—the correct memory, in Leveen's formulation. Unusual lexical choices in v. 39, part of Yahweh's explanation of the fringe communicated through Moses, also clearly allude to more deadly memories, past or yet to come.

> And you will have the fringe, and you will see it, and you will remember all the commandments of Yahweh and you will do them. And you will not spy after (תָתֻרוּ אַחֲרֵי) your hearts and after your eyes, which you are whoring after (אֲשֶׁר־אַתֶּם זֹנִים אַחֲרֵיהֶם).

Leveen offers an extended discussion of the way in which this verse's unusual use of the word for 'spy out, scout'—תור—connects the memorial object with the failure of the Israelites to journey directly into Canaan because of the fear induced by the those who spied out the land. תור is used thirteen times in the report of the spying out and the people's response to it in chs. 13 and 14. The 'remembrance' of the fringe is designed to invoke the wrong kind of memory about doubting God and longing for Egypt as a warning that will induce the right kind of memory about God's commandments.[14]

The use of the root זנה, 'to whore', in 15.39, however, is also unexpected. Leveen notes, but does not otherwise comment on, the prior use of זנה in 14.33, where Yahweh first announces the punishment: 'And your children will be shepherds in the wilderness for forty years, and

---

13. For further discussion of the Hobab passage, see Camp, *Wise, Strange and Holy*, pp. 268-71.

14. Leveen, *Memory and Tradition*, pp. 108-10.

they will bear the burden of your whorings (זנותיכם) until the last of your corpses lies in the wilderness'. But what whoring, besides the imagined activity of the suspected adulteress, has taken place at this point in the tale? The people have complained, doubted, and rebelled, but they have not yet 'whored'. זנה, in other words, is not an allusion to a memory but rather a foreshadowing of things to come, namely, the later incident of 'whoring' with the Moabite women and their gods at Shittim (25.1-4). That passage metaphorically identifies bad sex—what's done *by* faithless wives as well as *with* foreign women—and bad religion—what's done with foreign gods—in a way that often is taken for granted in the Hebrew Bible.[15] The foreshadowing use of זנה ('whoring') in relation to the 'remembrance' of the fringe, however, metonymically extends the metaphor by associating the harlotrous choices the men will later make with the Moabite women and their gods with the underlying memory of the 'original sin', the longing for Egypt, which led to the death of the entire Exodus generation in the wilderness. Gender ideology thus informs this text in two directions: only men will wear the *zikkaron* of the fringe, while women embody all the reasons they are going to need it.

The second wilderness 'remembrance' consists of the plating for the altar that Eleazar hammers from the bronze censors of the incinerated Levite Korah and his followers in ch. 16. The plating will cover the front of the altar, forever dividing the priest from the congregation; in this sense it is also a materialization of the role of all the Levites, whether rebellious or not, who stand between the priests and the people, at risk to their own lives.[16] The priests, again, do not simply assert authority with this action but build themselves an identity as separated, holy as the people are not, now with a bronze boundary as well as a human one between them and the congregational זרים. This episode depicts, however, one of the two closest approaches that non-priests ever make to the

---

15. And today as well, one might add, as we see in the overlapping religious and sexual uses of the words 'faithful' and 'faithless', though this has now become virtually a dead metaphor.

16. Leveen, *Memory and Tradition*, pp. 114-32. Leveen (pp. 128-29) stresses the connection of Korah's rebellion, especially the use of firepans, with the deaths of Aaron's sons, Nadab and Abihu, with their 'strange fire' (אש זרה; Num. 3.4; 26.61; Lev. 10.1-2). The demise of Korah, whose cry that 'all the people are holy' is not an inconsequential one vis-à-vis the claims of the Aaronites to special holy status, reiterates the danger of drawing too near to that holiness. At the same time, it reconfirms the need for the Levites to hold the protective line on behalf of the collective congregational Israelite strange man (איש זר in Num. 17.5) by replacing the sacrifice of the firstborn (Num. 3.12-13, 40-51).

holy: the ironic fact that 'Korah, even if only in memory, resides in the tabernacle'.[17]

While the gendered nature of this second זכרון is less obvious than that of the first and third, this aspect may be seen by considering where women appear and do not appear in the episode. Despite his offense and punishment, Korah, the male representative of the Levites, who themselves represent the male Israelites, lives on in cultic space and memory. Though sin and death have encroached, the male sphere of the priests remains intact and even capable of memorializing the sinner. Korah's accomplices, Dathan and Abiram, however, suffer a different fate. Sons of Reuben (16.1), they are neither priests nor Levites. They represent the זר-Israelites—the gender-mixed Israelites—and thus meet their end alongside their wives and children (16.27), swallowed up by the earth without remainder or memory (16.30-33). Korah's family and possessions are included in this end, but Korah himself has been carefully separated from it.[18]

The last זכרון, Aaron's rod, is created in ch. 17, marking the end of the rebellion against his priesthood. Alone among the twelve rods symbolizing the twelve tribes, the rod of the tribe of Levi, with Aaron's name inscribed as its head, sprouts, bears blossoms and then nuts. Thus does Yahweh confirm Aaron as the man he has chosen. But the nut-bearing rod does more than provide a divine imprimatur to priestly authority. For this unmistakable phallic symbol flowers and fruits without the aid of any woman. It thus recalls the male fantasy of the first part of Numbers, a patrilineal order impossibly perpetuated by men alone.

This point comes into further focus through the narratives of women near the beginning and at the end of the second part of Numbers. The story of Miriam, the sister of Moses and Aaron, in ch. 12 and those of the Moabite women and Midianite woman in ch. 25 effectively frame this major section of rebellions. This placement exactly corresponds, as we shall see below, to that of the two episodes involving Zelophehad's

---

17. Ibid., p. 131.

18. My thanks to Diana Edelman for the observation that, although Dathan and Abiram receive no memorial within the story world of Numbers, their names are in fact recorded in the written text, their memory thus renewed for every new generation of readers along with the memory of their dead wives and children. They could in this sense be viewed as another form of Leveen's countermemories, examples to be avoided by those readers. Perhaps we could even see them, rather literally, as *mises en abyme* of the countermemory theme. Those victims of the abyss are also, though, perpetual reflections of the inescapably—and, in the view of Numbers, dangerously—dual-gendered reality of the non-priestly congregation.

daughters in Part 3. If the latter arrangement is, as Leveen suggests, a structuring device for Part 3, then I think it is safe to see the same sort of feminized structuring in Part 2.

Consider the sister. Compared to potentially adulterous wives, sisters might seem relatively innocuous as a social group,[19] which is what makes the story of Miriam's punishment in ch. 12 so striking, given that she and Aaron had jointly protested Moses' authority—or perhaps his strange wife. The fleeting reference to Moses' Cushite wife in 12.1 is an interpretive crux, since the text immediately turns instead to the siblings' challenge to Moses' pre-eminence. For my purposes here, though, all we need notice is how mention of the Cushite wife cues the strange woman music, because that is where it all is headed. As I have argued at length in *Wise, Strange and Holy*, Miriam, the sister of Moses and Aaron—that is, the quintessential insider woman—is narratively estranged, identified as Other, struck with the impurity of skin disease, and set outside the camp. This cutting off of Miriam from Aaron is a definitive moment in establishing Aaron's priesthood insofar as it affirms his relationship with Moses, the two brothers joined as one authority, while suppressing, if not eliminating, the sister. Here we see the mythic realization of a practical impossibility with respect to the gendering of priestly identity, namely, the denial to priestly sisters not just of priestly status but, indeed, of membership in the lineage itself. The lineage of Aaronite priests is all male all the time. As was also true of the contrast between the Levite Korah and the זר-men, Dathan and Abiram, in Numbers 12, the totalizing maleness of the priesthood contrasts precisely with the rest of the people, who align and thereby identify themselves with Miriam, waiting out her leprosy before agreeing to move camp again. The estranged sister becomes an icon of the strange people—all are זר or, perhaps better, זרה, to the priests.

It is not until ch. 25 that actual foreign women finally appear, first Moabite women who invite the Israelite men to a banquet of bad sex and bad religion; 'the people' (העם, 25.1, 2), paradoxically now male-defined, whore with the women and bow down to their gods (synony-mously as well as simultaneously). In quick narrative succession, we are then told of an Israelite man, Zimri the Simeonite, bringing his Midianite wife, Cozbi, before the tent of meeting, an encroachment that provokes Phinehas, Aaron's grandson, to up and run them through with his spear. Along with Korah's, this is the second of two non-priestly encroach-ments on holy space. Comparing the two episodes, we can again see the

___

19. Every man knows, of course, that any wife can go bad: the possibility of their sexual misconduct is built into the system that makes their sexual constraint so vital.

difference that gender makes. Despite his crime, Korah is entirely male-identified and is finally materially memorialized, while Cozbi and Zimri—the mixed-gendered, זו-couple—die without obvious trace.[20]

Phinehas, however, for his deadly gesture, receives Yahweh's 'covenant of peace, the covenant of eternal priesthood' (25.12-13), suggesting once more the degree to which the male priesthood is defined over against Woman as Strange—here, in the form of a truly foreign woman, capable of further estranging the זו-Israelite man. Indeed, the covenant of priesthood is initiated precisely when the priest eliminates the Strange Woman. Again, unusual vocabulary and word play reinforce the gendered point, while perhaps also allowing a small glimpse of a remaining female trace. Phinehas, we are told, went after the Israelite man, into the tent (אֶל־הַקֻּבָּה), and he pierced the two of them, the Israelite man and the woman, into her womb (אֶל־קֳבָתָהּ[21]) (25.8a).

Both קֻבָּה (*qubbâ*, 'tent') and קוֹבָה (*qōbâ*, 'womb') are hapaxes, and must certainly be read in metaphorical association with each other. From the pierced קוֹבָה of the 'strange woman', the covenant of eternal priesthood emerges, bringing forth the 'priestly man' who will thenceforth define and control the holy womb of the קֻבָּה. The two contiguous episodes involving strange women in ch. 25, ending in Phinehas's receipt of the covenant of eternal priesthood, thus complete Numbers' gendered narrative process of priestly authorization and identity construction.

In the process, Phinehas's annihilation of the Strange Woman marks the priests of his generation as arbiters of an equally gender-defined identity for Israel as a whole. Before ch. 25, the women in Numbers all begin as members of the family: the Israelite wife in ch. 5 and the Israelite sister in ch. 12 must be constructed as 'strange' in the interests of the all-male priestly utopia. But such constructions defy the lived experience of real men and women; they are thus inherently unstable, and both texts display ambivalence about their representations. The Sotah ritual begins with but a suspicion and ends without full closure, while Miriam's crime and punishment are fraught with ambiguities, and

---

20. The observations in n. 18 regarding the textual memorialization of Dathan and Abiram could apply, *mutatis mutandis*, to Cozbi and Zimri. Later readers are again reminded both of the choice of proper memory that they can make and of the problematic dual-gendered identity of the congregation that it cannot escape.

21. Unlike BDB, *HALOT*, and other lexicons, *DCH* distinguishes the form of the word in this verse (קוֹבָה) from קֵבָה in Deut. 18.3 and various Qumran texts. The latter seems to mean 'stomach' (cf. the LXX's ενυστρον, 'fourth stomach of a cow'), while *DCH* assigns *qōbâ* the meaning 'female genitals, or breast', also corresponding to the LXX translation of Num. 25.8, which reads μντρα, 'womb'.

their effect on her future goes unstated. Numbers 25 makes a further move. The wife and sister are replaced by women who are strangers in all ways: sexually, religiously, nationally, and, if we take the root of Cozbi's name as meaningful,[22] in terms of language as well, representing deceit rather than truth.[23] All this strangeness is vanquished with one thrust of Phinehas's spear. What this priest ultimately clarifies, then, is Israelite identity itself, defined through the construction of the Strange Woman who is definitively not Us. The stories of the Moabite and Midianite women, foreigners, and worshippers of other gods whom all can gladly condemn, consolidate and reify the ambiguous Otherness of the wife and the sister, insider women who must either be ritually constrained (for the congregation) or mythically cut off and suppressed (for the priests). What cannot be entirely purged from the inside can be cleanly cut off on the outside. Phinehas's murder of the intermarried couple thus marks the outer boundary of Israelite identity over against the זרה. For *this* he receives the covenant of eternal priesthood, with the line between male-identified priest and the Israelite זר now also impassibly incised.

Part 3: Numbers 26–36

The last major literary unit of the book comprises priestly hopes for life in the land. Daughters appear twice in this section, in chs. 27 and 36. Episodes involving the brotherless brood of Zelophehad thus prominently bookend this new priestly vision, following the second census in ch. 26, to provide what Leveen regards as a 'mini-frame' for the practical, hopeful vision of the final priestly editor.[24] In ch. 27, Zelophehad's daughters insist to Moses and Eleazar and the other leaders that they should inherit from their dead father in order that his name not be lost. Moses consults Yahweh, who agrees with the women. The question is reopened in ch. 36, however, at the very end of the book, when the heads of the fathers' houses complain that land inherited by daughters will be taken into the inheritance of their husbands' tribes if they remarry outside. Moses responds with a new word from Yahweh, restricting inheriting daughters to marriage within their father's tribe.

22. Verbal forms of כזב mean 'to lie, be a liar'; the nominal כָּזָב means 'lie, falsehood'.

23. This point is particularly relevant to Leveen's emphasis on profligate, misdirected speaking—murmuring—as central to the wrong choices made by the people in the wilderness.

24. Leveen, *Memory and Tradition*, p. 178.

It is not hard to see the mixed blessing here as far as women are concerned. On the one hand, the possibility of women inheriting is recognized and the five bold daughters of Zelophehad are named no less than three different times in the account. On the other hand, their right to inherit is limited by the presence of even one brother and their marital choices are restricted in the interests of the patrilineage even if they do inherit. But what is this female-centered issue doing in such a prominent position in Numbers? Leveen offers a two-part explanation. First, the revision of Moses' initial judgment, the last and thus memorable event in Numbers, is itself important in showing that legal rulings are subject to review and revision. The very last event, an event that leaves an indelible impression in the mind of the reader because it *is* last, informs us that Israel is entering the land with the most important possession of all: the knowledge that the community will be governed by law and legal stipulations but that such rulings are subject to legal review and revision.[25] The fact that this momentous point is made on the backs of women is 'unfortunate', in Leveen's view, but compensated for by a second key function of the ending, the goal of having the father's name remembered (lit: not diminished or withdrawn, Niphal of the root גרע, 27.4), which has the happy result of having the daughters' names remembered as well. With this ending, she says, 'the narrator personifies the core concern of Numbers—the preservation and transmission of collective memory—and the ultimate resolution of that concern in the new generation'.[26]

But why, the inquiring feminist mind wants to know, given everything that has gone before, would this editor want to personify the book's 'core concern' in female form, when it could have been done any number of other ways? I suggest we read Zelophehad's daughters in light of the gender ideology we have examined thus far. The texts on the Sotah and Miriam show the devilish problem that insider women present to constructing the right sort of identity, insofar as they disrupt the priestly vision of an all-male utopian community in the one case and undermine the perfect maleness of the priestly lineage in the other. Phinehas's spear seems to resolve such matters, but the memories of women remain and, of course, real women remain as well!

The account of Zelophehad's daughters seems to recognize this reality. Like the rest of Part 3, it focuses on more mundane matters in a more realistic sort of way. But there is a less than harmonious undercurrent in the apparently straightforward account of ch. 36. The leaders

25. Ibid., p. 180
26. Ibid., p. 181.

who object to Moses' first ruling ignore the daughters' expressed concern for the remembrance of their father's name; the men focus instead on the tribal assignment of lands, carried out by lot in 26.52-56, which could be disrupted by inheriting women.[27] For these men, lost land (also Niphal of the root גרע, 36.3) trumps lost name. But what this tension unveils is the usually repressed recognition that inheritance, which should provide the basis for the memory of male names, may end up competing with it. This is the profoundly disruptive possibility that women both present and represent, and which Moses must revise his legislation to control. The memory of the daughters' names, I would suggest, does not represent a straightforward honouring of them but rather a textual trace of the danger they present, even in the very act of controlling them.

The reiteration of the daughters' names at the very end of the book, then, hints at something more than straightforward, consciously maintained memory. Again let me cite and then twist a bit of Leveen's conclusion about Numbers' conclusion:

> It is fitting that at journey's end, and the very ending of the book, we are left with the names not of those bound by the desert but those who will at any moment leave it behind.[28]

Like the wife who teeters on the brink between faithfulness and adultery, however, and like the sister who is pushed over the line from insider to outsider, the names of Zelophehad's daughters can be seen as lining up at the edge of the book—five names, a line of text. Translated into spatial terms, Mahlah, Tirzah, Hoglah, Milcah, and No'ah line up at the boundary between the wilderness and the promised land, between Israelite men and strange women, partaking of the identity of each—Israelite women who will enter the land but who will stand always at the defining margin of Israelite identity. They will not wear fringe on the edges of their garments because they are themselves the fringe, the reminder of rebellion. With women's names the priests reinscribe the quintessential sin of Numbers, the people's longing for Egypt.[29] They may enter the land but, in remembering the name of their father, they look backward to wilderness, a pillar of salt, perhaps, *their* 'remembrance'.

---

27. Leveen notes this point but does not pursue its undermining implications.

28. Leveen, *Memory and Tradition*, p. 181.

29. The fact that Zelophehad is from the clan of Gilead—a Reubenite in other words, a tribe that ends up in TransJordan, against the wishes of Moses and God—further reinforces this marginality, both part in and part out of the promised land, and part in and part out of full commitment to God's will.

WOMEN ON THE EDGE

Carey Walsh

The Concept of the Woman as Other

Since biblical narratives were presumably written by a host of anony-mous, male scribes within the patriarchal culture of ancient Israel, the portrayals of women in the narratives bear indications of difference and separation from the normative male position. Under the androcentric gaze, that is, a perspectival orientation that presumes male privilege, woman is different from the male; she is in some way strange or other. The process of Othering another occurs in a variety of ways in the Bible and is not always or even primarily gender based. Ethnic identities that are not Israel, for instance, such as the Canaanites or Moabites, are marked off as 'other': they are to be avoided wholesale or conquered (Exod. 23.23-28; Deut. 7.1-4; Judg. 10.6).[1] Ethnic distinctions beyond the in-group, in this instance Israel, are 'outsider others', in contrast to the insider Others that are distinctions made among members of the in-group.[2] Persons with various physical conditions in ancient Israel, for example, such as a man with crushed testicles, or leprosy, or a menstru-ant, are put at a distance from the community, as Other, temporarily, as in the case of the menstruant, or on a more permanent basis, as in the case of the leper and genitally injured male.

The Other status of these persons is understood and maintained within the community, often with intricate rules that go unnoticed to those outside of it. Since insider Others are within the community, special care is given to demarcating their differences from other members. Where biblical law simply prohibits the entry of Moabites and Ammonites,

---

1. One difference lies in the nations or ethnicities that are perceived to be in the ancient past versus those that are contemporaneous neighbours of Israel during the monarchy. Exod. 23.23-28 lists six nations to be destroyed, while Deut. 7.1-2 lists seven. Judg. 10.6 lists contemporaneous nations to Israel, such as Moab.

2. Lawrence M. Wills, *Not God's People: Insiders and Outsiders in the Biblical World* (Lanham, MD: Rowman & Littlefield, 2008), p. 40.

ethnic outsiders, into the community (Deut. 23.3), the legislation for the man with crushed testicles must be detailed: 'He whose testicles are crushed or whose male member is cut off shall not enter the assembly of the Lord' (Deut. 23.1). In Leviticus, his Otherness is listed alongside other evident types of physical Otherness, such as the 'hunchback, or a dwarf, or a man with a defect in his sight or an itching disease or scabs or crushed testicles' (Lev. 21.20). Proximity with regular members of the community occasions specification for these examples of insider Others, especially if the difference is not visually apparent.

Marking differences within a communal arrangement is a vital function for societal definition, as F. Barth asserts: '...a group maintains its identity when members interact with others. This entails criteria for determining membership and ways of signaling membership and exclusion.'[3] The marked articulation of difference helps a social group define and affirm itself. If the insiders can be clearer on who is excluded from the assembly, namely, the man with the crushed testicles, then they can also be clearer on who is representative of Israel, that is, the undamaged male, and the value he upholds for the community in the form of healthy, male virility. Othering is an important practice for the social maintenance of distinct statuses and communal identity. It helps establish who We are by who We are not and who is not quite like Us. Othering also performs a regulatory function in determining who, though within the community, is nevertheless outside the bounds of normativity.

The distinguishing of woman as Other is a special case, since there is purportedly nothing deficient about her except that she is both different from man and necessary to the health and continuance of the community. Woman, then, under the androcentric view, is placed in the odd position of being both essential and Other. This dual aspect to her Otherness can at times occasion a strong ambivalence. Woman as Other is a construct that the male scribal tradition encodes throughout the biblical materials. For instance, while the Mosaic laws are meant for all Israel, they are addressed to propertied males in second person, masculine, verbal forms.[4] This syntactical detail is meant to include all persons, of course, but it assumes a heterosexual, male perspective. This becomes clear, for example, in the tenth commandment against coveting a neighbour's wife (Exod. 20.17), or in the Levitical law that prohibits men from having sex with one another without a parallel prohibition for females

3. Fredrik Barth, 'Introduction', in *Ethnic Groups and Boundaries: The Social Organization of Cultural Differences* (Boston: Little, Brown, 1969), pp. 1-26 (15).

4. Judith Plaskow, *Standing Again at Sinai: Judaism from a Feminist Perspective* (New York: HarperSanFrancisco, 1991).

(Lev. 18.22), until Paul later corrects for this androcentric omission in Rom. 1.26. Males are the assumed audience of biblical texts and so the woman becomes Other in their production and reception. *She* is not directly addressed.

From the beginning, in the creation accounts, the difference within gender is evident. Adam recognizes that the woman is part of man when he exclaims: 'This at last is bone of my bones and flesh of my flesh; she shall be called Woman, because she was taken out of Man' (Gen. 2.23). For all of Adam's intimate identification with the woman—'bone and flesh'—there is also a distancing construction of her as Other. For, in this Yahwist account (J), the creation of the woman occurs well after the man's and then only after Adam names the animals, without finding a suitable helpmate among them. As E. Lévinas has argued, 'Woman does not simply come to someone deprived of companionship to keep him company. She answers to a solitude inside this privation and—which is stranger—to a solitude that subsists in spite of the presence of God.'[5] Woman, then, is essential in ways even God cannot be!

By naming the animals, Adam has exercised a degree of authority over them and they are subject to him at least in terms of their taxonomic identity. He then names the woman, too (Gen. 2.23; 3.20). This action aligns woman with the beasts apart from the man, who is also a creature, but the one empowered to name all the others. In the woman, Adam recognizes the helpmate he will need, but it is *he* who gets to. The power dynamic rests with the male to whom she is subject. She is Other. She is certainly not Adam, the authoritative, speaking voice. And later, in their sexual congress, Adam 'knew Eve his wife' (Gen. 4.1): Eve is the object of his verb, with no narrative indication that she in turn 'knew' him. She is 'his' wife, a possession.[6]

The example of Eve illustrates S. de Beauvoir's general point about woman in Western civilization, namely, that 'she is defined and differentiated with reference to man and not he with reference to her; she is the incidental, the inessential as opposed to the essential. He is the subject,

5. Emmanuel Lévinas, *Difficult Freedom: Essays on Judaism* (trans. Seán Hand; Johns Hopkins Jewish Studies; Baltimore: The Johns Hopkins University Press, 1997), p. 33.

6. The wife of Job is portrayed in similar terms. She is the nameless wife, a fruitful mother of his ten children, and as helpmate, silently enjoys all his prosperity. Yet, she breaks from the role when she advises her husband, 'Do you still hold fast your integrity? Curse God, and die' (Job 2.9). With one verse, she is catapulted outside the text, as a bitter Other to Job in his suffering. She does not even return at Job's issuance of ten new children at the book's end. Those new children then are truly miracle children, without a mother, but with YHWH's sanction.

he is the absolute—she is the Other.'[7] While the Priestly account (P) of creation portrays gender as a complementarity in the human, viz., 'in the image of God he created him; male and female he created them' (Gen. 1.27), the J account differentiates woman from man, as both same and 'other'. In fact, the juxtaposition of these two sources gave rise in Judaism to the legend of the escaped first wife, Lilith.[8] The redactional inclusion of the Priestly and Yahwist accounts, then, adds yet another layering of Otherness to the woman, this time a textual one, since she is made stranger by the collage effect of multiple views. The first woman does not quite add up: she is like a Picasso woman. We could regard the rabbinic myth of Lilith to be an extreme act of Othering, since she is beyond the confines of the text. But she, a combination of viewpoints, is still hinted at by the textual juxtaposition of accounts that occasioned the myth in the first place.

Androcentric bias skews how woman's voice and character is portrayed in biblical stories involving women, but not in a monolithic way. Feminist interpretation has long mined the ideological indications of Otherness in biblical portrayals of women. In large measure, the intent of feminist hermeneutics has been to recover biblical women from textual androcentric bias and imagine their narrative action freed from such constraints.[9] Both feminist and the more recent postcolonial criticisms emphasize how power is asserted in texts and at what costs to the subordinated or subjugated voices; hence, the recovery of a woman's suppressed agency in a male-authored text is a shared goal. In postcolonial criticism, however, it is *power* rather than *gender* that most deeply

7. Simone de Beauvoir, *The Second Sex* (trans. H. M. Parshley; New York: Alfred A. Knopf, [1949] 1980), pp. xxxix-xl.

8. Kristen E. Kvam, Lind S. Schearing, and Valarie H. Ziegler, *Eve and Adam: Jewish, Christian, and Muslim Readings on Genesis and Gender* (Bloomington, IN: Indiana University Press, 1999), p. 204.

9. See especially, Carol A. Newsom, Sharon H. Ringe, and Jacqueline E. Lapsley (eds.), *Women's Bible Commentary* (Louisville, KY: Westminster John Knox, 3rd edn, 2012); Elisabeth Fiorenza, *In Memory of Her: A Feminist Theological Reconstruction of Christian Origins* (New York: Crossroad, 10th edn, 1994); Claudia V. Camp, *Wise, Strange and Holy: The Strange Woman and the Making of the Bible* (JSOTSup, 320; London: Sheffield Academic Press, 2000); Alice O. Bellis, *Helpmates, Harlots, and Heroes* (Louisville, KY: Westminster John Knox, 2nd edn, 2007); Alice Bach (ed.), *Women in the Hebrew Bible: A Reader* (London: Routledge, 1998); individual biblical books in Athalya Brenner's *Feminist Companion Series* (variously, with Sheffield: Sheffield Academic Press; London: T&T Clark International); Ilana Pardes, *Countertraditions in the Bible: A Feminist Approach* (Cambridge, MA: Harvard University Press, 1993); Plaskow, *Standing Again at Sinai.*

influences narrative. Its perspective sheds considerable light on the subjective power exercised by women characters within biblical constructions of Otherness, which run the range from resistance to acquiescence.

It should be said at first that deciding who is an Other and who is not in any given cultural context is a game played only by those who view themselves as not-the-Other. It is a game for the insiders, the We, to play against and at the expense of the Other, the outsider. And it often becomes a very serious game, requiring theoretical intervention: 'post-colonial criticism bears witness to the unequal and uneven forces of cultural representation involved in the contest for political and social authority...'[10] The We and the Other are inextricably linked. And, to clarify, the Other is quite different from the unknown stranger. It serves an *oppositional* purpose for the self-understanding of the insiders. The stranger, by contrast, is simply distant and different,[11] and does not exercise a polarizing influence. The Other, though, is pushed out or cast adrift from communal acceptance or full status. There is an exertion of power in delimiting the Other that the stranger does not occasion. Instead, Othering is really a means to render someone who is too *similar* as strange and different. The real stranger does not summon this kind of energy. As de Beauvoir argued, the male author in Western civilization plays the role of Othering in relation to the female: 'Only the intervention of someone else can establish an individual as an *Other*'.[12]

Hence, dominance of the insider group is clear in that we are the ones who name the Other, as Adam had named the animals. But it is also curtailed, since we are dependent on an Other for self-definition. We need the contrast of an Other to exercise our full authority, and so we share in a symbiotic relationship with the excluded Other. The Other is not simply not-Us; it is the not-Us to which We are nevertheless forever tied.

Given this reciprocal relationship, it is not surprising that the Other would provoke ambivalence and hostility rather than indifference as the distant stranger would, when political and emotional tensions escalate. There is in the construal of the Other a continuing power vortex, of fear and of desire, since the We and the Other are paired necessarily.[13] Of course, it is also true that the Other is an abstraction. It is a label only, which the scribal tradition on occasion well recognizes in narratives that

10. Homi K. Bhabha, *The Location of Culture* (Routledge Classics; London: Routledge, 1994), p. 171.
11. Wills, *Not God's People*, p. 12.
12. De Beauvoir, *Second Sex*, p. 281.
13. Wills, *Not God's People*, p. 13.

subvert or play with notions of the Other, as we shall see in the stories of Rahab and Vashti. All of the narratives investigated in this essay challenge or destabilize the notion of Other in the woman, often to the benefit of all Israel. Whereas de Beauvoir emphasized the process of rendering the woman as Other in patriarchal contexts, postcolonial criticism enables us to see modes of resistance and acquiescence in the biblical woman as Other. It provides insight into the power dynamics in texts, where we discover that woman is not always a victim but is often a skilled and lauded player.

The Other on the Edge

The present essay explores biblical women caught on the edge of inclusion and exclusion in terms of Israel's views of Otherness. That is, it explores women characters not for their Otherness *per se*, but in how they press ideological assumptions about Otherness into reexamination. There is, we shall find, a surprising dexterity in how biblical women carry their Otherness. This essay examines instances where women wield their very Otherness for the sake of a more expansive communal identity. The preservation of these examples by the male scribal tradition demonstrates a critical self-awareness of the power dynamics involved in social definition and offers heuristic caution. For power does real social damage, as R. Schwartz warns: 'Violence is not only what we do to the other. It is prior to that. Violence is the very construction of the other.'[14]

We see from the actions of select, women characters—Rahab, Jael, Ruth, Jezebel, Vashti, and Esther—that social power is fluid. These women contest the male dominance of their situations and secure gains as a result of negotiating their Otherness in Israel's midst. And they are each the Other in two ways: being woman and being foreign to their context. As such, they are able to transgress the boundary of Israel's community and are momentarily freed from its restraints and regulations. *How* they cross the boundary is an exercise of their power as Other. *That* they are shown doing so by the male scribal tradition means they have become transgressive examples for a subsequent insider group, that of biblical readers. The presumed audience is seeing the laudatory value of circumventing boundaries and listening to marginalized women. The oppositional code is formed by including subordinated voices, despite the fact that the text is being produced by those with a vested interest in

---

14. Regina Schwartz, *The Curse of Cain: The Violent Legacy of Monotheism* (Chicago: University of Chicago Press, 1997), p. 5.

patriarchy. A marginalized voice differs from a silenced or erased one, in that it is preserved in memory for a reason. In this sense, biblical Israel is a healthy, open system able to incorporate and instruct on difference.

These are all women on the edge of Israelite (or Persian) identity. They do not quite fit and are, therefore, marginalized and at risk. Esther is right to be concerned that she may be at risk of death for the movements she makes to save her people: 'I will go to the king, though it is against the law; and if I perish, I perish' (Est. 4.16). Yet therein lays their advantage. The Other on the edge often has nothing left but her own resources and these are discounted precisely by virtue of her being an Other. Ironically, their power goes further because it is undetected in the dominant structure. These marginalized women demonstrate self-reliant grit and trust in exercising their human agency in complicated situations. Their actions become, then, didactic illustrations of how to manoeuvre through circumstances where difference matters, and that tends to be most situations. Their Otherness works for them in many ways because no one expects it to. That enables these women a degree of freedom and agility denied those who are regulated insiders.

These biblical examples of marginalized women in part destabilize the regulatory efforts of communal definition by calling attention to the elasticity of the boundary. Marginalized people employ stratagems to work around the system. Such stratagems may, indeed, be how women would need to get ahead in patriarchal societies. Subjugation by a power structure breeds a kind of street intelligence to move about in the system. Depicting these stratagems as successful reveals momentarily that the dominant power is vulnerable. There is a subversive hope bred in these tales. Assumptions about received wisdom are upended with hints of some newer advance. The efforts of marginalized women to secure liberation for themselves in oppressive situations speaks to the larger biblical concern with liberation in general, for in the long run, to be God's people is to belong to no one else. Subjugation, even if customary, is always being subverted in biblical narrative, given the transcendent horizon, God, who exists beyond custom. Even being a secure insider can be a kind of cage itself that stunts liberation. When the widowed Tamar cannot obtain her legal rights in Israel from her father-in-law, Judah, she disguises herself as an outsider, a Canaanite prostitute, in order to secure them. She is freed to her full rights by becoming the outsider, but so, too, is Judah. For, he is not angry that Tamar duped him. He publically admits that 'She is more righteous than I, inasmuch as I did not give her to my son Shelah' (Gen. 38.26). Judah is also freed by his willingness to learn beyond the status quo that, as patriarch, he is enjoying. He acknowledges that the disguised prostitute has bested his patriarchal power and privilege. Power is rarely secure in the Bible, as it is always being checked or thrown over by a larger, divine power that frees.

Rahab, the Canaanite Prostitute

Often the status of a female character as Other is marked symbolically by her physical position in the story, near the city gate or wall (Deut. 22.15; Judg. 9.53, of a tower; Ruth 4.11; 2 Kgs 6.26; 9.33; Song 8.9-10; Est. 2.19; Ezek. 8.14; 2 Macc. 6.10; Tob. 11.16; Jdt. 8.33). Rahab lives in the city wall and is an Other in three ways: she is female, enemy, and prostitute. Early on, walls were built simply by placing houses adjacent to one another, so that one side of each house would also function as part of the city wall. Later, the architecture could incorporate dwellings or partial dwellings within the wall structure. As a prostitute, Rahab would benefit from near access to the potential customers arriving through the city gate. The safer, interior parts of the city would be reserved for community members of higher social status, like the king and other administrative officials. If attacked, those living in the wall would be the first victims. Rahab, then, is an outlier in her own community, living on the literal margins of the city. She performs a service for her male clientele that undoubtedly improves the overall market activity in Jericho, yet this goes unacknowledged. It is invisible, yet real to the community's functioning.

Rahab's attachment to Jericho is only provisional, given her location and profession. Her marginal status creates opportunities of free or at least unnoticed movement inside and outside her society. Her vulnerability on the wall provides the opening for Rahab's heroism. She can aid the spies' escape because she lives in the wall: 'Then she let them down by a rope through the window, for her house was built into the city wall, so that she dwelt in the wall' (Josh. 2.15). Her real asset, acknowledged by the narrator, is that she is an Other in her own community of Jericho, and so can identify, perhaps even empathize with, the Other in the Israelite spies. When word spreads that visitors from Israel are inside the city walls, Rahab answers the king first with a half-truth and then a lie:

> 'True, men came to me, but I did not know where they came from; and when the gate was to be closed, at dark, the men went out; where the men went I do not know; pursue them quickly, for you will overtake them'. But she had brought them up to the roof, and hid them with the stalks of flax that she had laid in order on the roof. (Josh. 2.4-6)

The king takes Rahab at her word because she is an incidental Other to him, incapable of the kind of subterfuge she in fact enacts.

Rahab's actions allow Israel to gain a foothold into the Promised Land. Though treasonous to her own community, she is acclaimed in Israel's memory as foundational to the nation. Rahab, the triple Other to her own people, then becomes the remembered hero of another people, Israel, the outsiders to this Promised Land. The marginal status of her social position has enabled her to see it in others, in the spies and, by extension, in their unknown God. Ironically, the instability of her social standing renders her receptive to this 'other' people and its God. She is praised in the book of Joshua for her wordless, quick fidelity to this God of the Other whom she cannot even yet know.

Rahab craftily uses her own Otherness in Jericho to advance the cause of the outlier spies. She lets them in through the window in the wall and posts a red thread there as her own makeshift Passover:

> Behold, when we come into the land, you shall bind this scarlet cord in the window through which you let us down; and you shall gather into your house your father and mother, your brothers, and all your father's household. (Josh. 2.18)

Symbolically, she also has ended her outsider status by retroactively joining in Israel's epic ritual of Exodus. Once this happens, the spies enter Jericho undetected and the tables are quickly turned. The insiders, the Canaanites, become the Other and the outliers, Israel, become the insiders. Rahab was instrumental in transposing Israel for Canaan as the legitimate insiders of the Promised Land. For her efforts, she and her family are spared destruction and commended in Israel's memory as the Other in Canaan who helped the great mass of Others, namely Israel, replace the insider population. Hence, while being an Other is a marginalized social status, it occasions opportunities for revolutionary movement and change that are not as easily available to insiders. In this instance, Rahab's power as Other enables her to save her family and transpose two entire nations and that is no small amount of power indeed.

Jael

Because there are so often power differentials existing between characters, biblical encounters are fraught with duplicity. Duplicity is a vital tool for an Other to employ to exercise her power, as it is for a number of biblical characters (e.g. Joseph, Gen. 44.2-4; Jacob, Gen. 25 and 27; Ehud, Judg. 3.19-21; Nathan, 2 Sam. 12.1-6; the old prophet of Bethel, 1 Kgs 13.18). As we saw above, Rahab used duplicity to treasonous effect since the king of Jericho assumed her incapable of it.

Jael's duplicity is also the result of a male, this time General Sisera, underrating her as a threat. Jael does not even have to lie to Sisera as Rahab had done to the king. She can simply manoeuvre within his presumptions about what women are for, namely, to care for men, especially those exhausted by battle. Sisera has escaped the rout of his army by the Israelites and seeks shelter from a people who are at peace with his own, namely, Heber the Kenite, the husband of Jael (4.17). Sisera is an arch traditionalist in his views of woman as Other, holding sentiments that are similar to those in the Talmud: she represents the hearth to a man.[15] The Other is nicely employed to subversive ends here in that Sisera, the enemy general, assumes that the woman in the tent is safe and nourishing. His neat assumptions about woman as the Other who is for him, for nurturance, costs him his life.

At first, Jael comes outside to greet Sisera and invite him in with the use of the deferential 'lord': 'Turn aside, my lord, turn aside to me; have no fear' (Judg. 4.18). She then warms him by covering him with a rug and provides him with a jug of milk even though he has only requested water. She is different from him, Other, and there to meet even a stranger's need for comfort. A woman's tent, like a hearth, offers warmth, safety, nourishment, and rest. There is even a maternal chord struck in Jael's tucking Sisera in with a rug and in her substitution of milk for water for the weary soldier. His guard is down and he falls asleep. But this female Other is, it turns out, not of the nurturing, maternal kind. Instead, Jael uses the tools of domesticity—milk, serving bowl, napping area, tent peg—for guerrilla aims, that is, to assassinate the unsuspecting general.

Jael has proven not so Other to Sisera; she has been too much the same, a warrior just like him. She takes the tent peg and hammers it into his skull 'till it went down into the ground' (Judg. 4.21), a chilling detail indicating her fierce resolve.[16] Jael acted as a warrior in felling the general and was even male-like in her choice to penetrate Sisera with a peg. She is memorialized as a heroic woman in this story in Judges 4 and then again in the Song of Deborah (Judg. 5): 'Most blessed of women be Jael, the wife of Heber the Kenite, of tent-dwelling women most blessed' (v. 24). Two biblical texts laud this remarkable woman, who, though Other to Israel, slays its enemy.

---

15. Lévinas, *Difficult Freedom*, p. 31.

16. When later it comes to Judith to kill the enemy general, Holofernes, with his own sword, she is in tears, praying twice for the Lord to strengthen her for the lethal deed (Jdt. 13.6-11). Jael, we note, needed no such divine assistance.

Jael is contrasted in Israelite tradition with Sisera's mother, who stands waiting at the window for her son's return from war. She assumes that the son can only be delayed by the time-consuming task of dividing all the spoils, from which she herself can expect 'two pieces of dyed work embroidered for my neck as spoil' (Judg. 5.30). Failure, still less death at the hands of a woman, is not even contemplated. Sisera's mother has no name in the text. She, too, is Othered as female; she exists only in relation to a male, her son. She has also assumed that the Other—both Israel and women—exist only to benefit the son. Women, in her view, are the Other and strictly for utilitarian gain. Either they are the spoil, 'a maiden or two for every man', or they merely effect 'two pieces of dyed work embroidered for my neck as spoil' (Judg. 5.30). From the mother's perspective, waiting at the window, we perhaps glimpse where Sisera learned his views of women.

The figures of Rahab, Jael, and later Judith, are all heroines in Israel's memory for their brave roles in saving or advancing Israel as a nation. That is, they are lauded for their heroism in patriarchal settings and so provide a subversive strand to Israel's memory of patriarchy, if only because they were so effective in it. For, as we champion the heroics of these women, we also wonder about the absence of male warriors. In the case of Rahab's bravery, we can wonder why the spies have been so timid about their entry into the city (Josh. 2.6). In Jael's case, we might wonder why the army has let Sisera escape if it has been such a powerful rout, and where Heber, her husband, is. Rahab and Jael step in because there is a vacuum of male power that allows it. And, from that vacuum, they are tactically quick and effective in their exercise of power.[17]

Both Rahab and Jael are double Others, in that they are foreigners and women. By including their stories in the Bible, the male authors esteem their power and even obliquely critique the absence of patriarchy's power, or the inherent instability that is dominance. These biblical stories are testimony that those without recognized social power nonetheless have it and can wield it to great political effect. At the same time, there is a tacit recognition that the stakeholders of patriarchal society—soldiers, spies, husbands, and kings—are sometimes lax. The tales of these outsider women illustrate the power of the marginalized and the fragility of insider, hegemonic power. By highlighting the marginalized in this way, postcolonial interpretation works 'to assert their denied rights and

17. Michel de Certeau argues that a tactic is the resource of power available to those without power since it is a short, contained act, operating in isolated actions, 'being without any base' (*The Practice of Everyday Life* [trans. Steven F. Rendell; Berkeley: University of California Press, 1984], pp. 37-38).

rattle the centre'.[18] In this case, then, **Rahab** and Jael are outside saviours who advance Israel and so merit acclaim in the narratives of Joshua and Judges. In addition, their bold decisive accomplishments 'rattle the centre' by obliquely critiquing the military preparedness and courage of Israel's male tactical teams of spies and soldiers who, for whatever reason, are missing in action. The insiders, it is clear, *need* the outsiders for their survival.

Ruth

Ruth is the consummate outsider who transitions to insider status as the great-grandmother of King David. She is a Moabite, one of the ethnic groups barred from entry into Israel (Deut. 23.3).[19] She has married an Israelite, Mahlon, who then leaves her widowed. Typically, the practice of intermarriage brings the Other into close proximity with insiders and so can elicit strong, negative reactions, as it does in Ezra, where the people have mixed with

> ...the Canaanites, the Hittites, the Perizzites, the Jebusites, the Ammon-
> ites, the Moabites, the Egyptians, and the Amorites. For they have taken
> some of their daughters to be wives for themselves and for their sons; so
> that the holy race has mixed itself with the peoples of the lands. And in
> this faithlessness the hand of the officials and chief men has been
> foremost. (Ezra 9.1-2)

Ruth's own Otherness is emphasized by her being referred to as 'the Moabitess' five times in the story. Her stranger status in Judah, of course, is situational. She does not have it in her homeland of Moab. In fact, we have no clue if her marriage to a foreign man, her mixed marriage, has occasioned a Moabite Othering of her. There is no indication from the text that she, Orpah, and Naomi live on the periphery of Moabite society because of their mixed marriages, though Ruth's readiness to leave might imply her marginalized status. The story focuses on Ruth as the highlighted Other, while all the other Others—Orpah, Moab, and foreign husbands, are dropped from view.

---

18. Sugirtharajah, *Exploring Postcolonial Criticism*, p. 13.
19. Three additional discussions of Ruth occur in this volume. For an analysis that sees her as both integral to Israel and yet a foreigner, see Ehud Ben Zvi, 'Othering, Selfing, "Boundarying" and "Cross-Boundarying" as Interwoven with Socially Shared Memories: Some Observations', pp. 20-40. For an analysis of Ruth using ethnic theory, see Anne-Mareike Wetter, 'Ruth: A Born-Again Israelite? One Woman's Journey Through Space and Time', pp. 144-62. For an analysis using literary theory, see Robert L. Cohn, 'Overcoming Otherness in the Book of Ruth', pp. 163-81.

Ruth's Otherness serves a different function in the narrative than it had for Rahab and Jael before her. It is not a tool for either duplicity or tactical, empowered action by the character. Whereas Rahab and Jael used their 'otherness' to exercise their own power, Ruth's 'otherness', by contrast, is domesticated into Israel. She does not express a subjective agency independent of the societal conventions that Naomi, Boaz, and the Bethlehemite women teach her. In other words, her power as Other is sublimated to the established gender relations of Israel. She folds into the power dynamics at play in Israel. At the same time, Ruth is remarkably adaptive and demonstrates an Israelite-like covenantal fidelity to her mother-in-law, Naomi: 'for where you go I will go, and where you lodge I will lodge; your people shall be my people, and your God my God' (Ruth 1.16). But her Otherness remains back in Moab once she begins her journey to Bethlehem.

Ruth shows herself to be submissive to Naomi, to Israelite customs of gleaning and the right of the redeemer, to the risk of male molestation in the fields, and to Boaz. Even in Boaz's bedroom, which might otherwise have been a brazen demonstration of female sexual power, Ruth quietly lies at Boaz's feet until he awakes. Sneaking into a man's bedroom might otherwise indicate some *hutzpah* on Ruth's part, but she then waits to take her cue from him. And even this action is the result of Naomi's instructions: 'go and uncover his feet and lie down; and he will tell you what to do'. And she replied, 'All that you say I will do' (3.4-5).[20] Ruth's own desire, if it is there, is masked by her obedience to Naomi.

When Boaz awakes, Ruth quietly receives her next set of instructions, namely, to wait for the right of the redeemer, since there is a kinsman closer than Boaz (3.13-14). Boaz, the next of kin, and the elders all gather at the city gate to decide Ruth's future without her. She is folded into a customary, package deal, 'the day you buy the field from the hand of Naomi, you are also buying Ruth the Moabitess, the widow of the dead, in order to restore the name of the dead to his inheritance' (Ruth 4.5 RSV). Her Otherness is folded, too, into these Israelite, customary trappings. It is fortunate that Boaz gets the right of redemption, since that is what he and Naomi want. He has even used Ruth's Otherness slyly, by defining her as 'the Moabitess', to discourage the kinsman from redeeming her. Hence, while the desires of Naomi and Boaz are clearly evident and met, we can only surmise Ruth's consent from her quiet acquiescence to their plan for her. Though foreign, she proves an exemplary submissive to Israelite hegemony.

---

20. Since 'feet' is a Hebrew euphemism for genitals, Naomi's advice is blunt, indeed, and presumes little of the male who is Other for her, than that he wants sex.

When Boaz declares them married, Ruth is Othered by being in the background as a purchase: 'Also Ruth the Moabitess, the widow of Mahlon, I have bought to be my wife, to perpetuate the name of the dead in his inheritance, that the name of the dead may not be cut off from among his brethren and from the gate of his native place; you are witnesses this day' (4.10). She would seem to be exchanging one Otherness, her foreign status, for another Otherness, that of seed-bearing memorial to the dead husband, Mahlon. In fact, when the entire town blesses her, they do so only by stressing the renowned fertility of earlier women of Israel, e.g., Rachel, Leah, and Tamar (4.11-12), and never once use her name. Ruth herself gets lost in this story about her. She is a vehicle, the womb that keeps one dead man alive through the levirate legal fiction and which will yield a future king. Her body is not her own but functions as a symbol in determining the boundaries of the group, as Mary Douglas has argued.[21]

When her son is born, Naomi and the Bethlehemite women supplant Ruth in the mother's role, even naming the child: 'then Naomi took the child and laid him in her bosom, and became his nurse. And the women of the neighborhood gave him a name, saying, "A son has been born to Naomi" ' (Ruth 4.16-17). Ruth then remains an Other even to these women around her, for they treat her as a discharged surrogate. She is just a womb to them; an important one, to be sure, but detached from the actual person, Ruth. Her ethnic Otherness has been effectively muted by her willingness to become another kind of Other, a womb for Israel. Ruth, then, though Other by ethnicity and gender, is not a woman on the edge for long and does not use her position to challenge, still less critique, the power structure of Israel. Instead, the narrators use her to serve their ideological agenda for the inclusion of foreigners. They advance that inclusion by receiving Ruth's foreignness and construing her womanhood to male conventions of utility to Israel. There is in this story a heightened and idealized construal of woman as productive womb, for Naomi and Ruth. And Ruth is praised along with previous women in Israel for their realized fertility.

Ruth's own agency as a marginalized woman is indirect, seen only in her compliance with the will of others. She, then, is not the kind of Other who 'rattles the centre' of patriarchal power structures. Instead, she serves it wholesale. She trades her Otherness, her foreign widow status, to become a mother for Israel. We know that Israel benefits because she gives birth to Obed, the grandfather of King David. But we can only

21. Mary Douglas, *Natural Symbols: Explorations in Cosmology* (New York: Pantheon, 1970), pp. 65-81.

surmise that Ruth herself is better off for joining the insiders as a wife and mother for Israel. Hers, then, is a domesticated Otherness, one serving the agenda of those in power, perhaps at her own expense. Ruth is esteemed in biblical memory for her fidelity to Naomi and for her willing receptivity to Israel's people, customs, and God. Both themes strengthen the self-identity of the community of Yehud in post-exilic times. The authors of Ruth, then, allow this outsider woman a voice in order to bolster their message of inclusion of foreign women married by Judeans. Ruth illustrates the agenda they wish to advance and remains tangled in the narrative constraints of Otherness.

Jezebel

Jezebel is another foreign woman in Israel and a powerful one in that she is the queen in northern Israel, beside her husband, King Ahab. Her Otherness is a continual threat to Israel and the biblical authors revile her (1 Kgs 16.30-32; 18; 19.1-3; 21; 2 Kgs 9.7-37). Ahab was already viewed as a wicked king, but he worsened simply by having married Jezebel, who incited him (1 Kgs 21.25). She illustrates the dangers inherent in the Other. Jezebel was an effective cipher for Otherness because she was a triple qualifier: she was a Phoenician, a Northerner (= Samarian), and a woman. While virtually all the kings of the North are reviled by the Deuteronomistic Historian, Jezebel and Ahab are in a class all by themselves:

> Ahab, son of Omri, did evil in the sight of the Lord more than all that were before him. And as if it had been a light thing for him to walk in the sins of Jeroboam, son of Nebat, he took for his wife Jezebel, the daughter of Ethbaal, king of the Sidonians. (1 Kgs 16.30-31)

While Ruth's Otherness was effectively subsumed into idealized Israelite notions of woman as Other, Jezebel becomes a female Other only at her death. Before then, of course, she was a woman—a daughter to Ethbaal, a wife to Ahab, a mother to Athaliah—but her other kinds of Otherness, particularly her religion, have occasioned more narrative attention. Ruth's sexuality was quickly domesticated in the story of her inclusion in Israel. Jezebel's sexuality remains latent until she meets her assassin, Jehu. And this, in itself, is an interesting narrative delay in Othering her as a woman. When Jezebel learned that Jehu was coming to kill her, she painted her eyes, adorned her hair, and waited by the window, all characteristically feminized gestures for ancient Israel (2 Kgs 9.30).[22]

---

22. The motif of the 'woman at the window' is well known, e.g. Judg. 5.28; 2 Sam. 6.16; Prov. 7.6.

Yet, these gestures are not put to their expected use of objectified beauty. Jezebel did not beautify herself in order to seduce or persuade Jehu. Instead, she was defiant, proud, and fearless. The beautifying, then, was not for the man's benefit. Nor was it for deception, as it was in Prov. 5.3-4. It was done for Jezebel herself as she readied for death. In other words, it was a demonstration of her power to leave on her terms. She stood in full command of her power and would look her best at the end. Jezebel plays up her femininity to macabre effect as it makes for a more jarring kill. At her end, Jezebel draws attention to the excessive use of force on the woman as Other. She resists by exposing the system's use of male dominance as overkill. There is a fair amount of gender play in this account of her death. Jezebel stands defiant before the soldier who announces her imminent death. She is fearless as a soldier herself, yet takes the time to make herself up and await the end. By forcing Jehu to acknowledge that he is killing a woman, Jezebel bequeaths a scathing critique of male violence toward woman. Her actions indict the dominant power structures that would need to assert control by violence. The insecurity of male dominance is then reinforced when the guards who manfully throw the Jezebel out the window are themselves eunuchs, men without testosterone.

As this story of Jezebel demonstrates, there is a pronounced sexual component to the construction of woman as Other. Woman is the sexualized temptress who lines the streets of Proverbs and prophecy, enticing Israelite males away from wisdom or YHWH (e.g. Prov. 5; 7.5-27; Eccl. 7.26; Jer. 2.33; Ezek. 16 and 23). Or, she is the gateway excuse toward religious apostasy. The Deuteronomistic scribes of Kings assigned blame, first for the division of the kingdom after Solomon, and then for the demise of the Omride dynasty, on religious syncretism fostered by the foreign wife. Solomon's foreign wives (1 Kgs 11.2) were the cause of Solomon's support for religious syncretism, as Jezebel was for Ahab's. The notion of woman as a temptress is a pernicious instance of Othering her. By way of contrast, women readers are nowhere cautioned about the seductive dangers of buffed males on street corners or in battle. Instead, the temptress motif occurs only with women figures, where it localizes blame and thereby diminishes male responsibility. For whatever unwanted action results, it is only the woman as temptress who is to blame. She is the one who draws Israelite men away from where they need to be. Temptress women are distractions and dangers, lasciviously draining off (male) Israel's fidelity to its God or its adherence to social boundaries. This is Jezebel. She remains the unforgiven Other who was outcast for the sake of Israel's betterment. She is a lesson on the danger of the Other who is proximate, on the inside, but she also exposes the vulnerability of a society that has to overreach so viciously to purge one woman from its midst.

Esther and Vashti

The queens of the book of Esther, Esther and Vashti, provide contrasting depictions of the power exercised from female Otherness. As a result, the insider, Vashti, becomes a banished outsider and the outsider, Esther, is welcomed in. Woman as Other in this tale is wholesale defined and constricted by male expectations of beauty. When Queen Vashti is summoned before the king's banquet, it is for the sole purpose of displaying her beauty:

> to bring Queen Vashti before the king with her royal crown, in order to show the peoples and the princes her beauty; for she was fair to behold. [12]
> But Queen Vashti refused to come at the king's command conveyed by the eunuchs. At this the king was enraged, and his anger burned within him. (Est. 1.11-12)

And for 'peoples' in v. 11, we should understand only the males, since another banquet is being held for the women elsewhere in the palace by Vashti herself (v. 9). Vashti embodies the conventional woman as Other. She is there to display her beauty, nothing more, and she refuses. By doing so, she brings into relief that woman is treated as the Other, that she has been made an object for male visual pleasure and can refuse to submit. Her entire value as a spectacle for the party lies in her Otherness. The men have no interest in seeing one of their own on display, the same, nor do they want conversation with Vashti. They summon female beauty, and they may even prefer it naked, as only her crown is requested (v. 11).

Vashti's refusal highlights her Otherness to the men, for though she is doing the same thing as them, namely, throwing an extended banquet, she must come for their enjoyment of their banquet. Her beauty is her commodity. It is clearly much more significant than her duties as hostess of her own banquet. Vashti's refusal demonstrates the power of the marginalized Other, that there is more to her than her beauty. She is more than the male gaze that seeks to restrict her. In fact, her refusal shatters the presumption of that male gaze. It even momentarily shatters the restriction of ideas about women to beauty alone, for here Vashti demonstrates that she has an opinion and a will of her own. She has transcended the role of Other that patriarchal power relations have put on her. Her refusal threatens that male dominance and explains the king's heated reaction. He is not miffed or put out or frustrated; he is *enraged* (v. 12).

In the figure of the king, then, man's ambivalence toward the woman he needs yet cannot control comes to the fore. Woman, in Beauvoir's existential view, inspires a man's 'horror of his own carnal contingence'.[23]

What Vashti has done is throw the entire power dynamics of Persia's sexual roles into question. Her exercise of power as the Other has destabilized the presumption of the male hegemonic order. And the men immediately grasp this for they are not merely disappointed that they have been denied the pleasure of gazing at female beauty. Instead, they intuit that their patriarchal privilege has been threatened. Immediately sobered, they exclaim:

> Not only to the king has Queen Vashti done wrong, but also to all the princes... For this deed of the queen will be made known to all women, causing them to look with contempt upon their husbands, since they will say, 'King Ahasuerus commanded Queen Vashti to be brought before him, and she did not come'. (Est. 1.16-18)

If the husbands' hold on their wives is this precarious, then Persia is, indeed, in trouble. The gathered men cannot let Vashti's disregard for male dominance go unchecked, for if other wives hear of it and do the same, the entire power structure crumbles. Theirs is a tacit admission that male dominance, patriarchy itself, is tenuous, a social construction erected by males. The gender dynamics—rejected by the queen, presumed by the king, relied upon by all husbands—are openly mocked by the narrator. His inclusion of Vashti and her deeds is deconstructive of power itself.

There is evident humour in the men's solution, when they send a statewide decree to be made into law throughout the land that Vashti can no more appear before the king (1.19). Since this is what Vashti wants anyway, in effect, they legislate female desire and broadcast their powerlessness to control it. Their overcompensating legislation makes public throughout all of Persia a wife's refusal of male dominance, the very event they wish to avoid. The exaggerated reactions and tumult that this one wife's refusal cause the palace represent a subversive commentary on the tenuousness of all power, male to be sure, but also monarchic and Persian, where you can be queen one day and nothing the next.

Esther begins her journey to the inside as a doubled Other in that she is a woman and foreign to the court of King Ahasuerus. Entry to this insider group is predicated upon meeting stringent, male criteria of beauty and sex. Women compete to be Queen, a spectacle of beauty for

23. De Beauvoir, *Second Sex*, p. 156.

the king to display at his whim. The women of this beauty contest are subject to strict standards of beauty, which the text indicates takes extensive work; 'this was the regular period of their beautifying, six months with oil of myrrh and six months with spices and ointments for women' (2.12). The exaggerated preparations for beautifying a woman parallel the exaggerated banquets that last six months each and lend a burlesque quality to this Persian palace. Yet the prolonged beautifying *necessary* to make a woman competitive in the eyes of the king exposes the male artifice in making woman Other. Becoming a woman is labor-intensive. It takes a long time, a lot of work, a harem, and a eunuch-in-waiting to construct a beautiful woman (2.3). She does not come naturally to the role but is instead fashioned to meet the male ideals of woman. This beauty pageant, then, is a subversive exposé of the societal, male construction of beauty and of the Othering of woman. It well illustrates de Beauvoir's famous point: 'One is not born, but rather becomes, a woman. No biological, psychological, or economic fate determines the figure that the human female presents in society; it is civilization as a whole that produces this creature, intermediate between male and eunuch.'[24]

Further, the woman is still not 'complete' after a full year of beauty treatments. She next is subject to the final test, namely, sleeping with the king: 'In the evening she went, and in the morning she came back to the second harem in custody of Shaashgaz the king's eunuch who was in charge of the concubines; she did not go in to the king again, unless the king delighted in her and she was summoned by name' (2.14). Sexual skill and beauty then qualify the woman to be a woman. She is a well-crafted Other who has passed rigorous inspection. As are all of the groomed women, she is a well-run, two-stage harem for the king's pleasure. The best Other, the one most constructed by male standards of beauty and sex, that is, 'the maiden who pleases the king' (2.4), will become queen of the land. And the narrator constructs this court, with its pageantry, harems, and endless banquets, as the Orientalizing, exotic Other.[25]

Esther handily wins the king's favour after a night with him and becomes his queen. She is now on the inside of the palace, privy to its opulence, comfort, and most importantly, its information. Esther replaces Vashti because she better suits the male notions of woman: that she be

24. Ibid., p. 281.
25. Though Edward Said does not discuss this instance, he offers a trenchant analysis of Othering Eastern cultures (*Orientalism* [London: Routledge & Kegan Paul, 1978]).

Other to men as beautiful and compliant. Though Esther is the fairest of all the maidens in the land, this is no fairy tale. Instead, it is a deft, prescient analysis of the costs of Othering. For the spectacle of Esther's Otherness, her beauty, will serve her other, subterranean Otherness, her identity as a Jew. Because Esther has so successfully assumed her role as subordinate woman, she is well positioned to act as saviour to her people. And Esther's fashioned Other, the beautified woman, means nothing next to her identity as a Jew.

The book of Esther draws a stark and poignant contrast about its Othernesses. While the woman as Other is treated with burlesque humour (e.g. a state-wide decree to control one woman, the extensive beauty regimen), the Jew as Other carries a lethal threat. Constructing the Jew as Other also elicits exaggeration, but this time in the form of hatred. Haman's Othering of the Jews has genocidal intent (3.9). Haman exemplifies the ugly, obsessive component to Othering another. The Jew now is not merely different and distant from him; he is, instead, an opposite and an object of obsession.[26] Mordecai is the proximate Other who causes Haman the 'stew of anxiety' that spills out as hatred.[27] The instigating incident is that Mordecai has refused to bow down to Haman, but the real problem is that Mordecai is the Other who is always in Haman's face. Here we are reminded of Schwartz's dictum, 'Violence is not only what we do to the other. It is prior to that. Violence is the very construction of the other.'[28] The tale of Esther is in no small measure a cautionary one about the dangers of Othering.

Esther uses her position as queen to thwart Haman's plot. She only got there by first assuming the role of the beautiful and beautified first lady of the kingdom. Having been Othered by male construals of woman, Queen Esther can act as an insider to stop the murderous Othering of Haman. In the climax to the story, Esther marshals no small degree of her subjective, tactful power. She chooses the moment of confrontation and prepares for it with prayer, food, and practice; she speaks out against impending violence; she betrays a powerful insider; and then deploys honesty by revealing her ethnic Otherness to the king:

---

26. Wills, *Not God's People*, p. 12. Prejudice is a pronounced instance of Othering another.

27. Jonathan Z. Smith, 'What a Difference a Difference Makes', in *'To See Ourselves as Others See Us': Christians, Jews, 'Others' in Late Antiquity* (ed. Jacob Neusner and Ernst S. Frerichs; Scholars Press Studies in the Humanities; Chico, CA: Scholars Press, 1985), pp. 3-48 (46-47).

28. Schwartz, *Curse of Cain*, p. 5.

> If I have found favor in your sight, O king, and if it please the king, let
> my life be given me at my petition, and my people at my request. For we
> are sold, I and my people, to be destroyed, to be slain, and to be
> annihilated. If we had been sold merely as slaves, men and women, I
> would have held my peace; for our affliction is not to be compared with
> the loss to the king. (Est. 7.3-4)

Before the king, Esther is finally stripped bare of the decorative props
that make her an object of beauty, the kind of Otherness he is used to.
She appeals to him not as this Other now, but as an intimate, privy to the
king's decision-making process. This is a risky transition in her status.
Indeed, Esther herself recognizes that death might be the result, 'if I
perish, I perish' (Est. 4.16). Like Jael, she dares to exercise her power in
one tactical action in order to benefit all Israel.[29] Her moment of truth and
power has come and she is ready for it.

Esther's action is the Bible's paradigmatic moment of speaking truth
to power and it averts genocide. It is heroic and shows that her subjugation as woman, including sleeping with the king, is, by comparison, a
mere trifle. She, too, is a heroine in biblical tradition, a warrior who
deployed her power under the guise of a beauty queen. Vashti and Esther
both transcend the confines of their Otherness and cross a vital, social
boundary as a display of their autonomous power. Vashti leaves the
kingdom, is expelled from the insider group, but desires it. And Esther
crosses a border into Persia, into its very power base. She is compliant
and accommodating as a woman yet uses her insider position to gain
safety for Israel. Had Esther done what Vashti had and refused to be
constrained by the male requirements of being woman, the Jews would
have been annihilated.

In a world where social identities are fashioned by systems of
inclusion and exclusion, the text would seem to be positing, first, that
Othering cannot be avoided, and second, that actions by the Other
require a kind of shrewd prudence that can effect great events. While
Vashti escaped the confines of being the woman as Other, Esther
achieved more by using her power as Other for a cause greater than
herself; indeed, a providential one, as Mordecai had claimed: 'And who
knows whether you have not come to the kingdom for such a time as
this?' (4.14). In the right circumstances, then, the Other becomes an
important, even salvific person for Israel.

---

29. For a sustained discussion on the use of tactics versus strategies by the weak,
see de Certeau, *Practice of Everyday Life*, pp. 36-39.

Conclusion

All of these Othered women—Rahab, Jael, Ruth, Jezebel, Vashti, and Esther—exercise their power as Other inside the hegemonic power in place and manage to accomplish a great deal from their marginalized or outsider status. They all exercise their personal power from positions of vulnerability and, by doing so, expose the power dynamics at work. A postcolonial perspective has allowed us to see these women's agency in terms of their autonomous power and skill rather than their gender. Even Jezebel is admirably free from societal constraints for acting on her own terms, and the narrator, who despises her, nevertheless allows her her moment, too. She suffers a gruesome death but not the loss of her dignity. The goal in analyzing how these women exercise power has not been to recover them and give them a voice. Instead, it has been to listen to those voices for wisdom about negotiating within hegemonic systems, and from places of vulnerability and risk, and by so doing, reveal a wisdom of global appeal.

Ruth: A Born-Again Israelite?
One Woman's Journey Through Space and Time

Anne-Mareike Wetter

Prelude

To apply the Christian idiom 'born-again' to the Moabitess Ruth must appear as a blatant anachronism at first sight. And the 'sin' of anachronism may not be the only problem. By phrasing Ruth's transition from Moab to Israel as an instance of being 'born again', religious connotations immediately come to the fore. However, my motivation for choosing this phrase is a very different one. In fact, the issue of religion plays a rather secondary role in my analysis, although religion can never be left out entirely when discussing the identity of Israel. But the pride of place in my inquiry belongs to concepts of *ethnic* identity.

Consequently, my reading of 'born-again' is a very literal one: it points to the way in which both Ruth herself and the community of Bethlehem erase Ruth's Moabite descent and re-inscribe her identity within an Israelite genealogy. Ruth thus travels in time as well as in space: in order to acquire a position in her new homeland, she must enter into a curious, imagined relationship with figures from Israel's remote past.

Introduction

Both ethnic belonging and the crossing of ethnic boundaries are thematized time and again in the book of Ruth. Scholars have responded to this issue very differently. Some, like G. Gerleman, focus on the 'problem' of a Moabite ancestress in King David's genealogy and propose that the purpose of the book is the 'ethnic cleansing' of David's pedigree.[1] Many others read Ruth as a voice that propagates ethnic, though not religious, inclusivity; thus, an opposing voice to the ethnic

1. Gillis Gerleman, *Ruth. Das Hohelied* (Biblischer Kommentar: Altes Testament, 18; Neukirchen–Vluyn: Neukirchener Verlag, 1965).

exclusivism of Ezra and Nehemiah.[2] Quite contrary to readings underlining the tolerant and inclusive worldview of *Ruth*, scholars approaching the narrative from a postcolonial perspective critically observe that Ruth's 'Moabiteness' is treated as an evil that must be overcome but which, nevertheless, clings to Ruth throughout the narrative.[3]

My own analysis is rather more theoretical and less evaluative than the examples enumerated above. Applying insights from ethnic theory to the book of Ruth, I will attempt to determine how the different groups in the narrative are construed in ethnic terms and if and how it is possible to cross the threshold between them. Focusing on Ruth's promise to stick with Naomi in 1.16-17 and on the blessing of the elders in 4.10-11, I read both parts of the text through the lenses of ethnic theory. I will try to point out how these different parts of the narrative complement each other, both in their understanding of Israel as an ideal community and in their contribution to the incorporation of Ruth into this community.

Looking at what both the utterances of the community and Ruth herself accomplish, I suggest reading them as 'speech acts' that bring about a change in the world of the text through the effective use of language. And since speech acts are always embedded in a social and discursive reality in order to be effective, this approach immediately brings us to what is perhaps the most interesting issue at stake here: Are the speech acts accomplishing Ruth's transition based on comparable discursive and social practices in the world *behind* the text? Or do they present a novelty, a practice that had yet to be invented?

2.   The contribution by Robert L. Cohn in this volume is an example of such a reading of Ruth as a literary example of overcoming otherness, which also considers its social setting from an anthropological perspective ('Overcoming "Otherness" in the Book of Ruth', pp. 163-81. Other examples are Marjo C. A. Korpel, *The Structure of the Book of Ruth* (Pericope, 2; Assen: Van Gorcum, 2001), and Neil Glover, 'Your People, My People: An Exploration of Ethnicity in Ruth', *JSOT* 33 (2009), pp. 293-313. For a reading using feminist and postcolonial theory in this volume, see Carey Walsh, 'Women on the Edge', pp. 122-43. For another brief consideration of Ruth in this volume, which sees her as both integral to Israel and yet a foreigner, see Ehud Ben Zvi, 'Othering, Selfing, "Boundarying" and "Cross-Boundarying" as Interwoven with Socially Shared Memories: Some Observations', pp. 20-40.

3.   See, for example, Judith E. McKinlay, 'A Son Is Born to Naomi: A Harvest for Israel', in *A Feminist Companion to Ruth and Esther* (ed. Athalya Brenner; FCB, 2/3; Sheffield: Sheffield Academic Press, 1999), pp. 151-57; and in the same volume Athalya Brenner, 'Ruth as a Foreign Worker and the Politics of Exogamy', pp. 158-162; and Laura E. Donaldson, 'The Sign of Orpah: Reading Ruth Through Native Eyes', in *The Postcolonial Biblical Reader* (ed. Rasiah S. Sugirtharajah; Malden, MA: Blackwell, 2006), pp. 59-170.

Ethnic Theory and Biblical Israel

From the first verse onwards, the book of Ruth delineates and describes two different ethnic groups: Moab and Israel/Judah. Though both groups had ceased to exist as independent nations at the time the book of Ruth was presumably written,[4] the text presents them as recognizable entities with well-defined borders. But how are these borders defined, other than geographically, and how does the narrative construe the 'stuff' inside the borders?

Primordial or Constructed?

'Ethnicity' is a relatively new term within anthropological and socio-logical studies, and a complex one at that. After just having established that 'ethnicity is one of the primary organizing principles of human history', P. Spickard and W. J. Burroughs lament that all the same, 'no one seems to understand very well how ethnicity works'.[5] A central issue that divides scholarship in this area concerns the choice between 'primordialist' vs. 'instrumentalist' approaches.

The primordial approach to ethnicity, associated with scholars such as E. Shils and C. Geertz,[6] takes its point of departure from givens of human life, such as language, religion, certain customs, and, most crucially, kinship, all of which are experienced by their adherents as 'at once over-powering and ineffable'.[7] According to this approach, human beings are born not only into a nuclear family but just as much into wider social and perceived kinship relations, with a particular language, religion, and set of customs. Primordialists hold that this 'being born into' acquires a measure of significance that is difficult to negate or to explain as the consequence of conscious choices of the individual, as instrumentalists contend.

---

4. Notwithstanding possible older versions of the text, the most recent analyses of the book strongly suggest a post-exilic date for the final version of the book of Ruth (see, e.g. Frederic W. Bush, *Ruth, Esther* [WBC, 9; Dallas, TX: Word, 1996]; Korpel, *Book of Ruth*).

5. Paul Spickard and W. Jeffrey Burroughs, 'We Are a People', in *We Are a People: Narrative and Multiplicity in Constructing Ethnic Identity* (ed. Paul Spickard and W. Jeffrey Burroughs; Asian American History and Culture; Phila-delphia: Temple University Press, 1999), pp. 1-19 (1).

6. Clifford Geertz, *The Interpretation of Cultures* (New York: Harper Torch Books, 1972).

7. John Hutchinson and Anthony D. Smith, 'Introduction', in *Ethnicity* (ed. John Hutchinson and Anthony D. Smith; Oxford Readers; Oxford: Oxford University Press, 1996), pp. 1-14 (8).

Two points are important to keep in mind. The first is that even for primordialists, ethnicity is essentially a narrative, albeit one that gains extra impetus through its proclaimed roots in physiological 'facts'.[8] The second point is that the focus of primordialist approaches is on the 'inside' of an ethnic group, not on ethnic boundary construction.

For instrumentalists, on the other hand, it is precisely the boundary between one ethnic group and another that is most interesting to analyze, especially where this boundary is contested or fluid. They are not so much interested in the exact nature of a group's culture, religion, or kinship patterns *per se*, but rather investigate when, how, and why the group adhering to them gives them an 'ethnic', that is, boundary-marking quality.

The main point of contention between primordialist and instrumentalist views on ethnicity is thus not the question whether ethnic bonds are 'true' in the sense that they refer to genuine blood relations or the like— both approaches affirm that this is not (necessarily) the case. Rather, it is the focus, inside or out, and the issue of conscious choice that divides the two viewpoints. A primordialist view entails that this choice is, at best, very limited; one does not simply shake off one's ethnic attachments or trade them for other, more opportune ones. However, for instrumentalists, ethnicity is neither natural nor stable but created— invented—through the more or less conscious choices of individuals.[9]

For the analysis of ethnicity in the book of Ruth, I suggest adhering to a revised form of instrumentalism. It seems clear that in this narrative, ethnic identity is negotiable rather than fixed: whether wholly or in part, Ruth the Moabitess is absorbed into the community of Israel. On the other hand, the change of ethnic identity is more than a matter of free choice of the individual agent: certain prerequisites apply, and they have everything to do with the 'stuff' that constitutes the self-understanding of the Israelite *ethnie*.

Defining Ethnic Identity

The difficulty remains how to define an *ethnie*. After just having established that ethnic identity is largely an invention and a process, a fixed list of ethnic markers seems a step back. On the other hand, even the

8. Stephen E. Cornell and Douglas Hartmann, *Ethnicity and Race: Making Identities in a Changing World* (Sociology for a New Century; Thousand Oaks, CA: Pine Forge, 2nd edn, 2003), pp. 251-52.

9. Fredrik Barth, 'Introduction', in *Ethnic Groups and Boundaries: The Social Organization of Culture Difference* (ed. Fredrik Barth; Scandinavian University Books; Bergen: University Press, 1969), pp. 9-38 (15).

most adamant advocate of a functionalist approach to ethnicity will admit that the borders between in-groups and out-groups are created out of *something*; some traits common to most members of the in-group or lacking in everyone else, which are then imbued with 'ethnic' significance. Which features of identity qualify as ethnic markers is debatable. The ones most generally acknowledged, besides kinship, are language, religion, and 'nationality', although certainly in a modern situation of large-scale migration and multi-ethnic nations, every one of these aspects may be subject to change and fluidity. Hutchinson and Smith provide a relatively extensive list of ethnic markers, without, however, including nationality. They distinguish six features:

> 1) a common proper name; 2) a myth of common ancestry; 3) shared historical memories; 4) one or more elements of common culture, which need not be specified but normally include religion, customs, or language; 5) a link with a homeland; and 6) a sense of solidarity.[10]

Of course, this list is based on and aimed at the analysis of current phenomena and cannot be taken at face value for understanding the biblical text. The first item, a 'common proper name', immediately raises several problems. The historical situation at the time the biblical sources were written results in a confusing co-occurrence of different terms for the same, or at least overlapping, entities.[11] However, for the present analysis, this issue will not be taken into account.

'Common descent' is perhaps the most generally acknowledged criterion of ethnicity. In the Hebrew Bible, the 'myth of common ancestry' is often conveyed by means of more or less extensive genealogies. These genealogies serve not only to prove the lineage of principal characters but also to supply them with a background that goes beyond the simple 'facts' of reproduction. Essentially, Israel construes itself as the descendants of Jacob/Israel. The narratives about the family of Jacob and about his ancestors (notably Abraham) and descendants (e.g. Moses) are an important part of their 'shared historical memories'. At the same time, they constitute the ideological basis of the current state of affairs.

---

10.   Hutchinson and Smith, 'Introduction', pp. 6-7.

11.   Willi's book *Juda, Jehud, Israel* bears witness to this confusion—all three terms can legitimately be used of approximately the same group of people, yet all three retain different nuances (political, geographical, religious) that would be lost if one decided to favour one of them at the expense of the others (Thomas Willi, *Juda–Jehud–Israel: Studien zum Selbstverständnis des Judentums in persischer Zeit* [FAT, 12; Tübingen: Mohr, 1996]).

Other nations, too, are retraced to an eponymous ancestor to whom they owe not only their name but also central character traits and a predefined relationship with Israel. The account of Lot and his daughters, from whose illicit union spring the Moabites and the Ammonites (Gen. 19.36-38), is a relevant example of this function of genealogy. A sense of sameness over time is implied: Moab is now, always has been, and always will be of dubious descent, prone to sexual misconduct, and, although related to Israel, intentionally separated from and opposed to the descendants of Abraham.[12]

Genealogy, or the 'myth of common ancestry', and 'shared historical memories' are thus tightly knit together in the biblical account. Put differently, the myths relating each new generation to its forebears by means of genealogy form an essential part of the 'shared historical memories' of the group.

Hutchinson and Smith's fourth marker consists of 'one or more elements of common culture, which need not be specified but normally, include religion, customs, or language'. Of all items in their list, this is perhaps the most problematic. Even a primordialist will agree that the decision as to which elements of a culture are viewed as ethnic markers is contingent upon various circumstances and perhaps even, to some extent, arbitrary.

In addition, the term 'culture' itself resists definition. The choice concerning what is to be counted as an expression of 'culture' is highly subjective. As a result, R. Wodak proposes an approach to culture based on rules rather than content. She 'understand[s] "culture" as a system of rules and principles for "proper" behaviour, analogous to the grammar of language, which sets the standards for "proper" speaking'.[13] This also implies that one can become proficient in more than one culture, just as one can learn to communicate in more than one language. Nevertheless, it is almost always possible to distinguish a native from a second-language speaker, and the same may hold true for those born into a culture and those joining it from the outside. The question, then, is whether Ruth confirms this near-impossibility to blend in perfectly, or whether she is an example of the opposite.

---

12. In Num. 25.1-3, for example, the Moabites are portrayed as a danger to both the sexual and the cultic purity of Israelite men.

13. Ruth Wodak et al., *The Discursive Construction of National Identity* (trans. A. Hirsch and R. Mitten; Critical Discourse Analysis Series; Edinburgh: Edinburgh University Press, 1999).

For reasons of space, I will omit a discussion of Hutchinson and Smith's fifth criterion, the 'link with a homeland'.

The last criterion by which to identify an *ethnie*—a 'sense of solidarity'—is especially relevant for the analysis of Ruth. Members of one ethnic group are more inclined to sympathize with and lend assistance to other members of their group than to outsiders. There are two ways to account for this observation. One seeks an explanation in alleged blood ties. To view other members as 'extended family' lays an emotional claim on the individual to identify with them and their problems. Not to show solidarity with another member of the same ethnic group would come close to abandoning one's father, sister, or child. A different approach leans toward the notion that *ethnies* are essentially groups arising from 'shared interests'.[14] This perspective emphasizes that solidarity is always also self-serving: by identifying with and helping others from my group, I also advance my own interests. Inner-group solidarity thus turns from a virtue into utilitarian adroitness. In the case of Ruth, we seem to be dealing with the paradoxical situation that the 'extended family' towards which Ruth displays such exemplary solidarity is, in fact, not part of her own ethnic group.

As stated above, Hutchinson and Smith's definition of an *ethnie* is not automatically applicable to the biblical texts. Still, I have found their list illuminating in my search for markers of Israelite identity in the book of Ruth, albeit with some revisions. In the following analysis I focus on the first three items, *name*, *ancestry*, and *historical memories*, as one closely connected cluster and then on *elements of common culture* and *sense of solidarity* as a second one.

Creative Speech

As already said, I read the process of Ruth's identity switch as a sequence of speech acts or performative utterances. Since J. Austin first coined these terms in the 1950s,[15] they have been developed in a number of directions. Here, however, I limit myself to some of the basic notions of Austin's original theory. Austin's most essential point is that language not only describes reality but, under certain circumstances, actually serves to create it. In order to sort the intended effect—to be 'felicitous', in Austin's own terms—a speech act has to occur under appropriate circumstances. Not only does the speaker's intention have to be sincere,

14. Spickard and Burroughs, 'We Are a People', p. 8.
15. John L. Austin, *How to Do Things with Words* (The William James Lectures, 1955; Oxford: Clarendon, 1962).

but the social and discursive context in which he or she makes the performative utterance has to recognize this intention. Both the comprehensibility and the legitimacy of an utterance depend on conventions of culture and language in any given context. To return to Ruth: in order for her to achieve Israelite identity through one or a sequence of speech acts, the social and discursive reality in the text—and perhaps even more importantly, behind the text—has to allow for such a change to occur in the first place.

Ruth's Transition into Israel: An Extreme Ethnic Make-Over

Before identifying the markers of identity present in the book of Ruth, I will probe how closed or penetrable the borders of the Israelite *ethnie* are, based on the use of two terms: גר and נכריה. I will then try to assess what role Ruth's promise to Naomi plays in her 'ethnic conversion'. Last but not least, I will ask whether this promise, as sincere as Ruth's intentions may be, is recognized as a feasible and legitimate performance in the world of the text. I suggest that this is indeed the case, but not before the community has recognized that Ruth is as good as her word.

Strange, Stranger, Strangest: The Use of גר and נכריה

The notion of 'strangeness' or 'familiarity' resurfaces continually throughout the Ruth narrative. Interestingly, two different words are employed to describe 'strangers'. In Ruth 1.1, the verb גור is used in reference to Elimelech and his family: due to the famine in 'the land', they went to 'sojourn' in the plains of Moab. In Ruth 2.10, Ruth depicts herself as a נכריה, a 'stranger', undeserving of Boaz's kind words.

In general, גר denotes someone who stays in a particular country or region without any property rights to the land there. The motivation to become a גר was 'the desire for or necessity of seeking out a new and potentially more favorable social setting elsewhere'.[16] גר/גור seems to have various connotations, depending on the perspective and the subject of גור; is the 'sojourner' an Israelite staying in a different country, or a non-Israelite living as 'stranger' among the 'holy people'? Applied to non-Israelites dwelling in Israel, the emphasis is usually on the way these 'sojourners' are to be treated. Calling to mind Israel's own sojourn in

---

16. Frank A. Spina, 'Israelites as *gerîm*, "Sojourners", in Social and Historical Context', in *The Word of the Lord Shall Go Forth: Essays in Honor of David Noel Freedman in Celebration of His Sixtieth Birthday* (ed. Carol Meyers and Michael O'Connor; Special Volume series, 1; Philadelphia: American Schools of Oriental Research, 1983), pp. 321-36 (324).

Egypt, the Israelites are admonished to deal kindly with the sojourner in their midst (e.g. Lev. 19.33-34). The latter are not automatically part of the assembly of Israel but may join it at will. The only condition is circumcision of all male members of a household (Exod. 12.48). However, what seems like the ideal multi-cultural society our modern world is struggling so hard to realize has a flip side as well. The accept-ance of 'strangers' into Israel was by no means unconditional. Numbers 15.16 states that 'one law and one rule shall be for you and for the sojourner who sojourns with you'. And while it sounds appealing that the law is unbiased against all who live in the land, this verse also suggests that the 'sojourner' could not remain a 'stranger' for long. With the privilege of living under the covenant came the duty to follow the rules of the country, to adapt, to leave one's own cultural and religious roots behind. Immigrants received a warm welcome in Israel (at least in theory), but the pressure to assimilate was as strong then as it is now.

Of course, גור/גר can be used from a different perspective as well, to describe the 'insiders' of Israel living as 'strangers' in another country. On several occasions, first Abraham (Gen. 12.10; 20.1; 21.23, 34) and later the sons of Jacob (Gen. 47.4; Exod. 6.4) are described as 'sojourn-ing'. In Gen. 12.10 and 47.4, the motivation for their move is a famine, just like it was for Elimelech. Genesis 12.10, shows particularly striking similarities with Ruth 1.1. On the one hand, to be put on a par with these revered patriarchs suggests a high degree of approval of Elimelech's actions. On the other hand, even though Abraham's and Jacob's family seem to have been able to retain their own lifestyle even in a foreign country, the outcome of their sojourns often proved disastrous. Thus, while גור is principally a neutral term indicating a stay in another country for whatever reason, it seems a practice not to be recommended for any descendant of Abraham. Trouble has come of it in the past, and trouble will come of it in the case of Elimelech as well.

Interestingly, Ruth's role in Bethlehem is not described using גור but a different word. Ruth herself uses the term נכריה in expressing her gratitude towards Boaz (2.10): 'And she fell on her face and bowed to the ground, and said to him: "Why have I found favor in your eyes that you should recognize me (להכירני), me, a stranger (נכריה)?"'

נכרי is a much more charged term than גר. It describes persons, habits, objects, or gods who are *unfamiliar* from the perspective of the author or the protagonists. The term implies both menace and inferiority. In Deuteronomy, foreigners described as נכרי are treated as a necessary evil, but they do not enjoy the same rights as the native Israelites (Deut. 14.21; 15.3; 23.20). And although it was sometimes possible for a נכרי to approach the temple of YHWH and pray to him (1 Kgs 8.41-43), this is an exception to the rule that generally, individuals, especially women who are described as נכרי, tend to lure believers away from YHWH (1 Kgs 11.1-8; Prov. 2.16; 5.20; 6.24). One might even wonder whether נכרי always denotes a 'foreigner' in the ethnic sense or simply someone who behaves in a 'strange' way.

In Ruth 2.10, the two aspects of familiarity (נכר) and unfamiliarity (נכרי) come together. Above, I have argued that גור implies acceptance, but also cultural and religious assimilation of foreigners into Israel. נכרי, on the other hand, seems to emphasize the Otherness of the other, and appears to leave it intact, despite the negative evaluation of this 'other-ness'. To assume, as I. Rashkow does, that Ruth's choice of words points in the direction of a desired 'acceptance into Boaz's clan' is to negate the connotation of 'strangeness' Ruth applies to herself with the use of נכריה.[17] From her own perspective, as well as that of the Bethlehemites who continue to call her 'the Moabitess', Ruth simply does not fit in yet.

Interestingly, there is one other case in which two women designate themselves as נכריות. In Gen. 31.15, Rachel and Leah ask, referring to their father, 'Are we not accounted by him as נכריות? For he has sold us, and he has even devoured our money.' Here, the opposite process is at work: two previously 'familiar' women turn into 'strangers' to their own father through their marriage with Jacob. Is it a coincidence that Ruth is likened to these two women, who 'together built the house of Israel' (Ruth 4.11)? Rachel and Leah had to become 'strangers' to their father before they could become foremothers of Israel. Likewise, Ruth must be familiarized into Israel (and, by implication estrange herself from her father and mother; see Ruth 2.11) in order to continue the line set out by them. To do so requires the willingness of Boaz, and the rest of Bethlehem, to 'recognize' her. That they do so in due time seems obvious, although the fact that Ruth fades out of the narrative and is replaced by Naomi as mother of Obed does give one pause. There are several moments marking Ruth's transition into Israel: her vow to Naomi, the encounter with Boaz, and finally, of course, the birth of Obed.

Your People, My People: Solidarity and Common Culture in Ruth
I want to focus on two markers of ethnicity that are difficult to identify in the book of Ruth: *elements of common culture* and *a sense of solidarity*. The entire narrative is conspicuously silent on anything that relates to

---

17. Ilona N. Rashkow, 'Ruth: The Discourse of Power and the Power of Dis-course', in *A Feminist Companion to Ruth* (ed. Athalya Brenner; FCB, 1/3; Sheffield: Sheffield Academic Press, 1999), pp. 26-41 (35).

Israelite 'folklore', with the odd exception of the custom of exchanging sandals to confirm a legal transaction (4.7-8). And while instances of *solidarity* are certainly present in the narrative, they rarely occur between individuals of the same ethnic group. A term that does appear at key moments in the narrative, and that has often been acknowledged as central to the identity of Israel developed there (and elsewhere), is the notion of *ḥesed*.

Its first occurrence is in 1.8, where Naomi commends her daughters-in-law's *ḥesed* towards her and her sons. The second is in 2.20, where it is YHWH's *ḥesed* that Naomi is acclaiming. The third and last occurrence is again connected to Ruth, in Boaz's exclamation of praise about the Moabitess' choice to court him instead of some young 'stud'. My thesis, then, is that both the *customs* and the *solidarity* that should characterize the community of Israel do not find their most eloquent expression in actions or utterances of *Israelite* characters, but in Ruth's promise of *ḥesed* to Naomi in 1.16-17 and in the way she then *performs* this utterance in the rest of the narrative. Interestingly and somewhat disturbingly, Ruth's praiseworthy behaviour is annexed as an expression of the Israelite ethical code. Ruth's promise to Naomi in 1.16-17 is too well known to quote in its entirety. In it, Ruth pledges her allegiance to Naomi and her God (or gods), causing some commentators to read her words as a very early proselyte vow. However, even a quick glance at the exact formulation reveals that religion is only one of the items Ruth addresses, alongside a whole list of features of ethnic attachment—people, homeland, and burial place.

I will attempt to show that Ruth's vow has little to do with religion at all, at least if 'religion' is understood in the sense of a personal devotion to YHWH. Rather, I approach Ruth's words as a speech act through which Ruth makes herself part of the Israelite *ethnie* by putting into practice a central ideal, or custom, of this *ethnie*: *ḥesed*. In terms of the text itself, it is the *ḥesed* Ruth exhibits that is the 'common culture' of Israel envisioned in the text, much more so than specific customs, style of dress, or the like.

So far, I have refrained from giving a translation of *ḥesed*. N. Glueck calls it a reciprocal 'rights-and-duties-relationship' that springs from legal rather than moral or religious duty.[18] K. D. Sakenfeld prefers to speak of responsibility rather than duty, arguing that *ḥesed* is performed

---

18. Nelson Glueck, *Das Wort hesed im alttestamentlichen Sprachgebrauche als menschliche und göttliche gemeinschaftsgemäße Verhaltensweise* (BZAW, 47; Giessen: Alfred Töpelmann, 1927).

by a 'situationally superior' on a 'situationally inferior party', with the superior party always retaining the freedom *not* to act.[19] Both scholars also recognize a religious component to *ḥesed*. As Glueck puts it:

> *Ḥesed* does not consist of correct sacrificial practices or outward piety, but rather of moral-religious conduct, of the devoted fulfillment of the divine ethical commandments. In that sense, there is no difference between *ḥesed* as inter-human practice and *ḥesed* of humans towards God.[20]

Similarly, in a linguistic analysis of *ḥesed*, G. C. Clark emphasizes that *ḥesed* 'is a characteristic of God rather than human beings'; nonetheless, 'Yahweh expects his people to emulate this quality that he so frequently demonstrates, even though people's expression of it can be only a pale reflection of Yahweh's'.[21]

Reading these reflections on the use of *ḥesed* in the Hebrew Bible against the background of ethnic theory, I would suggest that *ḥesed* forms a bridge between the ethnic markers of *solidarity*, on the one hand, and *common culture*, on the other. *Ḥesed* is specifically Israelite, divinely inspired solidarity. Ideally, it is not grounded in blood ties or common interests but based on YHWH's example and commandments. As such, it cannot be conceived apart from the notion of *common culture*, of which religion is an important aspect.

By remaining loyal to Naomi, and later to Boaz as well, Ruth becomes the book's most prominent practitioner of *ḥesed*, the particularly Israelite version of *solidarity*. She displays, in the words of Bush, that 'quality of kindness, graciousness, and loyalty that goes beyond the call of duty'.[22] 'Beyond the call of duty' is, in the case of Ruth, beyond ethnic boundaries. Solidarity within one's own ethnic group is not surprising; it is, in fact, one of the markers of an *ethnie* without which the group as a whole could hardly hope to survive. As already elaborated, this 'unexceptional' solidarity is based both on the notion of common ancestry, appealing to an emotional bond, and/or on the more mundane notion of common interests. It is this intra-ethnic solidarity on which the laws of the levirate and redemption depend. However, neither one of these motivations applies to Ruth. And yet, she shows far-reaching solidarity with the fate of at least one individual from a different *ethnie*, thereby not only

19. Katharine D. Sakenfeld, *The Meaning of Hesed in the Hebrew Bible* (HSM, 17; Missoula, MT: Scholars Press, 1978), p. 234.

20. Glueck, *Wort hesed*, p. 23 (author's translation).

21. Gordon R. Clark, *The Word Hesed in the Hebrew Bible* (JSOTSup, 157; Sheffield: JSOT, 1993), p. 267.

22. Bush, *Ruth, Esther*, p. 52.

declaring a share in the kinship bonds and common interests of that *ethnie* but also in their very own definition of solidarity: *ḥesed* as a human act imitating a divine quality.

And thus we are back where we started, with Ruth's pledge of loyalty to Naomi. I suggest reading her words as more than 'just' a profession of faith in Naomi's God or a summary of all the items Ruth is ready to accept as part of her life with Naomi. Rather, it can be construed as a speech act not only marking, but actually accomplishing—at least in part—Ruth's transition into the Israelite *ethnie*.

The Blessing of the Elders: An Invitation into the House of Israel
Ruth's transition can never be complete without the consent of the community she is trying to enter. It is up to this community to decide whether her speech act, and the acts following it, are felicitous or not. Of course, we all know that Ruth succeeds in the end. The consent of the Bethlehemites finds its most eloquent expression in the blessing the elders pronounce on her—or more precisely on Boaz—in 4.11-12, after Boaz has claimed Ruth as his future wife. It is here that the three first items of ethnic identity, a *common proper name*, a *myth of common ancestry*, and *shared historical memories*, are projected onto or inscribed into the character of Ruth:

ויאמרו כל־העם אשר־בשער והזקנים עדים יתן יהוה את־האשה הבאה אל־ביתך
כרחל וכלאה אשר בנו שתיהם את־בית ישראל ועשה־חיל באפרתה וקרא־שם
בבית לחם:
ויהי ביתך כבית פרץ אשר־ילדה תמר ליהודה מן־הזרע אשר יתן יהוה לך
מן־הנערה הזאת:

> And all the people who were in the gate and the elders said: 'Witnesses! May YHWH give [that] the woman who will come into your house [will be] like Rachel and Leah, who have built the house of Israel, the two of them, and may you do strong deeds in Ephratah and may your name be called in Bethlehem. And may your house be like the house of Perez, whom Tamar bore to Judah, from the seed that YHWH gives you from this young woman.'

In just two verses, the elders move with giant steps through the history of Israel. And here and elsewhere in the narrative, Ruth is connected implicitly or explicitly to characters from Israel's past.

The names mentioned here explicitly—Rachel, Leah, Tamar, Judah, and Perez—are all connected to the process of building the house of Jacob/Israel. The characters implied in other parts of the narrative, notably Abraham and Rebekah, symbolize the willingness to follow a divine calling into an unknown country. I suggest that, together with Ruth, they encompass the past and the future of Israel, construed both as a kinship-group and a community sharing specific historical memories. In these memories, the ethical principle of *hesed* is supplemented by the ideal of leaving behind one's native country, whether in response to a divine calling or because an ethics governed by *hesed* demands it, and of building the house of Israel.

Building the House of Israel and Living in It

Let me start with the last point, the construction of the house of Israel. All individuals mentioned by the elders—Boaz, Rachel, Leah, Tamar, Judah, and Perez—are explicitly connected to a 'house', whether that house is a household in the literal sense or a more metaphorical entity (Israel). Even Bethlehem as the 'house of bread' could be construed as one more variation of this theme. בית has a range of connotations here, which overlap in part but also differ on significant points.

Interestingly, the term בית אב is absent in Ruth.[23] K. Butting argues that one of the main themes of the book is the failure of the בית אב ('father's house') to provide a future for Naomi and Ruth, and, effectively, for Israel as a whole.[24] Paradoxically, Boaz's house is not a בית אב in the true sense until Ruth enters it and helps Boaz become a father. In the book of Ruth, then, the houses of individual fathers (Elimelech, Boaz, Judah, and Perez) cannot be conflated with the concept of the בית אב as the physical and ideological place where *male* identity is formed and cherished.[25]

---

23. This absence is all the more surprising considering the mention of a mother's house (בית אם) in Ruth 1.8. Here, Naomi urges her daughters-in-law to return to their 'mother's house', much like Rebekah ran to her mother's house after her encounter with the servant of Abraham (Gen. 24.28). This has been read as a hint that Ruth is written from a female perspective (see Athalya Brenner and Fokkelien van Dijk-Hemmes [eds.], *On Gendering Texts: Female and Male Voices in the Hebrew Bible* [*BibInt* Series, 1; Leiden: Brill, 1993], pp. 94, 103; Irmtraud Fischer, 'The Book of Ruth: A "Feminist" Commentary to the Torah?', in Brenner [ed.], *A Feminist Companion to Ruth and Esther*, pp. 24-49).

24. Klara Butting, *Die Buchstaben werden sich noch wundern: Innerbiblische Kritik als Wegweisung feministischer Hermeneutik* (Alektor-Hochschulschriften; Berlin: Alektor, 1993), p. 45.

25. The social, ethnic, dynastic, and gender implications of the בית אב as the physical and breeding ground of Israelite (male) identity are well researched. Shunya Bendor offers a thorough study of the structure and social role of the בית אב in different stages of the history of ancient Israel (*The Social Structure of Ancient Israel: The Institution of the Family [beit ʾab] from the Settlement to the End of the Monarchy* [Jerusalem Biblical Studies, 7; Jerusalem: Simor, 1996]).

The ideological component of the בית אב has been pointed out and criticized in studies by, e.g. Carol Meyers ('"To Her Mother's House": Considering a

This is not to say, however, that in the book of Ruth the 'house' has nothing to do with *Israelite* identity. At least one house mentioned by the elders has a crucial double role to play in this regard: the house of Israel, which can refer to the literal household of Isaac's son Jacob/Israel or to the people that would eventually construe themselves as his descendants. Strikingly, the elders describe it as a house built by two *women*: Rachel and Leah, the wives of Jacob/Israel. Like the notion of 'house' itself, these women, too, function on at least two different levels. Literally, they have 'built' the household of Jacob/Israel by bearing his children. On a more ideological level, as the tribes of Israel started to trace back their roots to the twelve sons of Jacob, Rachel and Leah were revered as the biological foremothers of the nation.

However, there is more at stake here than biology. Much like Ruth and Rebekah, Rachel and Leah were willing to abandon their own father's house in order to help found a new one. I suggest that through the speech of the elders, Ruth's Moabite genealogical roots are replaced with more fitting Israelite ones. What seems quite a challenge biologically is rather unproblematic on the level of the narrative. After all, Rachel, Leah, Rebekah, and Ruth all embody (literally) the same core values: they are willing to let their fertility contribute to the household of their respective husbands and thus, more importantly, to the house of Israel as a whole. In order to do so, they leave behind their own father's (or mother's) house. This parallel is even confirmed on the level of vocabulary: as already mentioned, in Ruth 2.10, Ruth refers to herself as נכריה, 'stranger'. The same word is used for Rachel and Leah, who are estranged from their father through their marriage to a relative outsider (Gen. 31.14-16).[26] These women's willingness to break with their previous attachments and become strangers, *gerim*, in the land of their respective husbands, puts each of them, including Ruth, the Moabitess, on a par with Abraham, the founding father of the nation whom God called out of Ur and into Canaan.[27]

Counterpart to the Israelite Bet ʾAb', in *The Bible and the Politics of Exegesis: Essays in Honor of Norman K. Gottwald On His Sixty-fifth Birthday* [ed. David Jobling, Peggy L. Day, and Gerald T. Sheppard; Cleveland, OH: Pilgrim, 1991], pp. 39-51).

26. Of course, Jacob was not an outsider in the strict sense of the word: he not only was Laban's son-in-law but also his nephew. But once again, narrativity wins over biology as the actions of both Laban and Jacob estrange the two men from each other.

27. In her reflection on the correlation between 'sojourn', 'ethnic homeland', and 'ethnic election', Elisabeth R. Kennedy argues convincingly that the patriarchal narratives emphasize the voluntary choice of each individual matriarch to join in the

Summing up, as the text jumps from Boaz and Ruth to Rachel/Leah and then on to Perez, the literal meaning of the household of one particular 'father' and the symbolic meaning of the past, present, and future community of Israel continually blend into one another. In the terms of Hutchinson and Smith, the *myth of the common ancestor*, namely Jacob/ Israel, provides the *common name* of the people Ruth is in the process of joining. Simultaneously, it points to some of the most central *shared historical memories*: the literal building of Jacob's family but also, the experience of foreignness that Ruth now shares in. She is adopted into the metaphorical 'father's house' of Jacob's descendants and will contribute to its survival. In this context, Ruth's 'pledge of allegiance' also gains new salience if one does not assume the God of Israel lies behind the אלהים Ruth adopts as her own but rather, Naomi's venerated ancestors.[28] This is, admittedly, an unorthodox reading but one, nonetheless, that accords well with what follows directly ('where you die, I will die, and there I will be buried'), as well as with the further development of the narrative, in which Ruth's ancestor's are replaced with Israelite forebears.

Of course, not just any stranger could have been joined to Israel in this way. But then, Ruth had shown herself well versed in exceptionally Israelite qualities even before she had entered the Israelite homeland. In their blessing, the elders confirm and praise her willingness to build the house of Israel. But long before this official performance, Ruth had proven that she has what it takes, not only to build the house of Israel but live in it as well: *ḥesed*, that untranslatable kindness of character and conduct.

Too Good to Be True?

Reading Ruth's transition from Moabite to Israelite identity through the lenses of ethnic theory, I think it is safe to conclude that Ruth crossed over from one ethnic group to the other. Religion is one facet of this transition, but—as far as the narrative goes—only in its most applied form. Ruth's practice of *ḥesed* towards individuals from the Israelite

---

sojourn of their (future) husbands and to trust that this sojourn will some day make way for a more lasting establishment in the Promised Land (*Seeking a Homeland: Sojourn and Ethnic Identity in the Ancestral Narratives of Genesis* [BibInt Series, 106; Leiden: Brill, 2011], pp. 130-38).

28. For the possibility of construing the אלהים as venerated ancestors, see Francesca Stavrakopoulou, *Land of Our Fathers: The Roles of Ancestor Veneration in Biblical Land Claims* (LHBOTS, 473; New York: T&T Clark International, 2010), pp. 17, 19.

ethnie enables her to function within this group as if it were her own. Whether or not she understands this practice as divinely inspired solidarity remains an open question. But she plays by the rules and can no longer be distinguished from a 'native speaker' of the Israelite cultural language.

Intriguingly, it appears that two aspects of Israelite identity, *ḥesed* and the willingness to leave the safety of one's home in order to build the house of Israel, only become visible in their performance by Ruth, the non-Israelite. It is through Ruth's crossing of the ethnic border that the 'stuff' inside the border is supplied with a name and a face. And in the process, the concept of 'us' vs. 'them' is partly deconstructed and partly filled with new meaning.

It would be nice to just leave it at that— an 'all's well that ends well' kind of story about how greatness of character wins over xenophobia and prejudice. However, such a conclusion would ignore the critical remarks from postcolonial readers that Ruth must leave behind her own ancestors and culture, only to disappear between the lines of the closing genealogy (Ruth 4.18-22).[29] The narrative breathes an air of Israel-centrism that is hard to ignore. Even though the Israelites in the narrative do not necessarily live up to their own standards or have to be reminded of these standards by an outsider, joining the Israelite *ethnie* is presented as infinitely more desirable than remaining a Moabite. Ruth's commendable actions and traits are given a typically Israelite label: *ḥesed*. Apparently, by refusing to leave Naomi or to be seduced by the young men in the fields, Ruth is not following the customs of her homeland but abides by the superior Israelite ethical code. Her actions are lauded but, at the same time, confiscated as expressions of Israelite rather than Moabite identity.

And there is a second objection to an all too idyllic interpretation of *Ruth*. How does the 'come-join-us' policy that seems to characterize this piece of literature fit in with the historical background in which it was conceived? Do not the roughly contemporaneous books of Ezra and Nehemiah shed a very different light on Israel's willingness to accept strangers, especially strange women, into its midst?

Perhaps at least part of the answer can be found in the second theoretical 'leg' of my essay: speech act theory. I have argued that Ruth's pledge to Naomi is a speech act that is felicitous both due to its rootedness in real actions (i.e. her *ḥesed*), which confirm Ruth's sincerity, and to the corresponding speech act of the community in ch. 4. Austin insists that speech acts must be rooted in social reality in order to be

---

29. See, e.g., Donaldson, 'Sign of Orpah', p. 159.

comprehensible in the first place and to be legitimate or effective in the second. The question, then, is whether Ruth—or rather the author of the book of Ruth—was able to make use of existing social practices and perhaps even of oral or literary conventions expressing *and* effecting the crossing of ethnic and/or religious boundaries.

The inelegant expression 'and/or' in the previous sentence cuts right to the chase. Was it feasible in the ancient world to imagine religious and ethnic identity as two separate concepts? And if so, was it possible to shed or adopt either one of them by choice? Even prior to the Christian era, mystery cults had already introduced the possibility of choosing one's religious identity independently from one's ethnic roots. However, the feasibility of projecting these later developments onto the first half of the Persian era, when the book of Ruth was presumably written, is not at all self-evident. There are some indications that at the time, 'Israel' had already taken some steps away from a religious identity inherently rooted in ethnic identity towards a more distinct and thus negotiable construal of religion. Indeed, texts like Isaiah 56 or 1 Kgs 8.41-43 seem to anticipate the day on which individuals from all *ethnies* will be the joined to Israel eagerly. Consequently, E. S. Gerstenberger argues that it was more and more the confession of YHWH as one's personal God, rather than an Israelite genealogy, that became the watermark of a true Israelite.[30]

Even if we accept this thesis, however, the case of Ruth remains peculiar. After all, the confession of YHWH constitutes only a small part of her integration into Israel. Much more important are ethnic markers like genealogy and shared memories. Religious conversion may have been feasible within the discursive and social world of Israel in the Second Temple period, but does this apply to ethnic 'conversion' as well? Jeremiah seems to voice a generally shared sentiment when he asks, rhetorically, 'Can an Ethiopian change his skin, or a leopard his spots?' (Jer. 13.23). It seems safe to say that in the ancient world, ethnic instrumentalists were few and far apart. Nonetheless, as N. Glover convincingly argues, the book of Ruth presents the Bethlehemites as just that: 'optimistic constructivists', in his own words, who will accept any stranger willing to adopt an Israelite lifestyle.[31] Perhaps Cohen is right in assuming that ethnic 'conversion' was not an established practice at the time the book of Ruth was written. But the fact that Ruth—and,

---

30. Erhard S. Gerstenberger, *Israel in the Persian Period: The Fifth and Fourth Centuries B.C.E.* (trans. S. S. Schatzmann; SBL Biblical Encyclopedia Series, 8; Leiden: Brill, 2012), pp. 332-34.

31. Glover, 'Your People, My People', p. 300.

incidentally, Rahab as well—are able to exchange their 'strange' identity for an Israelite one suggests that such a cross-over was at the very least conceivable in the world behind the text. Whether it was common as well, and whether the conditions were always similar to those in *Ruth*, remains subject to discussion.[32]

32. Another discussion concerns the question whether gender figured into the equation. Were foreign women more easily accepted into the community than men, or was the perceived inherent strangeness of women *per se* an additional reason to guard against contact with them? I discuss this in my doctoral dissertation, 'Judging by Her: Reconfiguring Israel in Ruth, Esther, and Judith' (Utrecht University, 2014). In connection with Ruth, see pp. 81-90, 97-114; for Esther, pp. 158-62; and for Judith, p. 234.

OVERCOMING OTHERNESS IN THE BOOK OF RUTH

Robert L. Cohn

Behind the deceptively simple story of a young Moabite girl searching for happiness in the home of her Israelite mother-in-law lies a rather forceful case for the inclusive potential of Israelite identity.[1] Set in the time of the judges, which, according to the book of the same name, was a period when the fledgling Israelite settlements were most on the defensive against cross-border attacks from neighbouring peoples, the book of Ruth depicts instead a moment of peaceful intercourse between Moab and Judah. It is a quiet, domestic tale in which tolerance and openness flourish, and no one says a mean word. An individual family from Bethlehem domiciles and intermarries in Moab and a Moabite widow, back in Bethlehem, is transformed into a proper Israelite matron. Through this transformation, the Other—a foreigner, a pagan, a widow—becomes one of us. But at the same time that the book traces the deconstruction of the Other, it shows the reconstruction of Israelite identity in response. When the Other is embraced, the book of Ruth avers, we change as well. Given that the book was surely read if not written during the post-exilic period, when 'mixed marriages' posed a critical problem for the small, struggling community in Yehud, Ruth offered a counter-view to the more chauvinistic perspectives in the books of Ezra and Nehemiah. By recasting the ancient past as an era of open borders, Ruth made a claim for a shift in the national memory to undergird a wider Israelite identity.

---

1. For a reading of the story from the perspective of ethnic theory, see Anne-Mareike Wetter's essay in this volume, Ruth–A Born-Again Israelite? One Woman's Journey through Space and Time', pp. 144-62. For a reading based on feminist and postcolonial theories, see Carey Walsh, 'Women on the Edge', pp. 122-43. For additional, brief observations about Ruth as a character, see Ehud Ben Zvi, 'Othering, Selfing, "Boundarying" and "Cross-Boundarying" as Interwoven with Socially Shared Memories: Some Observations', pp. 20-40.

First, let me stake out a general position on the widely theorized categories of identity and the Other. Following anthropologist S. Hall, among others, I take cultural identity to be processual rather than essential. That is, rather than view identity as a fixed essence, a collective true Self based on national memory, transmitted cultural codes, and sense of destiny, and thus largely impervious to the vicissitudes of history ('the Jewish experience' say), Hall argues that cultural identities are constantly in flux, 'subject to the continuous play of history, culture, and power'.[2] As such, they are highly dependent on those elements of national memory foregrounded in order to legitimate current ideological positions. 'Identities', Hall says, 'are the names we give to different ways we are positioned by, and position ourselves within the narratives of the past'.[3] The book of Ruth offers not only a different perspective on the time of the judges but also a new narrative of Israelite–Moabite relations within which to position post-exilic Jewish identity.

Integral to the establishment of a group's identity is its construction of the Other, those who are not Us. A culture defines itself against those whom it demarcates as different. But if identity is a moving target, so is the Other. Perceptions of difference change. Otherness is less an objective reality than it is a way of relating. While there are clearly phenotypal, ethnic, social, cultural, and religious differences among human groups, the perception of difference is functional, not essential. The same qualities that distinguish the Other from Us today may bind Us to the Other tomorrow. As J. Z. Smith puts it, 'Otherness is not a descriptive category... It is a political and linguistic project, a matter of rhetoric and judgment.'[4] Labeling and defining the Other is a means of control. Furthermore, the geographically close Other is a greater threat to identity than the more distant Other. It is there that the 'political and linguistic project' is most acute, there where the objective differences—language, culture, appearance—are least visible, there where cultural boundaries are most vulnerable to slippage.

2. Stuart Hall, 'Cultural Identity and Diaspora', in *Identity: Community, Culture, Difference* (ed. Jonathan Rutherford; London: Lawrence & Wishart, 1990), pp. 222-37 (225).
   3. Ibid.
   4. Jonathan Z. Smith, 'What a Difference a Difference Makes', in *To See Ourselves As Others See Us: Christians, Jews, 'Others' in Late Antiquity* (ed. Jacob Neusner and Ernest S. Frerichs; Scholars Press Studies in the Humanities; Chico, CA: Scholars Press, 1985), pp. 3-48 (46).

Clearly the Moabites are among Torah's classic Others: 'No Ammonite or Moabite shall enter the assembly of the Lord, none of their descendants, even in the tenth generation', the Deuteronomist insists (Deut. 23.4), basing his prohibition on Moabite refusal to provide food and drink to the 'Exodus' wanderers.[5] This 'historical' reason for placing Moabites beyond the pale is supplemented by the rhetoric of sexuality: the Other is often sexually deviant. Moab's eponymous ancestor was the product of the incestuous union between Lot and his daughter (Gen. 19.36-37), while generations later Moabite women seduced Israelite men in the wilderness (Num. 25.1-2). Yet, the Otherness of the Moabites, like that of the other Others of the Tanakh, is not racial but moral, the product of human choices. The possibility of joining the Lord's people remains open, a possibility that the book of Ruth, along with Third Isaiah (chs. 56–66) and Ezra 6.21, for example, exploits. In Isa. 56.1-7 YHWH assures foreigners that if they hold fast to his covenant, he 'will bring them to my sacred mount/and let them rejoice in my house of prayer' (v. 7) and will welcome their sacrifices on his altar. And despite Ezra's exclusivistic demand that husbands divorce their non-Jewish wives, he embraces those 'who had separated themselves from the uncleanness of the nations of the land' (Ezra 6.21). Ruth, by joining her fate to Naomi, does exactly that. She separates herself from her family, her people, her gods, and her land to support Naomi and ultimately redeem Naomi's family.

In fact, Ruth's speech to Naomi on the road between Moab and Bethlehem programmatically sets out the elements of Otherness that she desires to overcome: geographical ('where you go, I will go'), gender ('where you stay, I will stay'), ethnic ('your people shall be my people'), religious ('your god is my god'), and temporal ('where you die, I will die'). Crossing the border (geographical), choosing to reside with an elderly and powerless woman (gender),[6] forsaking her people for another

---

5. On the other hand, a different tradition in Deut. 2.26-29 indicates that the Moabites did provide food and water.

6. J. Cheryl Exum argues that each of the three main characters in the book crosses symbolic gender and sexual boundaries. In the case of Ruth, for instance, both Naomi and Boaz call her 'my daughter', yet Boaz becomes Ruth's husband. And by 'cleaving' to Naomi (1.14), Ruth takes the part of a husband 'cleaving' to his wife (Gen. 2.24), while by supplying her with grain and a child, Ruth also functions as Naomi's 'wife'. This symbolic border crossing destabilizes our familiar gender categories. See 'Is This Naomi?', in *Plotted, Shot, and Painted: Cultural Representations of Biblical Women* (JSOTSup, 215; Sheffield: Sheffield Academic Press, 1996), pp. 129-74 (168-74).

(ethnic), pledging loyalty to her husband's family's god (religious), and promising a life-long commitment until death (temporal), Ruth aims to transcend her Otherness. Indeed, the Targum presents this speech as a catechism that, sentence by sentence, overcomes Naomi's stated objections formulated as commandments that Jews must follow.[7] Over the course of the narrative, each of these dimensions of otherness comes into play and is destabilized. By the end, not only Ruth but Boaz and Naomi as well have been transformed, and the seed of the royal line has been planted.

Here I want to highlight three frameworks or contexts in which the book of Ruth can be read. Each framework exposes in a different way the reconstruction of identity to which the book bears witness. The first of these is rhetorical. By means of a series of questions lodged in the book's highly dialogical prose,[8] individual identities are interrogated. The answers that these questions provoke chart a path toward self-redefinition. The second framework is intertextual and exegetical. Through both direct references and allusions, Ruth is aligned with and compared to Israelite and Moabite forbears. In fact, the links appear so purposeful that the book might be read as a commentary on Torah and a revisioning of sacred history. Thirdly, the story may be seen as a representation of a social process of identity transformation, which takes place during liminal intervals. Features of the tale jibe tellingly with theories on the processes of immigration, the 'carnivalesque', and rites of passage. In each, social structure gives way to openness before reconstituting itself in a new form.

First, then, the rhetorical framework. In a perceptive essay on Ruth, E. Lee contends that individuals form their identities in dialogue with others in a process of confirmation and disconfirmation of one's self-image.

---

7. For example: 'Naomi said, "We are commanded not to dwell together with the nations". Ruth replied, "Wherever you dwell, I shall dwell". Naomi said, "We are commanded to observe six hundred and thirteen commandments". Ruth replied, "Whatever your people observes, I shall observe, as though they were my people originally". Naomi said, "We are commanded not to engage in idolatry". Ruth replied, "Your God is my God"' (Ruth 1.16). See Étan Levine, *The Aramaic Version of Ruth* (AnBib, 58; Rome: Biblical Institute, 1973), p. 22.

8. Fifty-six of the eighty-five verses of the book are dialogue, notes Eunny Lee ('Ruth the Moabite: Identity, Kinship, and Otherness', in *Engaging the Bible in a Gendered World: An Introduction to Feminist Biblical Interpretation in Honor of Katharine Doob Sakenfeld* [ed. Linda Day and Carolyn Pressler; Louisville, KY: Westminster John Knox, 2006], pp. 89-101 [93 n. 8]). See also Jack M. Sasson, 'Ruth', in *The Literary Guide to the Bible* (ed. Robert Alter and Frank Kermode; Cambridge, MA: Harvard University Press, 1987), pp. 320-28 (320).

Accordingly, she emphasizes three questions of identity posed to or about Ruth. Ruth's answers lead progressively, in my terms, to the diminishing of Ruth's Otherness. The first is Boaz's question to his overseer in the field when he notices Ruth: 'To whom does this woman belong?' (2.5). The overseer answers in term of her ethnicity: 'She is a Moabite woman', though he adds that she is the one who has returned (literally 'the returner') with Naomi, an identification that rings a bell with Boaz.[9] When Boaz meets Ruth, she asks her own question, 'Why are you so kind as to acknowledge me (להכירני), my being a foreigner (נכריה)?' (2.10). Playing on the root נכר, Ruth calls attention to her status as 'other', which has unexpectedly drawn out Boaz's kindness. Ruth uses the term נכריה in a self-abnegating way, as a foreigner who had no natural connection to the land or its god and thus, no expectation of kindly treatment.[10] Yet, if this self-designation points to difference, it also suggests potential inclusion. In Isa. 56.3-7, the בן־הנכר is one who joins himself to YHWH, who brings him to his holy mountain and accepts his sacrifices. For Deutero-Isaiah, and ultimately for Ruth as well, religious loyalty trumps ethnic difference.[11] Indeed, Boaz then responds by highlighting the geographical, ethnic, and religious transformation about which he has already heard: she has left her homeland, come to a new people, and embraced the God of Israel. But he goes beyond acknowledgment to acceptance. By inviting Ruth to lunch—commensality marking communion—he welcomes her to his world.

The second question to Ruth is also Boaz's, this time not at midday in the open field but at midnight on the threshing floor. 'Who are you?' the suddenly awakened, likely hung-over, elder asks the now anonymous woman who lies at his feet. In the darkness of the night when they cannot see each other, the narrator drops the characters' names, referring to them as 'the man' and 'the woman'. With only gender indicated, they are free to fashion new identities. Boldly, Ruth goes beyond Naomi's instruction

---

9. Aviva Zornberg points out that the root שוב ('return') is used twelve times in the first chapter and again here. But how, she asks, can Ruth return to where she has never been? Zornberg sees this repetition as indicating that Ruth is attaching herself to a past that is not her own. See 'The Concealed Alternative', in *Reading Ruth: Contemporary Women Reclaim a Sacred Story* (ed. Judith A. Kates and Gail T. Reimer; New York: Ballantine, 1994), pp. 65-82 (72). Indeed, positioning Ruth in a new narrative is precisely what taking on a new identity is about.

10. Kenton L. Sparks argues that in Deuteronomy the נכריה was always a foreigner, unlike the גר, which was not an ethnic designation but a social one that could apply to both Israelites and non-Israelites. See *Ethnicity and Identity in Ancient Israel* (Winona Lake, IN: Eisenbrauns, 1998), p. 240.

11. Ibid., p. 317.

for seduction, which was to let the man take the lead, and instead herself issues a request. By identifying herself as 'your maidservant Ruth' and Boaz as 'a redeeming kinsman' (גואל), Ruth seeks to overcome the remaining barrier to full Israelite identity: essentially, she proposes marriage. She thus proclaims a new identity for the man as well. 'She wrenches Boaz out of his ethnocentricity, his insecurity, his passivity, and dramatically alters his self-understanding'.[12] When, in his response, he calls her an אשת־חיל, we remember that the narrator had termed Boaz complementarily a גבור חיל. Like characters in a Shakespeare comedy or a Gilbert and Sullivan operetta clothed in costumes of the same color, these parallel epithets confirm that these two belong together. For his part Boaz, who never put the moves on Ruth during the gleaning season, now must overcome another barrier, that of age difference, in order to espouse the one he calls 'my daughter'.[13]

Naomi asks Ruth the third question when she returns from the threshing floor: usually translated 'How is it with you, my daughter?' (3.16), she literally asks the same question as Boaz: 'Who are you?' Lee reads this question as not simply a request for a report on the threshing floor ruse but also a concern for herself and her own well-being now that her provider, Ruth, has connected with Boaz. The grain that Ruth brings at Boaz's behest is one response; it is an assurance of ongoing sustenance. Another will be the child whom Ruth conceives, who will also be given to Naomi. So the blossoming of Ruth the Moabite into an Israelite wife will transform the self-professed, empty, and bitter Naomi into a fulfilled matriarch.

The several interrogations of identity trace the reshaping of each of the principals. Naomi grows toward the meaning of her name, 'pleasant', from her self-nomination as 'bitter' (מרא) by accepting the help and provisions offered by the Other, her Moabite daughter-in-law. By acknowledging Ruth's sacrifices and then taking her as his wife in order to carry on Mahlon's line, Boaz enriches the meaning of the 'substance' (חיל, 2.1) with which the narrator credits him at the outset. By so doing, Boaz becomes a link in the genealogy of David. And after the marriage,

---

12.   Lee, 'Ruth the Moabite', p. 98.

13.   Mieke Bal notes that Boaz also transgresses a boundary by extending the levirate law. The elders support his transgression by praising him for 'building up the house of Israel' and comparing him to Perez (breach- or rule-breaker), whom we soon find out is his ancestor. At the city gate he mediates between genders, classes, and people by adopting Ruth's perspective (*Lethal Love: Feminist Literary Readings of Biblical Love Stories* [Indiana Studies in Biblical Literature; Bloomington: Indiana University Press, 1987], p. 78). See discussion below.

the narrator at last drops the ethnicon 'Moabite', the mark of Otherness that has shadowed Ruth from the beginning. Though there are no references in the book to the evils of Moabites, in her actions Ruth counters the image of Moabites found elsewhere in the Tanakh. Unlike the Moabites who did not provide bread and water to the wandering Israelites, she provides bread for Naomi. Unlike the lascivious Moabite women who entice Israelite men, she is forthright in her approach to Boaz. However seductively she 'uncovers his feet', she immediately references the law and wants to be made a legal woman and wife. Through Ruth's actions and not only her professions, she has answered the question of who she is.

When we move from the text itself to its wider intertextual context, the overcoming of Otherness takes on an exegetical dimension. Ruth functions as a kind of commentary on Torah narrative and law.[14] A Genesis motif is sounded at the very beginning: because of famine in the land of Israel a family emigrates to a foreign land and when the famine is over returns. In this case, however, it is not the ancestress of Israel who is in danger, but rather the menfolk who die. And it is not an enriched patriarch who returns, but rather an impoverished widow. The employment of this patriarchal motif sets up a series of comparisons between Moabite Ruth and Israelite forebears.

Although Boaz does not mention Abraham's name, he alludes to the patriarch directly in his first encounter with Ruth: 'You left your father and your mother and the land of your birth' (Ruth 2.11, cf. Gen. 12.1). If Ruth's choice recalls Abraham, then Naomi's plight echoes that of Sarah. Both Naomi and Sarah are older women beyond child-bearing age, each accompanied in her journey by a person who will eventually give her an heir. Boaz's praise of Ruth is heightened by the allusion. Not only is Ruth the outsider compared to the ultimate insider, the father of the nation, but in one sense her courage is even greater than his. Whereas Abraham left his family and homeland on the strength of a divine promise, Ruth follows her heart only, in defiance of Naomi's wishes and what Naomi experiences as YHWH's express strike against her (1.13). She accompanies bitter Naomi, who does not even acknowledge her presence when they encounter the women of Bethlehem (1.20-21). Unlike Abraham, Ruth heads into an unknown future with no visible

14. Irmtraud Fischer raises several of the exegetical points I discuss here in 'The Book of Ruth: A "Feminist" Commentary to the Torah?', in *Ruth and Esther: A Feminist Companion to the Bible* (ed. Athalya Brenner; FCB, 2/3; Sheffield: Sheffield Academic Press, 1999), pp. 24-49.

means of support. In her 'patriarchal' role, she transgresses gender expectations.

Irmtraud Fischer also notes parallels between Rebekah's departure from Paddan-Aram and Ruth's from Moab.[15] For example, Naomi's blessing of Boaz (2.20) echoes that of Abraham's servant's upon meeting Rebekah (Gen. 24.27). 'Blessed be YHWH...who has not failed to keep kindness (חסדו)'. This intertextual framework serves to underscore the novelty and bravery of Ruth's exodus. Undertaken not at the behest of the deity, as with Abraham, or of a kinsman, as with Rebekah, Ruth sets forth toward the unknown land against the wishes of Naomi, who does all she can to dissuade her. Unlike Abraham, who seeks to exclude the local Other by importing a bride for his son, Ruth stands by her husband's family despite her Otherness. Here we have an Other who throws in her lot with the Israelite people and god, come what may.

Skipping for a moment to the end of the book, we find not just allusions but direct references to the Genesis matriarchs. When the townspeople invoke YHWH's blessing on Ruth, 'the woman coming into your house', they liken her in prospect to Rachel, Leah, and Tamar, all of whom 'built up the house of Israel' (4.11-12). By adopting her into this lineage, the writer argues that the children of this foreign mother should be considered fully part of Israel. Against Deut. 23.4-5, which forbids the admission of a Moabite 'even in the tenth generation', the book admits Ruth not only to the 'congregation' but to the chosen genealogy.[16] The child is 'given' to Naomi, named by the women neighbours, and claimed as the grandfather of David.[17] True, though the 'son is born to Naomi', the androcentric ten-generation genealogy leaves both mother and

---

15. Ibid., pp. 42-43.

16. Perhaps one of the purposes of the concluding genealogy in Ruth (4.18-21) is not only to create a ten-generation span between Perez and David but also to legitimate Ruth by placing her in the eleventh generation after Lot in a hypothetical Moabite genealogy. If Ruth is understood as one generation younger than Boaz, that would place her in the eighth generation after Perez's Moabite contemporary. Counting back to Judah, Jacob, and Isaac, the eponymous Moab's 'cousin', puts Ruth in the eleventh generation and thus admissible under some interpretation of Deut. 23.4-5. Some rabbinic sources, however, solve the problem more easily by stating that the ban applies to Moabite men but not Moabite women (e.g. *Ruth Rab.* 2.9).

17. And lest there be any doubt, the concluding genealogy places Boaz auspiciously seventh in the line between Perez and David (4.18-22). The writer adopts the *toledot* formula and the ten-generation span of Genesis to evoke those earlier lists and mark the new epoch that begins with David (Ron Zvi, 'The Genealogical List in the Book of Ruth: A Symbolic Approach', *Jewish Bible Quarterly* 38.2 [2010], pp. 85-92 [85]).

grandmother out of the picture. Still, in the shorter lineage of three—Obed, Jesse, David (4.17)—it is tempting to agree with Fischer that mother Ruth is standing in for the first seven generations, given that the women tell Naomi that Ruth was better to her than seven sons (4.13).[18] Against Deut. 23.4-5, a Moabite woman is admitted not only to the 'congregation' but also to the royal genealogy. If Ruth's female identity is finally swallowed by the male family tree, it is also the case that Ruth's arrival in Bethlehem widens Israelite identity by making possible the continuation of the Genesis family line leading to David the king.

In addition to allusions, references, and motifs linking Ruth to Genesis, the book rings a fascinating variation on a biblical type-scene. The type-scene may be defined as a fairly fixed ordered series of plot elements or motifs, which recur in a number of different episodes. The stories of the patriarch's wife handed off to the foreign king, the birth of the long-awaited son to the barren mother, and the meeting of one's future wife at the well are a few well-studied examples. By deploying a type-scene, the writer takes a story familiar to his or her readers with a fixed sequence of events and adapts it creatively to his or her own purposes. Against the background of convention, the new version spins the tale differently, implicitly commenting on earlier renditions. Moreover, as R. Alter notes, 'it is also a means of attaching that moment to a larger pattern of historical and theological meaning'.[19]

The type-scene behind the book of Ruth is the tale of a young woman who seduces an older man in order to preserve the man's family line. Ruth plays off earlier episodes in Genesis and, by so doing, underscores the book's new construction of identity. In the first of these 'May–December' liaisons, Ruth's own ancestor, the eponymous Moab, issues from the union of Lot with his older daughter (Gen. 19.30-38). In the second, Perez, twice referenced in Ruth as Boaz's forefather (Ruth 4.12, 18-21), issues from Judah and his daughter-in-law Tamar (Gen. 38.27-29). The elements of the type-scene may be abstracted as follows:

1. Family tragedy as the backstory: deaths of two husbands and a parent.
2. Survivor declares that there appears to be no way for the widows to find husbands.
3. Fearful father figure temporizes rather than offers solutions.

18. Fischer, 'Book of Ruth', p. 45.
19. Robert Alter, *The Art of Biblical Narrative* (New York: Basic Books, 1981), p. 60. For a less-noticed example, see Robert L. Cohn, 'Convention and Creativity in the Book of Kings: The Case of the Dying Monarch', *CBQ* 47 (1985), pp. 603-16.

4. Widow schemes to entrap vulnerable father figure into sex.
5. Senior acknowledges righteousness of widow.
6. Conception and birth of significant progenitor.

1. *Family Tragedy as the Backstory: Deaths of Two Husbands and a Parent*

In both the Lot and the Judah episodes, the husbands' own behaviour brings on their demise. Lot's two sons-in-law do not take Lot's frantic plea to flee God's wrath seriously: he seemed 'as one who jests' (כמצחק, Gen. 19.14). Both of Judah's sons 'displease the Lord', Onan by spilling his seed and the first-born Er in some unspecified way, so God is credited with taking their lives. Thus, whether as collateral damage in Sodom or the victims of divine punishment, these deaths are given clear motivation. In the case of Naomi's two sons, however, the narrator offers no explanation for the deaths and so prompts rabbinic commentators to suggest that they were punished for leaving the land of Israel or for marrying Moabite women.[20] But the contrast with the earlier tales, which give explicit reasons for the deaths, is striking. In fact, openness to the Other is already hinted at in the uncriticized relocation of Elimelech's family to Moab and his sons' taking of Moabite wives.

2. *Survivor Declares that there Appears to Be No Way for the Widows to Find Husbands*

3. *Fearful Father Figure Temporizes rather than Offers Solutions*

Lot's older daughter sizes up the situation in which her whole world has been destroyed and declares that she and her sister can carry on the family line only by sleeping with their father. Judah sends the widowed Tamar back to her father's house 'until my son Shelah grows up' (38.11), though in an aside, the narrator reveals that Judah has no intention to follow through.[21] Although there is a clear and legal way (the levirate

---

20. For example: *Ruth Rab.* 1.5: 'And a certain man went—like a mere stump. It is as if he went alone because he was leaving the land. He deserted his people during a time of famine and so was punished.'

21. According to 1 Chron. 4.21, Shelah eventually married and had children, though not with Tamar. In fact, his oldest son is named Er, thus perhaps, according to the Chronicler, fulfilling his levirate obligation. See the discussion of Larry L. Lyke, 'What Does Ruth Have to Do with Rahab? Midrash *Ruth Rabbah* and the Matthean Genealogy of Jesus', in *The Function of Scripture in Early Jewish and Christian Tradition* (ed. Craig A. Evans and James A. Sanders; JSNTSup, 154; Sheffield: Sheffield Academic Press, 1998), pp. 262-84 (279).

law) for Judah to give Tamar a husband, he puts off the solution indefinitely. In Ruth, these elements of the type-scene are highly developed and in a way that shows, in contrast to the first two tales, the daughter-in-law and the husband's family reaching out to each other. Both Judah and Naomi temporize by posing the problem of a too young or not yet born son as the reason for discouraging the young widow from waiting. Naomi wants Ruth to return to her mother's house, while Judah sends Tamar back to her father's house. The declaration by Naomi, the sole survivor of Elimelech's family, that she cannot provide a husband for Ruth arises not from fear but from compassion for a woman for whom she believes she has nothing to offer. This heartfelt effort to turn Ruth back, then, serves as the occasion for Ruth's own declaration of loyalty to Naomi and, perhaps, her intention to wait for Naomi's theoretical third son.[22] Whereas Judah sends Tamar away, Boaz, the father figure here, extends a helping hand to Ruth in his field. Though he does not fully engage with her until the end of the harvest season, his temporizing is born not of malevolence but of insecurity, as he admits when he evinces surprise that Ruth would go after an older man such as he (Ruth 3.10).

4. *Widow Schemes to Entrap Vulnerable Father Figure into Sex*
The desperation of both Lot's eldest daughter and Tamar makes them resort to seemingly illicit behaviors to carry on the family line and trick the fathers into sex. Drunken Lot and sex-starved Judah sleep with their daughters and daughter-in-law, respectively but not respectfully, without knowing what they are doing. In contrast, Ruth's plan is initiated by Naomi and carefully worked out.[23] And though both the strong drink that made Lot vulnerable and the disguise that fooled Judah are present in the Ruth story—an inebriated Boaz approached in the darkness of midnight—Boaz becomes fully aware of Ruth's presence and accedes to her proposal. Unlike Lot and Judah, Boaz was not unwilling and once confronted by Ruth, was intent on fulfilling what he took to be a familial obligation. In fact, his apparent quick thinking on the threshing floor about the nearer kinsman suggests that he had already contemplated marriage to Ruth. As L. Lyke puts it, 'In the case of Ruth, Naomi is unable to provide offspring and Boaz steps in for an unwilling redeemer. In Gen. 38 Judah, unwilling to provide his offspring, steps in as an unwitting "redeemer".'[24]

22. Ibid.
23. Professor Yu Takeuchi notes that Tamar, too, has an adviser, the anonymous person who alerts her to Judah's journey to Timnah (Gen. 38.13). Personal correspondence.
24. Lyke, 'What Does Ruth Have to Do with Rahab?', p. 279.

5. *Senior Acknowledges Righteousness of Widow*

Though the Lot story lacks this element, Lot having been silent throughout the episode, Judah belatedly acknowledges Tamar's righteousness
only after he has shown himself to be a brutal bully and hypocrite. He
himself has slept with a 'harlot', yet then condemns his pregnant
daughter-in-law to death for having been one. But he affirms her honour
only after being confronted with the evidence and then speaks of her only
in the third person: 'She is more in the right than I' (Gen. 38.26).
Furthermore, having impregnated Tamar, he has no further contact with
her. Boaz, on the other hand, not only invokes God's blessing upon Ruth
and calls her a woman of substance but also agrees to do whatever she
asks and subsequently takes her as his wife. His declaration to the townspeople functions as an official incorporation of 'Ruth the Moabite', as
she is still called this late in the tale (4.10), into the family and their child
as the heir of Mahlon the dead kinsman.

6. *Conception and Birth of Significant Progenitor*

Moab and Ammon are the sons of two sisters, Moab of the older and
scheming daughter. Perez and Zerah are the twin sons of Tamar, Perez
the second son who, however, emerged first. Obed is the only child of
Ruth. Double births in the earlier tales give way to a single birth in Ruth.
Here alone the birth is followed by two genealogies, the first simply
naming Obed, Jesse, and David (4.17), the second reaching back to Perez
and tracing the family line not through Mahlon but through Boaz (4.18-
21). The first follows on the story that honors Ruth, 'who loves [Naomi]
and is better to you than seven sons', and marks the full acceptance of
the 'other'. By also celebrating Obed as 'a redeemer' divinely sent
through Ruth, the women underline the salvation wrought by Ruth's
inclusion.

In an important essay, H. Fisch analyses parallels and links between
these three tales, though not as versions of a type-scene. Approaching
them as a structuralist à la C. Lévi-Strauss, he outlines the binary codes
visible in a synchronic analysis of the stories.[25] But unlike most struc-
turalists, he proceeds to a diachronic reading, showing the clear moral
advance that the tales map as we move from cave-dwellers (Lot) to sheep
farmers (Judah) to an agrarian society of law and order (Boaz), from

---

25.   Harold Fisch, 'Ruth and the Structure of Covenant History', *VT* 32 (1982),
pp. 425-37. For a representative statement of the method, see Claude Lévi-Strauss,
The Savage Mind (Nature of Human Society Series; Chicago: University of Chicago
Press, 1966).

incest to subterfuge to proper marriage. He also insightfully suggests that in the 'reunion between Ruth and Naomi the old sad break between the families of Lot and Abraham is repaired', out of which will issue 'a new birth of salvation'.[26] The story is thus about redemption—of land, of Ruth's widowhood, of Naomi's emptiness—but also of Ruth's unnamed foremother and Judah's unredeemed pledge, and it points ahead to the Davidic covenant. In my terms, by offering a counterhistory, a tale of union rather than dissolution, the book provides a fresh basis for legitimating an inclusive post-exilic Jewish identity.

The juxtaposition of the three versions of the type-scene spotlights other dimensions of the construction of identity in Ruth. On the ethnic plane, the explicit and repeated identification of Ruth as a Moabite stands against the ambiguous ethnic background of Tamar.[27] Against Judah's fear of Tamar, the story of Ruth is explicitly about acceptance of the ethnic 'other'. On gender identity, the respect shown for Ruth as a woman differs from the dismissive treatment of the women in the earlier stories. Lot was only too willing to hand his daughters over to the violent Sodomites, while Judah not only keeps his son Shelah from marrying Tamar, but calls for her to be burned for harlotry. In contrast, Ruth is treated respectfully both by Naomi, even in her attempt to turn her and Orpah back, and by Boaz. True, all the women resort to subterfuge to get their men, and both Lot's daughters and Ruth prey on them when they are sleeping and inebriated. As Bal comments, 'The sleep of the male is seen as a *sine qua non* of woman's access to her femininity'.[28] Yet, while Judah acknowledges Tamar's righteousness, her admirable effort to carry on her husband's line, he does so belatedly and only when caught with his zipper down. In contrast, Ruth identifies herself as soon as Boaz begins to stir and boldly tells him what he needs to do, her feminine indirection giving way to assertiveness. Within this androcentric environment, Ruth steps forth and is recognized as a woman of substance. Furthermore, as Bal notes, the solidarity between Ruth and Naomi gives 'social security and posterity to the one by means of the sexuality and fertility of the other'.[29] Finally, in terms of religious identity, the repeated

---

26. Fisch, 'Ruth', p. 435. Both family legacies, that of Boaz (Tamar) and that of Ruth (Lot's daughters) thus have in them desperation about the end of the family line. See Mona Fishbane, 'Ruth: Dilemmas of Loyalty and Connection', in Kates and Reimer (eds.), *Reading Ruth*, pp. 298-308 (301).

27. Though most commentators assume that she is supposed to be a Canaanite, like Judah's wife Shua, there is little basis for such a view.

28. Bal, *Lethal Love*, p. 75.

29. Ibid., p. 85.

invoking of the deity—by Naomi, Boaz, and the town choruses—in fact, by everyone except Ruth—affirms YHWH's encompassing of Ruth in response to her confession of loyalty to him.

Beyond the world of words created by Ruth's author, does the way the story portrays the acceptance of the Other and the concomitant shift in Israelite identity capture the dynamics of actual social processes? Two recent studies come at this question from different perspectives. Political theorist B. Honig reads Ruth's story as a lesson in the politics of immigration. While others see Ruth as an example of the extraordinary convert who 'reinvigorate[s] the Israelite order without at the same time threatening to corrupt it', Honig imagines Ruth as an immigrant Other with more conflicted emotions toward her past and present.[30] What if Orpah, the ordinary woman who stays at home, is meant to represent that part of Ruth that remains a Moabite even in Bethlehem, Honig asks? If it is Ruth's foreignness that so enchants and reinvigorates Bethlehem, her assimilation must remain incomplete. And like so many immigrants who are nostalgic for the homeland long after their successful immigration, so Ruth's story gives hints of immigrant ambivalence. Honig points to the repeated use of the ethnicon 'Moabite', the disappearance of Ruth from the narrative in ch. 4, and Naomi's assumption of the role of nursemaid. She suggests that Ruth's choice for Naomi over return to her people, her gods, and her mother's house might represent immigrant practicality rather than pure altruism. Would Moabites accept back into their fold a woman who had married into an Israelite family? While Ruth's Otherness shores up Israelite identity, like leaven in the bread of community it must also be managed lest her Moabite dimension, kept outside the border and symbolized by Orpah, flare up within and threaten Israelite hegemony. In the post-exilic context, perhaps Ruth is not so far from Ezra. Ezra demands that foreign women be put away, while the book of Ruth might be seen as a story of the purging of Ruth's foreignness. Yet is it too postmodern to interpret this story as showing that diversity and not uniformity is what gives life and strength to a nation, that immigration is a source of new blood? If, as the rabbis will later insist, a convert's past is never to be spoken of again, then why the preservation of a story of Ruth the Moabite as the ancestress of David?

---

30. Bonnie Honig, 'Ruth the Model Émigré: Mourning and the Symbolic Politics of Immigration', in Brenner (ed.), *Ruth and Esther*, pp. 50-74 (58). She cites Cynthia Ozick as an example of one who expresses the quoted view ('Ruth', in *Congregation: Contemporary Writers Read the Jewish Bible* [ed. David Rosenberg; New York: Harcourt Brace Jovanovich, 1987], pp. 361-82).

From another perspective, N. Aschkenasy interprets the tale in terms of M. Bakhtin's analysis of the 'carnivalesque'.[31] She reads the barley festival and the scene on the threshing floor as a mini-carnival, a time when social hierarchies are upended, subversive views aired, serious subjects mocked, and the bawdy valorized. Carnival season permits the expression of rebellious sentiments that would be considered dangerous at another time but which conclude with the restoration of peace and harmony. The comic spirit, evident everywhere in Ruth in Aschkenazy's reading, carries an antinomian critique of patriarchal society. Boaz on the threshing floor, for instance, is a comical character: intoxicated, asleep, uncovered by Ruth in the dark. Ruth breaks social boundaries by addressing him and telling him what to do, naming him as 'redeemer', and teaching him a lesson in the humanitarian interpretation of the law. This, Aschkenasy suggests, signifies a carnivalesque reversal of roles: the woman asks the man to marry her. She finds the dialogue between the two in the wheat field equally humorous. Ruth's tone is 'playful, even teasing', while Boaz's speech is stilted and formal. We can imagine his 'young workers laughing and sneering at their old master behind his back'.[32] The carnivalesque brings about social transformation according to Bakhtin; accordingly a Bethlehem that has accepted a foreign woman and integrated her into the lineage of Israel is a different place than it was before. Still, I see the tone less comic and the transformation more radical than a carnivalesque interpretation would imply. This particular barley festival was not, like all the others, simply an interlude of mocking reversals. Rather, as a commentary on the role of the Other, it marks a significant shift in social memory, a rewriting of the sacred history to include the formerly detested Moabite within the lineage of the great King David himself.

Let me suggest a third social framework, which I believe better suits the book's data: anthropologist V. Turner's analysis of social dramas such as rites of passage and the pilgrimage process. Turner terms these events 'liminal', intervals that lie 'betwixt and between' the fixed social positions assigned by law and custom. In the liminal phase of initiation rites, for example, the ritual subject occupies a realm apart, possesses nothing, and passively accepts the instruction he is offered. Somewhat similarly, pilgrims leave their usual lives behind and journey with others

31. See, for example, Mikhail M. Bakhtin, *The Dialogic Imagination: Four Essays* (ed. M. Holquist; trans. C. Emerson and M. Holquist; University of Texas Press Slavic Series, 1; Austin: University of Texas Press, 1981).
32. Nehama Aschkenasy, 'Reading Ruth Through a Bakhtinian Lens: The Carnivalesque in a Biblical Tale', *JBL* 126.3 (2007), pp. 437-53 (446).

to a sacred place where previous social classifications do not matter. Having contacted the sacred, both initiands and pilgrims return to society but with a new status. Turner calls the atmosphere reigning in liminal intervals one of communitas, a blend of 'lowliness and sacredness, of homogeneity and comradeship'.[33] 'Communitas strains toward universalism and openness'.[34]

The book of Ruth clearly chronicles a social drama and even one written in dramatic form, if we consider the four chapters as acts, with each act divided into several scenes. As a kind of 'conversion' narrative, the book of Ruth may be read as an extended rite of passage. In A. van Gennep's three-stage analysis of the rite of passage,[35] the first stage is separation, detachment from a fixed point in the social structure. Ruth's initial speech defines the terms of that separation, the breaking of the geographic, ethnic, gender,[36] and religious ties that had bound her to Moab. Having plighted her troth to Naomi, she is yet unrecognized either by Naomi or the women who come to greet her in Bethlehem. The second, or liminal, phase begins, broadly speaking, when she follows Naomi to Bethlehem, on the road betwixt and between her 'mother's house' and that of Naomi. Liminality continues when, on her own initiative, Ruth goes out to glean. When she becomes the provider, the relationship between Ruth and her mother-in-law, between foreigner and native, is reversed. Subordinating herself to and serving Naomi, Ruth assumes a position of humility characteristic of liminal beings that are 'ground down to be fashioned anew'.[37] Also, as in other liminal social dramas, rules and expectations are ignored: extra stalks are put out for her to glean and she eats and drinks with the boss man. While not yet communitas, the destabilization of social structure has begun. On the threshing floor communitas breaks out radically. In the darkness at midnight all are equal; even names are dropped: Boaz and Ruth become

33. Victor Turner, *The Ritual Process: Structure and Anti-Structure* (New York: Aldine, 1969), p. 96; idem, 'Liminality and Communitas', in *The Performance Studies Reader* (ed. H. Bial; London: Routledge, 2004), pp. 79-87 (79-81).

34. Victor Turner, 'The Center Out There: Pilgrim's Goal', *History of Religions* 12.3 (1973), pp. 191-230 (216).

35. Arnold van Gennep, *The Rites of Passage* (trans. M. B. Vizedom and G. L. Caffee; Chicago: University of Chicago Press, 1960).

36. In rejecting Naomi's advice that she return to her 'mother's house', Ruth breaks the natural daughter–mother bond in favour of a socially constructed one with her mother-in-law.

37. The story of the haughty Syrian general Na'aman who is healed only when he obeys Elisha and dunks himself in the Jordan river is another example of 'conversion' of the Other that requires the humility of liminality (2 Kgs 5).

'the man' and 'the woman'. Turner remarks that liminality is frequently likened to death, invisibility, and darkness. Here in the darkness is a moment of pure possibility in which former identities are upended and a new relationship is formed. The woman takes the lead and tells the man what to do. As threshold people, they slip through the normal social classifications. His status as elder and landowner gives way to the prospect of a May–December marriage. Ruth breaks out of her otherness and female humility by instructing Boaz, and Boaz recognizes her free, unconventional choice of an older man. Boundaries of age, gender, and ethnicity are cast aside. Whereas in the cases of Lot and Judah conniving women forced such a union upon vulnerable seniors, here, as simply man and woman, Boaz accepts Ruth's proposal and overcomes the difference in age between them. Of course, even before the night is out, structure reimposes itself, as happens in the final phase of a rite, when Boaz cites the law and the city gate as the proper sites for resolution of the problem.

Yet the resolution itself indicates how much things have changed in Bethlehem, how tradition bends to encompass the Other. Though communitas is fleeting, the experience changes all of the actors. Against the formal legal backdrop of the city gate with ten elders present, Boaz flummoxes the hapless and nameless nearer kinsman. He first pressures the kinsman to redeem Elimelech's land and then pulls the deal out from under him by announcing, without any clear legal justification, that he 'must also acquire the wife of the deceased, so as to perpetuate the name of the deceased upon his estate' (4.5). When the nearer kinsman backs out, Boaz moves in. Scholars have long read this requirement as a form of levirate (brother-in-law) marriage, the Deuteronomic solution for a married man who dies childless: his brother is to marry the widow and raise a child in the name of the deceased (Deut. 25.5-10). More recently, however, some scholars, including T. Eskenazi, have argued against understanding the Boaz–Ruth marriage in this way. She ably summarizes the reasons.[38] Among them are the facts that the word יבם (brother-in-law), present in the Bible only in Deut. 25.5-10, is absent here and that Boaz is not a levir but a more distant relation. In addition, redemption of land in the Bible has nothing to do with marriage, and Ruth requests from Boaz redemption, not marriage. The 'sandal' ritual, which the narrator in Ruth assures us was used to 'validate any transaction', is also markedly different from the sandal ritual described in Deuteronomy, which, in any case, applies only to the man who refuses to marry his brother's widow. Finally, the whole point of the levirate marriage

---

38. Tamara Cohn Eskenazi and Tikva Frymer-Kensky, *Ruth* (The JSP Bible Commentary; Philadelphia: The Jewish Publication Society, 2011), pp. xxxv-xxxviii.

appears jettisoned in Ruth, where the child of Ruth and Boaz is counted in the genealogies as a son of Boaz rather than as a son of the deceased Mahlon, whose name was to be perpetuated.

Yet, the number of allusions to the levirate law in Ruth suggests rather that with the legal ceremony in Ruth, the writer means to modify the tradition in order to justify Boaz's marriage to the Moabite Ruth. So although Boaz is not called a יבם, Naomi uses the feminine form of the word, יבמתך (your sister-in-law), in referring to Ruth's relationship to Orpah, the only place outside of Deuteronomy where the word appears. Naomi's reference to a potential third son also clearly brings the levirate custom to the reader's attention.[39] Furthermore, by freely interpreting levirate obligations to include near kinsmen, Boaz extends the law creatively and then, with equal *chutzpah*, hooks marriage onto the formerly independent right of redemption of the land.[40] To legitimate this new interpretation, he echoes the levirate law by declaring ponderously twice, to both the nearer kinsman and all of the people, that he does so to 'perpetuate the name of the deceased upon his estate' (להקים שם־המת, 4.5, 10; cf. Deut. 25.7). As for the sandal ceremony, the Ruth version plays off the one in Deuteronomy. In the gentler world of Ruth, there is no more spitting and lifetime shame upon a brother-in-law who chooses not to marry his brother's widow. By taking off his sandal and handing it to Boaz, the nearer kinsman completes a simple business transaction and is not judged the poorer for it. Boaz is blessed with Ruth and she, with conception by direct divine intervention. If the genealogies forget about Mahlon, it is because the story leads to the redemption of Naomi, whom the womenfolk celebrate as the mother of Obed. The tight links between Ruth and Deuteronomy suggest that Ruth represents an alternative tradition showing how the spirit of family redemption in the levirate law could be embodied in a human and inclusive way.

Though Judaism in the post-exilic era had no formal rite of conversion, the story of Ruth charts at least some of the dynamics of this later rite of passage. In the unfolding of character through dialogue, we can see the transformation of Naomi and Boaz as Ruth follows out the consequences of her decision to accompany her mother-in-law to Bethlehem.

---

39. Aschkenasy, 'Reading Ruth', p. 452.

40. In his discussion of legal history as a literary trope in the book of Ruth, Bernard Levinson concludes that, 'The representation of the past, along with the allusions to the legal protocols (levirate marriage, land acquisition, formalization of legal transactions), is a romanticized construction with scant foundation in legal history' (*Legal Revision and Religious Renewal in Ancient Israel* [New York: Cambridge University Press, 2008], p. 45).

As the Other becomes one of Us, We open ourselves to change as well. Boundaries of geography, ethnicity, belief, gender, and age crumble as Ruth's behaviour challenges assumptions about outsiders. Set in the period of the judges, when raiding enemies crossed borders, here a philo-Israelite crosses the border. Ruth's appearance and behaviour become the occasion for Jewish identity to show itself able to absorb a Moabite, resolve the poverty and helplessness of a widow, and extend the levirate mercy beyond brother to kinsmen. Here tolerance and openness flourish despite the initial hesitance of Naomi. On a deeper level, as the book invokes the Genesis ancestors, it positions Ruth as a latter-day matriarch whose story comments on theirs. Here the type-scene of the desperate daughter and fearful father is transformed into a tale in which חסד, rather than deception, reigns. Thanks to the intervention of Ruth, the genealogy of Perez, left off in Genesis, continues. The levirate law, assumed but distorted in the Lot and Judah episodes, here receives a workable interpretation. Finally, the book affirms that identity is not a fixed essence but a social process. Whether understood as illustrating the dynamics of immigration, the status reversals of the periodic carnival, or the destabilizing and reconstructing effects of liminality and communitas, the book of Ruth functions to valourize the overcoming of Otherness.

As an archaizing tale that intervenes into Israel's genealogical past, the book of Ruth presents a counterhistory, which could serve to legitimate the position of those post-exilic circles unwilling to write off foreign women altogether. Ruth is not alone in such an intervention. R. Hendel calls our attention to the 'countermemories' of Abraham by means of which various groups sought 'to refute, revise, and replace a previously compelling or accepted memory of the past'.[41] Ezekiel, for instance, presents a countermemory of Abraham by using him to argue against the Judaeans who claim that they, not the Jews in exile, are the authentic descendants of Abraham and thus the proper inheritors of the land (33.23-24). Ezra, on the other hand, disenfranchises the people of the land by making the returnees the legitimate heirs of Abraham (Ezra 4.1; 10.7). The book of Ruth similarly makes a claim on Abraham's memory by refracting Abraham's faith, journey, and new beginning through Ruth the Moabite, the great-grandmother of David, thus showing how the Other enriches and transforms us. If identity is the way we position ourselves in relationship to narratives of the past, Ruth stands as a powerful incentive to an altered post-exilic identity.

41. Ronald Hendel, *Remembering Abraham: Culture, Memory, and History in the Hebrew Bible* (Oxford Scholarship Online; Oxford: Oxford University Press, 2005), p. 41.

Imagined and Forgotten Communities: Othering in the Story of Josiah's Reform (2 Kings 23)*

Terje Stordalen

The story of Josiah's reform in 2 Kgs 23.1-25[1] seems suitable for reflecting on the Other whose religion was 'reformed'. This essay explores literary and mnemonic mechanics of Othering anchored in this text. By Othering I mean discourse producing a social Other as an excluded or mastered subject in order to imagine a stable social Self.[2] In order to perceive the process of Othering, we need to see the text in relation to ongoing collective remembering that located it in a specific space and time—in this case: early Persian Jerusalem. At that point, the memory of Josiah was used to imagine a particular version of the early Persian Hebrew *ethnos* and to marginalize people associating themselves with places and practices that challenged this imagination. These people are Othered in order to be disciplined into becoming more like the imagined self. More distant Others in the story remain ethnic Others in a classical sense. Before going into all this, in Part I I sketch aspects of the genealogy of the text, its composition, and its context in the early memory of Josiah and in the Deuteronomic History.

* I would like to acknowledge my indebtedness in this essay to Kåre Berge, Bergen, for years of conversation on these and cognate matters. Also, I am deeply grateful to Birgit Meyer, Utrecht, for her generous response to an earlier version of this essay.

1. Henceforth, simply '2 Kings 23'. It is common to take vv. 1-3 as the report of the discovery of the scroll; vv. 4-14 as the report of the reform, vv. 21-23 as a note on *pesah*, and to align vv. 15-20, 24-25 with one or another redactional layer.

2. Cf. Bill Ashcroft, Gareth Griffiths, and Helen Tiffin, 'Othering', in *Post-Colonial Studies: The Key Concepts* (ed. Bill Ashcroft, Gareth Griffiths, and Helen Tiffin; Routledge Key Guides; New York: Routledge, 2nd edn, 2007), pp. 156-58.

I

The History of a Memory
The most significant feature of 2 Kings 23 is its place in the religious memory and imagination of successive Yahwistic communities. The story is central to Deuteronomic ideology, and its view of Yahwism as non-iconic monolatry became the classical definition of biblical religion. It enshrines a memory that has been significant for centuries, even millennia, and which now consists of layer upon layer. Exploring these mnemonic layers—earlier as well as later ones—and their contribution to the production of textual sense—earlier as well as later—is an important aspect of biblical studies. It amounts to writing the history of the text as collective memory.

Josiah apparently occupied a significant space in collective remembering early on, at least in some ancient Hebrew communities. The extensive editing of the text bears witness to this.[3] Secondly, the author of the Chronistic History promoted Hezekiah rather than Josiah as the central reformer. Still, by the early fourth century BCE Josiah was so firmly associated with the emergence of 'true Yahwism' in the late Iron Age that the Chronicler could not avoid reporting his reform and celebration of *pesaḥ* (Easter) (2 Chron. 34–35).[4] Thirdly, the memory of Josiah is scant in the prophetic books and the perception of his time is generally negative.[5]

My interpretation would be that there was a positive ideological memory of Josiah early on; it was not universally shared but made its presence felt outside of its inner mnemonic circles. This memory, in

3. See the updated presentation in Juha Pakkala, 'Why the Cult Reforms in Judah Probably Did Not Happen', in *One God–One Cult–One Nation: Archaeological and Biblical Perspectives* (ed. Reinhard G. Kratz and Hermann Spieckermann; BZAW, 405; Berlin: de Gruyter, 2010), pp. 201-35 (217-29).

4. See the discussion in Hee-Sook Bae, *Vereinte Suche nach JHWH. Die Hiskianische und Josianische Reform in der Chronik* (BZAW, 355; Berlin: de Gruyter, 2005); Louis C. Jonker, *Reflections of King Josiah in Chronicles: Late Stages of the Josiah Reception in II Chr. 34f.* (Textpragmatische Studien zur Literatur- und Kulturgeschichte der Hebräischen Bibel, 2; Gütersloh: Gütersloh Verlagshaus, 2003) and especially Ehud Ben Zvi, 'Observations on Josiah's Account in Chronicles and Implications for Reconstructing the Worldview of the Chronicler', in *Essays on Ancient Israel in Its Near Eastern Context: A Tribute to Nadav Na'aman* (ed. Yairah Amit et al.; Winona Lake, IN: Eisenbrauns, 2006), pp. 89-106.

5. Ehud Ben Zvi, 'Josiah and the Prophetic Books: Some Observations', in *Good Kings and Bad Kings* (ed. Lester L. Grabbe; LHBOTS, 393; London: T&T Clark International, 2005), pp. 47-64.

successive versions, would have been the *Sitz im Leben* for the development and editing of 2 Kings 23. Since collective remembering overlay tradition with ever-updated significance,[6] a historical reading must consider this mnemonic process. Below is my attempt to do so for one particular period, but first, I must sketch my view of the larger history in which this remembering took place.

Historical Traces of Religious Change

Taken at face value, 2 Kings 23 dates Josiah's reform to 622 BCE. The historiographical problem in verifying the incident is that no contemporary primary sources unequivocally testify to the reform, and the biblical text is so heavily edited and ideologically charged it is difficult to assess its value as a historical witness to the narrated incidents. It seems the historicity of the event only can be evaluated in indirect ways.

N. Na'aman has made a case for placing King Josiah's agency in the brief geopolitical vacuum between the Babylonian revolt against Assyria in 626 BCE and Egypt's appearance in the Levant in the late 620s or shortly thereafter as the ally of Assyria.[7] In his view, the territory Josiah controlled was not much larger than the traditional tribal area of Judah. Geba, mentioned in 2 Kgs 23.8, seems to be a site just north of Jerusalem,[8] and it is unclear whether Josiah would have been able to exert influence in Bethel and further north into the hills of Samaria.[9] This provides the perceivable historical and topographical window for the kind of events narrated in 2 Kings 23.

No one doubts that the kind of cults targeted by the Josiah narrative existed in Palestine in the seventh century BCE. The problem is the historicity, extent, and nature of any religious reform in that time and space. J. Pakkala, who rejects most of the text as an unreliable source for recreating historical events, points to the apparent removal of Assyrian-influenced cult objects from the temple in Jerusalem as generally credible.[10] Assessing primarily the archaeological record, C. Uehlinger

---

6. For remembering the past as suitable and relevant, see, for instance, Eric Hobsbawm, 'Introduction: Inventing Traditions', in *The Invention of Tradition* (ed. Eric Hobsbawm and Terence Ranger; Cambridge: Cambridge University Press, Canto edn, 2006), pp. 1-14.

7. Nadav Na'aman, 'Josiah and the Kingdom of Judah', in Grabbe (ed.), *Good Kings and Bad Kings*, pp. 187-247 (210-17).

8. Cf. Oded Lipschits, '"From Gera to Beersheba": A Further Consideration', *RB* 111 (2004), pp. 345-61.

9. Na'aman, 'Josiah and the Kingdom of Judah', pp. 217-19.

10. Pakkala, 'Why Cult Reforms', pp. 229-31.

argues there is a tendency toward less figurative iconographic representations of deity in Judah in the late seventh and sixth centuries, accompanied by a discernible concentration on the deity Yahweh.[11] It seems to me this tendency is neither momentary nor absolute, but I assume Uehlinger is correct when locating it in that medium-range time perspective that he calls conjunctural history, following F. Braudel.[12] It indicates that religious change in Jerusalem was not limited to the reign of Josiah. Uehlinger thinks the archaeological record reflects cultic purification rather than centralization of the cult.[13] The sources do not indicate whether or not these changes were the result of a planned 'reform' by a named prince.

I would add to Uehlinger's account that the source material he discusses seems primarily to emerge from religious discourse at high social levels, associated with overarching national or regional processes.[14] Records related to religious discourse in households and towns might look different. I. Wilson has argued that Judean pillar figurines were a vehicle for popular Judahite identity in the reign of Josiah.[15] He still thinks, however, they could have been subject to religious purification, while R. Byrne has argued that these figurines were not targeted by any reform policy or practice of the time.[16] Byrne's view explains why symbols of fertility and reproduction would be particularly important in Neo-Babylonian Judah. Given that the archaeological record has yielded a few pillar figurines after the reign of Josiah, and that artefacts in general from the period after the fall of Jerusalem are sparse, it seems to me that Byrne has the better argument.

11. Christoph Uehlinger, 'Was There a Cult Reform Under King Josiah? The Case for a Well-Grounded Minimum', in Grabbe (ed.), *Good Kings and Bad Kings*, pp. 278-316 (updated version of an argument made in German in 1995).

12. Fernand Braudel, *The Mediterranean and the Mediterranean World in the Age of Philip*, vol. 2 (trans. S. Reynolds; New York: Harper & Row 1972), p. 21. The level of conjunctures involves changes that take place over decades to centuries.

13. Now corroborated by the argument of Ernest Nicholson, 'Once Again Josiah and the Priests of the High Places (II Reg 23,8a.9)', *ZAW* 124 (2012), pp. 356-68. Cf. Pakkala, 'Why Cult Reforms', pp. 229-31.

14. See Terje Stordalen, 'Locating the Textual Gaze–Then and Now', *Material Religion* 8 (2012), pp. 521-24, and Uehlinger's response on the following pages.

15. Ian D. Wilson, 'Judean Pillar Figurines and Ethnic Identity in the Shadow of Assyria', *JSOT* 36 (2012), pp. 259-78.

16. Ryan Byrne, 'Lie Back and Think of Judah: The Reproductive Politics of Pillar Figurines', *Near Eastern Archaeology* 67.3 (2004), pp. 137-51 (145-48).

The Story of Josiah's Reform
The surface structure of the narrative in 2 Kgs 23.1-25 reflects a complicated process of growth. The brief report about Josiah in Bethel (2 Kgs 23.15-18) is introduced as a separate unit (using וְגַם) set in a different space (and perhaps time). The incident is modelled on 1 Kgs 12.31–13.32 and is so dense it seems to presuppose the *reader's* recognition of that legend. The same formula (וְגַם) formula opens the section on Samaria (vv. 19-20), which is set in a different space and probably at a later time. The report on the renewal of *pesah* is thematically (and temporally?) distinct (vv. 21-23), as is the report of the action against mediums, and so on (v. 24), even though it also uses וְגַם to mark its beginning.

Underneath this surface are indications of a linguistic, pragmatic, literary, and historical nature that have inspired generations of scholars to ponder the literary growth of the narrative.[17] A recent attempt by C. Hardmeier to untangle the various strands and the process of their introduction is strongly argued but remains basically arbitrary.[18] If, say, variations between Isaiah scrolls in Qumran reveal something about earlier scribal practices, we simply do not have the criteria by which to identify textual alterations and additions. For example, the criterion of coherence plays a role for Hardmeier. On the one hand, scribes in Qumran were evidently able to maintain textual coherence when altering an earlier text, and yet, on the other hand, they could transmit a text that seems to us to be incoherent.[19] In short, '[t]he problem of sources and dating can only be noted but not resolved'.[20] It remains clear, though, that the story of Josiah's reform was a long time in the making before the closure of the Deuteronomic History.

17. For the earlier phase, see Erik Eynikel, *The Reform of King Josiah and the Composition of the Deuteronomistic History* (OTS, 33; Leiden: Brill, 1996), esp. Chapters 1, 5, and 6. For a recent discussion, see Pakkala, 'Why Cult Reforms'.

18. Christof Hardmeier, 'King Josiah in the Climax of the Deuteronomic History (2 Kings 22–23) and the Pre-Deuteronomic Document of a Cult Reform at the Place of Residence (23.4-15*): Criticism of Sources, Reconstruction of Literary Pre-Stages and the Theology of History in 2 Kings 22–23*', in Grabbe (ed.), *Good Kings and Bad Kings*, pp. 123-63.

19. For correction procedures and practices in Qumran manuscripts, see Emmanuel Tov, *Scribal Practices and Approaches Reflected in the Texts Found in the Judean Desert* (STDJ, 54; Leiden: Brill, 2004), pp. 222-30.

20. Lester L. Grabbe, 'Introduction', in Grabbe (ed.), *Good Kings and Bad Kings*, pp. 3-24 (10).

The Deuteronomic History

The Deuteronomic History underwent several versions and received a makeover no earlier than the release of King Jehoiachin of Judah from his prison in Babylonian captivity around 560 BCE (2 Kgs 25.27-30). As far as I can understand, there are traces of editorial activity later than this, too, apparently down to the early Persian period.[21] The religion of the exiled Yahwistic community underwent serious change, in part because there emerged new spaces for social interaction, and religion seems to have become an important vehicle for constructing the collective identity of the Yahwistic minority.[22] The later layers of Deuteronomy and the Deuteronomic History reflect these changes.

During the final editing of the Deuteronomic History or a little later, members of the Jewish expatriate society in Babylonia returned, with some sense of imperial support, to rebuild the Persian province Yehud.[23] In their ideology, or perhaps their memory, the land of Judah had been practically 'emptied' of people during the Neo-Babylonian destruction and deportation.[24] While this view was not groundless,[25] it also was not entirely accurate (see below). The returning expats encountered the kind of religion that Josiah was supposed to have terminated. Their interpretation, reflected in Ezra 9.1-2, seems to have been that this religion was 'foreign' in origin.

Remembering Neo-Assyrian Judah as Early Persian Yehud

2 Kings 23 may reflect developments during the reign of King Josiah of Jerusalem, but the story was rewritten by scribes engaged in collectively

---

21. See the review of recent discussion in Rainer Albertz, 'Why a Reform Like Josiah's Must Have Happened', in Grabbe (ed.), *Good Kings and Bad Kings*, pp. 27-46. He assumes DtrH was written between 562 and 547, and finally closed before 520 BCE (p. 40). While this may be too specific, I think the general picture would be adequate.

22. See already Daniel L. Smith, 'The Politics of Ezra: Sociological Indicators of Postexilic Judaean Society', in *Second Temple Studies 1: Persian Period* (ed. Philip R. Davies; JSOTSup, 117; Sheffield: Sheffield Academic Press, 1991), pp. 73-97. For the transition from בֵּית־אָב (lit. 'father's house', and according to Smith a term referring to a 'basic familial unit') to בֵּית אָבוֹת (lit. 'ancestors' house' and according to Smith a term referring to a 'fictionalized familial unit') and the social symbolism of exilic laws of pollution, see pp. 80-86.

23. See the discussion in Diana Edelman, *The Origins of the 'Second' Temple: Persian Imperial Policy and the Rebuilding of Jerusalem* (BibleWorld; London: Equinox, 2005), pp. 332-52.

24. 2 Kgs 24.14; 25.11; 26.

25. See Avraham Faust, 'Judah in the Sixth Century B.C.E.: A Rural Perspective', *Palestine Exploration Quarterly* 135.1 (2003), pp. 37-53.

remembering Josiah as the initiator of a 'pure' Yahwistic cult; thus, it was continuously overlaid with new significance ascribed to it by subsequent writers and periods.[26] Different elements of the text have been formulated according to the communicative competences of different readers. However, once entered into writing, the text invites subsequent audiences to make sense of all its elements. The modern scholarly interpretation of the phrases הַנָּשִׁים אֹרְגוֹת and בָּתֵּי הַקְּדֵשִׁים אֲשֶׁר בְּבֵית יְהוָה שָׁם בָּתִּים לָאֲשֵׁרָה in v. 7 illustrates nicely how this works. Readers in the nineteenth and twentieth centuries were unable to make sense of this part of the text because they lacked the cultural knowledge required to decode the phrases adequately. To compensate, scholars mined out historical, philological, and other knowledge, which eventually rendered the readings even more *modern*. Texts must engage the *current* readers' communicative competence and mnemonic habits. Studying the memory enshrined in a given text, one must ask: Memory for whom, at what time, and in what situation?

Obviously, it is more difficult to reconstruct an earlier phase of remembering and editing in 2 Kings 23 than a later one. If the literary process ended in the early Persian period, this setting seems to be a suitable beginning point for exploring the history of the biblical memory of Josiah. Clearly, this is not the only possible way to read the story, but it is a reading that tries to respect the nature of the evidence and to see collective remembering as historical, localized, and embodied. This choice leaves us working with a text that was probably not *very* different from the textual versions we know today.[27] For practical purposes, I will use the text of Leningradensis, even though it seems evident this was not the exact text in the Persian period.

26. This is common for collective memory; see the introduction in Benedict Anderson, *Imagined Communities: Reflections on the Origin and Spread of Nationalism* (New York: Verso, rev. edn, 2006), pp. 1-7 (4). For the distortive effect of 'reading with canonical glasses' upon the apprehension of 2 Kgs 23, see Diana Edelman, 'Cultic Sites and Complexes Beyond the Jerusalem Temple', in *Religious Diversity in Ancient Israel and Judah* (ed. Francesca Stavrakopoulou and John Barton; London: T&T Clark International, 2010), pp. 82-103.

27. These are the Masoretic *ketib* and *qere'* (with minimal differences), the LXX, and the *Vetus Latina* in addition to the Chronistic account. See Adrian Schenker, 'Die Textgeschichte der Königsbücher und ihre Konsequenzen für die Textgeschichte der Hebräischen Bibel, illustriert am Beispiel von 2Kön 23.1-3', in *Congress Volume, Leiden 2004* (ed. André Lemaire; VTSup, 108; Leiden: Brill, 2006), pp. 65-79.

In that time, the act of collective remembering took place in a situation of conflict where returned expatriates saw religious practices among local inhabitants of Yehud as illicit. Therefore, my study of 2 Kings 23 pays special attention to what might have been a *controversial* memory or a conflicted site of memory. I look for places, installations, or habits that were imbued with mnemonic significance because of earlier practice, whose significance may have become contested through a contextual reading of 2 Kings 23.[28]

Provisionally, I distinguish between three trajectories in the textual process. Expressions like 'the historical Josiah' refer to historical incidents in the reign of Josiah. 'The narrated Josiah' refers to constellations in the narrated text. 'The contextual Josiah(s)' is a cipher for topographical and other realizations of the narrative in the contextual world of specific readers processing the text on the basis of their communicative competence and mnemonic habits. One important purpose in distinguishing among them is to discover ways in which they may interact.

II

Imagined Community

B. Anderson argues that *imaginations* of community are, in themselves, politically powerful in terms of the nature of relations or limitations that people imagine to exist in a given community and similarly, for imagined social power, desires, or fears.[29] Shared imaginations provide models for how to perform social interplay. Or, in the words of C. Taylor, they circumscribe social imaginaries that make members of a society perceive a sense of moral or metaphysical order in the way they practice social formation.[30]

It is easy to see how the narrative world of 2 Kings 23 generated a Yahwistic social imaginary in the early Persian era. It portrays an imagined Jerusalemite society that unanimously enters the covenant 'to kee [God's] commandments...written in this book [read by the speaking

28. The focus on conflicted topography rather than venerated texts is a point where this study adds to the similarly oriented and important study by Ehud Ben Zvi ('Imagining Josiah's Book and the Implications of Imagining It in Early Persian Yehud', in *Berührungspunkte. Studien zur Sozial- und Religionsgeschichte Israels und seiner Umwelt* [ed. Ingo Kottsieper, Rüdiger Schmitt, and Jakob Wöhrle; AOAT, 350; Münster: Ugarit-Verlag, 2008], pp. 193-212).

29. Anderson, *Imagined Communities*, esp. pp. 6-7. Anderson studied European nationalism but indicates a general dynamic.

30. Charles Taylor, *Modern Social Imaginaries* (Public Planet Books; Durham: Duke University Press, 2004), pp. 24-25, cf. Chapter 2.

prince]' (v. 3). The image of a society headed by a princely religious leader was historically powerful.[31] The narrated society demonstrates its participation in social formation by celebrating *pesaḥ* according to novel princely regulations (v. 21). Apparently, the early Persian Yahwistic community of Jerusalem did the same.[32] Also, the fears and animosities ascribed to the narrated Josiah could have political potential, possibly being played out in the encounter between Persian-era locals and repatriates. On a general level, there seem to be easy links between the narrated Josiah and the Josiah contextually imagined in the early Persian age province of Yehud.

Contested Places and Practices in a Persian-Era Reading
a) We can realize immediately that the narrated account of Josiah's purge of the *temple* in Jerusalem (vv. 4 and 6) would have had no evident site of memory in Jerusalem in the Persian period. The temple had been sacked by the Neo-Babylonians and the items referred to in 2 Kings 23 were gone in the Persian era. The same goes for the house and practices mentioned in v. 7, the *bamot* of the gates (v. 8), the horses by the entrance to the temple (v. 11), and the altars on the roof (v. 12).

b) The case is largely similar for the *wider topographies of Yehud and Samaria*. In v. 5 the king discontinues sacrifices at 'the *bamot* in the cities of Judah' and in v. 8 he defiles 'the *bamot* where the priests had burned sacrifice, from Geba to Beer-sheba'. Many towns of Judah were still in ruins in Yehud in the early Persian period. Beer-sheba, for instance, seems to have been deserted from the sixth to the fourth century BCE.[33] Other places had been rebuilt. But as K. Valkama notes, there was an evident lack of monumental buildings in the post-collapse society.[34] The general impression gained from the archaeological record is of a severe decline in settlement and population.[35] The rebuilt towns could

31. Cf. the depiction of priestly and scribal rulers in Ezra 9; Neh. 8; Sir. 50, etc.
32. This is the implication in Leonhard Rost, 'Josias Passa', in *Studien zum Alten Testament* (BWANT, 1; Stuttgart: Kohlhammer, 1974), pp. 87-93; and now also in Volker Wagner, 'Eine Antike Notiz zur Geschichte des Pesach (2 Kön 23,21-23)', *BZ* 54 (2010), pp. 20-35.
33. Zeev Herzog, 'Beersheba', in *The New Encyclopedia of Archaeological Excavations in the Holy Land*, vol. 1 (ed. Ephraim Stern; New York: Simon & Schuster, 1993), pp. 167-73 (172-73).
34. Kirsi Valkama, *Judah in the Mid-Sixth Century BCE: Archaeological Evidence for a Post-Collapse Society* (Helsinki: Helsinki University, 2012), pp. 272-75.
35. Edelman, *Origins of 'Second' Temple*, pp. 281-331; Oded Lipschits, *The Fall and Rise of Jerusalem: Judah Under Babylonian Rule* (Winona Lake, IN: Eisenbrauns, 2005), pp. 185-271.

have featured *bamah* cults, but there seems to be no positive evidence for that dating to the Persian period. Any use of the memory of Josiah to imagine derogatory action in the context of early Persian Yehud would have been controversial, as it would have been a century later.[36] Given the general claims in the text and the probability that parts of the area were deserted, it might seem that even this part of the text, if used as a political charter, would not have been very contested in the late sixth century.

The same is the case for Josiah's agency in Samaria (vv. 19-20). The question is not whether the historical Josiah would have been able to reform Samaria, which seems implausible. The point is that Persian Samaria was a separate province competing with Yehud for prominence. The capital city, Samaria, was more populated than Jerusalem and included a palace garden, limestone altars, and imports from the Aegean.[37] There is no way a governor in Yehud could be imagined to have influenced cultic life in Samaria.

The case is less clear for Bethel, where the narrated Josiah pulls down and defiles the altar and *bamah* (vv. 15-16). Scholars debate whether or not the historical Josiah might have had influence in Bethel.[38] Unsurprisingly, during the seventh century this border town had a noticeable Judahite cultural presence.[39] During the early Persian period, the area seems to have been ruled by Yehud.[40] Apparently, the town was not destroyed during the Babylonian crisis, but the archaeological record indicates at best a 'possible, very weak Persian-period activity'.[41] Again, the potential to imagine Yahwistic action in the context of Persian Bethel was perhaps not very controversial.

36. Edelman, 'Cultic Sites and Complexes', mentions a fifth-century solar shrine at Lachish (p. 92) and of course, that of Elephantine (p. 96).

37. Ron Tappy, 'Samaria', in *OENEA* 4, pp. 463-69 (465). Cf. William G. Dever, 'Bethel', in *OENEA* 1, pp. 300-301.

38. See recently Na'aman, 'Josiah and Kingdom of Judah', pp. 217-19.

39. Israel Finkelstein and Lily Singer-Avitz, 'Reevaluating Bethel', *ZDPV* 125 (2009), pp. 33-48 (39-41); Lipschits, *Fall and Rise of Jerusalem*, pp. 181-84, passim.

40. See Ezra 2.9; Neh. 7.32; Zech. 7.2, and cf. Yohanan Aharoni et al., *The Carta Bible Atlas* (Jerusalem: Carta, 5th edn, 2011), p. 134 (no. 187).

41. Finkelstein and Singer-Avitz, 'Reevaluating Bethel', p. 42; cf. Klaus Koenen, *Bethel. Geschichte, Kult und Theologie* (OBO, 192; Freiburg, Switzerland: University Press, 2003), pp. 61-62, esp. pp. 59-64. A somewhat brighter picture for the area in the Neo-Babylonian and Persian periods is drawn throughout Lipschits (*Fall and Rise of Jerusalem*).

Summing up, processing the topography of 2 Kings 23 in the context of Persian Yehud would not intensely contest current sites of memory. Many textual claims were located outside Yehud's influence, and much of what was inside was either not very specific or related to already deserted places.

c) Turning to the *mnemonic topography around Jerusalem*, we encounter a more complicated situation. First, there are the general references to *bamot* that may or may not have been thought to have historical referents around Jerusalem in the Persian era (vv. 5, 9). If the story was used to imagine religious evaluation or action against such sites, it was, of course, controversial. There is, however, no positive indication of this.

Next, the story mentions a number of shrines that give the impression of having been historically significant in the Neo-Assyrian period. First is the shrine for Molech in the Hinnom Valley (v. 10). I remain sceptical about the claim that this site was used for child-offering, but it still seems possible that biblical texts reflect the historical presence of a cult in the Tophet.[42] Secondly there are three *bamot* for the foreign national deities Astarte, Chemosh, and Milcom, all located near the Mount of Olives. It is difficult to verify their historicity.[43] If, indeed, all were major cult sites, it is likely the Neo-Babylonians destroyed them, too, during the two-year siege before Jerusalem fell. They do not reappear in the textual or archaeological record and so might not have been important sites of memory with stakeholders in the Persian period.

The single topographic memory in 2 Kings 23 that would have been most contested in the context of Persian-era Jerusalem are the several points relating to graves in the Kidron Valley on the east slope of the city and in the Hinnom Valley south of the temple mount. The textual Kidron is soaked in remains of what Josiah sees as illicit cult objects and installations (vv. 4b, 6, 12). These areas serve as a burial ground in v. 6, and narrative Josiah's choice of location perhaps was motivated by the remembered graves and chthonic associations that 'would have rendered [the area] ritualistically marginal'.[44] The same goes for the references to the Hinnom Valley and the Tophet. There is a complicated relation

---

42. Othmar Keel, *Die Geschichte Jerusalems und die Entstehung des Mono-theismus* (Orte und Landschaftern der Bibel, 4/1; Göttingen: Vandenhoeck & Ruprecht, 2007), pp. 492-504.

43. W. Boyd Barrick, *The King and the Cemeteries: Toward a New Under-standing of Josiah's Reform* (VTSup, 88; Leiden: Brill, 2002), pp. 196-215.

44. Ibid., p. 33, discussion on pp. 31-35.

between the Kidron, the Hinnom, and the Tophet.[45] In the text, the motif of pollution through the remains of human corpses unites the three. If we follow W. B. Barrick and associate the graves of the Kidron with the later graveyard of Silwan, there is evidence for the continuous use of these sites for burial from the Neo-Assyrian period at least through the Persian period.[46] K. Valkama argues that installations for inhuming the dead are among the few traditional structures that remain in use in post-collapse, subsistence-level societies, and she reviews documentation for this around Jerusalem in the sixth century BCE.[47] Evidently, any attempt at imagining Josiah's reform as a religio-political charter against burial sites in Persian-age Jerusalem and practices would be challenged by families or clans connected to these sites (cf. below).

d) Finally, two sets of *practices* being targeted in 2 Kings 23 might also have inspired controversy in a Persian-period processing of the text. The first is the 'removal' (בִּעֵר) of 'the mediums, wizards, teraphim, idols, and all the abominations that were seen in the land of Judah and in Jerusalem' (v. 24; NRSV). Much has been written on the terms in this series (אֹבוֹת, יִדְּעֹנִים, תְּרָפִים, גִּלֻּלִים and שִׁקֻּצִים) and their historical refer-ents. Following B. Schmidt, I take them to refer to items, practitioners, or practices in ancestor cult, often with a mantic character and frequently taking place in graves and family shrines.[48] Such cults were carried on throughout the classical Hebrew period (throughout the first century CE and even beyond). They would have been present in early Persian Yehud—likely located at the kind of burial precincts targeted by the narrated Josiah. Such practices were set in household and family forma-tions, and these might have objected to using 2 Kings 23 as a charter.

Secondly, there is the practice of *pesaḥ* celebration (vv. 21-21). *Pesaḥ* was traditionally conducted in household and family settings (cf. Exod. 12.1-29). The narrated Josiah instituted a new practice.[49] Peculiarly, the actual habits are not mentioned: the only qualification is that *pesaḥ* be

---

45. A fairly complicated argument and disentanglement is proposed by Barrick (ibid., pp. 80-103, 106-11).

46. Ephraim Stern, *Archaeology of the Land of the Bible*, vol. 2 (Anchor Bible Reference Library; New York: Doubleday, 2001), pp. 340, cf. pp. 337-41.

47. Valkama, *Judah in Mid-Sixth Century*, pp. 273, 106-13, 116.

48. Brian B. Schmidt, *Israel's Beneficent Dead: Ancestor Cults and Necromancy in Israelite Religion and Tradition* (FAT, 11; Tübingen: J. C. B. Mohr, 1994), pp. 220-41 (and the wider framing); cf. similarly Elizabeth Bloch-Smith, *Judahite Burial Practices and Beliefs About the Dead* (JSOTSup, 123; Sheffield: JSOT, 1992), pp. 109, 121 (and the framing).

49. See again, Wagner, 'Notiz zur Geschichte des Pesach', pp. 22-27.

194   *Imagining the Other*

celebrated 'in Jerusalem' (v. 23). We can safely assume that such geo-graphical centralization was not practiced in early, post-collapse Judah.[50] Using centralized *pesaḥ* as a religious charter would challenge Persian-era groups that used to celebrate *pesaḥ* in a family and household setting, headed by their elders (as implied in Exod. 12.1-28, etc.). As opposed to this, 2 Chron. 35.1 etc. reflect a *pesaḥ* celebration overseen by the *bet-abot*, a 'representative' group of family leaders unknown in Israel before the Babylonian exile. That probably tilted the expats toward one, central (symbolic) celebration. A controversy between a centralized vs. decen-tralized *pesaḥ* makes for a fairly clean distinction between newly arrived settlers, whose traditions were in any event reconfigured, and the local population in Yehud living on the soil. Again, the social conflict would be between central religious expertise and guardians of household and family religious habits.

e) Having attempted to identify what would have been contested sites of memory for Josiah when imagined as a Persian-era political charter, we are left with a profiled result. Most of the areas and practices covered by the narrated Josiah were either still in ruins or out of political reach for a Hebrew polity in the early Persian period. The sites and practices that would stand out as contested seem primarily to have been set in household, family, and township religion around Jerusalem, with much of it related to ancestor and funerary cult.

III

Remembering a Revolution
a) The story of Josiah's reform reflects strategies that are characteristic of violent social change. In the narrated world of Josiah, Moses had decreed Yahwism and, we may note on the basis of Exodus 24 or Deut-eronomy 29–30,[51] all Israel had accepted it. Its stipulations had been forgotten, were rediscovered, and are now re-instituted by Josiah, with the elders unanimously accepting this on behalf of the nation (cf. vv. 1-3). Historically, the idea that a book ascribed to a major religious figure[52] would have been forgotten is, of course, unrealistic, as is the idea that

50. Cf. the description of that society in Valkama, *Judah in Mid-Sixth Century*, pp. 272-75; Lipschits, *Fall and Rise of Jerusalem*, pp. 258-71 and passim.
51. Cf. further Deut. 5.1; 26.16-19, etc.
52. For 'Moses' as an institution (I would say: 'icon'), see Frank Crüsemann, *Die Tora: Theologie und Sozialgeschichte des alttestamentlichen Gesetzes* (Munich: Kaiser, 1995), pp. 76-131 (126-31 on the Persian period).

such a book would be unanimously accepted after some 500–600 years. If there were any historicity in the report, one would be inclined to speculate either that Moses was not a generally accepted authority at the time, or the 'rediscovered' book was a partisan memory of the Moses heritage. For our purpose, the historicity of Josiah is not the main issue. Rather, I would focus on two characteristics of this story that confirm its historical memory of revolutionary change.

First, there is the paradoxical tendency for revolutionary movements to claim historical heritage to legitimize radical change.[53] In 2 Kings 23 the heritage occurs through a book ascribed to the icon Moses, and radical change is prescribed in the book. The story also reflects another typical strategy of radical change: '[a]ll successful revolutions end with statues coming down'.[54] After the fall of Saddam Hussein and Moammar Gadaffi it should be evident that revolutions often demand the destruction of iconic installations and the production of new alternatives. The narrated Josiah dismantles earlier places and reorganizes new religious formations (vv. 8-9, cf. 17-18, 21-23). So, it seems likely that the text reflects drastic historical change—although I would not profess to know whether this change occurred in the reign of Josiah or over a period in subsequent times.

b) In terms of textual pragmatics, processing 2 Kings 23 in Persian-era Yehud makes a characteristic statement. The narrated Josiah successfully takes on major religious and political power throughout the classical Hebrew homeland. However, processing that textual Josiah as a political charter for the early Persian era does not seem to produce very strong political claims. The more violent parts of the story in particular seem to have little resonance. Those sites and religious practices that *are* targeted by the contextual Persian Josiah are mostly hit *indirectly.* They are areas in the Kidron being 'polluted', according to Josiah, by ashes from 'illicit' cult objects. They are graves providing bones for Josiah's defiling of the shrines on the Mount of Olives. The only items directly targeted are the אֹבוֹת, יִדְּעֹנִים, תרפים, גִּלְלִים, and שִׁקָּצִים. These are 'removed', not crushed or burnt, and there is no report of killing practitioners. On a pragmatic note, one may say that the Josiah read and

---

53. See, for instance, Jacques le Goff, *History and Memory* (trans. S. Rendell and E. Claman; European Perspectives; New York: Columbia University Press, 1992), p. 9: 'Nationalist movements…[that] inaugurate a completely new "order", present themselves as…returning to the past'.

54. Adrian Forty, 'Introduction', in *The Art of Forgetting* (ed. Adrian Forty and Susan Küchler; Materializing Culture; Oxford: Berg, 1999), pp. 1-18 (10).

remembered in a Persian-era context promotes a charter for cautious religious reform and backs it up with an ideological narrative of a wildly violent Yahwistic past that was primarily directed towards Samaria and other foreign polities.

Forgetting the Other—Through Time

a) One salient feature of individual as well as collective remembering is forgetting.[55] Politically, the most poignant act of memory in 2 Kings 23 is forgetting the people engaged in the cults targeted by Josiah. The effectiveness of that strategy is documented in the corresponding amnesia of a long stream of scholarly reading: I cannot remember having read any commentary on 2 Kings that addresses this issue. In light of other biblical literature, however, this forgetfulness is conspicuous. For instance, when Gideon destroys the Ba'al altar and the *asherah*, there is ample report about local objections (Judg. 6.27-31), and this would be the typical format of such heroic reports. In 2 Kings 23, there is not a single word reflecting the reaction of the people being targeted.

Historically, it is evident that a place having been imbued with cultic and religious significance remains a site of memory for its mnemonic community despite attempts to exterminate it.[56] It is also clear that graves were such sites in Jerusalem in the Persian period.[57] Even if the historical Josiah discontinued ancestor worship there, that worship would not have been forgotten some four or five generations later. Indeed, one would expect the cults would have been taken up during the vacuum following the fall of Jerusalem some thirty-five years after the alleged reform. 2 Kings 23 came into being during the century following the reign of king Josiah. Historically, people would have been practicing religion in those cult places around Jerusalem while the text was being composed. Yet, it remembers the named locations as *former* cult places only. This is the point where we must start searching for the text's Other.

b) The forgetfulness in 2 Kings 23 is created and legitimized through the construction of an enveloped temporal universe, one that produces what J. Fabian famously termed a denied coevalness of the other to the self. Fabian demonstrated how modern anthropological theory construes

---

55. Forty gives further background ('Introduction').

56. A good case in point would be the *Dresdner Frauenkirche*, cf. ibid., pp. 9-10.

57. See again Schmidt, *Israel's Beneficent Dead*; Saul M. Olyan, 'Family Religion in Ancient Israel and the Wider Levant of the First Millennium BCE', in *Household and Family Religion in Antiquity* (ed. John Bodel and Saul M. Olyan; Ancient World–Comparative Histories; Malden: Wiley-Blackwell, 2008), pp. 113-26; Valkama, *Judah in Mid-Sixth Century*.

the cultures studied as being distant and 'other'. It does so by mobilizing partly implicit, temporalizing, theoretical assumptions ('primitive', 'pristine', 'backward', etc.) that sustain a hegemonic relation between anthropology and its 'object' that mystifies their actual co-existence. In a sentence: 'The Other's empirical presence turns into his theoretical absence...'[58] The one part of this seminal insight that I would bring into my discussion of a very different intellectual regime is this: 2 Kings 23 projects moral justification for violent change back into a world where only the self, not the Other, is narratively (and logically) represented. This narratological structure is a cornerstone in the social imaginary that allows the narrator and the reader to perform their collective denial of coevalness with the Other.

To a Persian-era audience Josiah is already iconic, remembered as part of the authoritative religious heritage. Moses, of course, is part of the charter myth, imagined already in the narrated world to be located far back in ancient history. The narrator 'forgets' that Josiah's reforms would have had some Other being 'reformed'. Using this text as a religious charter in Jerusalem in the Persian period amounts to denying narrative representation to those Others empirically celebrating ancestor cult in the Kidron and the Hinnom. To twist Fabian: the narrated Josiah's logical Other is narratively absent, making the empirical Other of the Persian context textually invisible. Importantly, the text's memory of Moses is even more forgetful: there is no mention of a reform, not even of a single practice that needs to be changed. There simply are the decrees, now available in Josiah's book. This memory of a conflict-free Moses is very different from what is found, for instance, in the golden calf story in Exodus 32. To keep using Fabian as a palimpsest: while the Josiah imagined in the Persian context in Yehud had an empirical Other, the narrated Josiah's logical Other is narratively absent, and the textually remembered Moses' conventional Other is narratively and logically erased.

Incomprehensibly, so the narrative has it, the rules of Moses were forgotten. Josiah reinstates a world chartered by the memory of Moses. His decrees are known exclusively through the book and interpretations of the book by King Josiah, the priests, and the prophet Huldah (2 Kgs 22.10-20). Reforms that would have become controversial in a reading of the charter in the Persian period are morally and religiously negotiated in a space where the Persian-era Other is not represented. This is textually explicit: the 'elders' in the narrative would have been likened to those

---

58. Johannes Fabian, *Time and the Other: How Anthropology Makes Its Object* (New York: Columbia University Press, 2nd edn, 2002 [original 1983]), p. xli.

family heads overseeing family religion at graves around Jerusalem in the Persian period. In the narrative, these elders only get to *confirm* Josiah's interpretation (vv. 1-3). If the elders were supernumeraries in the narrative, we may assume they were kept outside the practice of canonical commentary in the Persian period.[59]

Othering and 'Sameing'

a) The empirical Other being produced and provisionally controlled in Persian-era reading seems to have been Hebrew speaking and traditional. Processes of Othering oneself or another occur commonly inside ethnic communities, including ancient Jewish culture.[60] I use 'ethnic' in a broad sense, denoting perceived linguistic, cultural, or religious cohesion and distinction, applied to self-definition by the group in question.[61] Two aspects of this process in 2 Kings 23 strike me as characteristic.

First, in 2 Kings 23 the Othering within the *ethnos* is embedded in a struggle over the very form of ethnic identity. For an audience in the Persian period, the speech act of 2 Kings 23 does not seem aimed primarily toward 'outing' the Other. Rather, it seems bent on convincing them that ancestor cult in the Kidron and the Hinnom is not 'really Yahwistic'. The elders' narrative confirmation would imply that Persian-era family heads should take the same stance. The more serious enemies in the narrative, the people in Samaria, would likely have been seen as ethnic Others by all Jerusalemite readers, local or settler, in the Persian period, but these ethnic Others are not really focused. Rather, it seems to me that the agency of Josiah in the context of Yehud in the Persian period would be to perform a temporary Othering for the purpose of ultimately 'sameing' the Others. The story has an internal missionary statement:[62] We (Hebrews) should not be like Them (Samarians, ancestor-worshipers, etc.) and therefore You (elders, ancestor-worshipers) must change. This, of course, would testify to the importance of this Yahwistic

---

59. On the significance of canonical commentary, see Terje Stordalen, 'Canon and Canonical Commentary: Comparative Perspectives on Canonical Systems', in *The Formative Past and the Formation of the Future* (ed. Terje Stordalen and Saphinaz-Amal Naguib; Oslo: Novus, forthcoming).

60. Cf. the educative study of Susan Niditch, 'Defining and Controlling Others Within: Hair, Identity, and the Nazirite Vow in a Second Temple Context', in *The 'Other' in Second Temple Judaism: Essays in Honor of John J. Collins* (ed. Daniel C. Harlow et al.; Grand Rapids, MI: Eerdmans, 2011), pp. 67-85.

61. As for the applicability of ethnicity to antiquity, see for instance Anthony D. Smith, *The Antiquity of Nations* (Malden, MA: Polity, 2004), pp. 181-210.

62. Uttered by missionaries, I admit, who do seem to have had some political power—which has usually been the case for missionaries.

imaginary also for the self. The conversion of the Other is important in order to confirm the self, both ideologically and politically. Interestingly, this discourse placed its 'imagined converts' in the same dilemma as Christian converts in Africa and Asia some two millennia later: how to relate to encultured traditions about the dead.

b) The narrated society is one where religious discourse on the state/ ethnic level intends to dictate religious practice in household, family, and township discourses. This integration of *ethnos* and family discourse is perceivable as an exilic, expatriate development.[63] In traditional Levantine societies, discourse in households, families, and town communities seems to have been fairly stable over time, following local patterns that were promoted by social bodies like the 'house of the father' or the 'elders of the town'.[64] The close alignment between 'ethnic' and family levels seem to have emerged as a result of religion becoming a prominent factor in performing Jewish identity in exile as a minority group. It seems evident that this orientation of 2 Kings 23, which permeates the entire present text, could not predate exilic times.[65] This is perhaps my strongest reason to date the current version of 2 Kings 23 in the early Persian period. It is also an important window onto the dynamics of 'sameing' in the text.

Epilogue

Writing the history of a biblical memory has proven to be a complicated exercise, demanding that we engage elements of historical knowledge (here: incidents, historical topographies), textual knowledge (the production of the text as well as the production of textual sense), and the history of ideology and mnemonic habits (successive imaginaries of the people producing or being addressed by the text). It requires that modern readers as well as ancient ones invest performative textual faculties in decoding speech-acts and perceiving imaginations encoded in the text, and also that they contextualize these in specific social and political environments. In principle, I would like to have been able to follow the mnemonic process through various redactional layers as well as early receptions of

63. See again Smith, 'Politics of Ezra'.

64. See recently Olyan, 'Family Religion in Ancient Israel'. While finding interaction between state and family religion, Olyan finds independency 'for family rites that occurred away from the sanctuary' (p. 116).

65. *Pace* the interpretation of 2 Kgs 22–23 offered by Leo G. Perdue ('The Israelite and Early Jewish Family: Summary and Conclusions', in *Families in Ancient Israel* [ed. Leo G. Perdue et al.; Louisville: Westminster John Knox, 1997], pp. 163-222 [211-22]).

the text, but, given space restraints and the chronological frame specified in the volume's title, I have only explored the memory played out at the point where the text was compositionally completed: in Jerusalem in the early Persian period.

The story of Josiah's reform took part in a process of collective remembering, and implications of the topographical memory of the reform varied for successive generations in the remembering community. Audiences reading the religio-spatial significance of the story would have performed their textual calculations using their own topographical communicative competence, not that of the historical Josiah or the modern scholar. Inserted into a narrative of Josiah, they inscribed the outcome of their reading onto his shared memory, adding to the significance and the complexity of this icon. So my analysis has had to distinguish between different trajectories in the text and its receptions. First, there were historical matters: topography, installations, practices, and beliefs that remained over centuries and were engaged in different ways at different points. Secondly, there was the memory of Josiah, continuously enriched and redefined by subsequent acts of remembering. Thirdly, there was the ever-contemporary text with its potential for continuous narrative and pragmatic application, being processed against the background of contemporary communicative and mnemonic competences. In the current essay, the heart of my analysis lay in tracing distinctions and interactions between these and calculating the speech-act performance emerging through their interplay. A focus on categories of space and time opened a window for viewing likely politics of sacred memory and of proto-canonical textuality in early Persian Yehud.

E. Gruen recently argued that apprehensions of the (ethnic) Other in antiquity are generally positive.[66] I am sorry to say I failed to find much openness to the Other in 2 Kings 23. More importantly, strategies of excluding, converting, convincing, and 'sameing' the Other through religious practice and thought are still powerful today. Perhaps they are more powerful now than in the more socially compartmentalized world of the narrated Josiah or the Yehudite reader. In so-called religions of the book, one may still imagine communities whose negotiations of moral and religious matters occur exclusively in past books and in closed spaces dominated by expert interpreters. I can only hope that insight into the mechanics of such denial of moral and religious covalence can help challenge such discourse.

---

66. Erich S. Gruen, *Rethinking the Other in Antiquity* (Martin Classic Lectures; Princeton: Princeton University Press, 2011).

JONAH AND THE OTHER:
A DISCOURSE ON INTERPRETATIVE COMPETENCE

Susanne Gillmayr-Bucher

The book of Jonah tells one of the most beautiful but also one of the most ambiguous and confusing stories in the Bible. Although the plot is quite simple, time and again the story evades a determination of its purpose or its focus.[1] Several gaps in the portrayal of the figures, in particular Jonah, require the readers to make presumptions to complete the story. Depending on the readers' selection of preconditions and contexts, different aspects of the story come to the fore.[2]

In this essay I will focus on the discourse about Others as it unfolds in the book of Jonah. I will approach this discourse from three perspectives. The first perspective situates the text in the wider context of the collection of prophetic books, especially the 'oracles concerning the nations' used in a number of them. The second focuses on the literary figure of Jonah and the way he is challenged by others throughout the book. The third and final perspective asks what significance the specific discourse in the book of Jonah might have in a larger discourse about interpretative competence during the Persian era.

1. Shaping the Background:
Jonah and the 'Oracles Concerning the Nations'

In several prophetic books other nations are given a special place within prophetic speech. In the so-called 'oracles concerning the nations',[3] they are used to review Israel/Judah's position within the community of the

---

1. Peter Weimar, *Eine Geschichte voller Überraschungen. Annäherungen an die Jonaerzählung* (SBS, 217; Stuttgart: Kohlhammer, 2009), p. 12.

2. The numerous and quite controversial interpretations of the book of Jonah give a vivid example of the variety of possible readings. Cf. Meik Gerhards, *Studien zum Jonabuch* (BThSt, 76; Neukirchen–Vluyn: Neukirchener Verlag, 2006), pp. 71-135; Ehud Ben Zvi, *Signs of Jonah: Reading and Rereading in Ancient Yehud* (JSOTsup, 367; Sheffield: Sheffield Academic Press, 2003), pp. 129-54.

3. E.g. Isa. 13–23; Jer. 44–51; Ezek. 25–32; Amos 1–2; similar also is Nahum.

nations. The portraits of the nations and their fate help reflect Israel/ Judah's construction of the past, ensure the present, and envision the immediate future. The occurrence of these oracles in a range of the prophetic books gives the impression that the 'oracles concerning the nations' form a specific discourse about other nations in prophetic contexts. When the book of Jonah chooses a setting that focuses on a prophet delivering a message to another nation, the discourse of these oracles could already have influenced the expectations of its readers. Thus, the first task will be to outline the types of anticipation the 'oracles concerning the nations' raise and to examine the story of Jonah against the background of these oracles.

Genre and Communication

Like most prophetic speeches, the 'oracles concerning the nations' are presented as divine words a given prophet must proclaim. The literary form of these oracles can be an announcement of doom and destruction, a lament or a dirge, but also a song of mockery. In all these forms, the distribution of communicative roles is one-sided. The deity alone talks about the nations, through his chosen agents, various prophets. Sometimes a few utterances of the nations are quoted, but the prophets are not allowed to speak up or react to the divine messages they relay. In most cases, the prophetic speeches present the nations and their announced futures to the prophets' audiences. This practice changes slightly in the book of Jeremiah. His prophecies speak about the nations, but more frequently, they address the nations in question directly. Direct speech is used to increase the dramatic effect of the prophecies. The nations, especially Babel, are depicted like an accused person during a trial (Jer. 50–51). Another rhetorical element used to include the nations in the conversation is the invitation to lament and mourn (e.g. Jer. 48.17; Isa. 23.1-2, 6, 14-16; Ezek. 32.16).[4] Nevertheless, even if the prophetic speeches address the nations directly, their immediate audiences are not the nations but Israelites, in the prophetic texts themselves as well as in their reception. They hear the divine message the prophet has to declare about the nations and perceive the resulting sorrow, shock, and terror or follow their trial.

---

4. Cf. Jürgen Kegler, 'Das Leid des Nachbarvolkes—Beobachtungen zu den Fremdvölkersprüchen Jeremias', in *'dass Gerechtigkeit und Frieden sich küssen (Ps. 85.11)'. Gesammelte Aufsätze, Predigten, Rundfunkreden* (Beiträge zur Erforschung des Alten Testaments und des antiken Judentums, 48; Frankfurt am Main: Peter Lang, 2001), pp. 56-71.

In the book of Jonah this element changes radically. Jonah not only speaks to the nations but travels to Nineveh and addresses its inhabitants directly. Instead of a mere introductory formula that announces an oracle to a nation, YHWH's instructions and the prophet's performance of them are given in detail. The story opens a narrated world where the prophet directly talks and interacts with foreigners. Thus, the foreground becomes the background as the oracle changes from hearing to showing.[5] Jonah slips through a loophole of the oracle genre and opens a quite different point of view. In contrast to other oracles, the words of YHWH that the prophet has to announce in Nineveh are only hinted at (Jon. 1.2; 3.2). But the message Jonah announces is never confirmed as YHWH's word (Jon. 3.4). Furthermore, Jonah only utters one statement, which lacks any detailed description of or reason for the events to come.

Point of View

Prophetic speech usually pretends to represent YHWH's point of view, which is understood to represent the ultimate, authoritative, and omniscient perspective. This is how the prophetic analysis of a situation gains its persuasive power. In most oracles Israel's situation is presented as distressed, threatened, or beyond hope.[6] The image of the other nations shifts between enemies and fellow victims. The nations are either depicted as enemies of Israel/Judah who will be punished or as fellow-sufferers and victims of another, more powerful force.[7] The destiny of Israel/Judah, its destruction, or the deportation of its inhabitants is reflected in the doom of the nations. Like Israel, they become the victim of other nations; they are destroyed and dispersed. The main focus of the 'oracles concerning the nations' is not their fate but the point of view that is making the pronouncements and evaluating the situation. These oracles ensure that Israel remains among the nations and that Israel/Judah and its deity still play a leading role in the community of nations. Contrary to the obvious events experienced by the prophet's audience, the prophetic message emphasizes a devastating fate awaiting all the

5. The genre of this prophetic book is not a collection of prophetic words but a narrative focusing on the figure of a prophet.

6. Quite often, however, Israel/Judah is presented not only as a victim but also is included as a target of prophetic critique. The books of Isaiah, Jeremiah, Ezekiel, and Amos do not spare Israel/Judah from harsh reproach for many perceived shortcomings.

7. This second perspective is typical, for example, of the oracles in the book of Ezekiel. This prophet addresses Israel after the destruction of Jerusalem; his dirges over the other nations mourn lost glory, thereby allowing his audience to relive shock, fear, and grief.

nations. Despite experienced powerlessness, the oracles depict the entire unfolding of world history from an 'insider' point of view that empha- sizes that Israel's perspective still exists. And even more, it is only this point of view that is able to make sense of all the events.

In the book of Jonah, Israel's situation is not mentioned, nor is the relation between Israel and Nineveh. The figure of Jonah is the only Israelite/Yehudite perspective explicitly present in the text. Nevertheless, Jonah's perspective is not held up as one that is able to explain the situation of the story; rather, it is a troubled perspective.

Dealing with the Others

In the 'oracles concerning the nations', the Others are regarded as a serious and threatening problem. C. Newsom points out how the dynamic of an encounter between self and Other may take on different strategies of exclusion: the Others can be eliminated, dominated, assimi- lated, or abandoned.[8] Most often, the 'oracles concerning the nations' dissolve the challenges the Others and their claims pose by envisioning their elimination. Sometimes the oracles give reasons for the harsh punishment they predict will befall the other nations. The most common charges are: arrogance, pride, and haughtiness or trusting in their own strength.[9] Sometimes the nations are accused of having acted against Israel/Judah (e.g. Jer. 50.17; Ezek. 25.12, 15; Amos 1.11), of misjudging its importance and the power of its deity (Isa. 14.14, 16; Jer. 48.27; Ezek. 25.8; 28.2), of gaining profit from Israel's tragedy (Ezek. 26.2; Amos 1.6, 9), or of rejoicing over its destruction (e.g. Ezek. 25.3, 6).

The opening scene in the book of Jonah features God declaring 'the evil of Nineveh': 'for their evil has come up before me' (Jon. 1.2).[10] God assumes the position of a judge, having recognized Nineveh's action to be evil; yet, no description of their evil deed(s) is forthcoming. Also, it is noteworthy that Israel is not part of this evaluation. It is not mentioned at all, not even as the victim of Nineveh's asserted misdeed(s).

---

8.   Carol Newsom, 'God's Other: The Intractable Problem of the Gentile King in Judean and Early Jewish Literature', in *The 'Other' in Second Temple Judaism: Essays in Honor of John J. Collins* (ed. Daniel C. Harlow et al.; Grand Rapids, MI: Eerdmans, 2011), pp. 31-48 (35).

9.   Enthusiastic appraisal of their own strength and resources leads to pride, arrogance, an exaggerated opinion of themselves, the imposing of their own interests on everyone else, and disdain of others (Charis Fischer, *Die Fremdvölkersprüche bei Amos und Jesaja. Studien zur Eigenart und Intention in Am 1.3–2, 3.4-5 and Isa 13.1–16.14* [Bonner biblische Beiträge, 136; Berlin: Philo, 2002], pp. 187-88).

10.   Lam. 1.22; Ps. 90.8.

Accusations against the nations usually lead to the announcement of YHWH's intervention that, more often than not, includes the elimination of the Others. Many oracles describe the predicted punishment and disaster in elaborate detail. The most common elements of an envisioned destruction are as follows:[11] (1) The land is to be laid waste, stripped of its culture and civilization, or given to foreign people. (2) The inhabitants of the land are terrified; they have to flee and are deported or die. (3) YHWH's harsh intervention accomplishes several goals simultaneously: he puts an end to human pride and glory,[12] he saves his people or enables their return from the exile,[13] and he protects the nations and redirects all people toward himself and away from their idols.[14] Divine intervention signals the rejection of the claims of the other nations, whose threat is eliminated with their destruction. The fate Israel fears most, namely to vanish from the earth, to vanish from history, and to be buried in oblivion, is projected onto the nations. In this way, Israel/ Judah's own destiny, its destruction or deportation, is reflected in the doom of the others.

Nevertheless, the elimination is not always complete; sometimes there is still hope for Israel/Judah as well as for the nations. The possible survival of the nations, however, is strictly envisioned from Israel's point of view. After they have been judged and punished, they can have no independent future; at most, they will be included in a new reality centred on Zion and YHWH. Thus, these nations are to be assimilated, and their still threatening potential in the audience's present is overcome by their anticipated subordination to YHWH and their acceptance of Israel's special role.[15]

Yet another variant form of assimilation of the Other can be found in the prophetic books. It is the idea that a foreign king not only can be a tool for divine punishment but also God's servant who is granted

---

11. Cf. Graham R. Hamborg, 'Reasons for Judgement in the Oracles Against the Nations of the Prophet Isaiah', *VT* 41.2 (1981), pp. 145-59 (156).

12. E.g. Isa. 13.11; 14.11-17; 16.6-14; 21.16-17; 23.7-9.

13. E.g. Isa. 14.1-8, 25; 17.12-14.

14. E.g. Isa. 17.7-8; 19.1, 16-25. Cf. Paul Raabe, 'Look to the Holy One of Israel, All You Nations: The Oracles About the Nations Still Speak Today', *Concordia Journal* 3.4 (2004), pp. 336-49 (339).

15. E.g. Isa. 19.25; 56.1-7; 66.18-19; Mic. 4.1-3. Cf. Georg Hentschel, 'Israel als Modell eines universalen Gottesvolkes', *ThG* 48.4 (2005), pp. 200-210 (201-205). For the impact of universalizing conceptions of YHWH on Israel's special status as an insider group that includes YHWH, see also the Diana Edelman's contribution to the present volume, 'YHWH's Othering of Israel', pp. 41-69.

responsibility for Israel, the nations, and even the whole of creation.[16] In this way, the foreign king is assimilated and turned into the one chosen by YHWH, 'his royal representative on earth'.[17] Although he still remains a foreign king, he is included in Israel's idea of world order.[18]

The book of Jonah contains yet a third variation to the two strategies presented above for dealing with other nations. It presents the idea that the nations will find salvation without being eliminated but also, without being chosen. Instead, the inhabitants of Nineveh and their king experience Israel's deity, who is merciful and accepts repentance, via his prophet, Jonah. In this way, Nineveh receives similar treatment to Israel/Judah, being warned about wrong-doing by a divine spokesperson and called to repentance. However, unlike other nations that are given a second chance, Nineveh is not included in a Zion-centred worldview. Although YHWH's responsibility and care for all creatures is emphasized, no new relationship between YHWH and Nineveh is established. The city reacts appropriately to Jonah's message but does not convert to YHWH. Likewise, no hierarchy between Nineveh and Israel/Judah is established; none is even mentioned.

Images of the Others

The prophetic texts interweave portraits of the nations with their envisioned futures. In many oracles, the foreign nations are shown as prosperous, powerful, respected, even feared; they are convinced of their security and they have confidence in their military and economic strength. While many oracles avoid any positive image of other nations, sometimes, as in the book of Ezekiel, the portraits allow sympathy for the nations and their rulers to surface, and occasionally, quite beautiful images of other nations are elaborated.[19] However, admiration of the power and beauty of the nations is usually a first, temporary step in the larger portrayal. As the prophetic speech continues, it begins to deconstruct this image, emphasizing the haughty self-assessment of the nations. If foreign rulers are mentioned, great significance is attached to them. Their image is drawn in vivid colours and their former beauty and power is particularly emphasized. But, similar to the nations, their portraits are drawn in hindsight. Their destruction is presented as a

---

16. E.g. the oracles concerning Nebuchadnezzar (Jer. 27.6) or Cyrus (Isa. 44–45; Ezra 1) (Newsom, *God's Other*, pp. 41-43).

17. Ibid., p. 42.

18. The hierarchical arrangement of: 'YHWH–Davidic king–Israel' is expanded to: 'YHWH–foreign king–Davidic king–Israel' (ibid., pp. 42-43).

19. E.g. Ezek. 27.3-25; 31.3-9; Jer. 46.20-21; 48.17.

reality that has already happened or will surely occur. In retrospect, the greatness of the king is exaggerated in order to heighten the contrast with the situation after his disempowerment. Since a change or reversal of their deeds is not anticipated, their behaviour is depicted as statically arrogant.

The image of a great and beautiful Other is only hinted at in the book of Jonah. Nineveh is explicitly presented as a large city, but no detailed description is offered (Jon. 1.2; 3.2-4). However, its size is emphasized from different perspectives. The information about the three days it takes to walk through the city presents a human point of view. This detail is complemented by a comment by the narrating voice emphasizing its size from God's point of view: Nineveh was even a large city by divine standards. At the end of the story, YHWH's speech once more repeats and even elaborates the image of the large city (Jon. 4.11).[20] Here the focus shifts from mere size to the city's large number of inhabitants. Nevertheless, compared to the Greek literary traditions that remember Nineveh as one of the great cities, if not the greatest that ever existed, the book of Jonah is muted and non-committal.[21] And in light of the presence of a few detailed, effusive depictions of foreign kings or capital cities in 'oracles concerning the nations', this gap in the description is also noticeable.

Nineveh's greatness is only hinted at. No beauty, no riches, no achievements are mentioned. Thus, a great fall is not anticipated for the city. What is more, Jonah's audience might be aware of the fact that Nineveh was destroyed a long time ago and was never rebuilt.[22] Thus, Nineveh is simultaneously the threatening and the eliminated 'other'. While the historical Nineveh fades into the background, the city called Nineveh in the story can become a cipher for various capitals, with their power and beauty.[23]

20. This image also refers to the city's similarity to Jerusalem (Zech. 2.8).

21. '...[W]e can see that in the Greek literary tradition Nineveh is acknowledged to be the capital of the great and ancient Assyrian empire, but the focus in Greek culture is not so much on the city's political or military prowess, but rather on the magnitude of its opulence. This opulence becomes personified in the figure of Sardanapallus, an individual so wealthy and eccentric as to be the ancient world's symbol of unbridled hedonism.' Thomas Bolin, '"Should I Not Also Pity Nineveh?" Divine Freedom in the Book of Jonah', *JSOT* 67 (1995), pp. 109-20 (115).

22. Ben Zvi, *Signs of Jonah*, pp. 15-17.

23. This becomes obvious when Nineveh comes into focus from a later perspective, e.g. the books of Tobit, Judith, and Jonah. The first world power Israel experienced became the archetype of every powerful nation that followed (Gerhards, *Jonabuch*, pp. 95-96, 100).

In the book of Jonah the Others are the inhabitants of Nineveh; the larger empire of Assyria[24] is not mentioned. Consequently, the 'evil of Nineveh' relates to the offences of its inhabitants but not to the cruel deeds of the Empire.[25] Since Nineveh is depicted solely in terms of an exemplary capital, its likely role as a cipher for Jerusalem becomes strengthened, and with it, an allusion to YHWH's dealing with his favoured, chosen city.

Nineveh's role as cipher for Jerusalem extends to its demonstrating the paradigmatic response to the warning words of YHWH delivered via his prophet, which Jerusalem should have followed.[26] These foreigners trust in Jonah's words; they accept their sin and immediately begin a liturgy of repentance (Jon. 3.5). The king even orders a communal repentance that includes animals as well as people.[27] Everyone is asked to perform an ethical reorientation, to 'turn from his evil way (מדרכו הרעה) and from the violence (חמס) that is in his hands'.[28] In his request, the king takes on a prophetic role and even quotes prophetic speech (cf. Jer. 18.11; 25.5; 35.15). Thus, this king orders the change Jonah has announced and the people take this radical turn. Like the prophet Joel (Joel 2.11-14), Nineveh's king knows the small chance the city still has (Jon. 3.9): 'who knows, maybe God will turn and change (נחם)'.

In his short appearance, the king of Nineveh is portrayed as someone familiar with the tradition and the deity of Israel. He is shown as a mirror image of an ideal Israelite king, even in contrast to King Jehoiakim (Jer. 36).[29] Thus Nineveh's ruler appears as a positive counterpart to the king

---

24. In biblical texts most occurrences of Nineveh refer to this city as the capital of the Assyrian empire. Although Nineveh does not become 'the evil city' *par excellence* like Babylon, it is nevertheless inseparably connected with the Assyrian empire and its politics.

25. Cf. Weimar, *Eine Geschichte*, p. 181.

26. 'The title "king of Nineveh", which the Assyrian kings never used for themselves, is found in both Jonah and the Greek writings' (Bolin, 'Should I Not Also Pity Nineveh?', p. 118).

27. Like the 'decree of the king and his great' (Jon. 3.7), the fasting of the animals is a reference to a common image of the Persians (Gerhards, *Jonabuch*, pp. 97-99).

28. So Martin Roth, *Israel und die Völker im Zwölfprophetenbuch. Eine Untersuchung zu den Büchern Joel, Jonah, Micha und Nahum* (FRLANT, 210; Göttingen: Vandenhoeck & Ruprecht, 2005), p. 138.

29. In Jer. 36, similar to the people of Nineveh, the inhabitants of Jerusalem begin fasting, but the king does not support them (Weimar, *Eine Geschichte*, pp. 194-98).

of Jerusalem.[30] In contrast to the image of the other kings in the 'oracles concerning the nations', this king is not arrogant or too self-confident. Quite the contrary, he is listening and he knows how to react appropriately.[31] Had the final kings of Jerusalem listened to Jeremiah, Jerusalem might also have been spared.

Like the book of Ezekiel,[32] the book of Jonah draws similarities between Israel and the Others, but it goes beyond Ezekiel's images. The Others in Jonah not only mimic pious Israelite behaviour; they serve as a shining example of how to respond to YHWH's prophetically delivered pronouncements. The identity of the Others, especially the inhabitants of Nineveh, is portrayed as a hybrid identity. Although they remain the Other, they still act according to the demands of Israel's deity.[33] As a result, the distinction between Nineveh, the exemplary Other, and Jerusalem/Judah is blurred.[34]

2. *Inside the Story: Jonah and the Foreign Worlds*

The plot of the story focuses on the journey of the prophet Jonah. Unlike the announcements of the 'oracles concerning the nations', Jonah literally has to deliver his message to a foreign land. Astonishingly, the message and its reception shift into the background, leaving Jonah and his experience of the Others the centre of the story. In an exemplary way Jonah sees, reflects, despairs, and maybe even learns from this experience.

Jonah's journey to foreign worlds starts right at the beginning. Receiving the order from YHWH, he immediately turns[35] to flee to Tarshish,[36]

30. Cf. Zeph. 3.1-2, where Jerusalem does not follow the warning it receives (ibid., p. 215).

31. A different image of Nineveh is presented in Zeph. 2.15. Here it appears as an exultant, overly self-conscious city.

32. The oracles in the book of Ezekiel depict the fate of the nations as mirroring Jerusalem's destruction. Ezekiel's audience can sympathize with all those who also mourn and tremble over their devastation. They might find some kind of comfort in not being the only ones. Cf. Susanne Gillmayr-Bucher, 'Selbstbewusstsein und Identität im Spiegel des Fremden', *ThG* 48.4 (2005), pp. 190-99.

33. However, which deity he sets his confidence in is not mentioned explicitly. Thus, the focus remains on an ethical reorientation; YHWH worship is not mentioned.

34. For a detailed discussion of the phenomenon of boundary-blurring between self and 'Other', see Ehud Ben Zvi's contribution to the present volume ('Othering, Selfing, "Boundarying" and "Cross-Boundarying" as Interwoven with Socially Shared Memories: Some Observations', pp. 20-40).

35. Jonah's urgency is reflected in the repetition of this plan (Jon. 1.3).

36. Tarshish cannot be located with certainty. Other biblical texts confirm that it is a location far away. Most probably it is located on the western edge of the

looking for a distant place far away from YHWH. Instead of carrying out his mission, he risks being far from God.[37] It is not only topographical distance but even more significant, distance from the divine order that initiates the development of the story.[38] From the beginning onwards, the relationship with the deity is the biggest challenge for the prophet Jonah, as YHWH repeatedly shakes his worldview and reveals himself as the ultimate Other.

Jonah and the World of the Sailors

The first strangers Jonah meets are the sailors on the ship to Tarshish. His confrontation with this world, especially his dialogues with the sailors, offers a first glimpse of his self-image (1.8-12). Asked to introduce himself, Jonah mentions his people (עברי, 'a Hebrew') and then adds information that has not been asked for: 'I fear YHWH the God of heaven, who made the sea and the dry land' (v. 9).[39] The reference to the deity is the most prominent element in his answer and it is this element that advances the dialogue. The verb ירא is used ambiguously: the fear of God is 'respect', but the sailors also interpret it as the fear that has led to Jonah's flight. With this ambiguity, the misunderstanding between God and Jonah that is later confirmed in the story is already hinted at, since 'to fear God' implies accepting God's decisions, which Jonah does not do. Jonah, however, claims to understand the situation (כי יודע אני, 'for I know') and accordingly, he defines the saving measure, which is that he must be thrown into the sea (Jon. 1.12).[40] Jonah's point of view embraces

---

Mediterranean Sea. *Tarsisi* (KUR *tar-si-si*) is referenced in an inscription of King Esarhaddon: 'All kings dwelling in the middle of the sea, from Cyprus (Iadanana) and Greece (Iaman) to Tarshish (Tarsisi), bowed down under my feet' (Reikele Borger, *Die Inschriften Asarhaddons Königs von Assyrien* [Archiv für Orientforschung Beiheft, 9; Graz: Weidner, 1956], p. 86).

37. 'To flee from the presence of YHWH (מלפני יהוה)' alludes to Cain in Gen. 4.16, who has to distance himself from YHWH (Gerhards, *Jonabuch*, pp. 140-42).

38. The setting of the harbour, Jaffo, might be a hint that Jonah received YHWH's order in Jerusalem, in the vicinity of YHWH's presence, from which Jonah now wants to flee. Whether or not Jonah assumes that a revelation of YHWH outside the land is not possible is disputed (ibid., pp. 145-63).

39. Both formulations point to post-exilic times. See Roth, *Israel und die Völker*, p. 142; Christoph Levin, 'Jonah 1: Bekehrung zum Judentum und ihre Folgen', in *Die unwiderstehliche Wahrheit. Studien zur alttestamentlichen Prophetie* (eds. Rüdiger Lux and Ernst-Joachim Waschke; ABiG, 23; Leipzig: Evangelische Verlagsanstalt, 2006), pp. 283-99 (289).

40. Cf. Ilse Müllner, 'Fraglos eine Frage? Zum Schluss des Jonabuchs', in *Fragen wider die Antworten* (ed. Kerstin Schiffner et al.; Gütersloh: Gütersloher Verlagshaus, 2010), pp. 286-304 (291-93).

quite a strict image of God, which then evokes an equally strict reaction: because he did not carry out the divine order, he will bear the consequences. He does not plead, nor does he try to negotiate.

The sailors represent a different point of view from Jonah's narrow one. Although they believe in different deities, the sailors are not portrayed as foreigners; rather, they mimic Israelite behaviour. They cast lots,[41] they call on their deities, they interpret the storm as punishment, and they hope for a salvation (cf. Ps. 107.23-29). The sailors are portrayed as capable, God-fearing people, who act according to the situation. They expect divine help, and since they seem not to mind which deity will help, they are open to Jonah's deity.[42] The sailors trust Jonah and readily accept YHWH's superior strength. They even ask for his forgiveness for throwing Jonah into the ocean (Jon. 1.14). When their pleas are answered, they even come to fear YHWH. Altogether, the sailors' reactions depict them as honest and open-minded men who try to act in an exemplary manner.

Their behaviour further emphasizes the universality of YHWH and shows that different people have their own approach to YHWH.[43] However, the sailors only gain an idea of YHWH from Jonah, the YHWH-worshiper.[44] And while the prophet obviously changes the sailors' perspective, they do not unsettle his narrow perspective of his God.

Jonah and the World Inside the Big Fish

The story of Jonah does not end when he is thrown into the sea but continues on into another, more foreign world: the belly of a big fish. When YHWH commissions (מנה)[45] the big fish to swallow Jonah, this is not a form of salvation. The fish is an image of personified chaos,

---

41. In contrast to other mantic practices, casting lots is an approved way for Israelites to reach a decision (e.g. Lev. 16.8; Neh. 10.35). 'These sailors cast lots…rather than engage in other kinds of ancient Near Eastern divination' (Brent A. Strawn, 'Jonah's Sailors and Their Lot Casting: A Rhetorical-Critical Observation', *Bib* 91 [2010], pp. 66-76 [74]).

42. Although the sailors offer sacrifices to YHWH and make vows (Jon. 1.16), they remain non-Israelites. Volker Haarmann considers them YHWH-worshipers from the nations (*JHWH-Verehrer der Völker. Die Hinwendung von Nichtisraeliten zum Gott Israels in alttestamentlichen Überlieferungen* [AThANT, 91; Zurich: Theologischer Verlag, 2008], p. 186).

43. Gerhards, *Jonabuch*, pp. 181-82.

44. Cf. Roth, *Israel und die Völker*, p. 126.

45. מנה means 'to commission, to appoint for a special role'. An accumulation of the verb מנה occurs only in the book of Jonah: God commissions a fish (2.1), a plant (4.6), a worm (4.7), and an east wind (4.8).

which then swallows the prophet.[46] In the strange world inside the fish, Jonah expresses his experience in a psalm-like prayer (Jon. 2.3-10).[47] It expresses a cry out of mortal fear, out of the fish's belly, which is experienced as the belly of the underworld (בטן שאול). The psalm is dominated by two motifs: YHWH destroys[48] and YHWH saves. While Jonah has experienced destruction, he still is confident that YHWH also saves (v. 10). His cry, however, is narrated retrospectively, and it is not formulated as an actual cry. This gives the impression that Jonah uses a psalm that already exists, adding to his image as a pious and knowledge-able person. The focus of Jonah's hope is also explicitly expressed: it rests on the temple (vv. 4, 7) and on YHWH (v. 10): 'salvation is towards YHWH' (ישועתה ליהוה). Despite the death-like situation, Jonah has no doubts about YHWH's reliability, even predictability. Jonah's beliefs are firmly rooted in tradition, which allows him to hold on to his God even in a seemingly hopeless situation. He recognizes the life-threatening chaos but remains confident.

In his prayer, Jonah again presents a very clear but un-nuanced point of view: God destroys and God saves. He does not rescue before disaster strikes, but he might save one from death in the disaster. But there is no word about fault, apology, or reversal. Even this utterly other situation does not seem to unsettle Jonah.

Jonah and the World of Nineveh

When Jonah enters the foreign world of Nineveh, his reactions to it are not conveyed. He walks into the city, a day's march, announces his message and leaves. The message itself is very short: 'Only forty days and Nineveh will be changed' (Jon. 3.4). The verb הפך means 'to convert, to change'. It can refer to a change for the worse, for example, turning a city upside down (Gen. 19; Deut. 29.22; Amos 4.11) or turning celebra-

---

46. Cf. Yolande Steenkamp and Gert T. Prinsloo, 'Another Look at Jonah 2', *Old Testament Essays* 16.2 (2003), pp. 435-52 (445).

47. Jonah's prayer contains several typical motifs and elements of a psalm: e.g. the motif of threatening water (Jon. 2.4-6; Pss. 69.2; 88.8); the motif of the deep (Jon. 2.4, 6, 7; Pss. 69.3, 15; 107.26; 130.1); the threat to be cut off from God's eyes (Jon. 2.5; Ps. 31.23); the hope to be brought up from the pit (Jon. 2.7; Ps. 30.4); YHWH's answering of prayers (Jon. 2.3; Pss. 31.23; 120.2); the holy temple as a centre and a refuge (Jon. 2.8; Pss. 5.8; 138.2); the נפש suffering from thirst (Jon. 2.8; Pss. 42.3; 63.2; 107.5; 142.4; 143.4); the enemies as those who worship empty things (Jon. 2.9; Ps. 31.7); and the motifs of gratitude (Jon. 2.10; Pss. 3.9; 26.7; 76.12) and sacrifice (Jon. 2.10; Pss. 50.14-23; 66.13).

48. The metaphors of the waters, the deep, the waves, and billows match the narrated situation.

tion into mourning (e.g. Amos 8.10), but also a change for the better: lamentation can be changed to joy (e.g. Jer. 31.14; Ps. 30.12) or curse into blessing (e.g. Deut. 23.6). While Jonah's message announces a fundamental change, it does not specify in which direction the situation will move, nor does it reveal who will initiate the change. Consequently, the intention of the announcement remains unclear. It could be an announcement of disaster, as in the 'oracles concerning the nations', but it also could be a warning that will lead to a change for the better.[49]

Jonah's attitude towards Nineveh is only revealed later, when he realizes YHWH is not going to destroy the city (Jon. 3.10–4.3). A short description offers insight into his perspective and his emotional reaction. YHWH's sparing of Nineveh is very evil (רעה גדולה) for Jonah and he becomes angry (Jon. 4.1). He is unmoved by the reaction of the city. Once again, the Others have no influence on or over Jonah's perception. It is at this point that God takes action toward Jonah again.

Jonah and YHWH

While Jonah sits outside Nineveh and waits for what will happen next, God demonstrates his overwhelming power and challenges Jonah's limited point of view (Jon. 4.6-8). As God shows his ability to change Jonah's situation from pleasant to intolerable in no time, Jonah's reactions to the changing situation are quick and intense: he goes through fierce anger (Jon. 4.1-9) to great joy (Jon. 4.6), to fatigue, and to the wish to die (Jon. 4.8). When the events do not unfold as he expected, he quickly gives up and is ready to die. Again, he does not plead, he does not fight, he does not negotiate.

The perspective Jonah represents is a black-and-white mindset that allows no adjustment. Events and actions are either right or wrong and they have predictable consequences. This attitude is also present in his prayer (Jon. 4.2-3), where he complains about God's inconsequent reactions. Jonah seemingly longs for a God of mere justice; although he knows that God is 'a gracious God and merciful, slow to anger and abounding in steadfast love, and relenting from disaster', he is not willing to adjust to this image. He is avoiding this kind of God.

---

49. Because the message includes an extension of forty days, it seems reasonable to assume that the forty days are the last chance for change. In this way, Nineveh is an example of a nation on trial (Roth, *Israel und die Völker*, p. 137). However, Jonah's message provides the city with a last chance to manoeuvre. Cf. Rüdiger Lux, *Jona—Prophet zwischen Verweigerung und Gehorsam. Eine erzählanalystische Studie* (FRLANT, 162; Göttingen: Vandenhoeck & Ruprecht, 1994), p. 131.

In this situation, God begins an argument about the קיקיון and Jonah's reactions: First God asks Jonah if his resignation, his wish to die, might be seen as justified anger. Jonah confirms this and emphasizes that his anger is justified, even until death (v. 9). In v. 10 God tries again and now calls Jonah's emotional response compassion (חוס):[50] '[Could it be that] you pity the קיקיון...?' Jonah does not answer. Could the most pleasant plant and its undeserved withering arouse Jonah's compassion? Perhaps Jonah would have wanted to spare it? Only if he is willing to consider this question and answer 'yes' might the final argument in v. 11 convince him. But again, Jonah's reaction is not mentioned. Reading vv. 10 and 11 as questions[51] emphasizes a tone of mockery in the divine argumentation. God asks Jonah if he possibly pities a plant he could not have saved. Not only did he not plant and care for this קיקיון, but he also could not do what YHWH had done: namely summon the plant, appoint a worm, or call the east wind; nor could he prevent these things from happening. Jonah is powerless; he cannot control even such a simple and ephemeral form of life. The next verse returns to the opening question of God's mercy. 'And [could it be] that I do not pity Nineveh...?' Compared to Jonah's compassion for the plant, YHWH's possible denial of mercy to Nineveh appears utterly out of proportion. And, what is more, YHWH is able to spare the city. This dialogue between Jonah and YHWH clearly is a discourse of power. YHWH claims sovereignty in dealing with his whole creation.[52]

3. *Jonah and a Discourse on Interpretative Competence*

The unusual image of the prophet and the equally astonishing pardoning of a foreign city, whose evil had come up to YHWH, sets this story apart from the 'oracles concerning the nations' in other prophetical books. The book of Jonah presents itself as a narrative reflection on such oracles.

The Prophet and the Others
In telling about the travels and troubles of Jonah, the role and function of a prophet are critically examined. Jonah is presented as someone who has a clearly defined picture of himself: he is a worshiper of YHWH and the centre of his world is the temple in Jerusalem. Throughout the story,

---

50. The verb חוס is usually used in a negative sense—'and no compassion/no pity' also would fit perfectly well for Jonah.

51. Neither question is marked in the Hebrew text as rhetorical; nevertheless, such an understanding might still be deduced from the context.

52. This kind of argument is similar to God's answer to Job (Job 38–42).

Jonah is presented as a prophet who assumes he knows God's intentions and who is familiar with Israel's traditions.[53] Nevertheless, the story does not present a mere retreat to strict positions and known traditions as a way to success. Jonah's self-assured ידעתי ('I know') is confronted by the מי־יודע ('who knows?') of Nineveh's king. Furthermore, YHWH challenges Jonah's centred view and opts for a more differentiated, decentralized picture. Jonah's deconstruction begins when he is forced to go in person to the addressees of his message. He is not able to deliver God's words from the safety of his own land and community, like the prophets before him. Rather, he has to expose himself to a foreign land and foreign people. Although it is not Jonah's intention, he extends the possibility of change to Others. Once Jonah has performed his mission, however reluctantly, his message is extremely effective. Now it becomes obvious that Jonah's success was only possible because he travelled to Nineveh in person. Only if the addressees get a chance to hear the message directly are they able to react. In retrospect, YHWH's order to go to Nineveh and deliver a message there, on-site, already prepared for this possibility. And Jonah might also have recognized this from the beginning. Despite all his efforts, Jonah fulfils the role of a prophet who issues a warning. In this way, he acts like his namesake, Jonah ben Amittai (2 Kgs 14.25-27), who was Israel's last prophet of salvation, proclaiming Israel's future against its enemies. Both stories show God's undeserved mercy towards sinful people.[54] From this perspective, Jonah comes close to the image of the prophet to the nations hinted at in the book of Jeremiah (Jer. 1.5; 18.7-8). This anticipated prophet brings orientation to the city and offers a new beginning. Jonah, however, is not willing to be part of such a concept and he is not willing to collaborate. Nevertheless, YHWH forces him to do so, which the prophet experiences as defeat. Like Elijah, Jonah's worldview—his knowledge, his obligations, the way he sees himself and his role as a prophet—is so badly shaken that he even wants to die (1 Kgs 19.4). On the whole, Jonah acts like a catalyst that spurs along reactions from the sailors and the people in Nineveh without being changed himself. However, although the Others Jonah meets on his journey do not make an impact on the prophet, step by step these events prepare the readers for the final challenge, when Jonah meets YHWH as the Other.[55] YHWH does not hesitate to demonstrate his power to adjust

53. Ben Zvi, *Signs of Jonah*, p. 107.

54. Gerhards, *Jonabuch*, p. 86.

55. Newsom refers to Lévinas, who describes this Other 'as that which is separate from me, that which is radically exterior to me, that which is utterly transcendent,

the world according to his plans or to shape it for Jonah's experience: the storm, the big fish, the plant, the worm, and the east wind are all appointed to challenge Jonah's perspective.[56]

A Discourse on Interpretative Competence

The traditional 'oracles concerning the nations' help reflect and reconstruct Israel's place in the community of nations. The prophetic announcements try to bring Israel and its perspective back into a discourse. But in the book of Jonah, Israel and the way Israel sees itself are not even mentioned. An Israelite perspective is only presented in the figure of the prophet Jonah. However, Jonah is not introduced as an exemplary Israelite but rather, as some Israelite prophet. While looking for the Other, it also became obvious that it was not the sailors, nor the big fish, nor Nineveh that represent the really challenging Other, but YHWH.

Although the struggle between Jonah and YHWH focuses on the position other (dominant) nations are granted, another question underlying this dispute is the relevance and validity of different interpretations. Against the background of the expectations raised by the standard motifs associated with 'oracles concerning the nations', Nineveh's elimination or a transition of power is set up in the readers' minds. Nevertheless, the story of Jonah frustrates these anticipations and proposes another solution. It stands back from imagining Israel's major importance to the nations and does not support visionary sketches of a great future.[57] In this way, it modifies a traditional prophetic perspective. Once the nations accept YHWH's dominance, an eschatological concept of judgment also is no longer necessary.[58] It is not stated why the literary figure of Jonah resists this idea. His anger and despair might be intended to reflect the demotion of a prophetic point of view.[59] Nevertheless, in the face of YHWH's display of power, Jonah retreats into silence (cf. Job 40.3-4).

When the story of Jonah encourages its readers to follow this prophet's journey, it does not ask them to leave Israel's traditions behind,

---

exceeding me. The encounter with the Other makes me aware that the world is not simply my possession or an extension of me, but that I share the world' (*God's Other*, p. 35).

56. Barbara Green, *Jonah's Journeys* (Interfaces; Collegeville, MN: Liturgical, 2005), p. 46.

57. Cf. Lux, *Jona*, p. 210.

58. Roth, *Israel und die Völker*, p. 171.

59. Some assume that Jonah resists because he fears negative consequences for Israel or fears being regarded as a false prophet (Gerhards, *Jonabuch*, pp. 120-21).

but instead to give up the idea they might be able to eliminate or dominate the Others. Confronted by YHWH, it becomes obvious that Jonah has to share the world and that YHWH cares deeply for all his creatures. The threatening Others still remain the Others, but they are also shown to be a part of YHWH's jurisdiction, responsibility, and care. Although the inhabitants of Nineveh do not become a part of Israel and do not orient themselves to Zion/Jerusalem, Nineveh is accepted as the Other in its own right and in its own space outside Israel.[60]

The book of Jonah was possibly part of a still ongoing discourse on the suitability or even legitimacy of a prophetic perspective. One of the problematic questions behind the story of Jonah could be a struggle for the sovereignty of interpretation. While prophetic voices still might have had hopes for Israel's political independence and might have envisioned the temple as the centre of the world and dreamed of peace and social justice for all people,[61] those in favour of assimilation into the prevalent empire[62] could be satisfied with steady political as well as religious conditions.[63] Furthermore, once the word of YHWH became a written word and prophetic speech continued in processes of reading and rereading and of composing and editing prophetic books, the role of the prophets was displaced by those who were able to interpret the tradition of the earlier prophets.[64] They had access to divine instructions by means of interpreting the authoritative voices handed down from earlier times and they were able to explain them.[65] Thus, not only the actual fate of the dominant nation was of vital interest but also the question about who

60. With this perspective, the narrator might also ask the audience to assume a conformist position within a dominant Empire.

61. E.g. Zech. 2.15; 6.8; 8.20-22.

62. Most exegetes assume the book of Jonah was written during the Second Temple period. More specific datings, however, range from Persian to Hellenistic times. See for example Ben Zvi, *Signs of Jonah*, p. 8; Lux, *Jona*, p. 204; Aaron Schart, *Die Entstehung des Zwölfprophetenbuchs* (BZAW, 260; Berlin: de Gruyter 1998), p. 286.

63. Rainer Kessler, 'Mirjam und die Prophetie der Perserzeit', in *Gotteserdung. Beiträge zur Hermeneutik und Exegese der Hebräischen Bibel* (BWANT, 170; Stuttgart: W. Kohlhammer, 2006), pp. 81-88 (85).

64. Armin Lange, *Vom prophetischen Wort zur prophetischen Tradition. Studien zur Traditions- und Redaktionsgeschichte innerprophetischer Konflikte in der hebräischen Bibel* (FAT, 34; Tübingen: Mohr Siebeck, 2002), p. 317; Ben Zvi, *Signs of Jonah*, p. 106; Frank-Lothar Hossfeld and Ivo Meyer, *Prophet gegen Prophet. Eine Analyse der alttestamentlichen Texte zum Thema: Wahre und falsche Propheten* (Biblische Beiträge, 9; Fribourg: Schweizerisches Katholisches Bibelwerk, 1973), pp. 159-60.

65. Ben Zvi, *Signs of Jonah*, p. 106.

had access to divine plans and who, consequently, was in charge of interpreting and evaluating the Others.

Against the background of the 'oracles against the nations', the story of the prophet named Jonah deconstructs well-known arguments in order to silence prophetic voices that envision a splendid future for Israel as the centre of the world.[66] Any idea of domination or exercising power is exclusively left to YHWH. If YHWH acts like the ruler of an Empire, assigning everyone his or her place within the Empire, there is no need for change. In the overall picture, every creature has its own designated space, and the only relevant relationship is between each individual, each city or nation, and YHWH. According to the book of Jonah, the typical biblical prophet is not willing or able to accept this new point of view. Although YHWH treats Jonah with love, forbearance, and care, it is obvious that his competence as a prophet is called into question. Jonah's self-assured statement, 'I know' (ידעתי), is deconstructed throughout the story. Instead of revealing an understanding of YHWH's will, Jonah himself experiences YHWH as the ultimate Other.

66. The story silences the prophetic voice twice: by reducing Jonah's message to one sentence and by challenging the prophet's interpretative competence.

DENIAL, DECEPTION, OR FORCE: HOW TO DEAL WITH POWERFUL OTHERS IN THE BOOK OF ESTHER*

Jean-Daniel Macchi

Introduction

Since people live in societies, the question of the exercise of power arises. One cannot fail to ask whether power is necessary, and if it is, who has the right to impose decisions on others. As power generally establishes a relationship of alterity between those who exercise power and those who perceive power as a constraint imposed on them, the exercise of power necessarily raises the question of limits. How much power is necessary to achieve one's goal, and where is the boundary between the necessary use of power and a tyrannical use of power? In complex societies that rule large territories, power may seem distant and uncontrollable to those who live at the periphery.

Beneath some humorous or even carnivalesque traits,[1] the book of Esther problematizes the issues and challenges faced by people confronted by a complex power that seems out of control. The Hebrew

---

* This is an adapted translation with a few new added paragraphs dealing with Othering more specifically of my article, 'Le refus, la ruse ou la force: le rapport au pouvoir dans le livre d'Esther', in *Le Pouvoir. Enquêtes dans l'un et l'autre Testament* (ed. Didier Luciani and André Wénin; Lectio Divina, 248; Paris: Cerf, 2012), pp. 195-206. Since the French original dealt with the question of imperial power, the matter of gender is hardly discussed, though I recognize its importance for the current focus on Others. I thank Diana Edelman, who helped me adapt this article to fit the framework of the present volume more closely.

1. See Erich S. Gruen, *Diaspora: Jews Amidst Greeks and Romans* (Cambridge, MA: Harvard University Press, 2002), pp. 135-48; Kathleen M. O'Connor, 'Humour, Turnabouts and Survival in the Book of Esther', in *Are We Amused? Humour About Women in the Biblical Worlds* (ed. Athalya Brenner; JSOTSup, 383; Bible in the 21st Century Series, 2; London: T&T Clark International, 2003), pp. 54-64; Carolyn J. Sharp, *Irony and Meaning in the Hebrew Bible* (Indiana Studies in Biblical Literature; Bloomington, IN: Indiana University Press, 2009), pp. 65-83; André LaCocque, *Esther Regina: A Bakhtinian Reading* (Rethinking Theory; Evanston, IL: Northwestern University Press, 2008).

version as we know it sets the story within the vast Persian Empire. In this short fictional story,[2] Esther is presented as a young Jewish girl who becomes queen at the court of King Ahasuerus. Thanks to her personal plea before the king, she is able to save her people, preventing the execution of a decree to exterminate all Jews. Prime Minister Haman issues the decree after a conflict with Mordecai, Esther's adoptive father. The story ends with the massacre of all the enemies of the Jews and the establishment of the festival of Purim. Through this narrative, which revolves around a situation of Us vs. Them, Jews are able to participate vicariously in an Othering process that temporarily distances them from the abusive side of royal and imperial power that many of them encountered on a regular basis in their daily lives under subsequent imperial regimes.

The Poorly Controlled Power of a Vast Empire

The governmental system of the Persian Empire is depicted ambiguously in the book of Esther.[3] The story opens with a presentation of an extensive empire of 127 provinces stretching from India to Nubia (Black Africa). The initial verses describe a luxurious banquet King Ahasuerus gives for all his officials, a banquet lasting 187 days. The supply of wine is unlimited. Further on in the narrative, one encounters the administrative apparatus of the sprawling Persian Empire. The king rules through a complex system of multilingual decrees published throughout the Empire (Est. 1.22; 3.13; 8.8-10). The government is virtually omnipotent; it can organize huge banquets and collect all the beautiful women of the kingdom for the royal harem (Est. 2.3).

---

2. See Michael V. Fox, *Character and Ideology in the Book of Esther: A Decade of Esther Scholarship* (Studies on Personalities of the Old Testament; Durham, SC: University of South Carolina Press, 1991), pp. 131-52; Jon D. Levenson, *Esther: A Commentary* (OTL; London: SCM, 1997); Adele Berlin, 'The Book of Esther and Ancient Storytelling', *JBL* 120 (2001), pp. 3-14; Harald-Martin Wahl, *Das Buch Esther. Übersetzung und Kommentar* (Berlin: de Gruyter, 2009), pp. 23-31.

3. See Hans-Peter Mathys, 'Der Achämenidenhof im Alten Testament', in *Der Achämenidenhof / The Achaemenid Court. Akten des 2. Internationalen Kolloquiums zum Thema 'Vorderasien im Spannungsfeld klassischer und altorientalischer Überlieferungen' Landgut Castelen bei Basel, 23.–25. Mai 2007* (ed. Bruno Jacobs and Robert Rollinger; Classica et Orientalia, 2; Wiesbaden: Harrassowitz, 2010), pp. 231-308 (244-65); Jean-Daniel Macchi, 'Le livre d'Esther: regard hellénistique sur le pouvoir et le monde perses', *Transeuphratène* 30 (2005), pp. 97-135.

Yet, the reader soon realizes that this impressive machinery is not free of inconsistencies. At the end of the magnificent banquet, an unexpected event occurs. Queen Vashti refuses to comply with the king's command (Est. 1.11). Immediately, the council of sages 'versed in law and custom' (1.13) meets to deliberate over how to deal with the act of disobedience (1.13-22). At first glance, the existence of such a council seems positive, since all power is not in the hands of the king. Several hints undermine this view, however. First, the process takes place when the king's heart is 'merry with wine' (1.10) and everyone else is also presumably intoxicated from the limitless wine on offer (1.8). Drunkenness may explain Memucan's rather absurd statement that if the queen does not obey Ahasuerus, women all over the Empire will follow suit and cease to respect their husbands.[4] His subsequent suggestion to publish a decree throughout the Empire that forbade Vashti to enter the king's presence and which removed her from her position of queen, implicitly as punishment for her disobedience, would likely aggravate the situation rather than resolve it in any satisfactory fashion. What if broadcasting the refractory queen's repudiation spurred all husbands throughout the realm to seek new wives to replace the existing ones who emulated the queen and disobeyed? Where would they find replacements, since ch. 2 notes that all the beautiful girls of marriageable age were to be taken to the palace for a beauty contest whose winner, chosen by the king, would become the new queen in place of Vashti?

The Empire's dysfunctional nature is underlined by the fact that the royal advisors systematically play an ambiguous role in the decision-making process. While the king always makes a decision only after consulting his advisers, these advisers are never depicted as neutral or objective. They carefully distil information at selected times to influence royal policy for their own benefit, to serve their personal interests. The most striking case is Haman, who obtains permission to proclaim a decree affecting all Jews (ch. 3). Driven by the desire to avenge a personal insult, he warns Ahasuerus that:

> There is a certain people scattered and separated among the peoples in all the provinces of your kingdom; their laws are different from those of every other people, and they do not keep the king's laws, so that it is not appropriate for the king to tolerate them. If it pleases the king, let a decree

4. See Levenson, *Esther*, p. 51; Carol M. Bechtel, *Esther* (Interpretation Bible Commentaries; Louisville, KY: John Knox, 2002), pp. 24-26; and Adele Berlin, *Esther* (JPS Bible Commentary; Philadelphia: Jewish Publication Society, 2001), p. 17.

be issued for their destruction, and I will pay ten thousand talents of silver
into the hands of those who have charge of the king's business, so that
they may put it into the king's treasuries. (Est. 3.8-9 NRSV)

Haman develops a strategy of Othering that discredits a particular people
in the eyes of the sovereign. He insists that an anonymous group is
threatening the Empire itself but is careful to remain silent about the
people's identity; the reader has already learned that the Jew Mordecai
had recently saved the king's life and that his act had been duly recorded
in the royal annals (2.21-23). Haman provides targeted, partially accurate information[5] to win the king over to his cause, adding a tempting
financial incentive to further his chance of success. Yet, in the Hellenistic
period when the book was likely written, the Jews did not constitute a
homogeneous group observing the same rules and the same way of life,
contrary to Haman's description. In addition, even if the Jews of the
Persian Empire had followed the rules of today's Orthodox Judaism, they
would not have been obligated to reject all royal laws, so the implied
ancient audience of the Esther Scroll, like modern ones, would instantly
have recognized that Haman's half-truths were half-lies intended to
deceive.

In the story world, however, the king falls into Haman's trap and a
mighty administrative apparatus is set in motion to destroy the ethnic
group of the man who had saved the king's life. The negative portrayal
of Persian power becomes clear when the blatant injustice of the royal
decree is presented as irrevocable. Since an edict written in the name of
the king and sealed with his royal ring supposedly cannot be revoked
(8.8), Ahasuerus cannot personally annul or overturn it when he realizes
Haman's mischief. Even after having Haman sentenced to death, the king
cannot accede to Esther's request to cancel the decree of extermination
(8.5).

The book of Esther thus describes the deeply problematic nature of
imperial power. The Persian Empire is huge, rich, and extremely well
organized, but the king is portrayed as the plaything of his advisors, who
is held hostage to their private interests. Royal decisions are depicted as
subject to the vagaries of court life. This critique of imperial power
creates an intentional distancing between the intended and actual Jewish

---

5. For Haman's speech, see André Wénin, 'Pourquoi le lecteur rit-il d'Haman en
Esther 6 TM?', *VT* 60 (2010), pp. 465-73 (466-67); Fox, *Character and Ideology in
Esther*, pp. 47-53; Linda M. Day, *Esther* (Abingdon Old Testament Commentaries;
Nashville: Abingdon, 2005), pp. 70-73; Joseph Fleishman, 'Why Did Ahasuerus
Consent to Annihilate the Jews?', *Journal of Northwest Semitic Languages* 25
(1999), pp. 41-58.

audiences of the story and the imperial power in place at any given time, represented in the story as the Persian Empire. It reinforces those in power as Other and not to be trusted by insiders.

Strategies of Resistance

Against an inconsistent imperial power whose unpredictable decisions lead to tyranny, the book of Esther features three strategies of resistance: denial, deception, and force.

Denial

Queen Vashti and Mordecai embody the refusal to submit to imperial orders. Vashti does not honour the invitation to the royal banquet. Mordecai refuses to bow at the feet of Haman. The reasons for these refusals are not explicit. We can assume that, for the authors and their original readers steeped in ancient culture, the reasons for such refusal were obvious. In Vashti's case, I have suggested elsewhere that she considered it below her status to appear at the end of a drunken banquet. In Mordecai's case, an unwillingness to bow before human power likely motivated his refusal.[6] Legitimate as their insubordination may have been in both instances, each refusal has disastrous consequences. Passive resistance is not an option against a power like the Persian Empire. Vashti loses her status as queen, and Mordecai sees his entire people threatened with extermination. The authors of the work present the reigning imperial power as a terribly repressive regime for those who refuse to comply.

Deception

Esther presents a second strategy of resistance: cunning. Mordecai charges his adoptive daughter to intercede with the king (ch. 4). While not indicating how to proceed, Mordecai stresses the absolute necessity of the appeal despite the rigid rules that prevail in the court, of which Esther is well aware:

---

6. Macchi, 'Livre d'Esther', pp. 116-17, 122-23 = Jean-Daniel Macchi, 'The Book of Esther: A Persian Story in Greek Style', in *A Palimpsest: Rhetoric, Ideology, Stylistics, and Language Relating to Persian Israel* (ed. Ehud Ben Zvi, Diana Edelman, and Frank Polak; Perspectives on Hebrew Scriptures and Its Contexts, 5; Piscataway, NJ: Gorgias, 2009), pp. 109-27 (114-19). I sought to show that the book of Esther shared with Hellenistic culture the idea that the last part of a banquet was reserved for concubines and that a free man could not worship men, however powerful they might be.

> All the king's servants and the people of the king's provinces know that if
> any man or woman goes to the king inside the inner court without being
> called, there is but one law—all alike are to be put to death. Only if the
> king holds out the golden sceptre to someone, may that person live. I
> myself have not been called to come in to the king for thirty days. (Est.
> 4.11 NRSV)

From the moment Esther decides to risk her life (4.16), the story
describes her as acting independently and becoming master of her own
destiny, no longer receiving instruction from anyone. Previously, she
had obeyed the eunuch Hegai (2.15) and Mordecai (2.10, 20), but now
her conduct becomes unexpected and clever. She makes the most of the
customs of the court to obtain a decision in her favour. Contrary to
Vashti, who had refused to obey the royal summons to appear before the
drunken king, Esther goes to the king uncalled. While Vashti had refused
to put in an appearance at the end of a banquet that featured heavy
drinking, Esther invites the king and Haman to a drinking banquet (5.4-
6). As if to erase the affront of Vashti's twofold refusal, Esther only dares
to formulate her query (7.2-4) during the course of the second banquet
she has organized for the king and Haman. In so doing, she recognizes
that, in antiquity, the banquet was an important place of power.

The formulation of the speech Esther addresses to the king uses subtle
rhetoric that is similar to that used earlier by the royal advisers. She
begins with the formula of deference, 'If I have won your favour, O king,
and if it pleases the king…' (7.3).[7] With some exaggeration, she adds
that if her people had been sold into slavery, she would not have had to
disturb the king, but in this case, it is a question of life or death (7.4).
Esther wisely avoids mentioning that the king himself is the author of the
decree against her people, whose identity remains in limbo, as it did in
Haman's discourse in ch. 3. For anyone who has read the previous
chapters, it is logical to assume the method used by Queen Esther will
succeed since she is employing the same strategy Haman used to convince the king. Having invited her nemesis as well as the king to the
banquet, she denounces Haman's *hubris* and suggests that he sees
himself the equal of her royal husband.[8] In so doing she sets Haman on a
pedestal from which he can easily fall, as the story of Vashti's fall
highlights. Esther's actions result in justice being rendered directly by

---

7. See also Est. 5.4, 8; 8.5; 9.13 (Esther), 1.19 (Memucan) and 3.9 (Haman).

8. The text suggests that this is how Haman understood the invitation. Indeed,
the theme of honour plays a central role in the story of the two banquets held by the
Queen. Upon his return from the first banquet, Haman brags about the great honour
he received (5.11-12).

the Persian king. Haman is executed and his property and functions are turned over to Esther and Mordecai (8.1-2). With cunning and courage, Esther uses the system to resist the oppression of that same system, or at least of some of its officials.[9]

The success of the cunning strategy used against those in power in the story of Esther emphasizes the alterity of the king and Haman, who are outsiders from the viewpoint of the writer and his readers. Such a use of deception presupposes a lack of confidence in those who are duped in this way and is perceived to be a justified means to an end when dealing with Others who cannot be counted on to follow the customs and rules of one's own ethnic group. Had the ruse been used against another member of the community to which the writer and the readers belonged, however, it would have been perceived negatively, as a rupture of group harmony and a threat to group integrity.

Force

Force appears as a third strategy at the beginning of ch. 8. As the crisis is seemingly resolved with Haman's execution and Mordecai's assumption of his place, the inability to repeal the royal decree sent across Persia introduces a new complication: the Jews are still likely to be exterminated. Unable to revoke the decree made in his name, the king invites Esther and Mordecai to send a new royal decree to the Jews themselves, leaving its contents to their discretion. The new decree stipulates that Jews will be permitted to kill anyone who threatens their lives and to plunder that person's goods on 13 of Adar (8.11-13). Faced with a dysfunctional power that is unable to regulate itself, the book ends with the description of a bloodbath that allows Jews to triumph over their enemies (9.1-19) and with the institution of the commemorative feast celebrating these events (9.20-32).

The use of force has often been seen as a form of glorification of violence and of Jewish nationalism.[10] But in fact, the story is constructed

9. For an analysis of mirror Othering between Israel/Esther/Mordecai and Haman/Amalek in Esther in the present volume, see Ehud Ben Zvi, 'Othering, Selfing, "Boundarying" and "Cross-Boundarying" as Interwoven with Socially Shared Memories: Some Observations', pp. 20-40.

10. The debate over whether or not to include Esther in the canon and the failure of the Church Fathers to cite the work except rarely probably resulted from concern over its contents. See Jo Carruthers, *Esther Through the Centuries* (Blackwell Bible Commentaries; Oxford: Blackwell, 2008), pp. 7-13; Frederic W. Bush, *Ruth, Esther* (WBC, 9; Dallas, TX: Word Books, 1996), pp. 273-77. The book of Esther is also frequently discredited by Christian writers. Luther said: 'I am so great an enemy to the second book of the Maccabees, and to Esther, that I wish they had not come to us

in such as way as to prompt a reflection over the legitimacy of the use of force more than it glorifies violence. In Esther, violence is an act of defence made necessary because the empire is incapable of ensuring justice within its own realm. The act of war is a last resort.

Different Social Milieux Reflected in the Text

As resistance literature vis-à-vis an imperial power that is perceived to be Other than the group transmitting the work, the book of Esther presents different options for resistance. It might seem logical at first to assume that a single, homogenous group endorsed the sequential application of the three strategies outlined above when under threat by outsiders. If expressing a simple refusal does not achieve the desired results, then cunning should be used and ultimately, violence, if nothing else works. In fact, however, a careful reading of the text, which takes into account its redactional history, indicates that the attitudes toward imperial power and the three strategies employed to deal with it are too divergent to reflect the view of a coherent social and ethnic group. Rather, the various options for resistance reflect solutions envisaged by different Jewish groups as to what they deemed appropriate behaviour in a historical situation in which one finds oneself dominated in unjust ways by a foreign empire. The story of the Jewish wife of the Persian king serves as a vehicle for reflection over which attitude to adopt.

After Mordecai's refusal led to disaster, Esther used the imperial system to her advantage. Her approach suggests that the imperial system was not to be viewed as inherently corrupt. Jews could use its mechanisms judiciously for their own interests, which suggests in turn that the group that endorsed such a tactic was not opposed to participation in official circles. For them, then, the ruling imperial power was not to be seen as radically Other. In contrast, the terrible battle staged at the end of the work suggests that, eventually, some Jews considered the institutions of the empire too dysfunctional to be able to be relied upon and that recourse to arms was necessary. This group presents imperial power as completely different from what it should be and as a result, any participation by Jews in its proceedings would be counter-productive. For

at all' (*The Table-Talk of Martin Luther Translated and Edited by William Hazlitt* [London: H. G. Bohn, 1857], p. 11). However, throughout his work, Luther's attitude toward Esther is more nuanced than it appears; see Hans Bardtke, 'Neuere Arbeiten zum Estherbuch. Ein kritische Würdigung', *Ex Oriente Lux* 19 (1965–66), pp. 519-49 (545-46).

those holding this position, involvement in official circles of the empire is illegitimate; imperial power is depicted as Other in a more radical way.

As often is the case with ancient texts, different versions of the story of the adventures of Esther and Mordecai co-existed. The text was written and rewritten several times in different venues and circumstances before reaching the current forms we know.[11] We have a Greek version of the book, the Alpha text, which suggests that one form of the story ended with the punishment of Haman and the salvation of the Jews, omitting the final massacre of the Jews' enemies.[12] In this version, the theme of the irreversibility of Persian laws was absent and the imperial system was viewed with relatively little scepticism. This variant of the story, perhaps the oldest to have survived, was probably mediated by social groups for whom Jewish life within an empire ruled by foreign powers did not pose insurmountable problems, provided one had good knowledge of how the system worked and how to behave within it.[13] In my opinion, those who produced the first version of the story of Esther had encountered Hellenistic culture and could not have written the Alpha text earlier than the Ptolemaic period.[14]

11. It should be noted that the story of Esther has had a relatively complex textual history. It is known in three different forms, a Hebrew form (MT) and two Greek forms (LXX and AT) that contain six long additions. The text used here is the Hebrew text. For a comparison between the three texts of Esther, see David J. A. Clines, *The Esther Scroll: The Story of the Story* (JSOTSup, 30; Sheffield: JSOT, 1984); Linda M. Day, *Three Faces of a Queen: Characterization in the Books of Esther* (JSOTSup, 186; Sheffield: JSOT, 1995); Karen H. Jobes, *The Alpha Text of Esther: Its Character and Relationship to the Masoretic Text* (SBLDS, 153; Atlanta, GA: Scholars Press, 1996). For a comparison between the LXX and the MT, see Hanna Kahana, *Esther: Juxtaposition of the Septuagint Translation with the Hebrew Text* (CBET, 40; Leuven: Peeters, 2005); Catherine Vialle, *Une analyse comparée d'Esther TM et LXX: Regard sur deux récits d'une meme histoire* (BETL, 233; Leuven: Peeters, 2010).

12. See my synthesis in Jean-Daniel Macchi, 'Les textes d'Esther et les tendances du Judaïsme entre les 3e et 1er siècles avant J.-Chr.', in *Un carrefour dans la Bible. Du texte à la théologie au IIe siècle avant J.-C.* (ed. Innocent Himbaza and Adrian Schenker; OBO, 233; Fribourg, Switzerland: Academic Press, 2007), pp. 75-92.

13. In the Hebrew Bible, a similar view is expressed in the story of Joseph; although Jewish, the character eventually integrates remarkably into the Egyptian court and claims to be a shrewd adviser of Pharaoh (see Gen. 37–46). A similar issue of how to be Jewish and serve at the imperial court is explored in Dan. 1–6.

14. Allusions and references to themes and motifs present in Hellenistic literature about Persia are widely present in the Alpha text of Esther. For this reason, I have situated the production of the first version of Esther in the Egyptian Diaspora of the Ptolemaic period (Macchi, 'Textes d'Esther', pp. 89-90).

With its bellicose ending, the Hebrew text shows an extensive rewriting of the story to express a virulent critique of imperial power. This version of the story of Esther probably reflects the opinion of Jews who considered life in a vast and tyrannical empire to be wrought with difficulties. For them, insurgency and self-defence were the only reasonable options against the policies of the vast empires that dominated most of the known ancient Near East and beyond, in succession. Among the ancient Jewish texts, the books of Maccabees are the most explicit in justifying recourse to arms to oppose the domination of a foreign empire. Hence, this rewriting of Esther probably presupposes the Hasmonean period.

The Masoretic book of Esther has been produced in two stages. A first version of the work was produced by a Jewish group that considered it possible to work with a Hellenistic imperial power. This text was later reworked by a group that viewed collaboration with much more scepticism. If the literary history of the book of Esther reflects the Hellenistic era, these different perceptions of the relationship with an imperial power neither began nor ended with the writing of the different phases of Esther.[15]

Thus, in the Hellenistic and Roman empires that dominated the ancient Near East, some Jewish groups made the most of the imperial structures that ruled their world by developing a working relationship with the bodies of imperial power. Other groups, like those living in the Holy Land during the domination of the Seleucid kings, had recourse to arms to resolve their differences with emperors and enemies. In its own way, the story of Esther bears traces of an important debate between different Jewish groups. Through the storyline of a Jewish queen who sought the support of her sovereign husband, the Hebrew text maintained a certain commitment to use the law of the empire to resolve conflicts, even if the final form of the text ends with the failure of this strategy.

The Othering process in the book of Esther is not homogeneous. When Esther acts with cunning to manipulate the king, the Other is a figure with whom it is possible to co-exist, communicate, and interact. When the story relates that the Jews eventually had to fight their enemies alone,

---

15. Textual diversity characterizes the book of Esther during the Roman period and reveals that the debate over the correct attitude to adopt in a world dominated by a foreign empire was not closed when the MT was reworked. Therefore, it is understandable that different versions of the pre-Masoretic text of Esther co-existed. The TA Greek, still in use in the Middle Ages in some circles, probably originated from a text that does not presuppose the final rewriting mentioned above, while the LXX presupposes a parent Hebrew text rather close to the Masoretic text of Esther.

collaborating with the imperial Other is perceived as impossible. In this case, an unbridgeable gap alienates the Jews from Persia in the story world as well as generations of Jews who experienced injustice or oppression under the successive Empires to Persia. These points of view, ultimately quite different but both responses to the power of Others, reflect the positions of different groups within Judaism in contexts where, in some ways, they are also quite different from each other. Thus, in the book of Esther, the different approaches to the power of imperial Others in the story reveal a form of diversity and otherness within the Jews, the We of the story.

Imagining the Other in the Construction of Judahite Identity in Ezra–Nehemiah

Tamara Cohn Eskenazi

> Cultural identity is a matter of 'becoming' as well as 'being'... Cultural identities come from somewhere, have histories. But, like everything which is historical, they undergo constant transformation. Far from being eternally fixed in some essentialized past, they are subject to the continuous 'play' of history, culture and power. Far from being grounded in a mere 'recovery' of the past,...identities are the names we give to the different ways we are positioned by, and position ourselves within, the narratives of the past.
>
> —Stuart Hall[1]

Is Barak Obama an American? Like some listed in Ezra 2.59-63 and its parallel in Neh. 7.61-65, Obama in the twenty-first century had to produce a document to prove he qualified as a citizen, and even then the issue was not settled to everyone's satisfaction.

Controversies over Obama's identity are a refreshing reminder that anxiety about inclusion and exclusion remains hotly relevant, especially when the stakes are high, as is the case with a responsible public office.[2] Ezra–Nehemiah (EN) presents a world in which this issue was a lively one. In doing so, it partakes in what seems to be a postexilic debate that is apparent also in Isaiah 56–66 (see especially 56.1-7), and probably serves as a backdrop to the book of Ruth. The concern underlying these texts and much else in EN revolves around questions such as these: What does it now mean to be 'Israel'? Who is to be included and on what basis?

---

1. Stuart Hall, 'Cultural Identity and Diaspora', in *Colonial Discourse and Postcolonial Theory: A Reader* (ed. Patrick Williams and Laura Chrisman; London: Harvester Wheatsheaf, 1994), pp. 392-401 (394).
2. One can add the current debates about immigration and citizenship.

We know enough about historical circumstances to understand why the stakes would have been high at this point in the history of the people with ties to the territory of Judah. As a colonized people, dispersed throughout the Persian Empire, new criteria for unity and cohesion needed to be devised. The political, geographical, and religious boundaries that typified pre-exilic life were no longer fixed. Whatever infrastructures held communities together previously were no longer available: indigenous monarchy was a thing of the past, and the land was, in the words of A. Faust, a post-collapse society.[3] Furthermore, at the beginning of EN's account, the temple in Jerusalem was gone, and the city itself remained in a dire condition even a century later (see Neh. 1 and 7). Extra biblical evidence, as well as EN itself, indicates that diverse groups and nationalities now lived under a single umbrella and at the service of an empire. Whatever community was gathering in Judah/Yehud,[4] it was small, mostly poor, and itself diverse, surrounded by other groups.

EN can be read as a response to such challenges in which identity is no longer a given, no longer automatically established by virtue of geographical location or even genealogy. Instead, EN shows that identity needs to be assessed and (re)defined within a panoply of existing options and categories, as well as diverse constituencies; it also shows that conclusions need to be re-evaluated as time goes on.

The Elephantine documents from Egypt in the fifth century BCE amply illustrate the fluidity or perhaps instability of identity, when, depending on the context, the same individual is identified legally as an ארמי

---

3. Some earlier studies claimed that the damage the Babylonians inflicted upon Judah was limited. This view has since been abandoned in favor of newer studies such as Avraham Faust's 'Settlement Dynamics and Demographic Fluctuations in Judah from the Late Iron Age to the Hellenistic Period and the Archaeology of Persian Period Yehud', in *A Time of Change: Judah and Its Neighbours in the Persian and Early Hellenistic Periods* (ed. Yigael Levin; London: T&T Clark International, 2007), pp. 23-51. For the purpose of this article, it does not matter whether one accepts Faust's reconstruction of the archaeological evidence or other views, like that of Diana Edelman ('Settlement Patterns in Persian Period Yehud', in the same volume, pp. 52-64). For an excellent recent analysis, see Ehud Ben Zvi, 'Total Exile, Empty Land and the General Intellectual Discourse in Yehud', in *The Concept of Exile in Ancient Israel and Its Historical Contexts* (ed. Ehud Ben Zvi and Christoph Levin; BZAW, 404; Berlin: de Gruyter, 2010), pp. 155-68.

4. The Hebrew portions of EN consistently refer to the province as יהודה best translated as 'Judah'. The Aramaic source, however, uses יהוד ('Yehud') 3 times (Ezra 5.1, 8; 7.14). Because my goal is to trace the imagined self and Other in EN, and because יהודה is the preferred 'in group' term in EN, I use 'Judah', except when referring to the official provincial designation.

on some occasions and as a יהודי on others.[5] EN gives content to the meaning of יהודי (or rather plural יהודים) by beginning with a presumed origin in the land of Judah as the defining category (Ezra 1–6); then, after an encounter with the Other, by commitment to God and Torah as decisive (Ezra 7–10), requiring separation from the people(s) of the land(s). Finally, as a result of another encounter with an Other, it concludes by asserting a level of politico-religious self-determination as the next necessary marker (Neh. 1–7).

In his landmark study of the subject, S. J. D. Cohen claims that the term יהודים, 'Judeans', first functioned as an 'ethnic geographic term'.[6] It referred to 'those who originally hailed from the ethnic homeland'.[7] This is the definition we find operating in Ezra 1–6, though I prefer to use the term 'Judahite' instead of 'Judean' for this phase and meaning in this part of the essay. Cohen, however, objects to equating the term יהודים with Jews prior to the second century BCE; he maintains that, at least in English, '"Jews" is a religious term: a Jew is someone who venerates the God of the Judaeans, the God whose temple is in Jerusalem... "Jew", then denotes culture, way of life, or "religion" not ethnic or geographic origin.'[8] According to Cohen, using the term 'Jews' prior to the second century BCE is usually wrong (note that most translations render the Hebrew or Aramaic plural forms, יהודים, in EN as 'Jews'; see, e.g., Ezra 5.1 and Neh. 1.2).

Contrary to Cohen, I suggest that the authors of EN seek to describe the process by which Judahites became Jews. Ezra 7–10 sets the process in the early Persian period. The next stage, Nehemiah 1–7, describes not merely a city with Jews, who now are not only Judahites, but shows

---

5.   Jon L. Berquist has argued that all Judaeans were, in principle, Persian ('The Constructions of Identity in Postcolonial Yehud', in *Judah and the Judeans in the Persian Period* [ed. Oded Lipschits and Manfred Oeming; Winona Lake, IN: Eisenbrauns, 2006], pp. 53-66). This statement ignores the extent to which both Judaean and Persian sources consistently deny such an organizing category. Being subject to Persian imperial rule did not amount to being Persian.

6.   Shaye J. D. Cohen, *The Beginning of Jewishness: Boundaries, Varieties, Uncertainties* (Berkeley: University of California Press, 1999), p. 104. Although I avoid using the term Jew at this point in the paper, I consider the community in Neh. 8–12 to be 'Jewish' in the religious manner in which Cohen defines Jewishness, with Ezra 1–Neh. 7 reflecting the stages leading to this identity ('The Missions of Ezra and Nehemiah', in Lipschits and Oeming [eds.], *Judah and the Judeans in the Persian Period*, pp. 509-29).

7.   Ibid., p. 105.

8.   Ibid., p. 105.

how a city with Jews became a Jewish city. The transformation of identity in the post-exilic era is traced definitively also by E. Ben Zvi.[9] He focuses on how 'Exiled Israel' became 'Israel', a term like יהודי or Jew in Cohen's definition.

> During the post-monarchic period, and within the corpus of the period that was later included in the Old Testament/Hebrew Bible, the concept referred to by the term 'Israel', the larger group, began to change. Instead of referring to Judahites (and to some extent to 'Ephraim'), the term began to refer to those who *belonged to a community characterized by a certain religious tradition, including 'biblical' texts (or biblical texts in the making) and their interpretations*.[10]

Ben Zvi's note adds that the term יהודי, Judahite, underwent a similar change to 'Jew' as is illustrated in the book of Esther.[11]

Studies of ethnic identity by F. Barth and G. Bauman[12] have enhanced the work of numerous biblical scholars by introducing helpful categories for analysis from the fields of anthropology and sociology.[13] Most relevant for this essay is their explanation of identity formation as processual, a view echoed also by Stuart Hall above.

Yet, although modern studies confirm that identity is a construct, many ancient texts present it as primordial. This is where EN differs. A distinctive feature of EN is the degree to which it exposes the developmental processes of identity formation. EN begins with a question about

9. 'Inclusion and Exclusion from Israel as Conveyed by the Use of the Term "Israel" in Post-Monarchic Texts', in *The Pitcher Is Broken: Memorial Essays for Gösta Ahlström* (ed. Steven W. Holloway and Lowell K. Handy; JSOTSup, 190; Sheffield: Sheffield Academic Press, 1995), pp. 95-149.

10. Ben Zvi, 'Inclusion and Exclusion', p. 122; emphasis added.

11. Ibid., p. 122 n. 75.

12. Fredrik Barth, *Ethnic Groups and Boundaries: The Social Organization of Cultural Difference* (Boston: Little, Brown, 1969); Gerd Baumann, *Contesting Culture: Discourse of Identity in Multi-Culture London* (Cambridge Studies in Social and Cultural Anthropology, 100; Cambridge: Cambridge University Press, 1996); and idem, *The Multicultural Riddle: Rethinking National, Ethnic and Religious Identities* (Zones of Religion; New York: Routledge, 1999).

13. See, for example, Lawrence M. Wills, *Not God's People: Insiders and Outsiders in the Biblical World* (Plymouth, UK: Rowman & Littlefield, 2008); Neil Glover, 'Your People, My People: An Exploration of Ethnicity in Ruth', *JSOT* 33 (2009), pp. 293-313. For a good discussion, see also Gary N. Knoppers, 'Nehemiah and Sanballat: The Enemy Without or Within?', in *Judah and the Judaeans in the Fourth Century* (ed. Oded Lipschits, Gary Knoppers, and Rainer Albertz; Winona Lake, IN: Eisenbrauns, 2007), pp. 305-31 (306-308).

identity, as per the declaration of Cyrus: 'Who is among you from all his people...?' (Ezra 1.3). EN then illustrates how such identity has to be negotiated and renegotiated in stages.

The construction of identity in EN unfolds, as do other social constructs, by strengthening the community's core through uniting ideologies and actions, as well as by cultivating a boundary and relation to the Other. In EN, the Other comes in two forms that, for the sake of clarity, I over-simplify with the labels the Other as friend and the Other as foe.[14]

J. L. Wright shows how constructing communal identity is central to the formation of EN.[15] As he illustrates, composing material like the Nehemiah Memoir (NM) was itself an act of (re?)building identity.[16] Wright carefully traces the layered developments of the text, showing how internal communal tensions influenced the particular expression embodied not merely in the NM but in EN as a whole. The present essay builds on Wright's contribution but shifts the focus specifically to the construction of the Other as a distinct subtext in developing communal identity. Moreover, whereas Wright's study is diachronic, I am working with the final text as a starting point for discerning the construction of the Other, and I look at the identity that emerges from the final version of EN.[17]

This essay is indebted to Lawrence M. Wills's book, *Not God's People*, and especially to his chapter on 'Redefinition of We and Other in Ezra–Nehemiah'.[18] Like Wills, I wish to highlight the construction of the

---

14. That Nehemiah in Neh. 13 battles the same issues alerts readers, in good biblical fashion, to the likelihood that such challenges will repeat. This repeated need to refashion ideals and practices is underscored in Michael Walzer's comment that the Jewish version of the Bible 'reflects an unfinished engagement with history' (*In God's Shadow: Politics in the Hebrew Bible* [New Haven: Yale University Press, 2012], p. xvi).

15. Jacob L. Wright, *Rebuilding Identity: The Nehemiah Memoir and Its Earliest Readers* (BZAW, 348; Berlin: de Gruyter, 2004).

16. Other diachronic studies of the material include those by Yonina Dor, who seeks to identify the composition layers of the marriage controversies ('The Composition of the Episode of the Foreign Women in Ezra IX–X', *VT* 53 [2003], pp. 26-47), and Juha Pakkala (*Ezra the Scribe: The Development of Ezra 7–10 and Nehemiah 8* [BZAW, 347; Berlin: de Gruyter, 2004]).

17. As I note in my book, *In an Age of Prose: A Literary Approach to Ezra–Nehemiah* (SBLMS, 36; Atlanta: SBL, 1988). The division into two books, Ezra and Nehemiah is a late stage in the transmission of this literature. The earliest sources consider the material in Ezra 1–10 and Neh. 1–13 to constitute a single book. In *In an Age of Prose*, I show how the unified work conveys messages.

18. Wills, *Not God's People*, pp. 53-86.

Other in EN by paying attention to the distinct messages of each unit. But I follow a different demarcation of the units. Wills organizes the sources in terms of three units: (1) Ezra 1–6; (2) the Ezra Memoir: Ezra 7–10 and Nehemiah 8–10; and (3) the Nehemiah Memoir: Nehemiah 1–7 and 11–13.[19] This approach represents a widely held consensus that each of these units was distinct in an earlier stage of the composition, before being combined as EN. Wills's goal is to avoid homogenizing the perspectives of the different sections.

I, too, wish to differentiate the different positions in the text, but to do so in terms of the presentation in the final form. Therefore, I follow the story as it unfolds in the book, since my goal is to track the process and the imagined world as EN presents and organizes them. I do not, thereby, grant the final version historical reliability. This is not a reversion to an earlier, naïve reading in which what is said is taken at face value, except insofar as it is an articulation of the views the final authors created or preserved for their readers. My goal is to trace this book's messages about how identity is formed and what roles outsiders have in the process.

I begin with Ezra 1–6 as Wills does, but I follow the subsequent units and subunits in the sequence given in EN as the basis for analysis. As I show elsewhere,[20] EN unfolds in the following way:

Ezra 1.1-4 introduces Cyrus's edict, which commissions God's people to build the house of God. Ezra 1.5-6 reports that the people did so. What follows all the way through to Nehemiah 7 is a record of the response to Cyrus's edict. The building of God's house is done in three stages: first, the people build the temple (Ezra 3–6); second, they build the community itself (Ezra 7–10); third, and finally, they build Jerusalem's walls (Neh. 1–7). Only then is the house of God re-established. These three stages are placed between two virtually identical lists of names of those credited with building the house of God (Ezra 2 and Neh. 7.6-72). Once the house of God is complete, encompassing temple, people, and city, the entire community celebrates by articulating its sense of identity as a community committed to God's Torah and to God's temple (Neh. 8–12; see particularly the pledge in Neh. 10).

In reading EN, it is relatively easy to discern that it posits foreigners as the Other(s). Two features of EN are worth noting as unusual for the Hebrew Bible:

19. Ibid., p. 58.
20. *In an Age of Prose*, pp. 37-126.

1. More than any other biblical book, EN posits foreigners as Other not only as foe but also as friend.

2. Both the We and the Other in EN are presented as identities in process, with definition and boundaries forming as the story unfolds. This processual understanding that underlies claims to normative criteria of communal identity is taken for granted in modern historical analysis. It is rare, however, to find such a process so overtly illustrated and acknowledged in a biblical book.[21] In other words, the fluidity and constructive nature of identity in EN (that is, the recognition that identity is processual) is not only visible as an etic perspective but is also presented as an emic one. In what follows I review EN to illustrate how the narrative communicates these patterns.

The present essay examines the three stages of identity formation in Ezra 1–Nehemiah 7. I consider these to be the building blocks in the ongoing process of constructing Judahite identity. Nehemiah 8–12 is an articulation, confirmation, and celebration of the newly established communal boundaries and self-definition. The fact that the community as a whole now assents to the Torah (Neh. 8), recites communal history (Neh. 9), and unilaterally pledges itself (Neh. 10) is a bold assertion of who they claim to have become. In other words, Nehemiah 8–12 is the declaration of the newly constructed communal identity. Ezra 1–Nehemiah 7 charts the steps that were undertaken to reach this point. Among other things, Nehemiah 13 reminds the reader and the community that vigilance is nonetheless needed in order to sustain such identity in the face of recurrent pressures.

* * *

Each section in Ezra 1–Nehemiah 7 represents the active construction of identity by means of three sets of relationships. The most significant is strengthening the group by means of uniting commonalities. The most explicit unifying feature in the stages of reconstruction (Ezra 1–Neh. 7) is the building activity involving the physical erection of different components of the house of God. The construction of identity in EN is inseparable from the construction of the house of God. This is the kind of 'core' building that S. J. D. Cohen writes about.[22]

---

21. Arguably, much of the polemic in Deuteronomy and the prophetic material can be marshaled to argue that identity is at stake. But EN's narrative repeatedly 'shows' how this struggle for identity unfolds.

22. Cohen, *Beginning of Jewishness*, p. 9. As noted, however, Cohen objects to the use of the term 'Jew' prior to the second century BCE period (see n. 6).

But as even a cursory reading of EN shows, a relation to the Other is very much part of carving out a sense of self in these chapters. EN recognizes the power of the Other to shape its community in tandem with ritual and practices that help cohere from within, as it were. As noted earlier, EN imagines two types of an influential Other: 'the Other as friend' and 'the Other as foe'.[23]

The Other imagined as a friend is most notably the Persian kings; the Other as foe most notably is imagined and defined as foreign 'people(s) of the land(s)'.

More than any other biblical book, Ezra–Nehemiah grants a positive, influencing role to an Other in the formation of Judah's identity, a fact that might seem jarring to the many scholars and readers who focus on what they term as EN's xenophobia. EN certainly objects to certain Others. But it is as assiduous, and in many ways more so, in highlighting the positive role of an Other in the reconstruction of life in Judah. No other biblical book gives so much credit to outsiders. Isaiah 44–45 and 56.1-7 come a distant second.[24]

23. The political thinker Carl Schmitt has been credited with formulating the roles of 'enemy' (or 'foe') and 'friend' in the shaping of 'political theology'; see for example *Political Theology: Four Chapters on the Concept of Sovereignty* (trans. G. Schwab; Chicago: University of Chicago Press, 2005). The use of such strategies, however, is well documented in ancient sources, of which EN is perhaps the most explicit or vivid biblical example.

24. Many scholars have considered the reforms in EN to be a proactive policy of the Persian government, and some still do. See Wills, *Not God's People*, pp. 57-58. Peter Frei's thesis on the subject has influenced such a perspective (e.g. 'Persian Imperial Authorization: A Summary', in *Persia and Torah: The Theory of Imperial Authorization of the Pentateuch* [ed. James W. Watts; SBLSymS, 17; Atlanta: SBL, 2001), pp. 5-40]). Closer analyses of the evidence and the thesis, however, have solidly invalidated the claim. It is more likely that a backwater, small province like Yehud in the Persian period would not have registered on the vast map of imperial concerns or politics, except when promoted by the inhabitants of the area or their representatives in the imperial court. In this respect, EN's picture of the exchanges, whether fictive or factual, reflects a credible pattern, familiar from other sources. It is the case that the Diaspora is featured as influencing events both in relation to the Persian court, as the portrayal of both Ezra and Nehemiah shows. But, at least in terms of EN's construction of the relationship, the Diaspora's value is as a point of departure for a journey that not only culminates in Judah but is played out in Judah. There are no volunteered exchanges back to the Diaspora. The return of Nehemiah to the court is presented as a royal decree, not a personal choice (Neh. 13.6). I concur with Jonathan E. Dyck that the impetus for restoration was the work of exile (*The Theocratic Ideology of the Chronicler* [BibInt Series, 33; Leiden: Brill, 1998], pp. 108-109). It is more difficult, however, to assess the extent of correspondence

The three stages of reconstruction of the house of God in Ezra 2–
Nehemiah 7 roughly unfold this way: the first stage begins with support
from the Other as friend, followed by an account of the community
uniting in their mission around a shared building project. This establishes
a foundational and founding identity. The Other as foe appears next.
*As a result, EN renders the encounter with the Other as friend as a
primary feature of identity construction, leading to communal cohesion;
and it presents the Other as foe as a secondary or even tertiary development in the formation of Judahite identity.* Moreover, the Other
as foe in Ezra 1–6 and Nehemiah 1–7 is cast as a deliberate reaction to
the cohering/consolidation of Judahite identity that preceded (i.e. the
prior positive encounter with the Other as friend, and the strengthening
internal cohesion).

In this essay I will not attempt to disentangle historical realities such
as who 'the people of the land(s)' represented or the other cruxes that
bedevil EN scholarship, such as compositional history, dates, and so on.[25]

---

between life in exile and life in Yehud. We lack information about the organizational
structures of the exilic community. It is possible, therefore, to claim that the project
in Judah/Yehud differed from the exilic one, which is why some people went to
Judah/Yehud.

25. I share the perspective of Jonathan E. Dyck that one 'point of interest,
especially in dealing with Ezra–Nehemiah, is not the sociological realities to which
the texts refers [*sic*] but the way in which the text presents them' (*Theocratic
Ideology*, p. 109). I find Ben Zvi's article on the subject to be a superb study
of diverse historical issues at work, as well as of the literary representations along
with the possible ideologies that they serve ('Inclusion and Exclusion'). I concur
with most of his arguments, although we differ in particular on the roles of the
Achaemenid rulers. In terms of the present discussion, I agree with Ben Zvi that
'[a]lthough there may have been tensions between the returnees and those who
remained in the land, it is unlikely that there was a long-term tension between them'
(p. 136). But whereas he emphasizes the case in EN for 'Exiled Israel' as *the* 'Israel'
(his formulation being 'EI=I'; see, esp. pp. 129-35), I am inclined to suggest that the
case being made is, instead, that 'Exiled Israel' is *also* 'Israel'. In other words, in the
formation of communal identity, those from outside the land are pitching their
defensive case as strongly as possible in portions of EN in light of the challenge to
their legitimacy by those in the land. Their exilic position is combined with the other
voices. And as the editors of the narrative corpus in the Hebrew Bible do when they
retain both Joshua and Judges with their different ethos about origins, so, too, does
EN combine both groups, with the NM representing as יהודים those who have not
left. A similar weaving of both communities is evident in Isa. 40–66, with the
'dialogue' between the Jacob/Israel passages and the Zion/Jerusalem ones. In other
words, to agree with Ben Zvi that EN claims that 'EI=I' is not necessarily to concur
that this means 'EI is the only I'. A great deal in EN reflects the weaving together of
different constituencies, most overtly in the presentation of the two distinctive

Instead, I will follow the unfolding story as it constructs the Other and attempt to highlight what kind of Self or 'Israel' results through this process.[26]

Stage One: Building the Temple (Ezra 1–6)

EN begins by introducing the Other as friend, a foreigner who, inspired by Israel's God and in conformity with a prophetic message of Jeremiah, commissions the building of God's house. Cyrus's edict (Ezra 1.2-4) is cast both as an exhortation and possibly as a rhetorical question: 'Who is among you of all his people...? Let him go up...and build the house of YHWH, the God of Israel, he is the God in Jerusalem...' (Ezra 1.3; my translation).[27] The statement is both an invitation and the challenge that will reverberate throughout the rest of the book. Who indeed belongs to 'God's people'? From this moment forward, building the house of God is intimately tied to the definition of identity. This claim will dominate all three stages that lead to the completion of the house of God (Ezra 1– Neh. 7).[28] The chapters that follow this introduction in Ezra 1.1-4 seek to answer and expound on this question of 'who is among you of all his

figures of Ezra and Nehemiah, as well as Haggai and Zechariah (when the books bearing their names show no contact between the two). For this and other reasons, it is worth considering that a similar conjoining is at work in the notion of 'Israel'.

26.   My attempt to follow the story as it is told is not a reversion to how we used to read the Bible as the work of a reliable narrator. Rather, in this article, I aim to re-read along the grain precisely because we now have clearer information, even if it lacks precision, that actual historical 'facts' were often different. This makes it valuable to revisit the ideology embedded in the narration as conscious messages rather than 'mere' recording. In this essay, however, I am looking at the unfolding account as a specific project of constructing identity, not as a record of what happened during the Persian period that EN covers. I trust that the distinction is useful in showing how a community understood itself or rather sought to 'invent' or construct itself. The question why goes beyond the scope of the present study. The same holds for the questions about the actual facts in the history of the recon-struction.

27.   The NRSV obscures some of the important messages by translating less literally as 'Any of those among you who are of his people—may their God be with them!—are now permitted to go up..., and rebuild the house of the LORD, the God of Israel—he is the God who is in Jerusalem'.

28.   For this reason, I identify the structure of EN, Ezra 2–Neh. 7, as a three-stage response to Ezra 1, with Ezra 1.1-4 setting the agenda for the entire book, fulfilled only when the walls of Jerusalem are rebuilt. The two lists of returnees in Ezra 2 and Neh. 7.6-72 frame the three stages and unify them. See my book, *In an Age of Prose*, esp. 'The Structure of Ezra–Nehemiah', pp. 37-126.

people...?' through a series of inclusions and exclusions. The exclusionary sections often receive center stage in the studies of EN,[29] and these will be important in the present essay; but one must not lose sight of the fact that an imagined Other, King Cyrus, begins the process, and other outsiders will also repeatedly offer unstinting support that will make building possible.

EN proceeds to answer the question of 'Who is among you...?' by making it clear that God's people are those who join together and go up to build God's house in Jerusalem (Ezra 1.5-6). They, like Cyrus, had been roused by God's spirit: 'And they rose up to build YHWH's house in Jerusalem...' (Ezra 1.5). Thus, although a Persian king commissioned the building, it is Israel's God who directly inspires the people themselves. While the people are cast as obedient to imperial laws, they take their marching orders from Israel's God.

The community is comprised of Judah and Benjamin, along with priests and Levites (Ezra 1.5; 4.1). Although it is customary to suppose that the call and response are aimed exclusively at the Diaspora, the language of the edict itself, and the overarching response in 1.5-6, do not make such a claim. The call applies as much to those dwelling in Judah and Benjamin who now must align themselves with the project of building God's house in Jerusalem.

The list of the 42,360 people who went up from captivity (Ezra 2.64//Neh. 7.66) further establishes those who belong. With this list, and its repetition in Nehemiah 7, EN identifies the people as a whole as the chief protagonists.[30] Their commitment to (re)building God's house is their defining feature at this stage. Returnees will be joined by others who separate themselves from the impurities of the nations of the land (Ezra 6.21).

Those unable to prove their genealogy are subject to an uncertain status. Priests among them are temporarily barred from service but apparently not excluded from the community. The status of the other 'undocumented immigrants' is not specified.

As these builders organize for action, they are assisted by the friendly Others in Ezra 3.7: the Sidonians and Tyrians, who provide material and talent to the building of the temple. The successful founding of the cult and the temple marks the uniting rituals that identify God's people (3.8-13).

29. Wills's excellent chapter on EN in *Not God's People* primarily examines the cases of the Other as foe, not friend, with one exception: Ezra 6.21; see below.

30. For details, see my book, *In an Age of Prose.*

It is only after these efforts to establish identities that the narrator introduces the major encounter with the Other as foe in 4.1-23.[31] With this episode, the construction of identity is augmented by yet another category. By defining the Other to be of foreign origin, brought to the land by imperial fiat, EN makes identity determined by point of origin in Judah and Benjamin.

The narrator introduces 'the adversaries of Judah and Benjamin' (4.1). The ground for their exclusion is their own testimony: they identify themselves as settlers from a foreign land. They also speak of Israel's God as 'your God', providing evidence of a different orientation. Ezra 4.4 refers to them as 'people of the land', and Ezra 4.8-9 further identifies them as settlers in Samaria who have come from other lands. Allowing these people to join in building will impute legitimacy to their presence in the land and assent to their claim as a people of God. But Judah and Benjamin are to be separate, and thus the Other is rebuffed.

As is well known, Ezra 4 combines various accounts, parts of which are inserted anachronistically, to underscore persistent opposition to the builders. The overt artificiality of the composition[32] highlights the book's intention to cast an Other as the sole obstacle to the rapid building of the temple.

The retort with which 'the adversaries' are rebuffed further illumines the construction of Judahite identity in EN: 'It is not for you and us to build a house for our God; for we, together [יחד] will build to YHWH, the God of Israel, as the king commanded us, Cyrus King of Persia' (4.3, my translation). The reference to יחד, translated here as 'together', has been a problem for translators. Most render it as 'alone',[33] but the word typically means 'together' and here explicitly expresses the idea that building unifies the community vis-à-vis those now classified as outsiders by their own admission. The unifying gesture on the one hand, and excluding one on the other, are both defended as a sign of loyalty to the Other as a friend: the builders are loyal subjects, and they execute the

---

31. Fear of the Other appears briefly in 3.2 as background to the building of the altar but is closely followed by the Other as friend in the form of Sidonians and Tyrians in 3.7.

32. I presume that the ancient reader, no less than a modern one, would assume that the sequence is out of chronological order. This assumption is confirmed by changes made in other early versions of the account, such as 1 Esdras and Josephus.

33. The NJPS translates it as follows: 'It is not for you and us to build a House to our God, but we alone will build it to the LORD God of Israel, in accord with the charge that the king, King Cyrus of Persia, laid upon us'. NRSV has 'You shall have no part with us in building a house to our God; but we alone will build to the LORD, the God of Israel, as King Cyrus of Persia has commanded us'.

command of King Cyrus, whose royal stature is emphasized by the repeated reference to him as king.

In the script that EN constructs, the obstructionist tactics of 'the people of the land', including the correspondence that follows (Ezra 4.4-23), successfully stop the united builders. As numerous scholars observe, this section first and foremost aims to show the perfidy of the Other as foe as the sole reason why the temple was not speedily built, which contrasts with Judahite apathy toward building in Haggai. This allows the writers to retain the image of an eager Judahite community, wholly committed to building its temple but helpless to overrule malevolent local opponents when the Other as friend is far away.

Yet, one should not overlook the many ways the testimony of the adversaries also bolsters the image and identity of the Judahite community. Through these letters, the Other, even as foe, affirms the continuity of the current Judahite community, described as יהודיא in 4.12, with the powerful kingdom in the pre-exilic era; the adversarial letters further establish the Judahites' belonging in the land and confirm the significance of building as the reassertion of such power (4.16), a point that Nehemiah 1–7 will develop without naming it as such.[34]

The rest of Stage One depicts the Other as friend who replaces the foe. Rebuilding resumes in Ezra 5.1 when Judahite prophets inspire the community to build again (Ezra 5.1), and their efforts continue unhindered. The Other who facilitates their efforts is Tattenai, the governor of the province, and his entourage, who investigate the activities in Judah and sympathetically report their findings to King Darius. Although Tattenai's report makes no reference to the adversarial letter in Ezra 4, it becomes a mouthpiece for Judahite defense in the face of allegations in Ezra 4 (Ezra 5.6-17). The letter emphasizes Judahite loyalty to the Persian crown and the crown's loyalty to the Judahites: King Cyrus himself had ordered the building (5.13-15), and the Judahites have been carrying out his orders throughout the intervening years (5.16).

Despite the lack of clear transition in the section from Tattenai's letter to Darius', the full correspondence between governor Tattenai and King Darius (Ezra 5.6–6.12) establishes the legitimacy of the builders as responsible subjects of the Persian king. It constructs a Judahite identity

---

34. This point is worth noting in light of scholarly debates between 'minimalists' (like Philip Davies and Keith Whitelam) and 'maximalists' about the origins of the Judaeans in post-exilic Yehud. Again, I do not imply in this paper that the letters are genuine. I am merely highlighting the messages as an attempt to grasp the book's final form, which for me serves as necessary, preliminary work for any excavation of these texts.

in which the most powerful Other proves to be a friend and generous supporter, and displays this support at great length. The twin gestures of loyalty to God's message and responsible adherence to royal decrees assure success despite interference from a foe.[35]

As Wills observes, Ezra 1–6 limits the conflict 'and Otherness to those who are presumed to be from the mixed nations neighbouring Judah to the north'.[36] At the outset, 'there is one external division, but no internal divisions within Judah. Nor conflict between returnees and those who were not deported. In fact, the latter, "who separated themselves from the abominations of the land" are welcomed into the Passover celebration.'[37]

Wills also notes that scholars often neglect Ezra 6.20-21 in their discussion of the relation to the Other in EN. It is significant, as he indicates, that the first section of EN concludes by including those who separated themselves from 'the impurity of the nations of the land to worship YHWH, the God of Israel' (Ezra 6.21). The passage might signal that once the temple was in place, there was a strong enough core to allow criteria for safely crossing boundaries. In any case, the concluding verses of this Stage One open a gate and define additional terms for entering. Such a gate exists, however, because a symbolic wall already demarcates identity and a relation to the 'other' as an outsider.

Stage Two: Building the Community as the House of God (Ezra 7–10)

…but you shall be for me a priestly kingdom and a holy nation. (Exod. 19.6)

Ezra 7–10 focuses on building the community itself as the house of God.[38] Ezra 1–6 established that God's people are those who build God's house. The excluded Others were those who did not originally belong to

---

35. The claim that they have been building continuously conflicts with the earlier report. This leads the reader to conclude that the successful rebuilding was accomplished in the end by Judahite determination, through the inspiration of Judahite prophets and leaders willing to overrule imperial instructions.

36. Wills, *Not God's People*, p. 64.

37. Ibid.

38. See Eskenazi, *In an Age of Prose*, pp. 71-73. The use of 'house' (בית) to refer to a family, people, or clan is sufficiently familiar from biblical and other ancient texts (see, e.g., Exod. 40.38; Lev. 22.18; Num. 2.29). Architectural metaphors for the community also emerge in Ezra's prayer when Ezra refers to a tent peg (Ezra 9.8) and fence (Ezra 9.9), a flimsy foothold and protection. In this section, the going up to Judah is 'founded' (7.9). The use of יסד is decidedly an architectural image. See for example 1 Kgs 6.7, where it refers to the founding of YHWH's house, meaning the temple. Here this word applies to the people who go up.

Israel (4.10). Once the temple was built, an additional criterion is introduced: purity. Those may join who 'have separated themselves from the
impurity (טֻמְאָה) of the nations of the land' (6.21). Ezra 9–10 places
purity at the forefront when defining Judahite identity. A holy temple in
the people's midst requires rigorous standards of purity. The Judahite
community is thus construed as a 'seed of the holy' (Ezra 9.2; usually
translated as 'the holy seed'). As S. Olyan and others note, 'purity
ideology of Ezra–Nehemiah functions as one of several significant tools
used to reconfigure the Judean community through the definition of who
is a Judean and expulsion of those classed as aliens'.[39]

With Ezra 7–10, especially 9–10, Judahite identity is no longer the
business of men only but comes to apply to women as well. The women
men marry determine membership in the community. Moreover, genealogy no longer suffices. Belonging requires the practice of a certain level
of purity.

Like Ezra 1, Ezra 7–10 introduces the Other first as a beneficent king.
Royal generosity, in the form of giving Ezra all that he requests, is first
summed up by the narrator (7.6) and then exemplified in the king's long
letter, which bestows great benefits upon Ezra and the cult (Ezra 7.12-26;
see also Ezra 8.26-27, with quantities of gold and silver that defy
credulity). The letter also places the law of Ezra's God and the law of the
king in tandem as sources of authority that must be obeyed. The reference to 'the law of *your* God' in Ezra 7.14 underscores, once again, the
Otherness of the king.

This time, however, we note a shift in the relation: the initiative begins
with Ezra, not as in ch. 1, with the foreign king: 'and the king granted
him all that he asked, for the hand of the LORD his God was upon him'
(Ezra 7.6b NRSV). The empire is subjected to the wishes of the Judahite
official.

Having introduced the Other as a friend, notwithstanding the same
name appearing as a foe earlier in Ezra 4.11-23, the story focuses on
strengthening the core internally through rituals and other activities that
create unities: the recruiting of Levites, communal fasting (8.21-23),
assigning authority and sanctity to clergy (8.24-29), and the transfer of
gifts to the cult leaders in Jerusalem (8.33-34). These unifying gestures
culminate in a ritual in which the *golah* community makes an offering,
symbolically and significantly on behalf of the twelve tribes of Israel.[40]

39.   Saul M. Olyan, 'Purity Ideology in Ezra–Nehemiah as a Tool to Reconstitute
the Community', *Journal for the Study of Judaism* 35.1 (2004), pp. 1-16 (1).
40.   This is the first time in EN when Israel stands for the entirety of the people.
In Ezra 2.2, the term 'Israel' pertains to non-cultic families; elsewhere in Ezra 1–6 it

Conflict with an Other emerges in Ezra 9.1-2. The challenge concerns marriages. Ezra is informed that leaders, priests, and Levites have married women whose practices are like the abominations of the proscribed, early inhabitants of the land (Ezra 9.1, an unmistakable allusion to Deut. 7.1-6). Through these unions 'the holy seed has mixed itself with the peoples of the lands' (Ezra 9.2 NRSV). In response, Ezra sets stringent standards for membership. Ezra claims that God forbade such unions (9.11-12) and that they jeopardized the nation's survival in the past and threaten to do so once again (9.13-14). Wills considers this passage as 'one of the most important in the Hebrew Bible in terms of the construction of the We and Other; the definition of boundaries of Israel is altered in a fundamental way'.[41]

Under Ezra's leadership, the community agrees that separation from such women is required (Ezra 10.11). Ezra 10.18-19 specifies that those of the high priest family from the house of Jeshua son of Jozadak agreed to remove ('bring out', 'take out', or 'expel' as in 10.2) their foreign wives[42] and to offer the reparation sacrifice (אשם).[43] The fate of the other families is not disclosed.[44]

---

is used only in reference to YHWH as Israel's God. On 'Israel', see further Ben Zvi, 'Inclusion and Exclusion'.

41. Wills, *Not God's People*, p. 65. While this subject occupies a little less than half of Ezra 7–10, it seems to occupy a much larger part in later studies of EN. In English translation, Ezra 7–8 has 1,795 words, whereas Ezra 9–10 has 1,534.

42. As I argue elsewhere, one may regard Ezra 9–10 as a response directed pointedly at violations by leaders, including priests ('The Missions of Ezra and Nehemiah'). The process that Ezra undertakes functions as a model for exerting pressure on the elite. What follows, therefore, may be less concerned with everyone who married so-called foreign women but specifically with priests and other community leaders. The public assembly in Ezra 10, then, is key to the unfolding story, and is one of several strategies to distribute power to a wider circle, with the Torah at the center.

43. Who in Ezra 10 brings the אשם? Some argue that both priests and lay persons do; see Jacob Milgrom, *Cult and Conscience: The Asham and the Priestly Doctrine of Repentance* (Studies in Judaism in Late Antiquity, 18; Leiden: Brill, 1976), p. 73, and Christine E. Hayes, *Gentile Impurities and Jewish Identities: Intermarriage and Conversion from the Bible and the Talmud* (Oxford: Oxford University Press, 2002), p. 29. Olyan distinguishes between the EM, where priests and laity are equated, and the third person in Ezra 10, which separates priests from laity; thus, only priests bring the *asham* ('Purity Ideology', p. 9 n. 7).

44. Ezra 10.44 comments that the preceding names refer to those who married foreign wives, some of whom bore children. In contrast, the rendition in 1 Esd. 9.36 claims that all these men sent out or released (divorced) their foreign wives and children. Although many scholars conclude that the version in 1 Esdras applies as

As C. Saysell observes,

> the leaders' complaint that the 'holy seed intermingled with the peoples
> of the lands' leaves the status of the 'foreign wives' and their effect
> tantalizingly open: are they profane or impure and consequently do they
> desecrate or defile? Ezra in his prayer alludes to Lev. 18.24-30 and states
> that the Canaanites have made the land unclean with their abominations
> and filled it with impurity; a repetition of which he fears in his own day.
> This suggests that the women are impure, which immediately raises the
> question what the nature of their impurity is.[45]

Saysell's excellent review of scholarly interpretations of the alleged
impurity in Ezra 9–10 illustrates the difficulty of explaining aspects of
the exclusions by reference to other biblical sources. As Saysell
concludes, it is difficult to determine whether genealogical, cultic/ritual,
or moral impurity accounts for 'why intermarriages are unacceptable
with these "foreign women"'.[46]

   The lack of scholarly consensus about the precise nature of the impurity, despite many rigorous and erudite studies, may itself be a clue that

---

well to Ezra 10.44, even if only implicitly, such a view is unwarranted. In the present
account, strictures are placed upon the officiating high priestly family, as is to be
expected on the basis of texts such as Lev. 21. EN's author need not have read
Lev. 21 to determine that a different, stricter degree or standard of purity applies to
the high priest than to others; Neh. 13 demonstrates this presumption. Nehemiah
says he removed a son of the high priest who married Sanballat's daughter (Neh.
13.28). But Nehemiah only punishes other men who intermarried and demands their
oath not to allow this in the future (Neh. 13.23-27). Wives are not expelled.

   45.   Csilla Saysell, *'According to the Law': Reading Ezra 9–10 as Christian
Scripture* (Journal of Theological Interpretation Supplement, 4; Winona Lake, IN:
Eisenbrauns, 2012), p. 97.

   46.   Ibid., p. 99. Saysell argues that 'foreign women' in Ezra 9–10 'are considered
"morally impure" and their effect is profanation without (ritual?) defilement affecting irrevocably the children of such mixed marriages' (p. 121). She finds a similar
message in Neh. 13. That whole chapter, she maintains, has in mind with the term
מעל 'the non-technical sense of simply getting rid of any foreign influence that led
Israel into disobedience away from her commitment to her God' (p. 121). The
language of 'holy seed' receives much attention from interpreters, who ask whether
this is about genealogy, purity, ritual purity, or moral purity (p. 108). Ritual purity
is favored by David P. Wright ('The Spectrum of Priestly Impurity', in *Priesthood
and Cult in Ancient Israel* [ed. Gary A. Anderson and Saul M. Olyan; JSOTSup,
125; Sheffield: Sheffield Academic, 1991], pp. 151-15) and Tikva Frymer-Kensky
('Pollution, Purification and Purgation in Biblical Israel', in *The Word of the Lord
Shall Go Forth: Essays in Honor of David Noel Freedman in Celebration of his
Sixtieth Birthday* [ed. Carol L. Meyers and Michael O'Connor; Winona Lake, IN:
Eisenbrauns, 1983], pp. 403-404).

the charges themselves are not systematic. More is concealed than is revealed in the allegation in Ezra 9.1-2. The biblical authors paint with broad strokes a wide spectrum of objections to make a single point: not separating from the practices of those in the land(s) renders a person foreign. When that person is a woman, she may not enter the household. Sexual contact with her is contaminating.

As C. Frevel and B. J. Conczorowski put it, 'Several terms and motifs link the narrative to Lev. 18 to underline the purity paradigm'.[47] They further note that in Ezra 9–10, 'aspects of religious deviance, covenant, monotheism, genealogy and purity are brought together in a complementary manner. The authors of Ezra 9–10 have created an integrative concept to reject intermarriage...'[48] And N. Koltun-Fromm observes, 'Ezra, having democratized holiness among all Israel...solidifies Israel's ascribed holiness...'[49]

What is often lost in the discussion of this subject is the fact that Ezra 9–10 does not prohibit other types of relations between Judahites and foreigners, however they are defined. Other types of contact with the Other are not opposed. Non-marital contacts with the Other as friend, especially when far away, are valued. The objection is cast solely in terms of marriage.[50] For EN, what transpires in the home is no longer a private matter, if ever it was, over which each man has absolute control;

47. Christian Frevel and Benedikt J. Conczorowski, 'Deepening the Water: First Steps to a Diachronic Approach on Intermarriage in the Hebrew Bible', in *Mixed Marriages: Intermarriage and Group Identity in the Second Temple Period* (ed. Christian Frevel; LHBOTS, 547; New York: T&T Clark International, 2011), pp. 15-45 (27).

48. Frevel and Conczorowski conclude the sentence with 'which is taken up in post-biblical tradition frequently' (ibid., p. 32). The statement is somewhat misleading. While intermarriage is typically opposed in post-biblical Jewish traditions, outsiders can become insiders by means of conversion. Such an option is not mentioned in Ezra 9–10. Ironically, the word מקוה, mentioned in Ezra 10.2, is part of later Jewish discourse about conversion. The word comes to refer to a ritual bath; immersion into it is part of conversion rituals in Judaism. The fact that Shechaniah proclaims that there is a מקוה is taken to mean in later Jewish sources that the women under consideration refused this option of conversion. The plain meaning of Ezra 9–10 does not carry this message.

49. Naomi Koltun-Fromm, *Hermeneutics of Holiness: Ancient Jewish and Christian Notions of Sexuality and Religious Community* (Oxford: Oxford University Press, 2010), p. 45. On the notion of 'ascribed holiness', see below.

50. I remain puzzled by the frequent use of the verb ישב in the hiphil in EN (Ezra 10.2, 10, 14, 17, 18; Neh. 13, 23 and 27), which translators render as 'marry', usually without comment. But see NJPS, which has 'bring home'. For one interpretative option, see my paper, 'The Missions of Ezra and Nehemiah', pp. 519-22.

rather, it influences a larger holy space with ramifications for the entire system. Moreover, wives are no longer absorbed into their husband's world without recourse to who they have been previously. Who they were and what they do have a role to play in defining Judahite identity.

The notion of זֶרַע הַקֹּדֶשׁ in Ezra 9.2 seems to be pivotal in discussions of Ezra 9–10. Scholars typically translate this as 'holy seed' and draw out the significance of the term for identity in terms of genealogical or moral presumption of purity.[51] Milgrom for example, concludes that the problem resulting from the status of 'holy seed' is the desecration of the sancta. Saysell considers desecration a secondary danger, placing covenant violation as primary.[52] As I note above, there is no need to confine meaning to only one possibility.

Yet, it is important to note that holiness in Ezra 7–10 is evidently acquired, not simply inherited. It is what Kolton-Fromm refers to as 'achieved holiness'.[53] The vessels that Ezra brings for the temple are not temple vessels now returned, as in Ezra 1.7-11, but rather, the donation of the king and his court (8.25-27). They become holy (8.28) because they are dedicated to the temple. Likewise, the people are holy in so far as they are dedicated to Israel's God, which is why Jerusalem itself is called holy in Neh. 11.1 only after the committed community has built the walls (Neh. 3, especially 3.1), and pledged itself wholeheartedly to God's teachings (Neh. 10).

In this sense, holiness is not genealogical in Ezra 9–10; nor is foreignness strictly genealogical. It is not that genealogy does not matter; rather, it no longer suffices. This line of reasoning may be especially relevant if the peoples of the land(s) can also claim genealogical links.

---

51. For a thorough analysis of the options in interpreting 'holy seed', see Saysell, *'According to the Law '*, pp. 81-95. She herself supposes that the seed here pertains to the children of the returnees. I am inclined to see this text in light of Isa. 6.3, where it refers to the remnant after disaster. See other images in Ezra 9 that support this conclusion. As with much else in this chapter, multiple meanings apply.

52. Among Saysell's reasons are her analysis of Lev. 21.7, 14-15 and the emphasis on 'moral impurity' as a condition that only defiles the sinner, which would not account for the measures in Ezra 9–10 (*'According to the Law '*, pp. 120-21).

53. Koltun-Fromm uses the term 'ascribed holiness' when discussing priestly notions of holiness. As she illustrates, when it comes to defining קֹדֶשׁ, 'Torah traditions carry conflicting understanding on the subject' (*Hermeneutics of Holiness*, p. 33). In P texts, she notes, holiness is ascribed (pp. 33-34); in H texts it is to be achieved (pp. 34-35). See her discussion of ascribed holiness (pp. 32-34) and holiness achieved (pp. 34-36), as well as 'Ascribed Holiness Solidifies' (pp. 42-45), which focuses on Ezra traditions.

The threat to the holy is linked to an identity that casts the community as fragile, which the term 'seed' also expresses, referring to something small and not yet established. Ezra's prayer (Ezra 9.6-15) combines a wide range of metaphors and associations to bring home the gravity of the crisis and its far reaching ramifications.

Most telling is the construction of identity as a פליטה, 'remnant' (Ezra 9.8, 13, 14, 15). The four-fold repetition of this word makes Ezra 9 the densest concentration of פליטה in the entire Hebrew Bible.[54] All uses of פליטה in the Bible refer to survival after devastation, such as war. By employing this typifying term for Judahite identity in this section, the writer heightens the sense of vulnerability and the precarious nature of the community; so does the language of tent peg (Ezra 9.8) and fence (9.9), since neither is a solid and complete structure able to secure possession or protection. From Isaiah's references one can construct some associations of פליטה with the holy.[55] Four of the five references in Isaiah (4.20; 10.20; 37.31-32) anticipate a remnant especially endowed with sanctity and devotion to God.[56]

This language of פליטה in Ezra 9, then, renders the Judahite community as 'an endangered species', wholly dependent and insecure. Nehemiah 1–7 will pick up this theme and change the identity to one of an empowered community.

In sum, imagining the Other in Ezra 9–10 adds another layer to the construction of Judahite identity. It reflects a shift from a self that is united and affirming to one that is divided. As such, the Other outside and the Other inside are intertwined. While the Other as outsider poses the threat, it is insiders who bring the danger home. In response, and it is important to note that this is a response in light of new developments, Ezra 9–10 refashions identity by tightening the boundary.

One notes the feminization of the Other: although the culprits are Judahite men, and the abominations belong to the peoples of the land(s), the most direct object are the women, classified as foreign, who come to represent all that is wrong (Ezra 10.2, 10). In Ezra 9.14, for example, the

54. The one book that uses פליטה as often as EN (four times in Ezra 9 and once in Neh. 1.2) is Isaiah, with five occurrences spread out throughout the book.

55. I do not imply that Ezra 9 is using Isaiah. My goal is to identify a semantic range and cultural associations that might have been available as background to the author of the prayer. Dyck, however, proposes that 'the author of Ezra–Nehemiah is dependent, to a certain extent, on Deutero-Isaiah's understanding of the restoration...' (*Theocratic Ideology*, p. 85).

56. Isaiah 4.3 calls the פליטה 'holy'; Isa. 10.20 speaks of a faithful פליטה that will depend on God (see also Isa. 27.31-32).

abominations are squarely placed on the peoples of the lands as a whole. Yet, women are the target, a point underscored by reference to נִדָּה, a term that technically applies to women alone, designating a menstruating woman, and only metaphorically to the land (itself a feminine noun and sometimes a feminine symbol).

Whereas the Other as foe in Ezra 1–6 and Nehemiah 1–7 gets to have his say and is heard, as it were, by the reader (Ezra 4.2), and on occasion named (Ezra 4.8-9), the Other as female in Ezra 9–10 is without a name or a voice. Her practices are abominable, although nothing specific is recorded beyond a generality. She poses a danger to the vulnerable community whose identity is construed as פליטה. Ezra 9–10 shows no interest in this female Other *per se* but only in convincing Judahite men and the community as a whole that their actions endanger everyone and that they must separate from any 'foreign' wives. To this effect, EN marshals an array of associations to render the women as foreign and thus Other, with whom intimate contact, like marriage, is forbidden. The danger is deemed extreme, given the precarious nature of the community. Yet with this move, the writer also establishes the choice of wife as a marker of a legitimate Judahite identity.

Stage Three: The City as the House of God (Nehemiah 1–7)

Social boundaries having been erected in Ezra 9–10, the Third Stage (Neh. 1–7) focuses on building physical boundaries—Jerusalem's wall—as the uniting activity. This task completes the building of the house of God mandated in Ezra 1.1-4. Like the first two stages, Nehemiah 1–7 begins by presenting the Other as friend before turning to the Other as foe. In this section, the community is repeatedly identified as יהודים, as if it were a well-defined group.[57] However, the group is soon on the verge of being attacked by an Other. The opposing Others are mainly Sanballat and Tobiah, who seek to undermine Nehemiah and the יהודים in their building efforts and to bring reproach/disgrace (חרפה) upon them.

Once again, the Other as friend is the Persian king. Nehemiah inquires about the פליטה (Neh. 1.2) and learns that '[t]he survivors there in the

---

56. As Knoppers points out, 'The evidence suggests that, when Nehemiah refers to the *yehudim*, he is almost always referring to the residents of the province of Judah' ('Nehemiah and Sanballat', p. 311). Ben Zvi observes that whatever underlying tensions existed between returned exiles and those who remained in the land (evident in Ezra 1–6 and 7–9), they have subsided by the time of the NM ('Inclusion and Exclusion', p. 116). Knoppers, however, highlights tension between different concepts of Israel in this section.

province who escaped captivity are in great trouble and shame (חרפה);
the wall of Jerusalem is broken down, and its gates have been destroyed
by fire' (Neh. 1.3 NRSV). Nehemiah, therefore, uses his position in the
court to remedy the situation, and King Artaxerxes favorably responds to
him. As Neh. 2.1-9 makes amply clear, initiative comes from Nehemiah,
who elicits the foreign king's consent.

Both as friend or foe, the Other in Nehemiah 1–7 is imagined in
personal terms, focusing on the relation to Nehemiah himself. Nehemiah
extracts personal support from the king to build the city of his (i.e.
Nehemiah's) ancestors. The king's generosity focuses on Nehemiah
himself. Other details are deemed not important enough to mention,
which magnifies Nehemiah's role.[58]

As in Ezra 1–6 and 7–10, the Other as friend is geographically located
at a distance, and fortunately so from the perspective of EN.[59] The sole
value of the imperial Other comes from his ability to transfer material,
political, and legal resources to the community in Judah and Jerusalem.[60]

---

58. Neither Nehemiah nor the king mentions Judah or Jerusalem. The reader
does not know, therefore, whether the location was understood as a matter of fact,
implying the king knew that Nehemiah was a Judahite by birth or, as I think more
likely, that this information was deemed irrelevant to the point being made. The
city's name and even the province would have meant nothing to the king, being too
small and distant to appear on the imperial radar screen. Possibly, the report about
Artaxerxes in Ezra 4 looms large in the writer's mind and the name is avoided for
this reason.

59. In the musical, 'Fiddler on the Roof', the rabbi is asked: 'Is there a blessing
for the Tzar?' to which comes the reply: 'A blessing for the Tzar? Of course: May
God bless and keep the Tzar—far away from us!' Something of the same sort may
play out, especially in the Nehemiah section.

60. I see a similar role for the *golah* community in EN: its value flows in one
direction: from the Diaspora to Judah. At no point does the Judahite community in
Judah, including its returned Diasporic component, reach out to those remaining in
the Diaspora. For a different view, see Gary N. Knoppers, 'Ethnicity, Genealogy,
Geography, and Change: The Judean Communities of Babylon and Jerusalem in the
Story of Ezra', in *Community Identity in Judean Historiography: Biblical and
Comparative Perspectives* (ed. Gary N. Knoppers and Ken A. Ristau; Winona Lake,
IN: Eisenbrauns, 2009), pp. 147-71. Dyck also emphasizes outside initiative as
central to EN (*Theocratic Ideology*, p. 90). But given the brevity with which EN
depicts the Diasporic initiative, it seems more likely that while recognizing the role
of the Diaspora, EN is eager to present its legitimacy only in so far as it sustains the
reconstruction in Judah. The Diaspora's proper role, according to Ezra 1.1-4 and
throughout the book, is 'to build the house of YHWH…which is in Jerusalem' (Ezra
1.3). Jerusalem, not the Diaspora, is the focal point and goal.

EN never describes voluntary *Judahite* communication from Judah back to the royal court.[61]

The Other as foe appears again, as in Ezra 1–6, as a response. This time, however, the focus rests first on Nehemiah himself: 'When Sanballat the Horonite and Tobiah the Ammonite official [עבד] heard this, it displeased them greatly that someone had come to seek the welfare of the people of Israel' (Neh. 2.10 NRSV). Nonetheless, Nehemiah is able to inspire the community (יהודים) to unite in building the wall (Neh. 2.17-18; 3.1-32, 38 [NRSV 4.6], etc.) despite repeated harassment (Neh. 2.19; 3.33-35 [NRSV 4.1-3]; 4.1-2 [NRSV 4.7-8], etc.). Although the animosity is triggered as personal opposition to Nehemiah (2.10), it spreads further (2.19) as a response to the united building efforts by the יהודים at Nehemiah's urging (2.17-18) before escalating into a 'global' opposition by foes, surrounding Judah all around (4.1 [NRSV 4.7]). However, in sharp contrast to the parallels in Ezra 1–6, specifically Ezra 4, the unified builders, now under Nehemiah's leadership, continue despite these many, persistent attempts at interference and sabotage. Thus, Nehemiah 1–7 depicts a development that reverses the previous position of vulnerability.

The Other is both definite and, at least to readers living millennia later, obscure: 'definite' in that Nehemiah 'names names', chiefly Sanballat and Tobiah, and 'obscure' in that the adjectives he uses for the foes are a challenge. Tobiah's 'Ammonite' designation imputes foreignness to one who appears to have good standing as a member of the Judahite community as well as a Judahite name. 'Ammonite' may refer to Tobiah's place of residence or a position within the Ammonite court. In Nehemiah's hands, the label 'the Ammonite עבד' (Neh. 2.10, 19; see also 3.35), meaning Ammonite official (so NRSV) or Ammonite servant (so NJPS), renders Tobiah as one in the service of Ammon, in contrast to Nehemiah, whose loyalties are to the welfare of Judah.[62]

---

61. Nehemiah seems to have been 'recalled' to the king's court, according to Neh. 13.6; and there is no specific turning to the king for further authorization once Nehemiah goes to Jerusalem in ch. 2.

62. Tobiah could simply be a member of the successful Judahite family that is known to have settled in Ammon. Their origin in Ammonite territory could go back to the exilic period, when many Judahites escaped to neighboring regions to avoid the Babylonian destruction and reprisals (Jer. 40.11). The relation of this family to the Tobiads, whose family tomb is in Iraq al-Amir (between Amman and Jericho) is likely and suggests the ongoing prominence of this family. For a detailed discussion of Tobiah's identity and the proposal that he is an Israelite, see Knoppers, 'Nehemiah and Sanballat', pp. 317-24.

More puzzling is Sanballat's designation as a 'Horonite'. Reading from the distance of millennia, we cannot be entirely sure of his imputed identity, that is, the full significance of being called a Horonite. It is well known from Elephantine and the Wadi Daliyeh papyri that a Sanballat was governor of Samaria. It is therefore difficult to ascertain why Nehemiah would avoid specifying a Samarian connection. The only hint at a link with Samaria appears in 3.34 (NRSV 4.1), when Sanballat taunts the יהודים in the presence of 'his brothers and the army of Samaria'. In any case, the persistent opposition of these two, at times joined by Geshem the Arab, defines the Other as foe in Nehemiah 1–7.[63]

Thus, the Otherness in terms of 'foreigner' is not as developed. Whereas the 'Other' as foe in Ezra 4 is clearly demarcated as foreigners, the reader of Nehemiah 1–7 as well as Neh. 13.4, 38 repeatedly observes signs that Nehemiah's opponents are not so clearly outsiders. Their contacts through marriage and friendship (6.18-19) show that distinguished members of the Jerusalem's יהודים, including the high priestly family, considered these opponents as kin. Only Geshem the Arab is unambiguously a non-Judahite or non-Israelite.

Such connections between the Other as foe and community members may account for the lack of clear genealogical or ethnic emphases in Nehemiah's attack against his opponents; it suggests that their Otherness could not be criticized along those lines. Therefore, their actions, namely ill will, define their Otherness and render them foreign.[64]

The challenge that Nehemiah places before his community is no longer 'Who are We?' as in who is in and who is out, but, rather, 'How are We to be perceived by the others?' In particular, it focuses on removing the stigma of disgrace, חרפה.[65] This motive applies not only to the uniting efforts of building the wall ('Come, let us rebuild the wall of Jerusalem, so that we may no longer suffer disgrace [חרפה]', 2.17). It also applies in order to unite the community within as a coherent people

63. For a fuller discussion of Sanballat, see Knoppers, 'Nehemiah and Sanballat', pp. 325-30. Knoppers suggests that Sanballat uses kinship language in his letter to Nehemiah (Neh. 6.6), which is one of several signs of their shared ethnicity, language being another. Sanballat and his supporters may have construed a broader sense of who 'Israel' was ('Nehemiah and Sanballat', pp. 330-31). With this, 'Nehemiah was battling not only the enemy without, but also the enemy within' ('Nehemiah and Sanballat', p. 331).

64. The clear foreignness in Neh. 13.23-27 is another matter. It is noteworthy that Nehemiah does not demand divorce in the case of these decidedly foreign wives but only a promise that such marriages will not be repeated.

65. For a fine discussion of חרפה, 'reproach', in NM, see Wright, *Rebuilding Identity*, pp. 58-61.

in Nehemiah 5: the reforms in Nehemiah 5 attempt, on the one hand, to solidify a core by reference to vertical affiliation and kinship (Neh. 5.7).[66] On the other, they are a response to outsiders' reproach (Neh. 5.8-9); note the statement, 'You ought to act in a God-fearing way so as not to give our enemies, the nations, room to reproach (חרפה) us' in Neh. 5.9b. In Nehemiah 1–7, disgrace, חרפה, along with contempt, require a show of strength in the presence of outsiders, calling for self-affirmation, not self-probing.

The identity under construction in this section heavily rests on how to be יהודים among the nations. In this sense, it builds on the challenges left unfinished in the previous stages. Nehemiah 1–7 concentrates on positioning a people in terms of power. This is why the parallel with Ezra 4 is important. Building efforts in Ezra 4 also trigger opposition by outsiders. However, Ezra 4 reflected powerlessness, forcing builders to relinquish their God-given, royally authorized efforts. But whereas opponents in Ezra 4 successfully blocked building efforts, this time Nehemiah can boast that nothing and no one succeeded in interrupting the work.

Vulnerability also marked Ezra 9, when Ezra diagnosed the state and status of the community as a fragile פליטה, seeking to enforce socio-religious boundaries to protect its very survival. In Nehemiah 1–7, Nehemiah presents himself as one able to undo such conditions. Repeated attempts by Others fail to intimidate him; his charisma and personal authority prevent the repetition of the earlier scenarios.

The physical vulnerability of the wall in Nehemiah 1 mirrors and symbolizes the vulnerability that Nehemiah reverses. The building, therefore, is an act of self-affirmation. Pride, show of strength, and collective determination now replace shame and reproach.

There is much sword rattling in Nehemiah 1–7, both literal and symbolic, but never an actual skirmish or recorded battle beyond the duel of words and letters. These features serve to intensify the magnitude of danger. By casting the drama of Nehemiah's efforts in military garb, Nehemiah 1–7 adopts the unifying posture that a threat of war provides for a fragmented or debilitated community: camaraderie. In confronting the foe, the community cultivates new muscles.

Thus, in Neh. 4.1-2 (NRSV 4.6-7), Nehemiah reports that Sanballat, Tobiah, the Arabs, the Ammonites, and the Ashdodites 'all plotted together to come and fight against Jerusalem and to cause confusion in it' (4.2 [4.7]). This 'global' danger emphasizes the need of the

---

66. See also Dyck, *Theocratic Ideology*, esp. pp. 109-17.

community to move from being an object of scorn to a united subject able to determine its history and boundaries vis-à-vis the world ('the nations').[67]

This emphasis is highlighted by the frequency with which the word for strength or power, חזק, appears in Nehemiah 1–7. There are 42 references to חזק in Nehemiah 1–7 alone, much more than in any other biblical book except Chronicles (48 times in EN as a whole and 52 in all of Chronicles). This term usually appears in the account of rebuilding the wall in Nehemiah 3, but not exclusively there. Strength, then, is tied to this building, not because the wall itself is invulnerable, which it apparently is not, but because in building it, the people strengthened one another; see, for example, 'Next to them repairs were made [החזיק, lit. "strengthened"] by Melatiah...' in Neh. 3.7 (NRSV).

Building the wall is building an identity rooted in strength, with the capacity to stand one's ground and with readiness to fight. It changes the image of the יהודים. The power of the adversary who has been rebuffed is a measure of the power now instilled in the community.

Conclusion

> Identity is a verb.
> —Tali Hyman Zelkowicz.[68]

The first three stages in EN, Ezra 1–6, 7–10, and Nehemiah 1–7, trace three journeys from exile and Diaspora to Judah. They also trace the gradual development of an identity in response to changed circumstances in the post-exilic era, when criteria that held a people together previously

---

67. For a fine discussion of subjectivity as a factor in the Nehemiah material, see Don Polaski, 'Nehemiah: Subject of the Empire, Subject of Writing', in *New Perspectives on Ezra–Nehemiah: History and Historiography, Text, Literature, and Interpretation* (ed. Isaac Kalimi; Winona Lake, IN: Eisenbrauns, 2012), pp. 37-59.

68. In a private communication. For fuller discussion of this insight, see Tali E. Hyman, 'The Liberal Jewish Day School as Laboratory for Dissonance in American Jewish Identity-Formation' (PhD diss., New York University, 2008). Hyman includes the insight that 'grammatically speaking identity is a noun, sociologically speaking and in lived reality, it functions as a verb' (p. 10, based on Siebren Miedema and Willem L. Wardekker, 'Emergent Identity Versus Consistent Identity: Possibilities for a Postmodern Repoliticization of Critical Pedagogy', in *Critical Theories in Education: Changing Terrains of Knowledge and Politics* [ed. Thomas S. Popkewitz and Lynn Fendler; Education, Social Theory & Cultural Change; New York: Routledge, 1999], pp. 67-83 [76]). This idea is further developed in Zelkowicz's forthcoming book, *Liberal Jewish Identity-Formation*.

were no longer self-evident. EN acknowledges the resulting ambiguity and charts the processes by which group identity was constructed along new lines.

The age-old strategies of using friends and foes to articulate and construct identity are played out, illustrating a positioning of the community in relation to imperial authority and local constituencies.

The opposing Other serves as both impetus for galvanizing a people and proof for Judahite relative independence within the confines of an empire. Culminating in Nehemiah 7, EN traces the process through which the community develops a sense of self and finds a way to balance self-affirmation as a colonized people without bringing the wrath of the Empire upon oneself by means of rebellion. It is no longer at the mercy of the surrounding forces.

Nehemiah 8–12 celebrates the success in creating such an identity. Nehemiah 9 articulates a shared vision of collective history and destiny, and Nehemiah 10 translates this vision into a shared commitment. The people of God are those who have built the house of God in its fullest sense of encompassing temple, community, and city, and now dedicate themselves to these pillars of identity with the Torah at the center.

EN shows how this sense is communicated already in the Persian period. EN's Stage One, Ezra 1–6, identifies the people as those of Judah and Benjamin. Their identity depends on belonging to the Land. However, in Stage Two (Ezra 7–10) they develop into 'Jews' who, to use Cohen's words, 'venerate the God of the Judaeans, the God whose temple is in Jerusalem...'[69] In Stage Three (Neh. 1–7), Jerusalem is no longer simply a city with Jews but becomes a Jewish city. Its inhabitants have taken control over their lives and stand ready and able to determine who may or may not enter. Nehemiah 8–12 celebrates this achievement by spelling out what such Judahite or Jewish identity entails. Nehemiah 13 continues the message about the processual nature of identity: it illustrates that the construction and maintenance of identity is an ongoing process, one that is in constant need of vigilance.

---

69. Cohen, *Beginning of Jewishness*, p. 105. For a fuller discussion of the term, and my disagreement with Cohen's limits of its use, see n. 6 in the present study.

PHINEHAS AND THE OTHER PRIESTS IN BEN SIRA AND 1 MACCABEES*

Tobias Funke

Analysis of the Hebrew and Greek versions of Ben Sira, as well as the First Book of the Maccabees, indicates an intentional use of proto-canonical figures like Aaron, David, and Phinehas by different priestly groups in the Hellenistic period to legitimate the combination of profane and cultic power in the office of the high priest both genealogically and theologically. Using proto-canonical traditions, a group of scribes constructed a common identity against which non-conforming groups could be ostracized as Others. The present essay examines the Othering of priestly groups in the Hellenistic period.[1]

The authors used central biblical texts by explicitly citing them or alluding to them. This process can be analyzed using intertextual methods.[2] Given our different worldview and our limited knowledge of

* This chapter represents the reworked version of a paper presented at the EABS conference 2011 in Thessaloniki. My thanks to Diana Edelman and Ehud Ben Zvi for editing it in this volume. The editors thank Philippe Guillaume for his additional help with revising the English.

1. The research group 'Religious Non-Conformism and Cultural Dynamics', funded by the Deutsche Forschungsgemeinschaft (DFG), defines non-conformism as a self- or external attribution, never as a deviance from a specified orthodoxy. See its research programme, which can be downloaded at www.uni-leipzig.de/ nonkonformismus. For a broader analysis of the usage of Phinehas, see Tobias Funke, 'Der Priester Pinhas in Jerusalem und auf dem Berg Garizim. Eine intertextuelle Untersuchung seiner Erwähnungen und deren literar- und sozialgesichtliche Einordnung' (Ph.D. diss., University of Leipzig, 2013), to be published by Mohr Siebeck in 2015 in the series Oriental Religions in Antiquity.

2. A 'citation' includes the occurrence of at least three parallel word stems, while an 'allusion' requires only a single term or phrase. For the current debate over the use of the term 'intertextuality' in biblical research, see David M. Carr, 'The Many Uses of Intertextuality in Biblical Studies', in *Congress Volume, Helsinki 2010* (ed. Marti Nissinen; VTSup, 148; Leiden: Brill, 2012), pp. 505-36, and Geoffrey D. Miller, 'Intertextuality in Old Testament Research', *Currents in Biblical Research* 9.3 (2011), pp. 283-309.

the ancient literary canon for biblical scribes, modern scholars cannot identify all the citations and allusions biblical authors have made nor all the allusions an ancient reader would have understood. Nevertheless, one can understand much of a given author's intention by identifying those biblical texts he has targeted and then analyzing the differences between his version and the original and shifts in stress that appear in the later composition. For example, Sira 45 draws on Exodus 28, Numbers 16–18 and 25, and Pss 89 and 106 and applies biblical formulations originally attributed to David to Aaron and Phinehas.

The first part of this essay constitutes an analysis of the occurrences of Phinehas in the Hebrew and Greek versions of Ben Sira and in 1 Maccabees, describing parallels with the proto-canonical Phinehas tradition and differences between the two. The second part will focus on an examination of the authors of the two books in their social settings. Known conflicts between priestly groups in the Hellenistic period will be investigated for their ability to match the controversies that might have stood behind the analyzed texts. In this context, the question of the extent of the power of the priests in the Hellenistic period, especially the high priest, will be raised. Special emphasis will be placed on the office of *prostates*.

I. *Intertextual Analysis*

1. *Phinehas in the Hebrew Text of Ben Sira*
Phinehas is mentioned twice in the Hebrew text of Ben Sira: after the acknowledgment of Moses and Aaron and at the end of the book after the praise of Simon.[3]

---

3. Two articles deal explicitly with the role of Phinehas in Ben Sira: Kenneth E. Pomykala, 'The Covenant with Phinehas in Ben Sira (Sir. 45.23-26; 50.22-24)', in *Israel in the Wilderness: Interpretations of the Biblical Narratives in Jewish and Christian Traditions* (ed. Kenneth E. Pomykala; Themes in Biblical Narrative, 10; Leiden: Brill, 2008), pp. 17-36; and Heinz-Josef Fabry, '"Wir wollen nun loben Männer von gutem Ruf" (Sir. 44.1). Der Pinhas-Bund im "Lob der Väter"', in *Für immer verbündet. Studien zur Bundestheologie der Bibel* (ed. Christoph Dohmen and Christian Frevel; SBS, 211; Stuttgart: Katholisches Bibelwerk, 2007), pp. 49-60. See also Helge Stadelmann, *Ben Sira als Schriftgelehrter. Eine Untersuchung zum Berufsbild des vor-makkabäischen Sofer unter Berücksichtigung seines Verhält-nisses zu Priester- Propheten- und Weisheitslehrertum* (WUNT, 6; Tübingen: Mohr, 1980), pp. 150-51. For the position of Phinehas in Ben Sira, see Otto Mulder, *Simon the High Priest in Sirach 50: An Exegetical Study of the Significance of Simon the High Priest as Climax to the Praise of the Fathers in Ben Sira's Concept of the History of Israel* (JSJSup, 78; Leiden: Brill, 2003), pp. 58, 217-18, 240, 344, 358-60.

And also Phinehas, son of Eleazar, in strength he inherited glory, in his zeal for the God of all. And he stood in the breach of his people, when his heart urged him and he made atonement for the sons of Israel. Therefore also He established for him a statute, a covenant of peace to maintain the sanctuary, which shall be to him and his descendants a perpetual high priesthood, and also His covenant with David the son of Jesse, of the tribe of Judah: an inheritance of fire in front of His glory; an inheritance of Aaron to all of his seed. (Sir. 45.23-25)

May his mercy continue to Simon and establish for him the covenant with Phinehas, which not could cut off for him and his seed as the days of heaven. (Sir. 50.24)

1.a. *Phinehas in the 'Praise of the Fathers'*. The 'Praise of the Fathers' (Sir. 44–50) summarizes the biblical past and culminates in the praise of Simon, the high priest, which allows the author to insert Simon into the history of Israel. Both occurrences of Phinehas are marked by an invitation to praise the Lord (Sir. 45.25-26 and 50.22-23).[4] The second reference is further underlined by the appearance of the root חסד, which is otherwise rare in the Hebrew text of Ben Sira,[5] thus placing special emphasis on Phinehas among the other fathers.

The term ברית, 'covenant', is a structuring theme in the Hebrew version of the Praise of the Fathers.[6] Most occurrences of the word are found in the first part of the 'Praise of the Fathers'. In the second part, it appears only once, in reference to the 'covenant of Pinehas' (Sir. 50.24). This is another way to single out Phinehas for extra attention. A comparison of the covenants made with various fathers in Ben Sira with the proto-canonical covenant traditions reveals a further dimension of the covenant with Phinehas advanced by the author of Ben Sira.

---

4. Pancratius C. Beentjes, 'The "Praise of the Famous" and Its Prologue: Some Observations on Ben Sira 44', *Bijdragen* 45 (1984), pp. 374-83 (376).

5. The central phrase אנשי חסד, 'pious men', is introduced as a *leitmotif* in Sir. 44.1 and 10. It is used subsequently for Joshua (46.7), Josiah (49.3), and Simon (50.24). See Jeremy Corley, 'Sirach 44.1-15', in *Studies in the Book of Ben Sira* [ed. Geza G. Xeravits; JSJSup, 127; Leiden: Brill, 2008], pp. 151-81 [161]).

6. See Johannes Marböck, 'Die Geschichte Israels als Bundesgeschichte nach dem Sirachbuch', in *Der neue Bund im alten. Studien zur Bundestheologie der beiden Testamente* (ed. Christoph Dohmen; QD, 146; Freiburg im Breisgau: Herder, 1993), pp. 117-98 (120); Benjamin G. Wright, *No Small Difference: Sirach's Relationship to Its Hebrew Parent Text* (Septuagint and Cognate Studies, 26; Atlanta: Scholars Press, 1989), p. 179; Pancratius C. Beentjes, 'The Book of Ben Sira: Some New Perspectives at the Dawn of the 21st Century' (paper presented at the International SBL Meeting, Amsterdam, 2012, forthcoming).

1.a.α. *The Differences Between the proto-canonical conception of covenant and the Hebrew text of Ben Sira.* In Ben Sira, Noah, Abraham, and Isaac receive a covenant, but not a perpetual one.[7] Moses gets no covenant at all. David receives a statute rather than a covenant (Sir. 47.11, compare 2 Sam. 23.5), but Aaron and his sons are the recipients of an eternal covenant (Sir. 45.15), an honour they never receive in earlier biblical tradition.[8] They continue to serve the עולם חק, 'eternal statutes' (Exod. 28.43), but Aaron's role extends beyond mere service to a living statute: he is installed by God as a perpetual ordinance (Sir. 45.7). The net result is that the new eternal covenant with Aaron and the perpetual covenant with Phinehas become the only covenants of enduring length and implied unconditionality.

The proto-canonical covenant tradition of Phinehas is enlarged in Ben Sira. In 45.24, Phinehas remains the recipient of a ברית שלום, 'covenant of peace', now described as the high priesthood for him and his offspring, which is explicitly related to the covenant of David (45.25). This mention of David is unusual; it disturbs the otherwise chronological organisation of the 'Praise of the Fathers'. It is a matter of debate whether the covenant of David is subordinated to the covenant of Phinehas,[9] if it is of equal standing,[10] or if Phinehas is subordinated to David.[11]

---

7. In Sir. 44.18 the author seems to avoid the phrase עולם ברית, 'eternal covenant', and instead uses עולם אות, 'eternal sign' (Benjamin G. Wright, 'The Use and Interpretation of Biblical Tradition in Ben Sira's Praise of the Ancestors', in Xeravits [ed.], *Studies in the Book of Ben Sira*, pp. 183-207 [190]). At least in combination with כרת, 'cut', the term ברית would be expected. With עולם אות the author also alludes to the rainbow as אות־הברית, 'the sign of the covenant', which is also described as 'eternal' (cf. Gen. 9.12). Jacob is equated with Israel in Sir. 44.23.

8. Pomykala, 'Covenant of Phinehas', pp. 27-28; Wright, 'Use of Tradition', p. 195; Friedrich V. Reiterer, 'Aaron's Polyvalent Role According to Ben Sira', in *Rewriting Biblical History: Essays on Chronicles and Ben Sira* (ed. Pancratius C. Beentjes, Jeremy Corley, and Harm van Grol; Deuterocanonical and Cognate Literature Series, 7; Berlin: de Gruyter, 2011), pp. 27-56 (33). One exception might be the ambiguous promise of a עוֹלָם מֶלַח בְּרִית, 'eternal covenant of salt', in Num. 18.19. See Reinhard Achenbach, *Die Vollendung der Tora: Studien zur Redaktionsgeschichte des Numeribuches im Kontext von Hexateuch und Pentateuch* (BZAR, 3; Wiesbaden: Harrassowitz, 2003), p. 162.

9. Stadelmann, *Ben Sira*, p. 155; Pancratius C. Beentjes, '"The Countries Marvelled at You": King Solomon in Ben Sira 47:12-22', *Bijdragen* 45 (1984), pp. 6-14 (11); Marböck, 'Die Geschichte', p. 107; Heinz-Josef Fabry, 'Jesus Sirach und das Priestertum', in *Auf den Spuren der schriftgelehrten Weisen* (ed. Irmtraud Fischer and Johannes Marböck; BZAW, 331; Berlin: de Gruyter, 2003), pp. 265-82 (274); Arie van der Kooij, 'The Greek Bible and Jewish Concepts of Royal Priesthood and Priestly Monarchy', in *Jewish Perspectives on Hellenistic Rulers*

Although the meaning of the expression אש לפני כבוד ('a fire before his glory'?) in Sir. 45.25 is disputed,[12] I understand the description of the covenant with Phinehas as follows:

> So that he [Phinehas] and his descendants should posses the high priesthood forever and even His covenant with David, the son of Jesse of the tribe of Judah; the inheritance of fire before his glory, the inheritance of Aaron for all his descendants.[13]

In Phinehas, priestly and kingly powers are unified in the office of the high priest, and Sir. 50.24 sets Simon in the covenant of Phinehas, a covenant unknown in the Tanak.

1b. *The Differences Between Phinehas in 'Proto-canonical' Tradition and in the Hebrew Ben Sira.* The parallels between Numbers 25 and Sira 45 are numerous: Phinehas himself (Num. 25.11; Sir. 45.23), his zeal (Num. 25.13; Sir. 45.23), atonement (Num. 25.13; Sir. 45.23), and the covenant (Num. 25.12-13; Sir. 45.24) reappear. By contrast, Sir. 50.24 only alludes to the covenant with Phinehas and to his seed.[14]

Phinehas gains new characteristics. He is third in גבורה, 'strength' (Sir. 45.23), either in the genealogical line after Moses and Aaron, or

(ed. Tessa Rajak; HCS, 50; Berkeley: University of California Press, 2007), pp. 255-64 (260); Benjamin G. Wright, 'Ben Sira on Kings and Kingship', in *Jewish Perspectives on Hellenistic Rulers*, pp. 76-91 (86).

10. John Priest, 'Ben Sira 45:25 in the Light of the Qumran Literature', *RevQ* 5 (1964), pp. 106-18; Martin Hengel, *Die Zeloten. Untersuchungen zur jüdischen Freiheitsbewegung in der Zeit von Herodes I. bis 70 n. Chr* (Arbeiten zur Geschichte des antiken Judentums und des Urchristentums, 1; Leiden: Brill, 1976), p. 155; Saul M. Olyan, 'Ben Sira's Relationship to the Priesthood', *HTR* 80 (1987), pp. 261-86 (283); and Kenneth E. Pomykala, *The Davidic Dynasty Tradition in Early Judaism: Its History and Significance for Messianism* (EJL, 7; Atlanta: Scholars Press, 1995), pp. 132-44.

11. Mulder, *Simon the High Priest*, p. 341.

12. Does this phrase refer to a fire or to a man in front of his glory? Stadelmann sees in this man the high priest (*Ben Sira*, p. 151). The fire would refer to the occurrence of the term in Sir. 45.19, 21-22, alluding to Num. 17.1-15. See Beentjes, 'Book of Ben Sira', pp. 10-11; Olyan, 'Relationship', pp. 283-84.

13. Pancratius C. Beentjes, 'Portrayals of David in Deuterocanonical and Cognate Literature', in *Biblical Figures in Deuterocanonical and Cognate Literature* (ed. Hermann Lichtenberger and Ulrike Mittmann-Reichert; Deuterocanonical and Cognate Literature, Yearbook, 2008; Berlin: de Gruyter, 2008), pp. 165-82 (170-71).

14. The reference to the covenant seems to rely more on Ps. 89.29-30, where it designates a central promise to David, than on Num. 25. The terms ברית, חסד, and נאמן ('covenant', 'piety', and 'faithfulness' respectively) found in Ps. 89.29 are used in Sir. 50.24.

third after Aaron and Eleazar.[15] To describe the zeal of Phinehas, Sir. 45.23 uses the phrase ויעמד בפרץ עמו from Ps. 106.23, where Moses averts divine wrath by 'standing in the breach of his people' during the Golden Calf incident (cf. Ezek. 22.30).[16] Phinehas gains 'noble status' (נדבו לבו, Sir. 45.23),[17] and Sir. 45.24 adds the term גדולה to his priesthood to insist that he is the *high* priest, while his covenant of peace is qualified as לכלכל מקדש, 'to support the sanctuary', to suggest that it encompasses broad political duties like Joseph's (see כלכל in Gen. 47.12).

1c. *The Aaronid Priesthood in Ben Sira.* Aaron and Phinehas are central figures in Ben Sira.[18] Beginning in Sir. 7.29, the reader is called to honour the priests, even to hallow them, and one can speak of a pan-Aaronid ideology.[19] The designation of Aaron in Sir. 45.6 as a holy man moves a tradition that is marginal in the Hebrew Bible (only Num. 16.7; Ps. 106.16) into greater prominence.[20] Aaron is granted 'stateliness' (הוד in Sir. 45.7). He is the receiver and teacher of commandments, statutes, and judgments (Sir. 45.17), roles that are elsewhere reserved for Moses (Exod. 24.12; Deut. 4.5; 28.1, 13), the Levites (Deut. 33.10), and Ezra (Ezra 7.10).

Aaron also receives Davidic royal traits.[21] Aaron's exaltation in Sir. 45.6 is modelled after David's (Ps. 89.20). Ben Sira's Aaron is even more clearly flawless than he is in the Torah,[22] while his David is not (Sir. 47.11).

15. Pomykala, 'Covenant of Phinehas', p. 21.

16. See the parallels between Sir. 45.4 // Ps. 106.22 (Moses elected by God); Sir. 45.6 // Ps. 106.16 (Aaron as holy); Sir. 45.18-19 // Ps. 106.16-17 (Dathan and Abiram); Sir. 45.23 // Ps. 106.23 (standing in the breach); Sir. 45.23 // Ps. 106.30 (Phinehas). See Pomykala, 'Covenant of Phinehas', p. 21.

17. Exod. 25.2; 35.29; 1 Chron. 29.9; 2 Chron. 17.16; Judg. 5.2, 9; Sir. 7.6; 8.2, 4; 11.1; 13.9; [20.27G]; 38.3; Pomykala, 'Phinehas', pp. 22-23; Robert C. T. Hayward, *The Jewish Temple: A Non-Biblical Sourcebook* (London: Routledge, 1996), p. 61.

18. הן occurs in Sir. 7.29, 31; 45.15, 24; 46.13; 50.1, 16 (ἱερεὺς, 7.29, 31; 45.15, 24; 50.1, 12).

19. Olyan, 'Relationship', p. 275.

20. Reiterer argues that this verse designates the holiness of the divine name rather than Aaron, but the many connections with Num. 16–18 and Ps. 106 argue against this ('Polyvalent Role', p. 31).

21. This is clear in Sir. 45.12-15, where Aaron receives the royal golden crown (Ps. 21.4), the priestly turban (Exod. 28.4, 27, 39; Ezek. 21.31) and diadem (Exod. 28.36), plus the Davidic promise of a covenant (Ps. 89.30; Sir. 50.24). See Friedrich V. Reiterer, *'Urtext' und Übersetzungen. Sprachstudie über Sir 44.16–45,26 als Beitrag zur Sirachforschung* (Arbeiten zu Text und Sprache im Alten Testament, 12; St. Ottilien: EOS, 1980), p. 168; Reiterer, 'Polyvalent Role', pp. 42-43.

22. Mulder, *Simon the High Priest*, p. 217.

The extensive allusions to Korah's rebellion in Sir. 45.16-25 turn this revolt explicitly into a revolt against Aaron and a fight between priestly families. Sira 45.18-19 plays with the metaphor of fire and prepares for the reading of the word אש as 'fire' rather than 'man' in Sir. 45.25.

1d. *The Other Priests in Ben Sira.* The use of the term זר ('alien', 'foreign', 'strange', and/or 'illicit') in connection with Korah, Dathan and Abiram in Sir. 45.18 is used for priests whom the writer considers illegitimate. To identify these illegitimate priests, the almost total absence of Levi and Levites in Ben Sira is crucial.[23] The only exception is in Sir. 45.6, where Aaron is described to have arisen from the staff or tribe of Levi. The designation of Aaron's genealogy with the term מטה, 'staff', instead of שבט, 'tribe', which is more commonly used in connection with Levi,[24] points to the staff of Levi, upon which the name of Aaron was engraved before it blossomed (Num. 17.23). The preference for the term מטה in Sir. 45.6 underlines the replacement of the house of Levi by the staff of Aaron in Numbers 17 with the consequences discussed above regarding the transfer of the Levites' prerogatives (Deut. 31.24-27; 33.10) to the Aaronide priest in Sir. 45.5, 17. The concealment of Levi and the Levites is not due to a lack of interest nor to a canonical orientation.[25] Rather, it reflects contemporary conflicts that also are documented in the Aramaic *Levi Document* 11.5-6, which can be described as a 'counterpart' for Ben Sira.[26]

---

23. Peter Höffken, 'Warum schwieg Jesus Sirach über Ezra?', *ZAW* 87 (1975), pp. 184-202 (187); Olyan, 'Relationship', p. 273; Christopher T. Begg, 'Ben-Sirach's Nonmention of Ezra', *BN* 42 (1988), pp. 14-18; Pancratius C. Beentjes, 'Hezekiah and Isaiah: A Study on Ben Sira 48, 15-25', in *New Avenues in the Study of the Old Testament: A Collection of Old Testament Studies, Published on the Occasion of the Fiftieth Anniversary of the Oudtestamentisch Werkgezelschap and the Retirement of Prof. Dr. M. J. Mulder* (ed. Adam S. van der Woude; OTS, 25; Leiden: Brill, 1989), pp. 77-88; Gary N. Knoppers, 'The Relationship of the Priestly Genealogies to the History of the High Priesthood in Jerusalem', in *Judah and the Judeans in the Neo-Babylonian Period* (ed. Oded Lipschits and Joseph Blenkinsopp; Winona Lake, IN: Eisenbrauns, 2003), pp. 109-33 (128); Harald Samuel, *Von Priestern zum Patriarchen Levi und die Leviten im Alten Testament* (BZAW, 448; Berlin: de Gruyter, 2014).

24. Exod. 6.16-20; Num. 26.57-59. See Reiterer, '*Urtext*', p. 144; Samuel, 'Von Priestern', p. 231; Achenbach, *Vollendung*, p. 481; Mulder, *Simon the High Priest*, pp. 216-17.

25. *Pace* Samuel, 'Von Priestern', p. 412.

26. Beentjes, 'Portrayals of David', p. 172; see *Jub.* 31.11-20; 45.16; *Test. Levi* 2; 4; 5; 8–9; James L. Kugel, 'Levi's Elevation to the Priesthood in Second Temple

Zadok and the Zadokites are only mentioned in Sira in 51.12: 'Give thanks to him who has chosen the sons of Zadok to be priests, for his mercy endures forever'. This phrase is often seen to be a late addition meant to compensate for the otherwise missing Zadokites.[27] Such a view is based on the unproven premise that Simon belonged to Zadokite circles like the Oniads.[28] If this were the case, one would have expected a greater emphasis on Zadok in the text of Ben Sira.

1e. *Simon as Ruler (Sir. 50)*. In the 'Praise of the Fathers', Phinehas is endowed with kingly powers, while kings are depicted critically.[29] In Sira 50, the finale to the 'Praise of the Fathers' and to the entire book, Simon's leadership extends to both city and temple. Simon is a builder; like Solomon and Hezekiah, he fortified Jerusalem.[30] Then, Simon's role as high priest surrounded by his sons, especially the Aaronites, is described at length in Sir. 50.5-20. The presentation culminates in the prayer of the high priest. This blessing in Sir. 50.22-24 contains parallels with Sir. 45.23-25 and ends with the promise that Simon might stand in the covenant of Phinehas for eternity. As both king and priest, Simon is thereby exalted as the climax of the constructed history of Israel.[31]

Writings', *HTR* 86.1 (1993), pp. 1-64; Robert A. Kugler, *From Patriarch to Priest: The Levi-Priestly Tradition from Aramaic Levi to Testament of Levi* (Early Judaism and Its Literature, 9; Atlanta: Scholars Press, 1996).

27. Fabry, 'Jesus Sirach', p. 276; Knoppers, 'Relationship', p. 128; Patrick W. Skehan and Alexander A. DiLella, *The Wisdom of Ben Sira: A New Translation with Notes* (AB, 39; New York: Doubleday, 1987), pp. 568-69.

28. Pomykala, 'Phinehas', p. 28; Gabriele Boccaccini, 'Where Did Ben Sira Belong? The Canon, Literary Genre, Intellectual Movement, and Social Group of a Zadokite Document', in Xeravits (ed.), *Studies in the Book of Ben Sira*, pp. 21-42; Richard J. Coggins, *Sirach* (Guides to the Apocrypha and Pseudepigrapha, 6; Sheffield: Sheffield Academic, 1998), p. 81; Fabry, 'Pinhas-Bund', p. 49; Friedrich V. Reiterer, 'Gott und Opfer', in *Ben Sira's God: Proceedings of the International Ben Sira Conference, Durham, Upshaw College 2001* (ed. Renate Egger-Wenzel; BZAW, 321; Berlin: de Gruyter, 2002), pp. 136-79 (156).

29. Apart from David, Hezekiah, and Josiah, all kings of Judah were sinful (Sir. 49.4-6). Josef Schreiner, 'Patriarchen im Lob der Väter (zu Sir 44)', in *Textarbeit. Studien zu Texten und ihrer Rezeption aus dem Alten Testament und der Umwelt Israels* (ed. Klaus Kiesow; AOAT, 294; Münster: Ugarit-Verlag, 2003), pp. 425-41 (437); Wright, 'Ben Sira on Kings', p. 87.

30. In vv. 6-7 Simon is compared with the sun and moon, like the king in Ps. 89.38-39.

31. Mulder, *Simon the High Priest*, p. 218; Alon Goshen-Gottstein, 'Ben Sira's Praise of the Fathers', in Egger-Wenzel (ed.), *Ben Sira's God*, pp. 235-67 (261).

2. *Phinehas in the Greek Text of Sirach*

The main differences between the Hebrew and Greek texts of Sir. 45.23-26 need to be discussed. In v. 23, the phrase, 'when the people turned back' (ἐν τροπῇ λαοῦ), is added to Phinehas's standing in the breach of his people.[32] In v. 24 the Greek version summarizes the apparent doubling of חק ברית, 'statute of covenant', with διαθήκη, 'covenant', while the 'covenant of peace' is 'for the people' in addition to the chief of the sanctuary. The verb προστατέω 'to stand before, to lead' strengthens the political dimension of leadership, which was already implied by לכלכל, 'to support', in the Hebrew text. This is underlined by the addition of καὶ λαοῦ αὐτου, 'and his people'.[33] In v. 25, the relation between the Davidic covenant and the priestly covenant (Aaron, Phinehas) is described more clearly. Both covenants are placed side by side, on equal standing.[34] In v. 26, the phrase κρίνειν τὸν λαὸν αὐτοῦ ἐν δικαιοσύνῃ, 'to judge his people in righteousness', is added, which is a citation of Ps. 71.2 (LXX). However, in the psalm, the phrase is applied to kings (1 Kgs 3.9) not to priests. In vv. 6-7, Aaron is explicitly described as the 'equal of his brother' (ὅμοιον αὐτῷ ἀδελφὸν), and his priesthood is described as ἱερατείαν λαοῦ, a 'priesthood of the people'.[35] In Sir. 45.16, the phrase ולכפר על בני ישראל, 'to atone for the children of Israel', is rendered as ἐξιλάσκεσθαι περὶ τοῦ λαοῦ σου, 'to atone for his people', omitting 'Israel'. In v. 17, the parallel with Deut. 33.10 is strengthened by a mention of Jacob. In Sir. 45.18 זרים, 'foreigners', is rendered with ἀλλότριοι, 'others' or 'strange', although in Sir. 45.13 זר is rendered as ἀλλογενής, 'another race', as in Num. 17.5; 18.4, 7 LXX.

In Sir. 50.1, the Greek version makes Simon high priest (Σιμων Ονιου υἱὸς ἱερεὺς ὁ μέγας). Verse 23b is expanded with the addition of ἐν ἡμέραις ἡμῶν ἐν Ισραηλ κατὰ τὰς ἡμέρας τοῦ αἰῶνος, 'in our days in Israel forever'. The main difference in Sira 50 is the complete omission of the reference to Phinehas and his covenant at the end of v. 24.

---

32. Pomykala, 'Phinehas', p. 30.

33. Ibid., p. 29

34. Fabry, 'Jesus Sirach', p. 275; Stadelmann considers David's covenant superior to the covenant of Phinehas in the Greek version (*Ben Sira*, p. 151). For Marböck, the royal and the priestly covenant are of equal standing in the Greek and Syriac version. He refers to Jer. 33.17-26, where the covenants of David and Levi are next to each other ('Geschichte', p. 188).

35. Mulder, *Simon the High Priest*, p. 264; Reiterer, '*Urtext*', p. 148. The term ἱερατεία is also used in Num. 25.13 (LXX).

In vv. 25-26, to 'those who reside on Mount Samaria' is added the 'foolish people that dwells in Shechem'. The Greek has a stronger anti-Samarian impulse than the Hebrew text.[36]

In sum, besides omitting the covenant of Phinehas in Sir. 50.24, the Greek version of Sirach goes even further than the Hebrew text in broadening the power of the office of the high priesthood. In addition, the outlook is more universal, since the name Israel is avoided.[37] Instead, phrases that include the term λαός, 'people', are added (Sir. 45.7, 16, 23-24; 50.4, 5). The various Hebrew covenantal designations are subsumed in the single term διαθήκη, while the covenant with Phinehas is deleted.

3. Phinehas in the First Book of Maccabees
3a. *Phinehas in 1 Maccabees.* Phinehas appears twice in 1 Maccabees:

> When Mattathias saw this, he was inflamed with *zeal*, and his reins trembled, neither could he forbear to show his *anger* according to judgment: wherefore he ran, and slew him upon the altar. Also the king's commissioner, who compelled men to sacrifice, he killed at that time, and the altar he pulled down. Thus dealt he *zealously* for the law of God like as *Phinehas* did unto Zambri the son of Salom. And Mattathias cried throughout the city with a loud voice, saying, 'Whosoever is *zealous* of the law, and maintains the *covenant*, let him follow me'. (1 Macc. 2.24-27)

> *Phinehas* our father in being *zealous and fervent* obtained the *covenant of an everlasting priesthood.* (1 Macc. 2.54)

In 1 Macc. 2.24, Phinehas serves to legitimate the zealous act of Mattathias.[38] In v. 54, he is listed as an exemplary ancestor as though the

---

36.　Pieter W. van der Horst, 'Anti-Samaritan Propaganda in Early Judaism', in *Jews and Christians in Their Graeco-Roman Context: Selected Essays on Early Judaism, Samaritanism, Hellenism, and Christianity* (ed. Pieter W. van der Horst; WUNT, 196; Tübingen: Mohr Siebeck, 2006), pp. 134-50 (140); Magnar Kartveit, *The Origin of the Samaritans* (VTSup, 128; Leiden: Brill, 2009), p. 146; Matthew Goff, '"The Foolish Nation that Dwells in Shechem": Ben Sira on Shechem and the Other Peoples in Palestine', in *The "Other" in Second Temple Judaism: Essays in Honor of John J. Collins* (ed. Daniel C. Harlow et al.; Grand Rapids, MI: Eerdmans, 2011), pp. 173-88.

37.　In Sir. 50.17 God is קדוש ישראל, 'the holiness of Israel', or τῷ κυρίῳ αὐτῶν παντοκράτορι, 'our Lord, the creator of All'. In Sir. 50.22 אלהי ישראל, 'the God of Israel', becomes τὸν θεὸν πάντων, 'the God of All'. See also the use of κόσμος in Sir. 50.9, 14, 19.

38.　See Jonathan A. Goldstein, *I Maccabees: A New Translation, with Introduction and Commentary* (AB, 41; Garden City, NY: Doubleday 1976), p. 6; Joseph Sievers, *The Hasmoneans and Their Supporters: From Mattathias to the Death of John Hyrcanus I* (South Florida Studies in the History of Judaism, 6; Atlanta:

writer had Ben Sira's 'Praise of the Fathers' in front of him.[39] The motifs of zeal, covenant, and divine wrath are repeated. The prelude to the Maccabean revolt in 1 Macc. 1.15 alludes to Numbers 25 in its use of the rare term ζευγίζω, 'to yoke',[40] to describe the surrender of the Hellenizers to the 'heathens' (צמד, Num. 25.3). The 'great plague' (πληγή μέγας) resulting from Antiochus's misdeeds in 1 Macc. 1.30 is inspired by Num. 25.8-9 and the desecrations in 1 Macc. 1.43 and 63 are described by using the verb βεβηλόω, 'to commit apostasy', from Num. 25.1 LXX.[41] The 'great wrath' that was upon Israel in v. 64 is another allusion to Num. 25.3. This motif is repeated in 1 Macc. 3.8 where the wrath is averted by Judas, as Phinehas did in Num. 25.11. In the testimony of Mattathias, Phinehas gets a prominent position as ὁ πατὴρ ἡμῶν, 'our father', so that the sons of Mattathias could also receive the promise of high priesthood (1 Macc. 2.54).[42] If the direct allusions to the story of Phinehas are indeed only found in the first chapters of 1 Maccabees, the reception of Phinehas is important for the entire book.[43] The description of the Maccabean high priesthood in 1 Maccabees is characterized by the combination of priestly and military attributes, in contradiction to Leviticus 21–22, where the priests are protected from the impurity resulting from the contact with corpses in battle. In 1 Maccabees, recourse to the figure of Phinehas solves this problem; the future priest Phinehas is present at the war of revenge against the Midianites in Numbers 31.[44]

Scholars Press, 1990), p. 30; Klaus-Dietrich Schunck, *Die Quellen des ersten und zweiten Makkabäerbuches* (Halle: Niemeyer, 1954), p. 80.

39. Pomykala, *Davidic Dynasty*, p. 159.

40. ζευγίζω is a *hapax legomenon* in the LXX. But in their translation of Num. 25.3, Aquila and Symmachus both use a form of ζευγίζω to render צָמַד instead of the more imprecise translation ἐτελέσθη used in the LXX (Origenes, Hexapla 1 257; Goldstein, *1 Maccabees*, p. 201). LSJ, p. 753 translates ζευγίζω as 'yoke in pairs' and refer only to PGrenf.I.1.1 (II.B.C); LXX 1 Macc. 1.15; Aq. Num. 25.3.

41. Mixed marriages are not criticized in 1 Maccabees. The men are killed in war, not the foreign wives, as in Num. 31. For a lengthier discussion, see the contribution to this volume by Claudia V. Camp, 'Gender and Identity in the Book of Numbers', pp. 105-21.

42. In 1 Macc. 2.65 Simon is called 'your brother' and 'your father'.

43. *Pace* Othmar Keel, *Die Geschichte Jerusalems und die Entstehung des Monotheismus 2* (Orte und Landschaften der Bibel, 4/2; Göttingen: Vandenhoeck & Ruprecht, 2006), §1735.

44. Warfare in 1 Maccabees is conceived more along the lines of revenge against the Midianites (Num. 31) than the defensive war of Deut. 20. See Tobias Funke, 'Pinhas und Anti-Pinhas? Priestertum und Gewalt im 1Makk und 1QM', in *Ex Oriente lux. Studien zur Theologie des Alten Testaments* (ed. Angelike Berlejung and Raik Heckl; ABiG, 39; Leipzig: Evangelische Verlagsanstalt, 2012), pp. 199-224.

3b. *From Priests to Kings in 1 Maccabees.* In 1 Maccabees, the sons of Mattathias are given increasingly important titles. Judas begins as a priestly strategist, receiving from his father the task of ἄρχων στρατιᾶς, 'head of the armed forces' (1 Macc. 2.66). Jonathan is chosen as 'ruler and military leader' (ἄρχων καὶ ἡγούμεν τὸν πόλεμον, 1 Macc. 9.30). He is also 'high priest and friend of the king' (ἀρχιερέα τοῦ ἔθνους σου καὶ φίλον βασιλέως, 1 Macc. 10.20) as well as general and governor (1 Macc. 10.65). Hence, he is the first among the Maccabees to hold priestly as well as military titles. All offices and titles culminate in Simon. He is appointed as high priest as well as ἐθνάρχης τῶν Ιουδαίων καὶ ἱερέων, 'ethnarch of the Jews and of the sanctuary' (1 Macc. 14.47; 15.1, 2), and he acts as 'chief of all' (προστατῆσαι πάντων).

3c. *Simon in 1 Maccabees 14.* Like Phinehas, who is also called 'our father' (ὑμῶν πατήρ, 1 Macc. 2.54), Simon is appointed by Mattathias as 'father of all' (αὐτὸς ἔσται ὑμῶν πατήρ, 1 Macc. 2.65). Simon is the avenger (1 Macc. 13.6; 15.21, cf. Num. 31.2) and receives the superlative titles of ἀρχιερεὺς μέγας, 'highest high priest' (1 Macc. 13.42), and ἱερεὺς μέγας, 'high priest' (1 Macc. 14.20; 15.2), two likely allusions to the διαθήκην ἱερωσύνης αἰωνίας, 'covenant of eternal priesthood', of 1 Macc. 2.54 and of his 'eternal' office (εἰς τὸν αἰῶνα) in 1 Macc. 14.41. Simon shall be 'chief for all' (προστατῆσαι πάντων, see Sir. 45.24 LXX), and he will free Israel from the yoke of the nations (1 Macc. 13.41). Hence, allusions to Phinehas legitimate the combination of priestly and military functions.

3d. *The Other Priests in 1 Maccabees.* The intention of 1 Maccabees has been described to be 'to establish the legitimacy of the Hasmonean dynasty, and this concern is reflected by its *damnatio memoriae* of other Jewish claims to the high priesthood'.[45] What are these 'other Jewish claims'? In 1 Maccabees, the author describes in detail how the 'evil Jews join the Gentiles' (1 Macc. 1.15), but he never says who these evil Jews are. 1 Maccabees 5.62 makes it obvious that genealogy is a crucial determining factor for being Us or Other; the deaths of Joseph and Azariah are explained by the fact that they 'came not of the seed of those by whose hand deliverance was given unto Israel'.

45. Daniel R. Schwartz, 'The Other in 1 and 2 Maccabees', in *Tolerance and Intolerance in Early Judaism and Christianity* (ed. Graham N Stanton and Guy G. Stroumsa; Cambridge: Cambridge University Press, 1998), pp. 30-37 (30).

Like Ben Sira, 1 Maccabees mentions neither Levi nor the Levites; however, Alcimus is assigned Aaronite lineage (1 Macc. 7.14), even though he falls short of the expectations this raises. In light of these considerations, a number of scholars have interpreted the references to Phinehas in 1 Maccabees to be a Maccabean strategy used to justify their claim to the high priesthood although they were not Zadokites.[46] Anti-Maccabean texts from the Dead Sea scrolls are often mentioned to bolster this claim, but it is significant that these texts ignore the matter of lineage and focus on the participation of the Maccabees in warfare. The perceived problem was the incompatibility of military leadership with the high priesthood.

4. Preliminary Conclusion

The final chapter of Ben Sira's 'Praise of the Fathers' and the last part of 1 Maccabees share a portrayal of the high priest Simon based on the use of the biblical figure of Phinehas to legitimize the combination of cultic and military powers.[47] That conflicts between rival priestly groups took place is undisputed, but the particular historical circumstances behind these conflicts remains unclear. It is not enough to claim that Ben Sira was a pro-Zadokite while the author of 1 Maccabees espoused an anti-Zadokite stance.

II. Social-historical Classification

1. The Religious and Political Power of the Office of High Priest in the Hellenistic Period

Having shown how the priesthood of Phinehas is used in Ben Sira and in 1 Maccabees in Othering strategies among different priestly groups, I will now attempt to locate a historical setting for these rivalries over the office of high priest, particularly in light of the limited reception of Phinehas in the Greek version of Ben Sira.[48]

46. Goldstein, *1 Maccabees*, 74; Keel, *Jerusalem*, §1731; Deborah W. Rooke, *Zadok's Heirs: The Role and Development of the High Priesthood in Ancient Israel* (OTM; Oxford: Oxford University Press, 2000), p. 281; Ulrike Mittmann-Richert, *Historische und legendarische Erzählungen* (Einführung zu den Jüdische Schriften aus hellenistisch-römischer Zeit, 1/1; Jüdische Schriften aus Hellenistich-römischer Zeit, 6 supplementa; Gütersloh: Gütersloher Verlagshaus, 2000), p. 32.

47. Ingrid Hjelm sees here and in Sir. 50 a praise of Simon Maccabee, but the lack of military decorum in Sir. 50 argues against it (*Jerusalem's Rise to Sovereignty: Zion and Gerizim in Competition* [JSOTSup, 404; London: T&T Clark International, 2004], p. 330).

48. Maria Brutti, *The Development of the High Priesthood During the Pre-Hasmonean Period* (JSJSup, 108; Leiden: Brill, 2006); Joachim Schaper, *Priester*

Reconstructing the history of the priesthood on the basis of claims made in Ben Sira and in 1 Maccabees must take into account the date and the character of each work.[49] On the one hand, the identification of Simon in Sira 50 is problematic.[50] I consider the Hebrew version to be written from the viewpoint of Onias III, the son of Simon II, with the intention of justifying the high priesthood held by the Oniad family. On the other hand, the presentation of the beginnings of the Maccabean revolt in the first chapters of 1 Maccabees constitutes a foundation legend for the Maccabees rather than a historical description of events. By constructing a story about Mattathias and his sons, the different groups that took part in the revolt were invited to accept the legitimacy of the Hasmonean leadership.[51]

In this respect, the term προστατέω, 'to stand before, to lead', is particularly relevant. It is used in the Greek version of Sir. 45.24 (for לכלכל) as well as in 1 Macc. 14.47 to describe a title assigned to Simon

und Leviten im achämenidischen Juda. Studien zur Kult- und Sozialgeschichte Israels in persischer Zeit (FAT, 31; Tübingen: Mohr, 2000); Lester L. Grabbe, 'The Gestalt of the High Priest in the Second Temple Period: An Anthropological Perspective', in *The Priesthood in the Second Temple Period* (ed. Alice W. Hunt; London: Bloomsbury T&T Clark International, forthcoming).

49.   The Hebrew version of Ben Sira is accepted as pre-Maccabean and so written between 190 and 175 BCE. The Greek version is dated around 130 BCE and is thought to derive from the Egypt Diaspora: Fabry, 'Pinhas-Bund', p. 51; Johannes Marböck, 'Der Hohepriester Simon in Sir 50. Ein Beitrag zur Bedeutung von Priestertum und Kult im Sirachbuch', in *Treasures of Wisdom: Studies in Ben Sira and the Book of Wisdom. Festschrift M. Gilbert* (ed. Núria Calduch-Benages and Jacques Vermeylen; BETL, 143; Leuven: Leuven University Press, 1999), pp. 215-29 (165); Hayward, *Temple*, p. 38. Georg Sauer, *Jesus Sirach/Ben Sira* (Das Alte Testament Deutsch Apokryphon, 1; Göttingen: Vandenhoeck & Ruprecht, 2000), p. 488. The Hebrew *Vorlage* of 1 Maccabees is usually dated between 135 and 100 BCE and the Greek translation between 103 and 63 BCE. Both are thought to have been produced in Jerusalem. See Angelika Berlejung, 'Die Makkabäerbücher', in *Grundinformation Altes Testament. Eine Einführung in Literatur, Religion und Geschichte des Alten Testaments* (ed. Jan Christian Gertz; Göttingen: Vandenhoeck & Ruprecht, 4th edn, 2010), pp. 573-81; Keel, *Jerusalem*, §1658, §1667.

50.   For James C. VanderKam, it is Simon I (around 300 BCE) ('Simon the Just: Simon I or Simon II?', in *Pomegranates and Golden Bells: Studies in Biblical, Jewish and Near Eastern Ritual, Law, and Literature in Honor of Jacob Milgrom* [ed. David P. Wright and Jacob Milgrom; Winona Lake, IN: Eisenbrauns, 1995], pp. 303-18 [305]); for Marböck, Simon II (218–192 BCE) ('Hohepriester Simon', p. 165), and for Hjelm, Simon Maccabee (*Jerusalem's Rise*, p. 330).

51.   Schunck, *Quellen*, p. 63; Étienne Nodet, *A Search for the Origins of Judaism: From Joshua to the Mishnah* (JSOTSup, 248; Sheffield: Sheffield Academic, 1997), p. 263.

in addition to that of high priest. Comparing these observations with Simon's sole role as high priest in Sira 50, it can be assumed that the first two texts reflect a controversy associated with the lucrative office of *prostates*, which probably entailed the collection of taxes and tributes on behalf of the occupying power.

2. *The Office of* Prostates

The term προστατέω can be translated 'to stand before', 'to head something', 'to be chief of', or 'to have authority over'.[52] To my knowledge, no systematic analysis of this term is available. The relevance of the office of *prostates* when attested in other Hellenistic contexts remains unclear.[53]

Josephus uses the verb προΐστημι, a form related to προστάτης, n his description of the leading role of the high priests in the affairs of the Jewish society (*Ant.* 11.111). This statement is general and describes the situation around 300 BCE:

πολιτεία χρώμενοι ἀριστοκρατικῇ μετὰ ὀλιγαρχίας οἱ γὰρ ἀρχιερεῖς προεστή-κεσαν τῶν πραγμάτων ἄχρι οὗ τοὺς Ἀσαμωναίου συνέβη βασιλεύειν ἐκγόνους.

[They] made use of a form of government that was aristocratic, but mixed with an oligarchy, *for the high priests were at the head of their affairs*, until the posterity of the Hasmoneans set up kingly government. (*Ant.* 11.111)

Hecataeus of Abdera also uses a form of the verb προΐστημι and the term προστασία to describe the office of the Jewish high priest:[54]

---

52. LSJ, §1526f. The verb προστατέω occurs only in these two places in the LXX (Sir. 45.24; 1 Macc. 14.47). In addition, the noun προστάτης is used infrequently, either to translate פָּקִיד, שַׂר or נְשִׂיא ('minister', 'principal', or 'prince'; 1 Chron. 27.31; 29.6; 2 Chron. 8.10; 24.11; 1 Ezra 2.8; 2 Macc. 3.4).

53. Klaus-Dietrich Schunck does not mention the parallels in Hecataeus and Josephus (*Ant.* 11.111) nor the relation between the terms ἐπιστάτης and προστάτης ('Hohepriester und Politiker? Die Stellung der Hohepriester von Jaddua bis Jonatan zur Jüdischen Gemeinde und zum hellenistischen Staat', *VT* 44.4 [1994], pp. 61-71). For the occurrences of the term προστάτης in the context of the Egyptian priesthood, see Martin Hengel, *Judentum und Hellenismus. Studien zu ihrer Begegnung unter besonderer Berücksichtigung Palästinas bis zur Mitte des 2. Jh.s v. Chr.* (WUNT, 10; Tübingen: Mohr, 1988), pp. 45-47 and Lester. L. Grabbe, *A History of the Jews and Judaism in the Second Temple Period.* Vol. 2, *The Coming of the Greeks— the Early Hellenistic Period (335–173 BCE)* (LSTS, 68; London: T&T Clark International, 2008), p. 170; Grabbe, 'Gestalt of High Priesthood', p. 6.

54. Victor Tcherikover, *Hellenistic Civilization and the Jews* (Peabody, MA: Hendrickson, 1999), pp. 58, 464; Achenbach, *Vollendung*, p. 138; Grabbe, *History of Jews*, pp. 190, 284.

He [Moses] picked out the men of most refinement and with the greatest ability *to head the entire nation* (τοῦ σύμπαντος ἔθνους προιστασθαι), and appointed them priests; and he ordained that they should occupy themselves with the temple and the honours and sacrifices offered to their god. For this reason the Jews never have a king, and *authority over the people* (τοῦ πλήθους προστασίαν) is regularly vested in whichever priest is regarded as superior to his colleagues in wisdom and virtue. They call this man the *high priest* (ἀρχιερέα) and believe that he acts as a messenger to them of God's commandments. It is he, we are told, who in their assemblies and other gatherings announces what is ordained, and the Jews are so docile in such matters that straight way they fall to the ground and do reverence to the *high priest* (ἀρχιερέα) when he expounds the commandments to them. (Diodorus 40.3, 4-6)

Since Hecataeus flourished in the fourth to third centuries BCE, his observations can be seen to indicate the existence in the Hellenistic administration of an office of *prostates*, which in Yehud/Judaea was sometimes filled by the high priest.[55] The position was probably similar to that of the פחה of Ezra 6.6-7. He represented the interests of the local population before the Hellenistic rulers and served as an interface between the two, dealing with fiscal matters.

Drawing on a Tobiad romance, Josephus reports in 2 Maccabees that the Tobiad Joseph saved the Jewish people after the high priest Onias (probably Onias II) endangered them by stopping the payment of tribute. In this context, Joseph accuses Onias of greed when he assumed the *prostasia* over the people (τοῦ λαοῦ τὴν προστασίαν) in addition to the office of high priest (τῆς ἀρχιερατικῆς τιμῆς, *Ant.* 12.161). The roles of *prostasia* and high priest seem to be held by the same person. Later in the narrative, Joseph is appointed tax collector for all of Syro-Phoenicia and seems to hold the title of *prostates* (τὸ πλῆθος εἶναι γὰρ αὐτοῦ προστάτην, *Ant.* 12.167).[56] Although the historical value of this story is impaired by Josephus's clear pro-Tobiad bias and by the many allusions to the biblical Joseph narrative he made,[57] nevertheless, it may provide reliable information about the ability of a high priest to serve concurrently as *prostates*.

---

55. See also Papyrus Rainer and the Zenon Papyri; Rooke, *Zadok's Heirs*, p. 251; Hengel, *Judentum und Hellenismus*, pp. 44-47; Keel, *Geschichte Jerusalems*, §1147.

56. Theophil Middendorp, *Die Stellung Jesu Ben Siras zwischen Judentum und Hellenismus* (Leiden: Brill, 1973), p. 153.

57. Dov Gera, *Judaea and Mediterranean Politics, 219 to 161 B.C.E.* (Brill's Series in Jewish Studies, 8; Leiden: Brill, 1998), pp. 49-52; Diana Edelman, 'Seeing Double: Tobiah the Ammonite', *RB* 113.4 (2006), pp. 570-84; Grabbe, *History of the Jews*, p. 77.

It is unclear whether the pro-Ptolemaic Hyrcanus, the son of the Tobiad Joseph, inherited the *prostasia* (*Ant.* 12.219)[58] at his father's death or if the office went back to the pro-Seleucid Oniads.[59] The second option would reflect the situation in the wake of the battle of Banias (198 BCE) when the Seleucids took over control of Palestine from the Ptolemies, enabling the pro-Seleucid Oniads to come back to power.[60] The conflict, however, continued during the rule of Onias III (196–175 BCE). In the framework of the Heliodorus controversy (2 Macc. 3.4), someone named Simon is called the προστάτης τοῦ ἱεροῦ 'the administrator of the sanctuary', while Onias III struggled to hold authority over the marketplace (ἀγορανομία).[61] Onias III no longer seemed to hold the office of *prostates*.[62]

Jason (174–171 BCE) then purchased the office of high priest by promising his superiors increased tribute (2 Macc. 4.7), and he may have occupied the office of *prostates* initially. Subsequently, however, he was outbid by Menelaus (171–162 BCE), the brother of the Simon who is described as holder of the position of προστάτης τοῦ ἱεροῦ in 2 Macc. 4.23-24; the passage explicitly states he was not an Oniad (and hence also probably not an Aaronide). To compensate for this deficit, Menelaus married the sister of Onias III.[63]

Antiochus IV Epiphanes seems to have limited the power of Menelaus by placing Philoppos, who was not a Jew, at his side as ἐπιστάτης (2 Macc. 5.22). Philoppos probably held extensive military powers, given that the Maccabean revolt had probably been underway since ca. 165 BCE. In 161 Menelaus was replaced for a few years by Alcimus, of Aaronide lineage, possibly in an attempt to pacify the rebels (*Ant.* 12.385; 1 Macc. 7.14; 2 Macc. 14.3, 7). The reconstruction of the list of high priests after Alcimus is impaired by the contradictions in Josephus's report (*Ant.* 12.414, 434; 20.237).

58. Theophil Middendorp thinks *Ant.* 12.219 points toward this understanding because Hyrcanus is said to have been in contact with Ptolemaios IV Philopator, receiving presents from him and possibly also the office of *prostastes* (*Stellung*, p. 153).

59. Schunck, 'Hohepriester und Politiker', p. 65.

60. Mulder, *Simon the High Priest*, p. 236.

61. Schunck, 'Hohepriester und Politiker', p. 66; Hengel, *Judentum und Hellenismus*, p. 46.

62. Simon, a Benjaminite, was possibly a pro-Seleucid Oniad but not a priest. Onias III seems to have shifted allegiance back to the Jerusalemite branch of the pro-Seleucid Tobiads; 2 Macc. 3.10 reports that he kept funds safe in the temple of Jerusalem belonging to the Tobiads (Keel, *Geschichte Jerusalems*, §1149).

63. He may have been supported by the Tobiads; see *Ant.* 12.239 (Schunck, 'Hohepriester oder Politiker', p. 68).

Josephus further reports that without occupying the office of high priest, Judas Maccabee received the προστασίαν τῶν πραγμάτων, 'the administration of public affairs', from Mattathias (*Ant.* 12.285). Subsequently, his brother Jonathan held both the office of high priest and the office of *prostates* for four years (*Ant.* 13.212). Finally, Simon is described as 'high priest, leader, and owner of the *prostasia*' (Σίμωνα αὐτῶν ἡγεῖσθαι καὶ ἀντὶ Ἰούδου καὶ Ἰωνάθου τῶν ἀδελφῶν αὐτοῦ τὴν προστασίαν ἔχειν ἔσεσθαι, *Ant.* 13.201), again in parallel to 1 Macc. 14.47. Regarding John Hyrcanus, Josephus reports he was high priest and *ethnarch* as well as προϊστῆται τῶν ἀδικουμένων, 'stands for those who are injured' (*Ant.* 14.196). The term *prostates* is found again in connection with the Hasmoneans (*Ant.* 20.158, 238, 244, 251). How the title found on Hasmonean coins, הכהן הגדל ראש חבר היהדים, 'the high priest [and] head of the Jewish community', corresponds to the offices of high priest and *prostates* must remain unanswered here.[64]

3. *Historical Settings*
What can be known about the inner-Jewish rivalries between the Oniads and the Tobiads? Around 200 BCE, the Tobiads split into pro-Seleucid and pro-Ptolemaic branches.[65] Simon II, the high priest (215–196 BCE), sided with the Seleucids, as did part of the Tobiad family in Jerusalem. On the other side was Hyrcanus, the son of Joseph, who probably succeeded Simon II in the office of *prostates* (*Ant.* 12.219).[66] The Hebrew book of Ben Sira probably reflects the point of view of the Oniad branch in Jerusalem, which saw itself of Aaronide lineage.[67] They claimed the position of *prostates* for themselves in addition to the high priesthood and considered Levitical and Zadokite candidates illegitimate. This concentration of political and priestly power is then actively endorsed in the Greek version of Ben Sira by suppressing Phinehas.

---

64. Hengel (*Judentum und Hellenismus*, p. 51) and Michael Krupp (*Die Hasmonäischen Münzen* [Jerusalem: Lee Achim Sefarim, 2011], p. 35) argue for an equation of the two titles. Against this argumentation stands the fact that the term προστάτης is rare in 1 and 2 Maccabees.

65. Berlejung, 'Makkabäerbücher', p. 183; Pomykala, 'Covenant of Phinehas', p. 28.

66. The latter had a base in Transjordan. See S. Gabriel Rosenberg, *'Airaq al-Amir: The Architecture of the Tobiads* (BAR, 1544; Oxford: Hedges, 2006).

67. Middendorp, *Stellung*, p. 159; Olyan, 'Relationship', p. 270; Benjamin G. Wright, 'Putting the Puzzle Together: Some Suggestions Concerning the Social Location of the Wisdom of Ben Sira', in *Conflicted Boundaries in Wisdom and Apocalypticism* (ed. Benjamin G. Wright; SBL Symposium Series, 35; Atlanta: SBL, 2005), pp. 89-113 (111).

Inner-Jewish tensions between pro-Hellenistic and anti-Hellenistic circles have been identified in the rivalries between Onias III and his brother Jason;[68] tensions that led, according to 1 Maccabees, to the Maccabean revolt. The deletion of Phinehas from the Greek version of Ben Sira implies that a pro-Maccabean author suppressed the connection between the Oniads and the Maccabees so that Phinehas could represent the Maccabees alone.

Another area of tension that may inform Phinehas' use in the Greek version of Sira is the rivalry between the temples of YHWH in Jerusalem and Samaria. The occurrence of his name five times in inscriptions on Mt. Gerizim suggests that Phinehas was an important figure there, too.[69] Considering the growing tensions between Samaria and Jerusalem at the time of John Hyrcanus, who eventually destroyed the holy place on Gerizim around 111 BCE, the omission of Phinehas in Sir. 50.24 and the harsher tone towards Samaria in the Greek version makes sense in this context.

III. *Conclusion*

To conclude, a hypothetical reconstruction can be suggested. The pro-Oniad author of the Hebrew Sirach (around 190 BCE) presented a pan-Aaronide tradition that consciously set itself apart from Levitical traditions.[70] He used the figure of Phinehas to legitimate Simon's status as high priest as well as his right to combine his cultic role with the office of *prostates*. His literary strategy and the underlying political

68. Stadelmann, *Ben Sira*, p. 150; Heinz-Josef Fabry, 'Zadokiden und Aaroniden in Qumran', in *Das Manna fällt auch heute noch Beiträge zur Geschichte und Theologie des Alten, Ersten Testaments. Festschrift für Erich Zenger* (ed. Frank-Lothar Hossfeld and Ludger Schwienhorst-Schönberger; HBS, 44; Freiburg: Herder, 2004), pp. 201-17 (204).

69. Yitzhaq Magen, Haggai Misgav, and Levana Tsfania, *Mount Gerizim Excavations I: The Aramaic, Hebrew, and Samaritan Inscriptions* (trans. E. Levin and M. Guggenheimer; Judea and Samaria Publications, 2; Jerusalem: Israel Antiquities Authority, 2004), pp. 25-27; Tobias Funke, 'Phinehas and Samaria: New Aspects in the Current Debate about Pentateuch/Hexateuch Formation', in *The Samaritan Pentateuch and Samaritan Literature* (ed. Stefan Schorch; Studia Samaritana, 8; Berlin: de Gruyter, forthcoming).

70. On the social setting of the Levitical traditions, see Friedemann Schubert, *Tradition und Erneuerung: Studien zum Jubiläenbuch und seinem Trägerkreis* (EHST, 771; Frankfurt am Main: Lang, 1998), p. 146; Schaper, *Priester und Leviten*, p. 269; Antje Labahn, *Licht und Heil. Levitischer Herrschaftsanspruch in der frühjüdischen Literatur aus der Zeit des Zweiten Tempels* (BThSt, 112; Neukirchen–Vluyn: Neukirchener Verlag, 2010), p. 69.

views it supports can plausibly be associated with the rivalries between the Oniads and Tobiads, centred in Jerusalem, in the third to second centuries BCE. The pro-Maccabean author of the 1 Maccabees (around 130 BCE) also used Phinehas to legitimate the Hasmonean high priesthood but, in addition, to justify the use of violence and the military campaigns of the Hasmonean high priest.

The author of the Greek Sirach (also around 130 BCE) was aware of both the Maccabean and Samarian receptions of Phinehas. Inscriptions found on Mt. Gerizim indicate that the Samarian priesthood considered themselves to trace back to Phinehas. Two reasons for his emendation of references to Phinehas in the inherited Hebrew Sira are possible. First, Phinehas was deleted from Sir. 50.24 to avoid any impression of a link between the Oniads and the Maccabees. Heightened tensions between the Hasmoneans and the priesthood of Mt. Gerizim would have been a second reason for deleting Phinehas in Sir. 50.24, once John Hyrcanus had destroyed the temple era on Mt. Gerizim.

The literary reception of the priest Phinehas in Sira, Sirach, Maccabees, and Samarian inscriptions provides insights into historical rivalries over the offices of high priest and *prostates* and the construction of the identities of different groups in the Hellenistic period.[71] Within Jerusalemite and Egyptian circles, he is used to represent those who are 'in' legitimate favour and power, creating Others in these communities who become illegitimate 'outsiders' because they are not of the correct lineage. At the same time, legitimizing claims of lineage to Phinehas made by the Samarian priesthood in inscriptions found on Mt. Gerizim are also denied, Othering the Samarians and rejecting their claims that Gerizim was the place YHWH chose to place his name to dwell within Israel in favour of Jerusalem and its Hasmonaean high priesthood.

---

71. The question arises whether the results reached in this article could also cast light on proto-canonical uses of Phinehas and provide further arguments that would associate Phinehas with the final redaction of Pentateuch/Hexateuch (see Funke, 'Phinehas and Samaria'; idem, 'Der Priester Pinhas', pp. 281-308). Similar rivalries between profane and cultic leaders and between different priestly traditions (Aaronites, Levites, and Zadokites) have clearly existed in earlier periods. The late formation of the book of Numbers seems to be particularly fruitful for such an analysis. So, for instance, Achenbach, *Vollendung*, pp. 628-29; Christoph L. Nihan, 'The Priestly Covenant, Its Reinterpretations, and the Composition of "P"', in *The Strata of the Priestly Writings: Contemporary Debate and Future Directions* (ed. Sarah Shectman and Joel S. Baden; AthANT, 95; Zürich: Theologischer Verlag Zürich, 2009), pp. 87-134 (116-17); Rainer Albertz, 'Das Buch Numeri jenseits der Quellentheorie. Eine Redaktionsgeschichte von Num 20-24', *ZAW* 123.2 (2011), pp. 171-83; *ZAW* 123.3 (2011), pp. 336-47; Samuel, 'Von Priestern', pp. 419-20; Funke, 'Der Priester Pinhas', pp. 309-35.

DISABILITY, IDENTITY, AND OTHERNESS IN PERSIAN-PERIOD ISRAELITE THOUGHT

Rebecca Raphael

The category of disability is still a relative newcomer to biblical scholarship. Disability studies proper has a history reaching back to sociological research in the 1950s but came into its own in literary and cultural studies in the 1980s and '90s.[1] The application of this criticism to biblical studies has emerged over the past decade.[2] One of the significant insights of disability studies is the distinction between actual bodies and ideological constructions, as well as the historical contextualization of the latter.

---

1. For thorough overviews, see Lennard J. Davis (ed.), *The Disability Studies Reader* (New York: Routledge, 4th edn, 2013); and Sharon L. Snyder, Brenda Jo Brueggemann, and Rosemarie Garland-Thomson (eds.), *Disability Studies: Enabling the Humanities* (New York: The Modern Language Association, 2002).

2. For the early application of medical anthropology to the ancient Near East, see Hector Avalos, *Illness and Health Care in the Ancient Near East: The Role of the Temple in Greece, Mesopotamia, and Israel* (HSM, 54; Atlanta: Scholars Press, 1995). Shortly thereafter, Judith Z. Abrams's *Judaism and Disability: Portrayals in Ancient Texts from the Tanach Through the Bavli* (Washington, DC: Gallaudet University Press, 1998), and Tzvi C. Marx's *Disability in Jewish Law* (Jewish Law in Context, 3; New York: Routledge, 2002), appeared; these are useful treatments, but neither engaged with disability studies scholarship in literary criticism. More recently, in biblical scholarship, we have two major collections: Hector Avalos, Sarah J. Melcher, and Jeremy Schipper (eds.), *This Abled Body: Rethinking Disabilities in Biblical Studies* (Semeia Studies, 55; Atlanta: SBL, 2007) and Candida R. Moss and Jeremy Schipper (eds.), *Disability Studies and Biblical Literature* (New York: Palgrave Macmillan, 2011). The following monographs focus on the Hebrew Bible: Jeremy Schipper, *Disability Studies and the Hebrew Bible: Figuring Mephibosheth in the David Story* (New York: T&T Clark International, 2006); Saul M. Olyan, *Disability in the Hebrew Bible: Interpreting Mental and Physical Differences* (Cambridge: Cambridge University Press, 2008); and Rebecca Raphael, *Biblical Corpora: Representations of Disability in Hebrew Biblical Literature* (LHBOTS, 445; New York: T&T Clark International, 2008). Schipper's more recent work on Second Isaiah will be treated below.

While reluctant to view the body as entirely socially constructed,[3] disability theorists have drawn attention to the strategies by which some body types are elevated to a highly valued status and others are devalued. Yet, valuation is not a binary quality but rather, is subject to complexities and gradients. Concepts of embodiment tend to be deeply set in a culture, interconnected with its major ideas, values, and expressions. Attention to embodiment—both the ideologically normal body and the disabled body—can thus enrich our understanding of a text, period, and culture. The present essay seeks to clarify the cultural understandings of disability in Israelite literature commonly thought to have been composed in the Persian period or, in any event, literature that was being read and reread by the late Persian or early Hellenistic period.

As a preliminary to this investigation, two central insights of disability studies need to be articulated. First, we must distinguish between the biological body and the ideological body. By the former, I mean the observable state of an organism, with whatever morphology, metabolism, and sensory capacities it has. By ideological body, I mean the nexus of constructed symbolism, valuation, and interpretation given to bodies. The ideological body is not merely a representation of the biological body; it is a socially driven image, experienced as attribution or aspiration.[4] This distinction applies to many areas and invites many intersectionalities. I shall focus here on the one between the ability/disability axis and religio-cultural identity articulated in Persian period Hebrew texts. In that context, we can make a distinction between a deaf priest, who evidently could still function as a priest, and a blind priest, who was explicitly proscribed from performing sacrifices (Lev. 21.18). Both have sensory deficits, but the blind priest also has a socially constructed disability in the form of restriction on his assigned role.[5] In addition to this distinction, disability studies scholars refer to different models of disability, which constitute different frameworks for defining and understanding it. Most typically, the medical and social models are distinguished in a way that approximates the previous distinction: the medical

3. See David T. Mitchell and Sharon L. Snyder, *Narrative Prosthesis: Disability and the Dependencies of Discourse* (Corporealities; Ann Arbor: University of Michigan Press, 2000), pp. 15-46.

4. The impairment/disability distinction is a subset of a broader distinction. See Rosemarie Garland-Thomson, *Extraordinary Bodies* (ACLS Humanities E-Book; New York: Columbia University Press, 1996), pp. 6-9; Lennard Davis, *Enforcing Normalcy: Disability, Deafness, and the Body* (ACLS Humanities E-Book; New York: Verso, 1995), pp. 11-14; and my discussion in *Biblical Corpora*, pp. 5-11.

5. The deaf priest probably had other forms of social disability, as did the blind one.

model locates disability in the variant organism and seeks amelioration or cure, while the social model views disability as an interface between body and social environment.[6] However, this mapping is only approximate, because the medical model embeds many social conventions, and social models have their varieties, including, for example, focusing on the built environment, linguistic difference, and subcultures. As I have noted elsewhere,[7] the models identified in disability studies emphasize the modern and the secular, an emphasis appropriate and useful for Western societies over the past 300 years. However, in addressing premodern periods and also for understanding some facets of the present, we must examine religious models. That is not to reify 'religion' but simply to indicate the need to examine a context for embodiment and for medicine and society in which human practices are situated in a non-materialist cosmology and a rich symbolic network.

In applying disability analysis to biblical texts, two further problems arise. The first is historical and is not conditioned by the scriptural status of texts: it is the question whether the contemporary concept of disability can be appropriately applied to documents for which this concept is not indigenous. That Hebrew biblical literature grouped conditions that we would call physical impairments has not been seriously disputed.[8] Whether these texts made the further grouping of physical impairments with emotional and cognitive differences is open to debate.[9] Perhaps the most contested area has been variant physical conditions that may or may not have been disabilities in the social sense.[10] Overall, scholars seem to favour use of the contemporary term, provided it can be adequately justified historically and analytically in a given context. The

6. See Tom Shakespeare, 'The Social Model of Disability', in *The Disability Studies Reader* (ed. Lennard Davis; London: Routledge, 4th edn, 2013), pp. 214-21.

7. Raphael, *Biblical Corpora*, pp. 5-13. See also Schipper's discussion in *Mephibosheth*, pp. 15-21.

8. Biblical terms for deafness, blindness, and lameness and their tendency to occur in pairs have played a major role in this discussion. See Schipper, *Mephibosheth*, pp. 64-67, Olyan, *Disability*, pp. 147-48, and Raphael, *Biblical Corpora*, pp. 13-18.

9. Olyan explicitly included mental illness along with physical disabilities, an approach I support (*Disability*, pp. 2-3, 62-66).

10. Schipper (*Mephibosheth*, pp. 21-26) and Raphael (*Biblical Corpora*, pp. 13-18) have argued for a significant enough concept to justify use of the term 'disability'. Olyan takes issues with some of the argumentation, but in other ways extends the usage to cognitive and emotional impairments (*Disability*, pp. 12-13, 147-48). Joel Baden has argued against Raphael and Avalos (*Healthcare*, pp. 331-34) on whether barrenness could be properly termed a disability ('The Nature of Barrenness in the Hebrew Bible', in Moss and Schipper [eds.], *Disability Studies*, pp. 13-27).

second difficulty pertains to the Hebrew Bible's status as scripture for several religious communities. Pressure to make the text acceptable to contemporary sensibilities can distort interpretation,[11] as can the desire to polemicize against its status. Alternatively, exegetes may relieve themselves of this dilemma unjustifiably by erasing the textual presence of disability.[12] In approaching key texts from the Persian period, I shall proceed inductively, casting a wide net for terms and pericopes that have potential bearing on the question how disability figured in Judaic identity construction at the time. This wide net includes both the obvious terms of physical impairment, deafness, blindness, and lameness, and also terms applicable to disease more generally, like חֳלִי ('sickness'), נֶגַע ('affliction', 'plague', 'disease'), and צָרַעַת ('skin disease'). Further, since disability can be understood only in terms of its differential from an ideological norm, a larger penumbra of terms and concepts must be included. Beauty and ugliness, strength and weakness, walking and stumbling, and others, all disclose facets of how bodies were viewed and valued. Finally, given the limits of the extant materials, our inferences will benefit from the largest possible scope of relevant concepts. In what follows, I do not intend to suggest that Hebrew culture in the Persian period had more, or more onerous, norms than any other culture; to an outsider, any culture's practices will seem intricate and perhaps rigid, while to the native, they are both second nature and somewhat fluid.

1. The P Stratum

When it comes to disability, the Priestly source has justifiably received the lion's share of attention. This stratum, represented by much of Leviticus and sections of Numbers, includes fascinating requirements for bodily form and regulation. מוּם, that is, a 'defect',[13] operates as a central category in Leviticus. In Numbers, chs. 12–14 include several uses of disease as punishment; although not directly related to disability, these passages provide an important context for understanding how the body was placed with respect to human behaviour and divine action. Taken together, the Priestly material articulates a certain body as most acceptable to or valued by God and other types as diverging in various ways.

---

11. The tension is between historical investigation and continued authoritative use. See my discussion in *Biblical Corpora*, pp. 137-43.

12. See Schipper's exhaustive discussion of this process in relation to Isa. 53 in *Disability and Isaiah's Suffering Servant* (Biblical Refigurations; Oxford: Oxford University Press, 2011), pp. 1-12.

13. I follow Olyan's translation of this term (*Disability*, pp. 5-6).

Let us first examine the ritual material in Leviticus. The program for bodily regulation has three major aspects: rules for sacrificial actors (priests and animals), strongly gendered rules for laypersons, and rules pertaining to skin disease. The fully vested, non-defective priest functions as a bodily ideal.[14] For a priest to be qualified to perform sacrifices, his body must contain no defect. The key passage in Lev. 21.18-23 simply lists disqualifying defects, and there has been much scholarly debate about an underlying principle. Milgrom simply found it parallel to and perhaps derived from the requirements for sacrificial animals (22.19-25).[15] Others find a visual principle in both lists. Olyan summarizes: 'Most "defects"…are visible, long lasting, or permanent, and characterized by somatic dysfunction, and several share asymmetry as a characteristic'.[16] Thus, the list of defects embeds a concept of disability at two levels, as bodily divergence from an ideological norm and also as social disability, meaning disqualification from a valued social role that the priest would otherwise expect to perform. The text's justifications for these exclusions are also revealing: the approach of a priest with a 'defect' (מום) to the holy place would profane it (21.23). It is unclear what, exactly, about a priestly 'defective' body (i.e. a body with a מום) profanes the sanctuary; at most, we infer that the texts see the highest degree of holiness as incompatible with the presence of a priestly body with defects.[17] The danger of profanation is not mentioned in the case of sacrificial animals. Defective animals are merely unacceptable (22.21, 23), and practitioners are enjoined not to place them on the altar (22.22). Yet no ritual is prescribed for remedy in the event that an animal with a defect was placed on the altar in error. The 'defective' animal (i.e. one with a מום), then, has less power to profane the holy place. That differential discloses the high valuation placed upon the ideal human form, which, for Leviticus, is priestly, male, and visually non-defective.

The bodily regimen for laypersons, male and female, is not directly related to physical impairments. No reference to the concept of defect occurs in the portions of Leviticus addressing bodily comportment. Instead, the main focus is on bodily fluids, how these affect ritual cleanness, and how ritual uncleanness can be remedied by purification.

14. Raphael, *Biblical Corpora*, p. 39.

15. Jacob Milgrom, *Leviticus 17–22* (AB, 3A; New York: Doubleday, 2000), pp. 1836-40.

16. Olyan, *Disability*, pp. 45-49. Asymmetry is morphological but strongly visual/visible. For a visual analysis focusing on the skin as smooth boundary, see also Raphael, *Biblical Corpora*, pp. 36-39.

17. That is not to say that the priest loses priestly status along with sacrificial function. See Olyan, *Disability*, pp. 31-32.

As I have argued elsewhere,[18] these rules cannot be regarded as pertaining to impairments, but can be analyzed as a temporary social disability in the technical sense. That the biological processes governed here are natural and valued (e.g. childbirth) does not mean that no ideology of the body is present. Indeed, one of the major ways in which social groups define themselves is precisely in the details of their bodily habits, including what is eaten and what is not; what alternations are prohibited, permitted, or required, like piercings, hair-cutting, or circumcision;[19] and how those processes universal to all human bodies are disciplined into socially sanctioned forms. Just as the Torah's dietary restrictions embed certain relationships to land and animals, the bodily regulations of Leviticus embed a relation to the body. Specifically, fluids that cross the body's threshold are understood as moving the body itself over the threshold of cleanness/uncleanness, and purification usually requires the use of water, an external fluid, in contact with the body.

The regulations about skin disease (צָרַעַת) merit special attention. Since the disease can affect anyone, it is not gendered and is independent of the priest/lay distinction (see 22.4). These conditions also lead us to the difficult distinction between disease and disability: while not synonymous, the terms overlap. Diseases can bring social disability and bodily impairments and thus become disabilities, depending on both the physical features of the disease and the social valuations of bodily variation. Also, many disabilities are not themselves diseases, but many cultures may associate the two strongly, primarily by grouping both as appropriate objects of action for the health care system, whatever that may be. In the case of Hebrew texts read in the Persian period, both diseases and disabilities are attributed to divine action (Lev. 26.16, 21, 25).[20] Diagnosing skin diseases and their remission is one of the functions of the priesthood, although healing does not seem to be included as a priestly function.[21] Indeed, the priest's function vis-à-vis skin diseases

18. Raphael, *Biblical Corpora*, pp. 31-39. I explored an intersectional gender analysis in 'Approaching the Altar: Gender, Disability, and Holiness in Leviticus', a paper presented at the conference, 'Who Do You Think You Are? Gender and the Transmission of Identity in the Hebrew Bible, Dead Sea Scrolls, and Other Related Literature', sponsored by Oxford Centre for Christianity and Culture, Oxford, July 2011.

19. But see Olyan's discussion of circumcision as the exceptional, intentional defect (*Disability*, pp. 36-38).

20. Divine causation is the only etiology recognized in the Hebrew Bible, except for conditions resulting from injury (Lev. 24.14-20).

21. Avalos, *Health Care*, pp. 311-17.

is to determine whether the condition renders the person ritually unclean or once again clean, pending a purification ritual. In these cases, the disease warrants exclusion from the group, which is a very severe social disability. Notwithstanding ancient intuitions about infection, the exclusion of persons with skin diseases encodes a social identity of the group as healthy in terms of the visual surface of the body. Seen in this light, the prohibitions on piercings cohere with the restrictions on priests, with the exclusion of those with skin diseases, and with the intense focus on discharges, which, whatever else they are, cross and thus disrupt the surface of the body.

The narrative of Numbers 12–14 provides a site for this nexus of disease, disability, and identity. In the course of several challenges to Moses' authority, complainers are punished with food poisoning (12.33), skeptics of the invasion plans are punished with plague (דֶּבֶר, 14.12), and the disobedient spies die by plague (14.36-37). This iteration of disease as a divine punishment does more than assert Mosaic authority: it assumes that God causes disease. Best known, perhaps, is the skin disease God inflicts on Miriam in punishment for her criticism of Moses (12.10-15). It is interesting that she and Aaron criticize Moses' marriage to a Cushite woman (12.1), since they take that as a boundary violation.

Beyond the cases of plague punishments, Miriam's skin disease is the one that entails the social disability of separation from the group. Indeed, Moses immediately requests that God heal her, but God separately stipulates a period of exclusion (12.14). Thus, social disability is bound up with the disease. Tacitly, the narrative compares two possible identity-defining actions, exogamous marriage and denial of Mosaic authority; the latter is presented as decisive, while the former may or may not matter.[22]

The Holiness Code says little about the etiology of plagues and diseases, focusing instead on their ritual effects and requirements. The narratives of Numbers exhibit a deeply embedded but nonetheless clear assumption, an etiology of plague and skin disease: God sends them. To be sure, this was the common explanation of disease in the ancient

---

22. Contrast the view toward intermarriage in Ezra–Nehemiah, where Mosaic authority is simply assumed, and intermarriage is a decisive breach of social identity (Ezra 9–10; Neh. 13). Even so, it seems that the mass divorce of Ezra 10 functions to legitimate the Mosaic authority claimed by the text. On intermarriage, see Lester L. Grabbe, *A History of the Jews and Judaism in the Second Temple Period.* Vol. 1, *Yehud: A History of the Persian Province of Judah* (LSTS, 47; London: T&T Clark International, 2004), pp 314-16.

Near East.[23] The particularities of the Priestly narrative link diseases and their social disabilities to divine punishment for disobedience to authority. To that extent, the narrative constructs both religio-cultural authority as aligned with both divine will and health and simultaneously constructs major types of diseased bodies as not merely sick but disobedient, in the sense of defiant toward authority. These narratives are highly coherent with those of Chronicles, to which we now turn.

2. *Chronicles*

The books of Ezra, Nehemiah, and 1 and 2 Chronicles comprise the major narrative material from the Persian period. While Ezra and Nehemiah contain material pertinent to identity, these works do not have much to say about disability, disease, medicine, or healing.[24] Even their metaphorical use of the relevant terms is minimal at best. Fortunately, the books of Chronicles offer several passages relevant to embodiment. Neither extensive nor particularly central, these passages reflect cultural assumptions. In particular, the consistent explanation for illnesses provides an additional context for the same motifs in other works from the period.

1 Chronicles is fairly light on obvious disability language. In terms of bodily imagery more generally, its two references to giants (11.23; 20.4-6) use an opponent's great stature to display an Israelite warrior's great prowess. In the first case, Benaiah kills a very tall and strong Egyptian, but the opponent is not identified specifically as a giant (11.23). Later, during the David narrative (20.4-8), Goliath of Gath appears no longer as an isolated case as he is in the books of Samuel; many descendants of giants have gigantic traits. These giants appear in a series of challenges to David's army. Goliath is mentioned in a descriptive phrase that clearly alludes to 1 Sam. 17.4-7; then a different giant appears, one who is not only very tall but who has additional digits on each extremity (20.6).

---

23. Avalos, *Health Care*: illness not necessarily punitive in Asclepian medical theology, pp. 73-74; divine causation of disease, with multiple entities involved at Gula, pp. 185-89; Yahweh as only cause of illness, pp. 239-45.

24. Even the sensory terms are mostly formulaic requests for open ears in Nehemiah's prayer (Neh. 1.6), the significance of hearing the Torah read out (Neh. 8.2-3), and the interesting connection between endogamy and physical strength (Ezra 9.12). These passages reflect an ideological norm of the body but at such a general level that little can be inferred about disability.

That verse on the unnamed giant's digital superfluity signals the anomalous quality that these bodies have for the author and implied audience.[25] Israelite warriors, by contrast, are strong but not so exceptionally large or digitally prolific. The closest in-group example of an extraordinary body would be David's ambidextrous archers (12.2); this skill is presented as impressive but not grotesque. As for the Israelite warriors, they are not represented as disabled relative to these larger and more powerful opponents. The warriors who slay these opponents gain reputation by doing so, but they themselves are not represented as anomalous or even marvelous on the grounds of bodily endowment.

In 2 Chronicles, we see an unusual concentration of illnesses. The ancient Near Eastern idea that gods cause illness is stated or implied in all cases. Solomon's prayer at the dedication of the temple in Jerusalem concisely states the general idea that plagues and illnesses, along with other difficult conditions, lie in the purview of the divine to cause and to remedy (2 Chron. 6.28-31; cf. 1 Chron. 21.12-27, Lev. 26.16-33, and Deut. 28.16-29). Japhet notes that the scope includes both private and public distress, and both physical and emotional afflictions.[26] Regarding the same passage, Klein observes that the term 'forgive' is used when the concept of sin is not previously specified;[27] however, the underlying assumption remains divine causation for both afflictions and their relief. With regard to specific cases, the brief notice of King Asa's foot disease does not mention causality but supports the idea that God, not physicians, heal (2 Chron. 16.12-13).[28] In the case of Jehoram's bowel disease, the illness occurs as a condemnation of this king's actions, especially in

---

25. I have proposed the anomalous body as an analytical category for all bodies that fall outside of the ideological norm ('Monsters in the Crippled Cosmos: Construction of the Other as an Anomalous Body in 4 Ezra', in *The 'Other' in Second Temple Judaism: Festschrift in Honor of John J. Collins* [ed. Daniel C. Harlow et al.; Grand Rapids, MI: Eerdmans, 2011], pp. 228-83). In the present case, note that the Israelite warriors are not defined as having height, strength, or digital deficits relative to a norm set by the bodies of these large warriors; but this construction is just as possible. Excess, like disability, can also be an anomaly.

26. Sara Japhet, *I & II Chronicles: A Commentary* (OTL; Louisville: Westminster John Knox, 1993), pp. 596-97.

27. Ralph W. Klein, *2 Chronicles: A Commentary* (Hermeneia; Minneapolis: Fortress, 2012), p. 95.

28. Klein notes that the Chronicler links Asa's foot disease to his imprisonment of the prophet Hanani (*2 Chronicles*, p. 242); evidently that detail is sufficient to moor the episode to an ideology of illness-as-punishment. The reference to the medical profession shall be discussed in the conclusion.

leading the people astray (2 Chron. 21.11-20).[29] The threatened plague among the people is not narrated, although an invasion is; and the depiction of Jehoram's death, although brief, is gruesome. The text does not indicate whether the king sought any healing either from physicians or religious professionals. Finally, the pericope regarding Hezekiah's illness again reflects the belief that healing is a divine prerogative (2 Chron. 32.24-26) and pride is a danger. Yet, this episode does not seem to be very important in the text's overall view of Hezekiah. These passages show a coherent belief about the cause of illness and healing both on the individual and social levels.[30]

Let us turn now to the longest passage about an illness, one in which social disability also figures: the case of King Uzziah's skin disease (צָרַעַת, 2 Chron. 26.16-21). The Chronicler treats the early period of Uzziah's reign positively but says that he became proud (v. 16). Specifically, Uzziah attempts to perform sacrifice in the temple and reacts with anger when corrected by a priest. For his refusal to accept correction, God strikes him (נֶגַע) with a skin disease on his forehead (v. 20). This detail places the skin lesion in a location that would be immediately visible and difficult to conceal later. Both priests and king recognize the new lesion as requiring his immediate removal from the temple (v. 20b). Uzziah lives for an unstated period after this episode, but he must live separately; because of his separation, his son Jotham rules. Olyan notes the clear causality in this passage:

> The tradition in Uzziah's skin disease is present in the Chronicler's source, 2 Kgs 15.5, but the Chronicler is responsible for the story of Uzziah's act of sacrilege. Clearly 'skin disease' is viewed by the Chronicler as a grievous punishment from Yhwh, and requires an equally grievous transgression in order to justify it.[31]

In addition to the etiology and ideology of severe skin disease, the episode demonstrates how an illness can result in the social experience of disability; as with Miriam, the punishment of disease and the social disability of spatial exclusion are separated into two steps even though both aspects punish the transgressor. Although the narrator describes Uzziah's sacrifice as a prideful usurpation of priestly function, it is not

---

29. Klein notes the significance of causative verb forms in the description of Jehoram's misconduct (*2 Chronicles*, pp. 306, 309).

30. This is not to equate all forms of disease with sin. As Schipper points out, various diseases render the bearer ritually unclean but having them is not sinful (*Second Isaiah*, p. 39). The passages in Chronicles join several ideas together and sequence them in a distinctive way.

31. Olyan, *Disability*, p. 56.

clear whether the king saw it that way. Further, the story serves to bolster priestly claims to authority by inflicting upon a transgressive king a condition that would disqualify even priests from sacrificial functions. In its own historical context, Chronicles's various stories of major figures made ill as punishment serve to reinforce the bodily ideal of the priesthood, an ideal closely tied to claims for Mosaic and priestly authority.[32]

3. *Wisdom Literature*

The Wisdom literature provides another source for Persian period views about disability and identity. Any discussion of health, illness, physical impairment, and social disability in the Hebrew Bible must engage the book of Job; yet Proverbs is equally revealing, if much less dramatic. Since scholars still tend to see Proverbs as a more conventional type of wisdom that Job calls into question, I shall begin with it. However, on the matter of embodiment, these two works share much.

That Proverbs sets forth a model of the good, wise man and, more briefly, the good, wise woman is a truism. Much less noted is the particular embodiment attached to this concept. In its representation of the wise man, the bodily imagery consistently favours a normative locomotion and hearing. The wise man stands upright and is able to walk a straight path (2.20-22; 4.11-12), whereas the wicked man stumbles (4.19). Stumbling encompasses unclear direction of motion and uneven gait. The description implies that a wise man has smooth gait. In 26.7, proverbs spoken by fools are compared to lame legs. Since the nouns compared are 'legs' and 'proverbs', the line does not refer to a speech impediment but to the inability to use something to which the text attributes inherent usefulness. In addition to the imagery of walking, hearing is used to draw a distinction between the wise and foolish. The wise man is not only able to hear but knows how to use his hearing in culturally specific ways: he hears reproof (15.13); his ears seek knowledge (18.15); he uses hearing to express deference to authority (22.17); and he acquires wisdom through hearing (23.9, 12, 19). Within the broad pictures of the wise and foolish body, locomotion and hearing are relatively more prominent than other features.

---

32. This is only to characterize Moses as an authoritative speaker in these texts, not to assume that his name indicates any canon. The types of authority bolstered by the ideology of embodiment cohere well with a period of cult-and-authoritative-texts postulated for the Persian period by Konrad Schmid ('The Canon and the Cult: The Emergence of Book Religion in Ancient Israel and the Graduate Sublimation of the Temple Cult', *JBL* 131.2 [2012], pp. 289-305).

Two passages set out fully imagined embodiments of the wise and
foolish person. In ch. 4, the wise man walks easily on the straight path,
avoids stumbling (v. 12), and the sayings of the elders, once heard, light
the path, making obstacles visible and avoidable (vv. 18, 20-21), so as to
maintain health (v. 22). By contrast, the wicked are nocturnal (v. 16),
unable to see the path (v. 19), stumbling and causing others to stumble
(vv. 16, 19). Words of wisdom provide light, which informs the sense of
sight. Since the teachings are received through hearing, audition is
treated as the primary sense upon which the ability to see properly relies.
In the other extended passage, 6.12-19, the wicked are embodied as
speaking crookedly (v. 12), having undisciplined motion in their eyes,
feet, and fingers (v. 13), and having a perverted mind (v. 14). Further,
God abominates these embodiments (vv. 16-19). Passing over these
images as transparent metaphors would be a mistake, because such a
move would trivialize or erase the body. These descriptions seem, on
balance, more likely to reflect an isomorphism of character and body:
both manifest the same wisdom or foolishness, and neither is merely a
signifier of the other. That said, even a metaphorical construal relies
upon a negative valuation of certain body types and performances.[33]

The book of Job provides the most extended account in biblical
literature of the socially disabling aspects of disease. To be sure, Job
faces several calamities; the one most pertinent to our topic is the skin
affliction (שְׁחִין רָע, Job 2.7). In addition to its painful quality (16.6), the
experience undermines his strength, sight, body, and mind (17.6-7).
Throughout the book, his motion and action are severely limited. Beyond
his physical condition, he is socially isolated (16.20–17.2): most people
avoid him, the interlocutors mock him, and he has no social interactions
other than frustrating discussion with the friends. His final statement
about the quality of his previous life shows what we might call able-
bodied privilege: he helped the blind and the lame (29.15) and feels
entitled to this role, even as he dislikes being in need of help. It would be
an absurd reduction to say that Job only has skin boils (bodily difference);
he has lost all social position and ability (social disability). Schipper
points out that the narrator does not say that Job's skin boils are healed;
perhaps he remains disabled or physically marked.[34] Although I am not

---

33. Schipper has recently pointed out that easy resort to metaphorical interpretation can erase disabled presences from the text (*Isaiah's Suffering Servant*, pp. 26-
30). See also my discussion in *Biblical Corpora*, pp. 131-33. I do not think that all
disability is non-metaphorical but urge that exegetes take care to question the interpretative use of metaphor to erase the historical concepts of embodiment in the text.

34. Schipper, *Isaiah's Suffering Servant*, p. 51.

convinced this is the case, I agree with Schipper that we cannot simply read in healing without a textual basis. This textual feature coheres with the sustained discussion of Job's speech and with God's vindication of speaking that strains beyond the breaking point the proverbial concept of wise speech being a function of a wise and healthy mind-heart-body. Job is a spectacular counter-example.

If we now compare Proverbs and Job to the passages in Chronicles, we see an array of ideas. First, Proverbs has rendered the cause of disease and disability more complex: one's character and habits form the body as either ideologically normal or disabled, which, in Proverbs, seems to mean unsubdued motion. However, God does not specifically strike people, as in Chronicles and Job. God remains the cosmic architect who set the plans and operations (ch. 8), but the individual's auditory and cardiac attentiveness, or lack thereof, to wisdom teachings is the proximate cause of bodily health and performance. Proverbs increases human responsibility without diminishing divine causality. When it comes to the reasons or justification for divinely caused illness or disability, Chronicles and Proverbs strongly assert the idea that people earn these through their actions, while Job even more strenuously demurs. To be sure, the book of Job coheres with other texts on etiology: no one disputes whether God causes Job's affliction, but they contest the grounds on which God would send illness. This divergence is about divine motives, not divine power and not the etiology of health or disease. In short, on this topic, we do not find the book of Job always by itself; each of these three documents overlaps and diverges from the other two.

4. *Prophecy*

Of the prophetic works from the Persian period, references to disability either do not occur at all (e.g. Haggai) or occur prominently; that is, passing reference is unusual. This variability probably depends the strands of tradition that most inform a given text, and whether disability already figures in those traditions..

a. *Zechariah 1–8*
In terms of its body imagery, this material is very reminiscent of Deuteronomy: hearing is the primary sense for human beings; to hear is to obey (6.5; 8.9), and to disobey is not to hear (1.4; 7.7-13). By contrast, vision is a divine function by which God perceives human behaviour (4.10). The most detailed passage occurs in ch. 7, where the prophet replies to a question about fasting with a summary of basic, religio-ethical requirements (7.9b-14a). The people reject these by refusing to listen, closing

their ears, turning a shoulder, and hardening their hearts to the 'words of
the former prophets'. That phrase shows a distance from an already
authoritative teaching, whether textual or oral; the whole perceptual
structure resembles Proverbs insofar as listening to authoritative words
enables the rest of the sensory and active functions. In response to such
behaviour, God refuses to hear, a motif that occurs in many Psalms and
expresses an elective disability as a temporary refusal of communication.[35] In addition to the auditory dominance, the passage embodies disobedience in strongly physical terms, where the ears, heart, and gesture
of the turned shoulder constitute a refusal of receptive communication.
Embedded in this refusal we find actions expected by God of the people
but not performed and the actions expected by the people of God but not
performed. Refusal to comply with the other's commands or requests is
encoded as loss of or refusal to use the sense of hearing.

   In its context, this passage and the other, briefer references to hearing
or not hearing make receptive communication central to its concept of
what Israelites should be: people who listen to God. The ethical demands
of kindness and care are closely tied to this ability to hear or to listen.
While the passage does not condemn visual-gestural priestly worship or
ritual observance, it appears to give them a secondary place.

b. *Ezekiel*
The book of Ezekiel stands out for its florid body imagery and its distinctive palette of disabilities, diseases, and assaults to bodily integrity. The
notion that God sends pestilence (5.15, 17; 6.12) occurs in earlier Deuteronomic literature and also throughout the ancient Near East. Hearing
is linked to obedience and not hearing to disobedience (12.2; 40.4).
However, Ezekiel is exceptional in its sustained interest in the weak,
dismembered, or dying body. This central image includes both individuals and corporate entities as bodies that can suffer rupture and decay, and
its most vivid image of healing is the re-memberment of bones (ch. 37).

   The prophet's muteness stands out as a disability motif. It occurs at
the end of his commissioning scene. He is confined to his house, bound
with cords, and rendered mute (3.24-27). The muteness appears to be
selective: Ezekiel cannot engage in ordinary conversation or speak in his
own voice.[36] Instead, he receives elaborate instructions for what we

   35. For disability as communication impediment or strategy in Psalms, see
Raphael, *Biblical Corpora*, pp. 109-19.
   36. Commentators have seen the lengthy period of muteness and prophecy as
inconsistent. For a discussion of the positions and an explanation of the text's
cogency, see Moshe Greenberg, *Ezekiel 1–20: A New Translation with Introduction*

would call performance art, that is, his silent enactment of fasting and grief before his model of the city. Yet, he may speak oracles when made to do so. The muteness is removed twice.[37] First, Ezekiel hears news of the destruction of Jerusalem and is then able to speak (24.26-27). The second time, a fugitive reaches Babylon with the news of Jerusalem's fall and Ezekiel regains his ability for ordinary speech (33.22).

It would be incorrect, in my view, to read Ezekiel's selective muteness as a metaphor; it is a representational fact.[38] Nothing differentiates his muteness from the other items in the divine orders (3.23-27). In the performance that follows, muteness plays a crucial role and influences how others interpret his actions. Further, the intervening text between the institution and removal of the muteness consistently represents Ezekiel as speaking only oracles and nothing else. Even the oracles are presented as speech received by Ezekiel; the narrative representation of his delivery to the people is terse (11.13, 25; 14.1-2, *et alia loc.*). This strange form of muteness imposes upon its bearer a social experience of disability. It would be simplistic and inaccurate to suppose that a person must either have an impairment *in toto* or not have it at all. The impossibility of communication due to imposed muteness, the audience's incomprehension (ch. 33), or the sheer difficulty of speaking about events so enormously grievous[39] runs through the book of Ezekiel as a mainstay, emotionally and conceptually. Ezekiel's isolation, frustration, and extreme grief are coherent with the literal representation of this muteness but very odd if it is metaphorical.

In addition to muteness, the book contains prolific imagery of bodily weakness, fragility, and corruptibility. Some passages refer to physical weakness brought about by shocking events or news (7.17; cf. 21.7). The references to pestilence and famine go beyond merely naming these events but dwell upon their impact on bodies (5.15-17; 6.12; 30.21-22;

---

and Commentary (AB, 22; New York: Doubleday, 1983), pp. 120-21. Like Greenberg, I think the text clearly represents a selective muteness that permits only one form of speech and does not violate this condition.

37. This dual occurrence is surely a sign of editorial history, but both are representationally significant. For a discussion of the text's consistency on Ezekiel's muteness and his speech acts during a period characterized as mute, see Greenberg, *Ezekiel*, p. 103.

38. This is not to assert historicity; I only mean that Ezekiel as represented in the text is selectively mute.

39. The text encompasses a grief-induced silence without making this feature the only explanation of Ezekiel's actions. See Greenberg, where the divine proscription from the reproving function is one of several factors contributing to exceptional grief (*Ezekiel*, p. 121).

34.4; 38.22). These examples include both Israelites and others and thus introduce some types of bodily corruption as an index of divine wrath, a distinction that cuts across ethnic or religious lines. In Israel's case, however, the body is also used to represent an internal distinction between those who properly enact Israelite identity and those who do not, while outsiders cannot, by definition, fail to be proper Israelites. By 'proper', I indicate the text's implied ideological body, which is a textual artifact relative to a historical-cultural milieu.

One of the most extended and intriguing passages in which bodily fragility figures prominently occurs in the adoption parable of ch. 16 (16.4-6). Israel is represented as an exposed infant, abandoned, unwashed, and with the umbilical cord uncut. The images of an infant's helplessness blend seamlessly with cultural requirements for bodily regulation. The expected actions of others would both protect the helpless infant and also groom her body according to the local concept of cleanliness.[40] If we can view an infant as disabled in the sense of being unable to perform certain crucial functions, its disability and its non-groomed state coincide to represent it as outside the social community. Physical care-taking does not occur until the betrothal (16.8-9), and then it is quite elaborate. At that point, the motif of prostitution without payment in 16.31b comes to dominate the parable.

The passage in 16.4-6 would bear sustained examination in terms of body criticism; two observations shall suffice for the present. First, the image of uncontrolled blood occurs with both the infant and the whore (16.36, 38). Second, the non-Israelite gentilic terms Hittite and Amorite also attach to these phases of the story. Thus, bodily weakness in the case of the infant, and unregulated bloodiness in the case of the whore explicitly encode the non-Israelite Other. Further, Israelite status here depends on performance of bodily norms, not on birth, and these norms function as boundaries that can be crossed in both directions. Non-Israelites function as hortatory examples in the normative rhetoric, signifying what the implied audience is not to perform.

c. *Second Isaiah*

The prophetic collection known as Second Isaiah employs disability and bodily imagery in ways that do not quite fit the patterns of the priestly and narrative literature. Earlier in Isaianic tradition, we have prominent use of visual, auditory, and locomotive impairments to denote willful refusal of proper teaching (6.9-10); some passages seem addressed to elites whom the prophet criticizes for poor moral leadership (29.4, 9-14).

---

40. The verb and pronoun forms referring to the infant are feminine.

The normative body depicted in 33.13-20 strongly overlaps with that of Proverbs. Finally, terms for disability appear in eschatological passages such as 29.18-21 and 35.3-6, although one must attend to indications that the language of healing simply continues the metaphorical use of sensory impairments for immoral or irreligious elites.[41] This material provides the tradition in which Second Isaiah works and the literary context in which a reader encounters striking new images of embodiment.

Second Isaiah picks up the Deuteronomic association of idols with physical disability (41.29; 42.7, 16; 46.7) while presenting God as the source of physical strength (40.29-31).[42] Chapter 43 pivots around the ingathering of Israelites dispersed elsewhere. The referent of v. 8 is ambiguous: it could refer to the dispersed Israelites or to the nations called to discussion in v. 9. In either case, 'the people who are blind yet have eyes, who are deaf yet have ears' appear to be those who worship idols (vv. 10-13). The polemic and the imagery continue into ch. 44, where the needs of the human craftsman are set against that of the idol to show both the human's reality and weakness and the idol's lack of reality and greater weakness. Again, the text associates the idolator's behaviour with impaired vision and cognition (44.18; cf. 44.9). In both cases, the idolaters appear to be non-Israelites; the passages advance claims to the reality of Israel's God in contrast to unreal idols. Neither passage deals with actual persons with disabilities, yet the terms are used in highly negative ways to advance a central religious claim.

In that fairly traditional context, two of the so-called suffering servant songs stand out for their innovative use of disability imagery.[43] The servant of Isaiah 42 is not himself a suffering figure but rather, an agent of rescue. He will 'open the eyes that are blind' (42.7) in a context where

---

41. In *Biblical Corpora*, pp. 119-28, I argued that the disability language of ch. 29 is metaphorical and applies to social leaders. I based this conclusion on the grounds that the initial use of the terms clearly do not apply to persons with disabilities, whereas ch. 35 presents an isomorphism of land and bodies, both transformed, and neither clearly anchoring the other. See also Olyan's discussion (*Disability*, pp. 87-89); he treats both passages as pertaining to persons with disability.

42. For fuller discussions of disability terms applied to idols and idolaters, which locates idols within an economy of ideological body norms, see Raphael (*Biblical Corpora*, pp. 40-43) and Saul Olyan, who applies his social analysis of stigma ('The Ascription of Physical Disability as a Stigmatizing Strategy in Biblical Iconic Polemics', in Moss and Schipper [eds.], *Disability Studies*, pp. 89-102).

43. The category 'suffering servant song' is contested. Although I am skeptical of this characterization, I use it here simply as a well-known term for a set of passages.

light signifies proper worship of the one God and darkness and imprisonment symbolize idolatry. Isaiah 49.1-6 includes light imagery, with the
servant functioning as 'a light to the nations' (v. 6). As in ch. 42, this
servant does not appear to suffer. He expends his strength on unworthy
projects that might involve idolatry but the meaning of the key term הֶבֶל
is ambiguous in 49.4.[44] At most, then, we have associations of lost
strength with improper purposes that possibly involve worship and of
worship of Israel's God with regained physical strength. In the third
song, Isa. 50.4-9, the servant does suffer, specifically from social abuse
(v. 6). His own physicality, however, is characterized by the proverbial
norm of attentive hearing (vv. 4-5) and extreme fortitude expressed by
the phrase 'a face like flint' (v. 7). Together, these three passages have
interesting speech imagery: the quiet servant does not harangue in the
streets (42.2); a mouth like a sword enables the servant's mission (49.2);
an educated tongue joins the concepts of wise speech with bodily discipline (50.4). The images do not converge on a single concept, but all link
prophetic speech with a bodily discipline of the organs of speech. This
discipline is strongly reminiscent of the ideal body–speech relation of
Proverbs. For a prophetic speaker, as for a wise person, knowing how to
speak goes beyond the mere words.

Isaiah 53 deserves separate treatment for two reasons: its servant is the
one who most clearly suffers, and its disability imagery has been thoroughly treated by J. Schipper. He argues that the language in vv. 3-4 best
supports an interpretation of the servant as one with a skin disease that
would incur ritual impurity and who perhaps also has bodily differences
on account of which social disability occurs.[45] In contrast to a history of
interpretation that tends to erase the disabled servant either by defining
terms metaphorically or introjecting a healing that is not really there,
Schipper suggests that Isaiah 53 depicts a disabled servant who fulfills
his mission. If this is correct, then the author of this passage offers a
striking but not unprecedented contrast to the priestly understanding of
diseased or disabled bodies: a disabled servant can serve, can be a divine
instrument in the body he has. Unlike a priest, however, his service is not
performing temple sacrifice. This approach aligns Isaiah 53 more with
Job than with our other sources from the Persian period. Note, however,
that this passage shares the prevailing understanding of disease etiology.

---

44. Verse 4. הֶבֶל is frequently used to refer to idols or idolatry; see the discussion
above.
45. Schipper, *Disability Studies*, pp. 33-42. The key terms are חֳלִי, 'sickness',
'infirmity', and נָגוּעַ, 'stricken'.

It differs by contravening the assumption that such a person might remain as is and still be of service, which is not construed as some other or lesser kind of service but as fully compliant with divine intention.

5. *Conclusions*

It remains to step back and assess first, the understanding of disability in texts generally thought to have been produced in the Persian period but which were being read and reread buy the late Persian or early Hellenistic period, and second, what these might tell us about Jewish identity in the period. The single largest common element was also common to the Near East generally: the idea that divine powers caused both disease and healing. Deficits of the senses and congenital variations of the body's form clearly fall within the scope of the many assertions of divine etiology. That the ancient world recognized acquired disabilities from warfare or other violence is beyond dispute; even so, our texts do not focus on these, except within the framework of divine action. Since the idea was widespread at the time, it alone cannot help toward any kind of identity definition.

Beyond bare causality, we can look at the question of motivation: for what reasons or purposes does God send disease, impairments, or social disabilities? On this question, our texts offer an array of possibilities: as punishment for violations of ritual or authority (Numbers, Chronicles); as the already-built-in consequences from a refusal of wisdom and of expected life habits (Proverbs); as inexplicable assertion of power (Job). Here, we find some distinctiveness in the specific conditions that might elicit bodily punishment, although not in the general idea itself. The Priestly literature provides a conceptual counterpart to the story of Miriam and those of Chronicles. In the former case, a socially disabling disease is punishment for some kind of violation or profanation, whereas in the latter, an already-defective body would profane the sanctuary and is therefore proscribed. Although both cases have different causal sequences in relating the variant body to the religious demand, they have the same structure: proximity to the holy is associated with a certain type of body, and separation from the holy is associated with a different bodily status. Specifically, the priestly, male, visually unruptured, gesturally capable body receives the closest association with the divine and thus, the highest value. In a shift away from the audio-centricity of Deuteronomic literature, the visual-gestural is the dominant modality in which markers are articulated. The body ideology of Proverbs is structurally similar to that of the Priestly, except that wisdom instead of

holiness occupies the central place, and hearing functions as a prerequisite to sight. At this point, one might ask how different holiness and
wisdom were thought to be in the period; both were clearly valued
qualities associated with God. Holiness seems to have a strong spatialization, concretized in the temple,[46] while wisdom is more temporally
oriented and spatially diffuse, as is sound, wisdom's key sensory mode.

In these two pathways of embodiment, we see the co-dominance of a
Judaism centered on sacrificial cult and one centered on devotion to
verbal performance, oral or textual. They are structurally similar and
share some elements but can be differentiated along several axes: the
favoured sensory mode (sight-gesture v. hearing); construction of sacred
boundaries on the person (bodily fluids or speech); and orientation to
spatiality or temporality. This is *not* to propose two social groups or sects
but only two imaginative and ideal constructions with different emphases, historically driven by the destruction of the first temple such that
Judaism begins to operate both with and without a temple, even after the
second is constructed.[47] Both converge on a set of habits for bodily
regulation; such regulations, including diet, regulation of bodily fluids,
concepts of cleanness, acceptable postural and locomotive performances,
and even the differentiation of better and worse ways to use one's senses,
function as strong cultural markers in Persian period Judaism, as they do
in cultures today. This is not to say that Israelites who fell short of the
performative expectations were excluded, although that is likely the case
for those with skin diseases; rather, the idealized bodily forms and
performances articulated central values, with the priestly body functioning as the main visual representation of the divine and the disabled body
functioning as a major signifier of refusal, more so than of the merely
non-Israelite. Disability is not mapped onto gentiles but onto non-
compliant Israelites. In Job and Isaiah 53, we find variations on this
theme: the potentially dangerous inside 'other' figures as a non-compli-
ant body, even as these texts polemically distinguish bodily performance
from performance of Israelite identity. Thus it does not signify the
cultural other, but rather the other inside—most intimately inside.

46. For a discussion of spatial categories in P relative to changing concepts of
divine embodiment, see Benjamin D. Sommer, *The Bodies of God and the World
of Ancient Israel* (Cambridge: Cambridge University Press, 2009), pp. 109-23.

47. Schmid, 'Canon and Cult', pp. 302-304. See also Grabbe, *History of the
Jews*, pp. 170-71, 238-43, 360.

THE OTHER OTHERS:
A QUMRAN PERSPECTIVE ON DISABILITY

Anke Dorman

Introduction

In the discourse about the Other, the Dead Sea Scrolls contain an abundance of material that can provide a complementary perspective from a later period. Recently, interest in the subject of Otherness from a Qumran perspective has increased, as demonstrated during the Fifth Meeting of the International Organization for Qumran Studies in Groningen in 2004 and the subsequently published volume, *Defining Identities: We, You and the Other in the Dead Sea Scrolls*.[1] All these essays focus on the community's self-perception as opposed to Jewish and non-Jewish groups, and how they define other groups as outsiders. The same applies to H. Harrington's recent article that studies the insider/outsider motif in the *Damascus Document* and in the *Rule of the Community*.[2] Within the Qumran context, where clearly set boundaries existed between the community and the rest of the (Jewish) world, this article explores how the group dealt with the issue of Otherness from an insider perspective. One category of persons clearly defined as Other in Qumran literature is disabled individuals. Five Qumran documents contain special rules for persons with disabilities, thereby categorizing them as Other within a society that categorized itself as separated from others.[3]

---

1. Florentino García Martínez and Mladen Popović (eds.), *Defining Identities: We, You, and the Other in the Dead Sea Scrolls—Proceedings of the Fifth Meeting of the IOQS in Groningen* (STDJ, 70; Leiden: Brill, 2008).
2. Hannah K. Harrington, 'Identity and Alterity in the Dead Sea Scrolls', in *Jewish Identity and Politics Between the Maccabees and Bar Kokhba: Groups, Normativity, and Rituals* (ed. Benedikt Eckhardt; JSJSup, 155; Leiden: Brill, 2012), pp. 71-89.
3. For the disabled as Other in mainstream biblical thought in the Persian period, see in this volume, Rebecca Raphael, 'Disability, Identity, and Otherness in Persian Period Israelite Thought', pp. 277-96.

The Otherness of disabled persons in the Qumran Scrolls is shown by several disqualifying regulations. On the one hand, these texts undoubtedly display a negative attitude towards persons with disabilities that impacted their participation in religious and social activities. On the other hand, the very existence of rules about disability indicates that disabled persons were members of the communities behind the texts.

Holiness and the Disabled Other

The Otherizing of disabled community members, pilgrims, or priests in the Qumran Scrolls arises in part from the rules in Lev. 21.16-23 that do not allow disabled priests to perform the sacrificial ritual. These rules apply to every priest who is blind, lame, disfigured, deformed, has a broken leg or a broken arm, a hunchback, is thin, has a discoloration of the eye or a scar, lichen, or a crushed testicle. The reason for the exclusion of blemished priests in Leviticus 21 has nothing to do with practical considerations. A priest who is thin or has a scar, for example, would be perfectly able to carry out the offering rituals. In Leviticus 21, the disability itself causes a threat to holiness. In some way, the physical blemish has the ability to profane what is holy. Leviticus's idea that disability profanes is reflected in some texts from Qumran dealing with disability, but not in all, as is shown below. Texts that attribute a profaning quality to disability are the *Rule of the Congregation* (1QSa) and the *Damascus Document* (CD). The rules in the *Temple Scroll* (11QT^a) even contain the idea that disability has the power to defile, that is, to make impure what is ritually clean.

Rule of the Congregation

As can be gathered from its title, the *Rule of the Congregation* (1QSa) is a book of rules that belonged to the so-called *Rule Scroll*.[4] This scroll contained the *Rule of the Community* (1QS), the *Rule of the Congregation* (1QSa), and the *Rule of the Benedictions* (1QSb). These three

---

4. For the history and text of the *Rule of the Congregation*, see for example Dominique Barthélemy and Józef T. Milik, *Qumran Cave 1* (Discoveries in the Judaean Desert, 1; Oxford: Clarendon, 1955), p. 108; Lawrence H. Schiffman, *The Eschatological Community of the Dead Sea Scrolls* (SBLMS, 38; Atlanta: SBL, 1989); James H. Charlesworth and Loren T. Stuckenbruck (eds.), *The Dead Sea Scrolls: Hebrew, Aramaic, and Greek Texts with English Translations*. Vol. 1, *Rule of the Community and Related Documents* (PTSDSSP; Tübingen: Mohr, 1994), p. 108; Florentino García Martínez and Eibert J. C. Tigchelaar (eds.), *The Dead Sea Scrolls Study Edition*. Vol. 1, *1Q1–4Q273* (Leiden: Brill, 1997), pp. 98-99.

works were initially composed independently. At a secondary stage they were combined into one document. The *Rule of the Congregation* is a sectarian text that can be dated to 100–75 BCE.

The core of the *Rule of the Congregation* (1QSa 1.6–2.11) contains regulations that were important for an existing earthly community. The secondarily added introduction in 1QSa 1.1-5 beginning with the words וזה הסרך לכול עדת ישראל באחרית הימים ('And this is the rule of all the congregation of Israel in the final days') and the description of the Messianic banquet at the end (1QSa 2.11b-22) place the entire document in an eschatological framework.[5] When it comes to Othering strategies in the *Rule of the Congregation*, it is important to understand that the rulings about the convocation of an assembly (1QSa 1.25–2.11) from which disabled persons were excluded were not eschatologically oriented, but instead, were valid for the lives of the Qumran members during its present time.[6]

The text can be translated as follows:[7]

25	(…) *Blank* And if there is a convocation for the entire assembly
26	for judgment or for the council of the community or for a convocation of war, they shall sanctify themselves during three days so that everyone who enters is pre[pared for the cou]ncil.
27	These are the men who are called for the council of the community from…*Blank* all
28	the w[ise men] of the congregation, those who have understanding, and those who are perfectly skilled in behavior, and the
29	noble men with [the leaders of the tri]bes and all their judges and their officials and the leaders of thousands and the leaders[of hundreds,]

bottom margin

5. Charlotte Hempel, 'The Earthly Essene Nucleus of 1QSa', *Dead Sea Discoveries* 3.3 (1996), pp. 253-69. Even the introduction and end of the document could be referring to the last days of the present time. The Essenes believed that they were already living in the end of time and, for that reason, the words באחרית הימים could be understood as the last period of history in the present time. For this interpretation, see Annette Steudel, 'אחרית הימים in the Texts from Qumran', *RevQ* 16 (1993), pp. 225-46.

6. This idea is supported by Hartmut Stegemann's argument that the rulings in 1QSa 1.25–2.11 would not have made sense in the ideal Messianic Age ('Some Remarks to 1QSa, to 1QSb, and to Qumran Messianism', *RevQ* 17 [1996], pp. 479-505 [494-95]).

7. This translation is taken from Johanna Dorman, 'The Blemished Body: Deformity and Disability in the Qumran Scrolls' (Ph.D. diss., University of Groningen, 2007), pp. 67-68. The dissertation is now available online: http://dissertations.ub.rug.nl/faculties/theology/2007/j.h.w.dorman/

1   And over fifties and over tens, and the Levites in the mid[st of his division of servi]ce. These are

2   the renowned men, called to the assembly, gathered for the cou[ncil of the communi]ty in Israel

3   in the presence of the sons of Zadok, the priests. But every man who is afflicted [with any on]e of the human impurities

4   may not enter into the assembly of God. And every man who is afflicted with [these may not]

5   take his stand in his office in the congregation. And every one who is afflic[ted in his flesh, lam[e in his legs] or

6   arms, limping, or blind or deaf or dumb or afflicted with a

7   blemish [in his flesh]

8   visible to the eyes, or a stumbling old man who does not stand firm in the assembly

9   these may not en[ter] to take their place [in] the midst of the congregation of the m[e]n of the name, because the angels

10   of holiness are in their [cou]ncil. And if there is someth[ing for someone of] them to say to the holy council, they will ask [him], but the man may n[ot] enter into [the assembly] for af[flicted is] h]e (...)

11

The section above can be divided into four units. The first unit (1QSa 1.25-27) explains the functions of the assembly and requires all participants to be ritually clean as preparation for the assembly. The second unit contains a list of men who are qualified to participate in the assembly. The third contains a catalogue of persons who are explicitly denied access to the gathering: persons with impurities, with physical deformities, and persons who are advanced in age (1QSa 2.3-9). The last unit contains a rule stating that a person who has something to say to the congregation but who is not allowed to enter can be questioned in private to express his case (1QSa 2.9-11).

The fact that the *Rule of the Congregation* has rules about persons with disabilities shows these persons were part of the community addressed by the text. If disabled persons were not allowed into the community, it would make no sense to have regulations about them in the first place. The regulations in 1QSa demonstrate that every time an assembly took place, special measures were taken for those afflicted with various kinds of disabilities.

The reason for denying disabled persons access to the assembly is the presence of holy angels. It may be hard to imagine communion with angels in a real community, but the members of the Qumran community thought this was possible. Their self-description was, to a significant extent, based on the image of the angelic priesthood in the heavenly sanctuary. Since the Qumranites strongly objected to the temple service in Jerusalem, the prototype of the ideal priesthood was to be found in heaven, not on earth. Not only did the Qumranites parallel their own liturgy and cult with those of the angels in heaven, but they also thought that the presence of the holy angels was possible in their community.[8] Regarded in this way, it is less remarkable that 1QSa 2.8-11 refers to the presence of the holy angels as the rationale for excluding unclean and physically deformed persons from the assembly.

Although it is obvious that during an assembly in which angels were believed to be present disabled persons would be seen as impacting holiness, it is more difficult to explain *why* they have the power to profane. C. Wassen sees fear of demonic power as the rationale for excluding disabled persons from meetings in the Qumran community.[9] In her view, the scrolls express the idea that disabled persons were under the control of evil forces. She concludes that because the Qumran community saw itself as a pure sanctuary in which humans could enjoy the company of angels, evil forces had to be banned from that holy environment. The fear that deformed body parts were caused by demonic forces might be present in some texts.[10] However, this does not mean this idea should be applied to every text mentioning disability, not even when those texts contain references to the demon's greatest enemies, the holy angels.[11]

8. Devorah Dimant, 'Men as Angels: The Self-Image of the Qumran Community', in *Religion and Politics in the Ancient Near East* (ed. Adele Berlin; Bethesda: University of Maryland Press, 1996), pp. 93-103.

9. Cecila Wassen, 'What Do Angels Have Against the Blind and the Deaf? Rules of Exclusion of the Dead Sea Scrolls', in *Common Judaism: Explorations in Second-Temple Judaism* (ed. Wayne O. McCready and Adele Reinhartz; Minneapolis: Fortress, 2008), pp. 115-29.

10. 4Q186, for example, links physical features to a person's spiritual qualities and his affiliation with good or evil. Yet, this text does not explicitly deal with physical disabilities. What is more, it is unclear to what extent 4Q186 impacted the communities associated with the scrolls. For a detailed treatment of this text and the interpretation of physical features as signs of spiritual qualities, see Mladen Popović, *Reading the Human Body: Physiognomics and Astrology in the Dead Sea Scrolls and Hellenistic–Early Roman Period* (STDJ, 67; Leiden: Brill, 2007); cf. Wassen, 'Angels', p. 125.

11. Likewise, it does not mean that texts referring to 'afflictions' have physical afflictions solely in mind. In the case of 1QS 3.23-24, for example, it is far from evident that the text refers to disabilities at all. It seems more likely that it refers to human hardships in general. In addition, the association of illness and demonic forces cannot be automatically paralleled with ideas concerning the relationship between demonic forces and disability, because illness and disability are not synonymous (contra Wassen, 'Angels', pp. 123-24).

It is likely that the combination of holy angels and exclusion of disabled persons in this text is also rooted in Leviticus 21. The *Rule of the Congregation* excludes 'every person afflicted in his flesh, who is lame in his legs or arms, limping, or blind or deaf or dumb or afflicted with a blemish in his flesh visible to the eyes' (1QSa 2.5-7) from communion with the holy angels because of fear of profanation. The excluded disabled persons form a threat to the sanctity of holy angels, just as deformity forms a threat to the holiness of מִקְדָּשַׁי when performing the sacrificial ritual in Lev. 21.23c. The idea of parallel reasoning in Lev. 21.23 and 1QSa 2.8-9 is strengthened if one recognizes that the author of 1QSa might have read the word מִקְדָּשַׁי, 'my sancta' or 'my sanctuaries', in Lev. 21.23c as מְקֻדָּשַׁי, 'my sanctified ones', referring to the holy angels. Support for this idea can be found in Isa. 13.3, in which the term מְקֻדָּשַׁי, is used to refer to YHWH's angelic host.[12]

In sum, the Othering of disabled community members in the *Rule of the Congregation* is not based on a concern for demonic powers or purity. The only thing that can be stated with certainty is that, parallel to the rulings in Leviticus 21, disabled persons in some situations somehow profane what is holy. If it is assumed that the Qumranites regarded themselves as holy in the same way that priests are holy in Leviticus, then disabled members of the community were probably regarded as holy, too. By virtue of belonging to that community, disabled and non-disabled members were Othered from the rest of the world. However, within that self-proclaimed Othered community of holy people, disabled persons were further Othered. Parallel to disabled priests in Leviticus 21, they were accorded a special position: they were not holy *enough* or qualified *enough* to partake in a specific activity.

Yet, although disabled community members were clearly Othered by the *Rule of the Congregation*, the excluded persons were still regarded as members of the community and the community protected their concerns. Together with the two other groups not qualified to attend the assembly, 1QSa 2.9-11 states that disabled persons may take a deposition to make their case in the council. This prescription also was inspired by Leviticus 21; v. 22 contains a special provision for disabled priests who are disqualified from offering sacrifices. Although they no longer can perform the sacrificial ritual, priests with a physical blemish may partake in the priestly emoluments. This prescription also makes clear that any priest who was unfit to carry out the special priestly task of offering was still regarded as a priest and could join his fellow priests in eating the holy food.

12. For a detailed analysis of this idea, see Dorman, 'Blemished Body', pp. 83-86.

Damascus Document

Angelic presence and Othering disabled community members are also linked in the *Damascus Document* (CD), which probably was not composed in Qumran but goes back to a group rooted in the same general movement from which the Qumran community arose. Thus, the group behind the *Damascus Document* and the Qumran community were related but not identical. This relation is best explained by assuming that the community behind the *Damascus Document* was an Essene group while the Qumran community represented a schism within the Essene movement.[13]

In the *Damascus Document* disabled persons are Othered for the same reason as in the *Rule of the Congregation*: persons with disabilities are excluded because of the presence of holy angels in the עדה, 'congregation'. The regulation in the *Damascus Document* is also rooted in the law disqualifying priests from offering in Leviticus 21. The ruling is worded as follows:[14]

> (15) And anyone simp[le], er[r]ant, (16) with dimmed eyes too weak t[o see,] limping, [or]lame, o[r deaf,] and an un[der-a]ge boy: no[ne (17) of these] may enter [the congregation, because the angels of holiness are…].

At first sight, it is not immediately clear what the context of the term עדה is. Some scholars think it refers to the community as a whole,[15]

---

13. Literature on the text and history of the *Damascus Document* is abundant. A good overview is given by Cecile Wassen, *Women in the Damascus Document* (Academia Biblica, 21; Atlanta: SBL, 2005), pp. 19-31, and by David Hamidović, *L'écrit de Damas: le manifeste essénien* (Collection de la revue des études juives, 51; Leuven: Peeters, 2011), pp. ix-xvi.

14. The translation is taken from Dorman, 'Blemished Body', p. 109.

15. See, e.g., Józef T. Milik, *Ten Years of Discovery in the Wilderness of Judaea* (Studies in Biblical Theology, 26; London: SCM, 1959), p. 114; Goran Forkman, *The Limits of the Religious Community: Expulsion from the Religious Community Within the Qumran Sect, Within Rabbinic Judaism, and Within Primitive Christianity* (Coniectanea biblica. New Testament Series, 5; Lund: CWK Gleerup, 1972), p. 63, and especially pp. 76-77; Michael Newton, *The Concept of Purity at Qumran and the Letters of Paul* (Society of New Testament Studies Monograph Series, 53; Cambridge: Cambridge University Press, 1985), p. 50; Florentino García Martínez and Julio Trebolle Barrera, *The People of the Dead Sea Scrolls* (trans. W. G. E. Watson; Leiden: Brill, 1995), p. 156; Charlotte Hempel, 'Community Structures in the Dead Sea Scrolls: Admission, Organization, Disciplinary Procedures', in *The Dead Sea Scrolls After Fifty Years: A Comprehensive Assessment*, vol. 2 (ed. Peter W. Flint and James C. VanderKam; Leiden: Brill, 1999), pp. 67-92 (70-73); idem, 'The Laws of the Damascus Document and 4QMMT', in *The Damascus Document, A Centennial of Discovery: Proceedings of the Third International*

which would imply that the persons excluded in CD 15.15-17 could not become members of the community. This idea must be rejected for various reasons.[16] The most important of them is that other passages in the *Damascus Document* presuppose the presence within the community of the categories of persons who are excluded in this rule. CD 13.6, for instance, speaks of a simple (פתי) priest, and CD 14.14-16 refers to a young boy (נער) and an afflicted person (איש אשר ינוגע). These are clearly references to persons who are members of the community. Consequently, it is unlikely that עדה in CD 15.17 and the community behind the *Damascus Document* are referring to the same term.

Because the exclusion cannot be from the community itself, the term עדה must refer to an aspect of community life.[17] To define more precisely the situation or situations from which certain people are excluded,[18] a closer look at the context in which the exclusion rule appears is needed. The regulation is part of a larger section in the *Damascus Document* (CD 15b-16:6a) that begins with regulations for 'entry into the covenant' (CD 15.5b) and ends with a reference to the book of *Jubilees* (CD 16.2b-6a). Because the statement בוא בברית, 'entering the covenant', heads the passage in CD 15.5b–16.6a, Hempel reads the entire pericope as a description of 'the entry into the movement that lies behind the communal legislations of the Laws of the Damascus Document by swearing the oath of the covenant'.[19] Although her idea that the ruling addresses entry into the community as a whole cannot be maintained, the covenantal context is crucial for identifying the specific circumstances from which disabled persons are excluded. It also helps answer the question about the situation in which the Othering of disabled persons takes place.

Symposium of the Orion Center for the Study of the Dead Sea Scrolls and Associated Literature (ed. Joseph M. Baumgarten, Esther G. Chazon, and Avital Pinnick; STDJ, 34; Leiden: Brill, 2000), pp. 69-84 (76).

16. Dorman, 'Blemished Body', pp. 110-14.

17. Schiffman, *Eschatological Community*, p. 48; Maxwell J. Davidson, *Angels at Qumran: A Comparative Study of 1 Enoch 1–36, 72-108 and Sectarian Writings* (Journal for the Study of the Pseudepigrapha, Supplement Series, 11; Sheffield: JSOT, 1992), p. 186.

18. Davidson and Schiffman think the exclusion applied to various circumstances. See Schiffman, *Eschatological Community*, p. 48; Davidson, *Angels at Qumran*, p. 186. According to Wassen, the congregation mentioned in CD 15.17 is not limited to the congregation that gathered for the initiation (*Women*, pp. 146, 150-51, 155). In this interpretation, the regulation in the *Damascus Document* could parallel the exclusion rule of 1QSa 2.3-9.

19. Hempel, *Laws*, p. 76.

Wassen agrees with Hempel that the passage discusses entrance into the community but describes it as formal initiation.[20] This means that she discerns different levels of membership within the specific, organized community reflected in the *Damascus Document*. In her view, the community consists of persons with full membership status and those who lack full membership status. As described in CD 15.5-15, initiation results in full membership in the community. A full-fledged member has two privileges: taking the oath of the covenant and attending communal meetings. From this it can be concluded that the exclusion of the categories of persons mentioned in CD 15.15-17 must be understood in this light: the excluded persons lack full membership status and may not enter the congregation, that is, a communal meeting. Unlike Hempel, Wassen points to the fact that, although the categories of persons mentioned in CD 15.15-17 cannot attend the initiation ritual, they are, nevertheless, members of the community. The initiation ritual contains two Otherizing mechanisms. Wassen puts it this way: 'While the oath of the covenant marked the separation between insiders and outsiders, it also served to distinguish between full members in the community and those who had not yet attained this status'.[21] In the case of most disabled persons, however, it was extremely unlikely they would ever attain this status.[22] They would always be marked as Other in relation to the full members of the community, who could be present in the עדה beside holy angels.

Wassen seems to imply that the Othering of disabled community members took place on more than one specific occasion. Their lack of full membership would have been visible every time they were banned from the עדה. Although it cannot be denied that the lower status of disabled persons impacted their lives, there is no textual evidence to support this view.

The exclusion from the עדה in CD 15.15-17 may well have occurred annually on a single, special occasion. There are reasons to assume that the exclusion rule addresses the celebration of the Feast of Weeks.[23] This interpretation fits very well within the larger context of CD 15.5b–16.6a, which contains a significant amount of covenantal vocabulary and allusions to the festival. It also fits the observations made by Harrington and

---

20. Wassen, *Women*, pp. 131-56.
21. Ibid., p. 154.
22. Wassen points to the fact that full members who later become disabled also will be excluded from covenant meetings ('Angels', p. 121).
23. For a detailed argument, see Dorman, 'Blemished Body', pp. 118-25.

Wassen about the character of the larger section in 15.5b–16.6a. During the Feast of Weeks, new members were initiated and people gathered to renew the Law of Moses by swearing oaths. Not all community members were present at the ceremony: persons with mental or physical deformities and youngsters were prohibited from participating in this ritual.

The reason for their exclusion was the same already seen in the *Rule of the Congregation*: holy angels were thought to be present. Persons with disabilities were not qualified to enjoy community with the angels. Because the *Damascus Document* also presupposes membership of disabled people, Othering them can only be confirmed in specific circumstances. Therefore, one could assume that in the everyday life of the community, the physical condition of members did not matter as much as during a gathering of the עדה.

Although Leviticus 21 served as a source text for CD 15.15-17, the latter passage does not contain a provision for disabled persons comparable to Lev. 21.22 or 1QSa 2.9-11. Elsewhere, however, CD 14.12b-17a contains a law prescribing financial support for the disabled:[24]

> *Blank* (12b) And this is the rule of the Many, to provide for all their needs: the salary (13) of two days each month at least. They shall give it in the hand of the Inspector and of the judges. (14) From it they shall give it to the <[in]jured> and with it they shall support the needy and the poor, and to the elder who (15) [is ben]t, and to the af[flic]ted, and to the prisoner of a foreign people, and to the girl who (16) had [n]o re[dee]mer, [and] to the <youth> [w]ho has no-one looking after him; everything is the task of the association, and (17) [the house of the association shall] not [be deprived of] its [means]. *Blank.*

This law indicates that the community behind the document treated its disabled members with respect and simultaneously conveys information about their social position. The need of financial care for disabled persons indicates they lived at an economically lower level than their able-bodied fellow-members.

---

24. The translation is taken from García Martínez and Tigchelaar, *Dead Sea Scrolls Study Edition*, p. 575. A similar call to be compassionate towards the poor and needy can be found in the Admonition of the *Damascus Document* in CD 6.21. The main difference between CD 6.21 and CD 14.12-17 is that the latter mentions the exact amount of money that should be donated each month and the fact that the Examiner and the judges are responsible for the collection and distribution of the funds.

Temple Scroll (11QT^a)

The *Temple Scroll* Others blind persons because it fears their ability to defile what is holy and pure. The *Temple Scroll* is a rewriting of parts of the Pentateuch running from the end of Exodus through to the end of Deuteronomy. The manuscript of 11QT^a is more than eight meters long and consists of nineteen thin sheets of animal skin, varying in length between thirty-nine and sixty-one centimeters. It was copied at the end of the first century BCE, most likely at Qumran. This can be concluded from the scribal techniques and the script, which are typical of the other Qumran manuscripts. Although it was probably copied in Qumran, it already existed prior to the foundation of the community.[25]

11QT^a 45.12-14 prescribes the exclusion of blind persons because they may defile the city in which YHWH resides:[26]

> 12 (...) *Blank* No blind person
> 13 shall enter it all their days, and they shall not defile the city in whose midst I dwell
> 14 because I, YHWH, dwell in the midst of the children of Israel for ever and always. *Blank*

The regulation marks the end of the first literary section of the document, which is concerned with the building of the temple. Several prohibitions regarding entry into the temple, temple cities, and other cities are listed. Men who had a nocturnal emission (11QT^a 45.7-10) or an emission of semen during sexual intercourse (11QT^a 45.11-12), blind persons (11QT^a 45.12-14), persons who had a discharge (11QT^a 45.15-17), persons who had contact with the dead (11QT^a 45.17), persons suffering from leprosy, and diseased persons (11QT^a 45.17-18) are not allowed to enter. All these groups are regarded as sources of pollution, and in each case, except for the blind, purification requirements are given. Characteristic of each law is the phrase לוא יבוא אל, 'he shall not enter', and the fact that each ruling is derived from biblical texts.

Several elements in the passage on the banning of blind persons from the temple city indicate that the *Temple Scroll*'s position towards the blind was stricter than other Qumran writings. The placement of the law prohibiting blind persons from entering the temple among other groups of people who cause pollution provides a strong indication that the

---

25. For the text and history of the *Temple Scroll*, see, for example: Johann Maier, *Die Tempelrolle vom Totem Meer* (UTB, 829; Munich: Ernst Reinhardt, 1978); Yigael Yadin, *The Temple Scroll* (4 vols.; Jerusalem: Israel Exploration Society, 1983); Sidnie White Crawford, *The Temple Scroll and Related Texts* (Companion to the Qumran Scrolls, 2; New York: T&T Clark International, 2000).

26. The translation is taken from Dorman, 'Blemished Body', p. 235.

Temple Scroll regarded these people as unclean. Their exclusion was not caused by the practical difficulties of blindness that could lead to accidental pollution.[27] The *Temple Scroll* excludes the blind and persons suffering from all sorts of ritual impurities from the entire city. Since a normal social life in a real city becomes impossible if every kind of impurity is prohibited, it is likely that the rulings in the *Temple Scroll* only apply to pilgrims. Avoiding impurities during pilgrimage is feasible; avoiding them in normal circumstances is not.

The *Temple Scroll* shaped its ideas on the basis of Leviticus 21 but made extensive modifications to the basic precepts of the text. First, it extended the categories of ban among priests to common Israelites and then made them applicable within the entire city, not the sanctuary complex alone. Secondly, the *Temple Scroll* modified the thought in Lev. 21.23 that disabled persons could profane, converting it to the idea that a blind person might pollute. As a result, the *Temple Scroll* contains a stricter position toward the blind than any other scroll.[28]

Practical Considerations

The three documents discussed above all contain disqualifying regulations for persons with disabilities who were regarded as Other because their disabilities became the focal point of their identity: as Other, they were not holy enough to be in the company of holy angels or to enter the city of YHWH. In the next two sections, two Qumran documents are discussed that Otherize disabled people for practical reasons. These people, too, are excluded and disqualified, not because of who they are

27. This means that the *Temple Scroll* does not take their inability to distinguish between clean and unclean into consideration, contrary to MMT, where blind and deaf persons are not regarded as intrinsically unclean. The latter text is discussed below.

28. Evidence from another passage in the *Temple Scroll* that deals with the exclusion of certain groups of people from the inner court (11QT^a 35.2-9), however, allows for a more tolerant interpretation. This passage also states that the groups are excluded because they possess the power to defile the sanctuary. To these groups belong priests who are not properly dressed and persons who are not a priest. Perhaps the text also mentions blemished and unclean priests, but since the fragment is so heavily damaged this remains unverifiable. In any case, the fact that a person who is not properly dressed but who is not unclean can *defile* the sanctuary indicates that defilement of the sanctuary or the city can result when persons enter who are not in themselves unclean but merely unqualified to have access to those precincts. Therefore, it cannot be proven definitively that the blind pilgrims in 11QT^a 45.12-14 were excluded because they were regarded as unclean.

but because of the dangers their disability could cause. Thus, in the *War Scroll* and in MMT, the rationale for labelling disabled persons as Other is purely practical.

War Scroll

The *War Scroll* (1QM) is a Qumran document that recounts a war between two parties that will take place at the end of times. The date of the original composition of the *War Scroll* is unknown, but a time close to the Maccabean wars is probable. The document was written by Qumran members and developed from different versions into its present form. The document relates that the 'Sons of Light' belonging to God will fight against the 'Sons of Darkness' belonging to Belial. In the end, God himself will intervene and the Sons of Light will defeat Belial and his followers.[29]

The *War Scroll* contains one reference to disability in the first part of the document that deals with practical regulations for warfare. 1QM 7.3b-8 relates strict rules on the selection of warriors allowed to participate in the holy battles. Women, minors, and persons with various kinds of bodily defects and skin ailments are deemed unsuitable for participating in the war and may not leave with the warriors to their camps:[30]

3b	And no young boy or any woman at all shall enter the camps
4	when they leave Jerusalem to go to war, until they return. And no lame, blind, paralyzed person nor any man who has an indelible blemish on his flesh, nor any man afflicted with an
5	uncleanness of his flesh, none of these will go out to war with them. All these shall be volunteers for the war, perfect in spirit and in body, and ready for the day of vengeance. And every
6	man who is not pure from his 'spring' on the day of battle will not go down with them, for the holy angels are together with their armies. And there will be a space
7	between all their camps and the toilet of about two thousand cubits. And no immodest nakedness will be seen in the surroundings of all their camps.
8	*blank*

29. See for editions and (annotated) translations e.g. Barthélemy and Milik, *Qumran Cave 1*, pp. 135-36, pl. XXXI; Yigael Yadin, *The Scroll of the War of the Sons of Light Against the Sons of Darkness* (Oxford: Oxford University Press, 1962); Jean Duhaime, 'War Scroll', in *The Dead Sea Scrolls: Hebrew, Aramaic, and Greek Texts with English Translations. Vol. 2, Damascus Document, War Scroll, and Related Documents* (ed. James H. Charlesworth et al.; PTSDSSP; Tübingen: Mohr, 1995), pp. 80-141, and idem, *The War Text: 1QM and Related Manuscripts* (Companion to the Qumran Scrolls, 6; London: T&T Clark International, 2004).

30. Translation from Dorman, 'Blemished Body', p. 156.

The holy angels also appear in the passage under consideration. It is very likely that the author of 1QM knew the tradition contained in the *Rule of the Congregation* and/or the *Damascus Document* and read this text in tandem with Leviticus 21. One could argue, therefore, that parallel to the *Rule of the Congregation* and the *Damascus Document*, the *War Scroll* also Others disabled people because they are regarded as antithetical to angelic presence.[31] A closer look at 1QM 7.3b-8, however, reveals that the text contains at least two different occasions when it would be decided who could join the warriors. The first occasion would be when the warriors were to leave Jerusalem to reside in the war camps. The second instance would be on the day of the battle (1QM 7.6), when a man who was unclean because of seminal emission would be barred from fighting in the war.[32] This means that disabled persons were already excluded from going to battle during the first selection. During the second selection in the camps, which is concerned with the presence of holy angels, disability is no longer a criterion for exclusion.

In the discussion about Othering strategies of disabled persons as well as the relation between them and the holy angels, this perhaps minor observation is very important. The presence of holy angels gives the battle a special status of increased holiness.[33] When disabled persons are excluded because of the presence of holy angels, this means that they are, in and of themselves, not holy enough to participate in the battle. This is the rationale contained in the *Rule of the Congregation* and the *Damascus Document*. If, however, the exclusion of disabled persons takes place when the warriors leave the home base Jerusalem, the rationale for the exclusion is rooted in practical military considerations.

The exclusion rule in 1QM 7.3b-8 also leans heavily on Leviticus 21, and this sheds light on how the author of the *War Scroll* interpreted the nature of the eschatological battle. It is implied that the battle fought by the Sons of Light will be a holy war. The persons who partake in the battle perform some kind of ministry comparable to the ministry of priests. Thus, a man who is unclean cannot participate in the battle, because uncleanness and cultic practice in the sanctuary are absolutely incompatible. However, unlike Leviticus 21, the exclusion of disabled persons in the *War Scroll* seems to be based primarily on practical military considerations. The statutes about the young boys and the women (1QM 7.3) and about the 'lame, blind, paralyzed person', any

31. Wassen, 'Angels', p. 120.
32. Dorman, 'Blemished Body', p. 159.
33. Note that 1QM 7.6 says that the holy angels are 'with their armies' and not 'in their camps'.

man 'who has an indelible blemish on his flesh', and any man 'afflicted with an uncleanness of his flesh' (1QM 7.4f.) must be read together and interpreted as equivalents.[34] These two remarks repeat the idea that all these people are physically unfit to take part in the battle in the first place and that for this reason, it is pointless to join the men who are 'perfect in spirit and in body' (1QM 7.5) in their war camps.

The text does not connect the disabled with those who are disqualified to fight on the day of the battle because they are unclean. The combination of uncleanness, the camps, and the battle occurs in a second stage. Uncleanness was something thought to be a normal accident. Because ritual impurity is easily attracted in daily life, it would be impossible to maintain stringent purity regulations inside the camps and to exclude every ritually unclean person from entering the camps. Especially in a war context, warriors would easily attract ritual impurity in the act of killing. Yet, the location of the toilet and the prohibition of immodest nakedness show that warriors needed to make an effort to maintain the highest level of purity possible and joining the holy angels in the actual battle while being unclean was unthinkable.

MMT

Practical considerations are also the rationale behind the disqualification of blind and deaf priests in *Miqsat Ma'ase Ha-Torah* (MMT), 'Some Works of the Torah'. MMT is generally interpreted as a letter sent by one of the Qumran community's leaders either to the priesthood in Jerusalem or one of its representatives, possibly the high priest. One could identify the author of the letter as the Teacher of Righteousness and the addressee as the so-called 'Wicked Priest'.[35] If the interpretation of MMT as a letter

---

34. The idea that the rules for disabled persons apply to the period when the warriors prepare to take up dwelling in the camps and not the time when they are already in the camps is supported by a comparison between 1QM 7.3b-8 and a similar ruling in the War Scroll-like documents from Cave 4 (4Q491 f1-3.6-10). It becomes clear that in 4Q491 the holy angels are only present in the actual battle and not in the camps. For that reason, a man who attracted ritual uncleanness in the camps could not fight in the eschatological battle with the angels unless he purified himself. This rule concerns a second selection of persons qualified for participating in the war. The first selection was already made at the time when the warriors left Jerusalem to reside in the camps. During the first selection it was decided who was clearly unfit for battle: women, minors, and disabled persons. For an extensive analysis of this idea, see Dorman, 'Blemished Body', pp. 159-72.

35. For more information on MMT and its textual history, see Zdzislaw J. Kapera (ed.), *Qumran Cave IV and MMT: Special Report* (Krakow: Enigma, 1991); Elisha Qimron and John Strugnell, *Qumran Cave 4, V: Miqsat Ma'ase Ha-Torah* (Discoveries in the Judaean Desert, 10; Oxford: Clarendon, 1994); John Kampen and

is correct, it must date from the very beginning of the Qumran community's foundation in the second half of the second century BCE, even
before the final separation from the priesthood in Jerusalem. This
proposed dating of MMT is based on the observation that the document
does not use typical sectarian language and does not employ the dualistic
ideology known from other community texts. With this understanding of
the document's genre, the letter has commonly been seen to provide the
reasons for the schism: there was a difference of opinion on certain
halakhic ideas.

In the last decade, however, while the idea that at least some parts of
the document could once have functioned as a letter written in the early
days of the community has remained the norm, additional qualifications
have arisen.[36] New interpretations have questioned the limitation of the
date range for extant MMT manuscripts from 75 BCE to 50 CE, noting the
composition was still important some 100 to 200 years later. As a result,
a new focus has emerged on how the document could have functioned
for the ongoing community that copied it, since, according to Pérez
Fernandéz, 'it is apparent that the letter has come to be understood as
"redirected" to the community'.[37]

MMT contains one regulation dealing with disability. This rule is only
addressed to blind and deaf priests and for that reason, nothing can be
said about MMT's attitude towards disabled persons in general. The
regulation is formulated as follows:[38]

Moshe J. Bernstein, 'Introduction', in *Reading 4QMMT: New Perspectives on
Qumran Law and History* (ed. John Kampen and Moshe J. Bernstein; SBLSymS, 2;
Atlanta: Scholars Press, 1996), pp. 1-7.

36. See Miguel Pérez Fernández, '4QMMT: Redactional Study', *RevQ* 18.2
(1997), pp. 191-205; Steven D. Fraade, 'To Whom It May Concern: 4QMMT and
Its Addressee(s)', *RevQ* 19 (1999/2000), pp. 507-26; Maxine L. Grossman, 'Read-
ing 4QMMT: Genre and History', *RevQ* 20 (2001), pp. 3-22; Florentino García
Martínez, '4QMMT in a Qumran Context', in *Qumranica Minora I: Qumran
Origins and Apocalypticism* (ed. Eibert J. D. Tigchelaar; STDJ, 63; Leiden: Brill,
2007), pp. 91-103; Hanne Von Weissenberg, *4QMMT: Reevaluating the Text, the
Function and the Meaning of the Epilogue* (STDJ, 82; Leiden: Brill, 2009); Emile
Puech, 'L'épilogue de 4QMMT revisité', in *A Teacher for All Generations: Essays
in Honor of James C. VanderKam*, vol. 1 (ed. Eric F. Mason et al.; JSJSup, 153/1;
Leiden: Brill, 2012), pp. 309-39. Charlotte Hempel, on the other hand, attempts to
leave traditional interpretations of the text behind and argues for a much broader
audience for the text as part of an exchange of halakhic ideas ('The Context of
4QMMT and Comfortable Theories', in *The Dead Sea Scrolls: Texts and Context*
[ed. Charlotte Hempel; STDJ, 90; Leiden: Brill, 2010], pp. 272-92).

37. Pérez Fernández, '*4QMMT*: Redactional Study', p. 193.

38. The translation is taken from Dorman, 'Blemished Body', p. 190.

49 Also concerning] the bl[i]nd
50 [*who cannot see as to beware of every single mixtur*]e:
51 they cannot see the offence *blank*
52 [*Also concern*]ing the deaf, who cannot hear law, or [*judg*]ment or precept and who cannot
53 [*h*]ear the judgments of Israel. Because who cannot see or cannot hear does not
54 [kn]ow how to act. And they app[roac]h the pure [objects] of the sanctuary. *Blank*

The addressees of this regulation are not immediately clear. The text has a cultic setting but could be directed to worshippers or to priests. A closer look reveals that the law is for priests only. The text focuses on acts carried out within the sphere of the sanctuary. Because the author of MMT was concerned about a blind person's active contact with mixtures in the temple sphere, it is reasonable to assume that these acts were related to performing ritual acts.[39] Worshippers come to the sanctuary, but they are not allowed to bring offerings, and it is precisely the possibility of offerings not being carried out properly that causes fear of profanation. This forms the motivation behind the law in 4QMMT B 49-54.

The ruling for blind and deaf priests in MMT also was inspired by Leviticus 21; although the resemblance is not immediately obvious, there are some clear parallels between the two texts. They both deal with the issue of a priest's disability limiting the proper performance of ritual acts. In Lev. 21.16-23 a priest with a physical blemish is disqualified from performing the sacrificial ritual. 4QMMT B 50-51 also cautions against illicit mixtures in a cultic context. Both texts attempt to safeguard the way in which priests bring offerings. The motivation behind this concern for proper offerings is the fear that an illegitimately performed sacrifice somehow might threaten the pure objects of the sanctuary. Leviticus expresses this concern in the concluding phrase of the law (Lev. 21.23c), which reads ולא יחלל את־מקדשי, 'and he may not desecrate my sancta'. 4QMMT B 54 reads באים לטהרת המקדש, 'they approach the pure objects of the sanctuary'. This example shows that the מקדשי in Lev. 21.23c and the טהרת in 4QMMT B 54 are parallels[40] and that MMT does not make a direct link between מקדשי and holy angels.

---

39. Ibid., pp. 206-14. Olyan and Berthelot also believe that the regulation is addressed to priests, although they come to their conclusion in a slightly different way. Katell Berthelot, 'La place des infirmes et des "lépreux" dans les textes de Qumrân et les évangiles', *RB* 113.2 (2006), pp. 211-41 (222-23); Saul M. Olyan, *Disability in the Hebrew Bible: Interpreting Mental and Physical Differences* (Cambridge: Cambridge University Press, 2008), p. 106 and 161 n. 13.

40. So Olyan, *Disability in the Hebrew Bible*, pp. 161 n. 13, and Berthelot, 'Infirmes et lépreaux', p. 221.

The reason for Othering priests with disabilities, however, differs in both texts. In Leviticus 21, the physical condition itself is the rationale for Othering. A priest's disability forms a threat to holiness. In MMT, the fear results from the limitation in functional capability caused by the priest's disability. This difference is underlined by the fact that MMT discusses only two kinds of disabilities, blindness and deafness, while twelve disabilities are listed in Leviticus 21. In the latter list, only blindness causes serious problems when the line between purity and impurity must be discerned. A scar, for example, does not impact on somebody's sensual perception, nor does a broken arm or a crushed testicle. Because MMT is concerned with the practical consequences of a disability, it also mentions deafness. Not being able to hear impacts, for example, on the proper understanding and proclamation of laws. Thus, for MMT a person's physical appearance seems to have no influence on the validity of an offering as long as it does not hinder a priest in the proper enactment of the sacrificial ritual.

Damascus Document

Besides the Othering of disabled community members in CD 15.15-17, the *Damascus Document* also contains a reference to the exclusion of disabled persons for practical reasons. The latter regulation, which is not preserved in the Genizah text, is addressed to priests prohibited from reading the Torah due to their speech impediment. A reconstruction of the manuscripts 4Q266 f. 5ii.1-4, 4Q267 f. 5iii.1-6 and 4Q273 f. 2.1-2; f. 4i.5-11 enables the following translation:[41]

> (1) [And a]nyone [   ]
> (2) [   ] and anyone with dim [eye]s or [anyone who is not]
> (3) quick to un[derstand. And anyone who has a soft v[oice or with a voice]
> (4) unsteady and who does not divide his words so that [his voice may be heard. Of these]
> (5) none shall read from the b[ook of the Law,] les[t he make an error in a capital matter]
> (6) [   ] congregation and [his brethren]
> (7) [the priests, in the servi]ce, but he shall not [   ]

Due to the fragmentary character of this text, the scope of the regulations cannot be determined in full. In line 2, for example, reference is made to someone with dim eyes, but it is uncertain whether this must be connected to the law concerning the reading of the Torah or whether it is

41. Joseph M. Baumgarten, *Qumran Cave 4. XIII: The Damascus Document (4Q266-273)* (DJD, 18; Oxford: Clarendon, 1996), pp. 49-102.

part of something else. What is clear, however, is that priests with speaking disabilities may not read from the 'book of the Law'. The rationale for these regulations is again practical: priests who read from the Torah in public cannot make a mistake in their pronunciation. Reading errors must be avoided at all cost to safeguard the proper interpretation of laws.[42]

With respect to the construction of ideas about the disabled Other in this passage, it is important to recognize that priests who had difficulties speaking apparently were not disqualified from the priestly office in general. Their disability only appeared problematic in the context of the public reading of the Torah. This was only one aspect of their job.

Conclusion

The answer to why disabled persons were regarded as Other in the Dead Sea Scrolls is found in the *Rule of the Congregation* and the *Damascus Document*. These texts define disability as a quality that is antithetical to the presence of holy angels. The idea of the incompatibility of disability and holiness is rooted in Lev. 21.16-23. This biblical text excludes priests with disabilities because they have the power to profane. Although these priests were still regarded as holy and ritually clean, their disability marked them off from their 'whole' colleagues. One could argue, therefore, that disabled priests were less holy and this idea is also reflected in the *Rule of the Congregation* and the *Damascus Document*.

Although the latter two texts do not refer to priests or the temple, they paralleled certain aspects of sectarian life with temple service. Their meetings could be compared to performing the sacrificial ritual in the sanctuary when divine contact was most intense. The idea of divine presence in the sanctuary paralleled the notion of community with holy angels in the Qumran texts. At the same time, the regulations in the *Rule of the Community* and the *Damascus Document* show that disqualification was probably partial: only in specific situations and for various reasons could a person's disability become problematic.

Although the *Temple Scroll* does not mention angelic presence, this text also Others disabled persons, in this case pilgrims, because they are a threat to the holiness of the city of YHWH. The disability itself causes

---

42. Joseph M. Baumgarten, 'The Disqualifications of Priests in 4Q Fragments of the "Damascus Document", a Specimen of the Recovery of pre-Rabbinic Halakha', in *The Madrid Qumran Congress: Proceedings of the International Congress on the Dead Sea Scrolls, Madrid 18–21 March 1991*, vol. 2 (ed. Julio Trebolle and Luis Vegas Montaner; Leiden: Brill, 1992), pp. 503-13 (508).

fear of profanation or even pollution. However, it is likely that this Othering mechanism was only valid during pilgrimage. For that reason, nothing can be said about the *Temple Scroll*'s attitude towards persons with disabilities in everyday life.

Three situations in three sources were identified in which disabled individuals were excluded for practical reasons. The sources include the *War Scroll*, the *Damascus Document*, and MMT. The three situations when disabled individuals were to be excluded from participation included war, and in the case of serving priests, reading from the Torah and bringing sacrifices.

Notwithstanding the negative attitudes towards disability, the Dead Sea Scrolls also show a tendency towards taking care of disabled persons. Although the *Damascus Document* excluded disabled persons from the celebration of the Feast of Weeks, CD 14.12b-17a contains a law prescribing financial support for the disabled. The *Rule of the Congregation* makes provision for disabled community members to make their case in the council (1QSa 2.9-10), parallel to the rule in Leviticus 21–22, which provides disabled priests with their share in the priestly food. This implies that just as disabled priests in Leviticus 21 were still regarded as priests, the excluded persons in the *Rule of the Congregation* were still regarded as community members. They were not qualified to attend the assembly, but their interests were not forgotten.

INDEXES

INDEX OF REFERENCES

HEBREW BIBLE/
OLD TESTAMENT

Genesis

1.27	125	17.12	100	27.38	71
2.23	124	17.19	50	28.3	50
2.24	165	17.21	50	28.4	50
3.1-5	45	17.23-27	100	28.14-15	50
3.16	50	17.23	100	28.14	45, 50
3.20	124	18.18	46, 50	28.15	51
4.1	124	18.19	45, 50	28.20	51
4.16	210	19	212	31.3	50, 51
4.19	45	19.14	172	31.5	51
9.9-17	65	19.30-38	171	31.13	50
9.12	260	19.36-37	165	31.14-16	158
9.25	72	20	71, 79	31.15	153
12.1-2	50	20.1	152	31.45-47	82
12.1	50, 169	20.6	71	32.9	50
12.2	46, 50, 83	21	71, 82	32.12	50
12.3	45, 66	21.12	50	34	85
12.6	72	21.23	152	35.3	51
12.7	50	21.34	152	35.11	46, 50
12.10	152	22.17	50	35.12	50
13.14-18	85	22.18	50, 66	35.29	97
13.14-15	50	23	72, 97	36.1	85
13.14	84	23.26	51	36.53	85
13.17	50	24.24.7	50	37–46	227
14	72	24.27	170	38	173
15.5	50	24.28	157	38.11	172
15.7	50	24.60	50	38.26	128, 174
15.18-21	50, 72	25	130	38.27-29	171
16	71	25.8	97	44.2-4	130
16.10	50	25.17	97	46.3	46
17.1-21	50	25.23	46	47.4	152
17.1	50	25.25	85	47.12	262
17.7	50	26.4	50	48.4	50
17.8	50, 72	26.5	50	48.19	46
17.9-14	50, 100	26.24	51	48.21	51
		27	71, 130	49.33	97
		27.11	85	50.20	50
		27.34	71		

Exodus		*Leviticus*		26.25	282
1–15	74	10.1-2	115	26.44	52, 53, 63,
2.8	72	16.8	211		69
2.18	113	16.29-34	99	26.45	98
2.25	45	18	247		
3	71	18.22	124	*Numbers*	
6.4	152	18.24-30	66, 246	1–10	107, 108
6.16-20	263	18.28-29	100	1–4	108-10,
12.1-29	193	18.29	101		112, 113
12.1-28	194	19.2	40	1.1	107
12.43-49	91, 100	19.33-34	152	1.48-53	107
12.43-44	100	20.2-5	98, 100	1.51	107
12.48-49	102	20.24-26	90	1.52-53	107
12.48	152	20.24	46	2.29	243
12.49	93	20.26	46	3.4	115
15.17	48	21–22	36, 267,	3.6-9	107
17.14-16	31		316	3.10	107
18	29	21	246, 298,	3.12-13	107, 115
19.5	46		302, 303,	3.34	108
19.6	36, 46,		306, 308,	3.38	107
	243		310, 313,	3.40-51	115
19.8	55		314, 316	3.40-45	107
19.15	24	21.7	248	4.17-20	108
199.6	46	21.14-15	248	5–7	109
20.17	123	21.16-23	298, 313,	5–6	108, 109,
22.19	62		315		113
23.11	58	21.18-23	281	5	110
23.23-28	122	21.18	278	5.1-4	109
23.23	72	21.20	123	5.3	108
23.31-33	72	21.22	302, 306	5.5-10	109
24	194	21.23	281, 302,	5.6	108
24.3	55		308, 313	5.11-31	108-10
24.7	55	22.4	282	5.14	110
24.12	262	22.18	243	5.15	110, 111
25.2	262	22.19-25	281	5.18	111
28	258	22.21	281	5.21	112
28.4	262	22.22	281	5.26	112
28.27	262	22.23	281	5.27	112
28.36	262	23	98	5.29-30	110
28.39	262	24.14-20	282	6.1-21	109
28.43	260	24.22	93	6.2	108, 109
33.5	51	25.23	98	6.3-4	109
33.13	46	25.44	100	6.5-12	109
33.16	51	25.47-54	103	6.18-19	109
34.11	72	26.16-33	285	7–10	108, 113
35.29	262	26.16	282	8.17	107
40.38	243	26.21	282	9.1	107

9.17-23	113
10.29-32	113
10.31	113
11–25	107, 114
11.20	51
12–14	280, 283
12	113, 116-18
12.1	117, 283
12.10-15	283
12.14	283
12.33	283
13–14	72
13	114
14	114
14.12	46, 54, 69, 283
14.33	114
14.36-37	283
15.15-16	93
15.15	93
15.16	152
15.26	93
15.29	93
15.38-41	114
15.39	114
16–18	258, 262
16	115
16.1	116
16.7	262
16.27	116
16.30-33	116
17	116, 263
17.1-15	261
17.5	107, 115
17.5 LXX	265
17.23	263
18.4	107
18.4 LXX	265
18.7	107
18.7 LXX	265
18.19	260
20.24	97
24.7	112
25	30, 113, 116-19, 258, 267
25.1	117
25.1 LXX	267
25.1-4	115
25.1-3	149
25.1-2	165
25.2	117
25.3	267
25.8-9	267
25.8	118
25.11	261, 267
25.12-13	118, 261
25.13	261
25.13 LXX	265
26–36	107, 119
26	110, 119
26.52-56	121
26.57-59	263
26.61	115
27	119
27.4	120
27.13	97
30	109
31	22, 114, 267
31.2	97, 268
36	120
36.3	121

Deuteronomy

2.26-29	165
4.1-40	74
4.5	262
4.6	46
4.7	46
4.29	61
4.34	46
4.37	45, 47
4.38	46
5.1	194
5.32	61
6.5	61
6.7	61
6.20-25	61
7	71, 73
7.1-6	245
7.1-4	122
7.1-2	122
7.1	46, 72
7.2-3	80
7.2	75
7.4	85
7.6-7	45
7.6	46
7.12-13	48
7.17	46
7.25-26	73
8.19-20	73, 85
9.1	46
9.14	46
9.24	45
10.12	61
10.15	45, 47
11.13	61
11.23	46
11.28	85
13	62
13.6	84
14.2	45, 46
14.21	152
15.3	152
15.21	36
17.1	36
17.11	61
17.20	61
18.3	118
19	85
20	267
22.15	129
23.1	123
23.3-8	65
23.3	123, 133
23.4-5	170, 171
23.4	165
23.6	47, 213
23.11	24
23.20	152
25.5-10	179
25.7	180
25.17-19	31
26.5	46
26.16-19	194
26.18	46
26.19	46
27.4-8	93

Deuteronomy (cont.)

28.1-14	55
28.1	46, 262
28.13	262
28.14	61
28.16-29	285
28.20-57	61
28.20-44	62
28.23	61
28.26-35	61
28.58-68	66
29–30	194
29.22	212
29.28	58
31	86
31.9-13	99
31.10	99
31.24-27	263
32.6	47
32.28	46
32.43-44	46
32.46	61
33.10	262, 263, 265
34.10	45

Joshua

2.4-6	129
2.6	132
2.15	129
2.18	130
3.10	51
6.13	53
7	55, 56
8.30-35	93
11.17	85
15.7	55
15.15	55
15.47	55
22.31	51

Judges

1.6	36
1.7	36
1.11	55
1.16	113

2.20	46
3.17	46
3.19-21	130
4.1	46
4.11	113
4.17	131
4.18	131
4.21	131
5	131
5.2	262
5.6	46
5.8	46
5.9	262
5.24	131
5.28	31, 136
5.30	132
6.27-31	196
9.53	129
10.6	122
10.13	46
14.3	36

Ruth

1.1	151, 152
1.4	26
1.8	154, 157
1.13	169
1.14	165
1.16-17	145, 154
1.16	25, 134, 166
1.20-21	169
1.22	26
2.1	168
2.2	26
2.5	167
2.10	151-53, 167
2.11	153, 169
2.20	154, 170
2.21	26
3.4-5	134
3.10	173
3.13-14	134
3.16	168
4	160

4.5	26, 134, 179, 180
4.7-8	154
4.10-11	145
4.10	135, 174, 180
4.11-12	135, 156, 170
4.11	129, 153
4.12	171
4.13	171
4.16-17	135
4.17	171, 174
4.18-22	160, 170
4.18-21	170, 171, 174

1 Samuel

4.9	33
8	30
8.5	46
8.7	33, 52
10.19	52
12.20-25	54, 68
14.6	36
15	31
17.4-7	284
21.5-6	24
21.8	25
22.9	25
22.18	25
28.18	31

2 Samuel

6.2-12	27
6.10-12	27
6.16	136
7.10	48
7.23	46, 47, 68
11.3	25
11.4	24
11.6	25
11.12-13	24
11.17	25
11.21	25
11.24	25

12.1-6	130
12.9	25
12.10	25
13.28	33
23.5	260
23.29	25
24.17	57

1 Kings

3.9	265
5.1-8	30
5.9-14	30
6.7	243
8.41-43	68, 152, 161
8.51	48
8.53	48
8.57	54
10.23	30
11.1-8	153
11.1-3	30
11.2	137
12.31–13.21	186
13.18	130
14.15	58
15.5	25
16.30-32	136
16.30-31	136
17.9	28
17.31	27
18	136
19.1-3	136
19.4	215
21	136
21.25	136
22.8	45
22.13	45
22.17	57

2 Kings

5	178
5.17	28
5.18	29
5.27	29
6.26	129
9.7-37	136
9.30	31, 136
9.33	129
14.25-27	215
15.5	286
17.15	52
17.20	52, 64
18.33	47
19.12	47
21.14	48, 53
22–23	199
22.10-20	197
23	182-84, 187-90, 192, 193, 195-200
23.1-25	182, 186
23.1-3	182, 194, 198
23.3	190
23.4-14	182
23.4	190, 192
23.5	190
23.6	190, 192
23.7	188, 190
23.8-9	195
23.8	184, 190
23.10	192
23.11	190
23.12	190, 192
23.15-20	182
23.15-18	186
23.15-16	191
23.17-18	195
23.19-20	186, 191
23.21-23	182, 186
23.21-22	193
23.21	190
23.23-23	195
23.23	194
23.24-25	182
23.24	186, 193
24.14	187
25.8-11	28
25.11	187
25.27-30	187
26	187

1 Chronicles

4.21	172
11.23	284
11.41	25
12.2	285
13.13-14	27
16.5	27
17.9	48
17.14	25
17.21	68
20.4-8	284
20.4-6	284
20.6	284
21.12-27	285
21.17	56, 57
26.4-8	27
27.31	271
28.5	25
29.6	271
29.9	262
29.23	25

2 Chronicles

6.28-31	285
7.20	58
8.10	271
13.5	25
13.8	25
16.10	24
16.12-13	285
17.16	262
18.16	57
21.11-20	286
24.11	271
24.19-22	24
25	26
25.24	26
26.16-21	286
26.16	286
26.20	286
32.14-15	47
32.17	47
32.24-26	286
34–35	183
35.1	194
35.22	29

Ezra		5.1	231, 232, 242	9.11-12	245
1–10	234			9.12	284
1–6	91, 92, 95, 99, 232, 235, 238, 239, 243, 244, 250-52, 255, 256	5.6–6.12	242	9.13-14	245
		5.6-17	242	9.13	249
		5.8	231	9.14	249
		5.13-15	242	9.15	249
		5.16	242	10	22, 245, 283
		6.6-7	272		
1	206, 232, 236, 239, 244	6.7	240	10.2	245, 247, 249
		6.19-22	3, 95		
		6.20-21	243	10.7	181
1.1-4	235, 239, 250, 251	6.21	22, 89-91, 95, 103, 165, 240, 243, 244	10.8	90
				10.10	247, 249
1.3	234, 251			10.11	90, 245
1.5-6	235, 240	7–10	232, 235, 243-45, 248, 251, 255, 256	10.14	247
1.5	240			10.16	90
1.7-11	248			10.17	247
2	235, 239			10.18-19	245
2.2	244	7–9	250	10.18	247
2.9	191	7–8	245	10.30-31	4
2.59-63	230	7.6	244	10.44	6, 245, 246
2.64	240	7.9	243		
3–6	235	7.10	262	*Nehemiah*	
3	99	7.12-26	244	1–13	234
3.2	241	7.14	231, 244	1–7	232, 235, 238, 242, 249-51, 253-56
3.7	241	8.21-23	244		
3.8-13	240	8.24-29	244		
4–6	95	8.24	90		
4	242, 251, 252, 254	8.25-27	248	1	231, 254
		8.26-27	244	1.2	232, 249, 250
4.1-23	241	8.33-34	244		
4.1-4	6	9–10	244-50, 283	1.3	251
4.1	181, 240, 241			1.6	284
		9	90, 99, 190, 248, 249	2	252
4.2	250			2.1-9	251
4.3	241			2.10	252
4.4-23	242	9.1-4	4	2.17-18	252
4.4	14, 241	9.1-3	90, 97, 99	2.17	253
4.5	4	9.1-2	133, 187, 245, 247	2.19-20	4
4.8-9	241, 250			2.19	252
4.10	244	9.1	90, 245	3	248, 255
4.11-23	244	9.2	244, 245, 248	3.1-32	252
4.12	242			3.1	248
4.16	242	9.6-15	249	3.7	255
4.19-22	95	9.8	243, 249	3.33-35	252
		9.9	243, 249	3.34	253

3.35	252	13.4	253	7.4	224
3.38	252	13.6	237, 252	8	225
4.1-3	252	13.23-31	10, 14	8.5	222, 224
4.1-2	252, 254	13.23-27	246, 253	8.8-10	220
4.1	252, 253	13.25	6	8.8	222
4.2	254	13.28	246	8.11-13	225
4.6-7	254	13.38	253	8.17	32
4.6	252	23	247	9.1-19	225
4.7-8	252	27	247	9.1	32
4.7	252, 254			9.13	224
5	99	*Esther*		9.20-32	225
5.7	254	1.8	221	9.29-32	33
5.8-9	254	1.9	138	9.29	33
5.9	254	1.10	221	9.32	33
6.6	253	1.11-12	138	10.2-3	33
6.18-19	253	1.11	138, 221		
7	231, 232,	1.12	138	*Job*	
	235, 236,	1.13-22	221	2.7	288
	238-40,	1.13	221	2.9	45, 124
	256	1.16-18	139	14.21	57
7.6-72	235, 239	1.19	139, 224	16.6	288
7.32	191	1.22	220	16.20–17.2	288
7.61-65	230	2.3	140, 220	17.6-7	288
7.66	240	2.4	140	29.15	288
8–12	232, 235,	2.10	224	38–42	214
	236, 256	2.12	140	40.3-4	216
8–10	235	2.14	140		
8	98, 99,	2.15	224	*Psalms*	
	190, 236	2.19	129	1.3	48
8.2-3	284	2.20	224	3.9	46, 212
9–10	248	2.21-23	222	5.8	212
9	256	3	221, 224	7.2	51
9.1-37	14	3.8	32	7.4	51
9.2	89, 92	3.9	141, 224	8.2	51
10	235, 236,	3.13	220	8.10	51
	248, 256	4	223	14.7	46
10.28	14	4.11	224	18.29	51
10.29	89, 92	4.14	142	20.8	51
10.35	211	4.16	128, 142,	21.4	262
11–13	235		224	26.7	212
11.1	248			27.10	47
13	22, 90,	5.4-6	224	30.3	51
	234, 236,	5.4	224	30.4	212
	246, 247,	5.8	224	30.12	213
	256, 283	5.11-12	224	30.13	51
13.1-9	14	7.2-4	224	31.7	212
13.3	90, 92	7.3-4	142	31.15	51
		7.3	224		

Psalms (cont.)		80.2	48	107.26	212
31.23	212	80.8	48	109.26	51
33.12	45-48	81.8	49	110.3	46
35.24	51	81.9	46	111.6	46
36.11	45	81.11	51	111.9	46, 49, 69
37.34-35	92	81.12	46	113.5	51
37.35	92, 93	81.14	46	115.5	49
40.6	51	83.4	47	120.2	212
41.14	51	85.3	46	122.9	51
42.3	212	85.7	46	130.1	212
44.2	48	85.9	46	135.4	45, 46
44.11	56, 57	88.8	212	135.12	46
44.12	48	89	258	135.14	46
44.13	46	89.16	46	138.2	212
44.18-20	49	89.20	262	140.7	51
44.22	56, 57	89.29-30	261	140.8	51
50.7	46	89.29	261	142.4	212
50.14-23	212	89.30	262	143.4	212
52.2	25	89.38-39	264	144.15	46, 51
55.14	46	89.50-51	25	146.5	51
59.6	51	90.8	204	147.20	46
63.2	212	92.14	48	149.4	46
66.13	212	94.5	48		
68.6	47	94.14	48, 59	*Proverbs*	
68.8	46	94.23	51	2.16	153
68.9	51	95.7	46, 48	2.17	49
68.21	51	95.10	46	2.20-22	287
68.36	51	99.5	51	3.12	47
69.2	212	99.8-9	51	4	288
69.3	212	100.3	46, 48	4.11-12	287
69.7	51	103.7	49	4.12-19	288
69.15	212	103.13	47	4.12	288
71.2 LXX	265	104.1	51	4.13	288
72.2	46	105.1	68	4.14	288
72.17	68	105.7	51	4.16-19	288
72.18	51	106	258, 262	4.16	288
74.1	48, 56, 57	106.8	68	4.18	288
74.20	49	106.16-17	262	4.19	287, 288
76.12	212	106.16	262	4.20-21	288
77.21	48	106.22	262	4.22	288
78.52	48	106.23	262	5	137
78.59	52	106.30	262	5.3-4	137
78.67-70	53	106.40	46, 48	5.20	153
78.67	52	106.47	51	6.24	153
78.71	48	106.48	51	7.5-27	137
78.72	71	107.5	212	7.6	136
79.13	46, 48	107.23-29	211	15.13	287

18.15	287	19.1	205	50.1	47
22.17	287	19.16-25	205	51.4	46, 47
23.9	287	19.16	33, 66	51.14	46
23.12	287	19.24 LXX	66	51.15	51
23.19	287	19.25	48, 205	51.22	46
26.7	287	21.16-17	205	52.4-6	46
31	56	23.1-2	202	52.12	51
		23.6	202	53	280
Ecclesiastes		23.7-9	205	53.6	57
7.26	137	23.14-16	202	54.5-8	34
12.13	24	26.2	47	54.5-6	47
		26.15	47	54.6	52
Song of Songs		27.31-32	249	55.3	25
8.9-10	129	36.18	47	55.5	51
		37.12	47	56–66	165, 230
Isaiah		37.31-32	249	56	67, 161
1.2-3	47	40–66	238	56.1-7	165, 205,
1.4	47	40.11	48		230, 237
2.2-4	66	40.17	46	56.3-8	66
2.3-4	37	40.24	48	56.3-7	167
4.3	249	41.8-10	53, 69	56.3-6	66
4.20	249	41.8-9	45	56.3	38
5.2	48	41.9	52	56.6-7	67
5.7	48	41.13	47, 51	56.6	67
5.21	59	41.17	51	56.7	67, 165
5.24	59	42.6	49	57.14	46
6.3	248	42.13-15	33	58.1	46
6.10	45	43.1	47	58.2	47
9.2	47	43.3	51	60.3	40
10.6	47	43.4	47	60.9	51
10.20	249	43.15	51	60.22	47
13–23	201	43.20	45	60.65	47
13.3	302	43.21	46	61.6	36
13.8	33	44–45	206, 237	61.9	66
13.11	205	44.1-2	45	62.3-5	34
13.13-14	58	44.6	51	62.4-5	36
14.1-8	205	45.3	51	63.12	68
14.1	45, 63	45.4	45	63.16	47
14.11-17	205	45.5	30	63.17	48
14.12	63	45.11	47	64.8	47
14.14	204	45.22-23	66	64.9	46
14.16	204	46.3	47	65.10	56
14.25	205	47.4	66	65.19	46
16.6-14	205	47.6-9	66	65.22	46
17.7-8	205	47.6	48	66.8	47
17.12-14	205	48.1	51	66.18-19	205
17.13-14	66	48.17	51	66.21	67

Jeremiah				*Lamentations*	
1.5	215	31.31-34	56, 69	1.10	65
2.2	34, 47	31.31	63	1.22	204
2.11	47	31.32-33	63	5.22	52, 53
2.21	48	31.32	34, 47		
2.33	137	31.35-37	53, 69	*Ezekiel*	
3.4	47	31.36	47	2.3	47
3.6-13	47	31.37	52	3.23-27	291
3.14	47	31.40	58	3.24-27	290
3.17	66	32.23	28	5.15-17	291
3.19	47	32.36-41	69	5.15	290
5.9	47	32.36-37	64	5.17	290
5.29	47	32.38	64	6.12	290, 291
6	52	32.39	64	7.17	291
6.1-2	52	32.40	63, 64	8.14	129
6.8	52	32.41	48	11.13	291
6.19	52	33.17-26	265	11.25	291
6.30	52	33.23-26	53, 69	12.2	290
7.28	47	33.24	45, 47, 52	14.1-2	291
7.29	52, 53	33.26	52	16	137, 292
8.3	47	35.15	208	16.58-63	63, 64
9.8	47	36	208	16.59-63	63
9.17	53	38.7-13	36	17.8	48
11.17	48	39.9	28	17.10	48
12.2	48	40.2	28	19.10	48
12.7	59	40.5	64	19.12	58
12.14-15	58	40.11	252	19.13	48
13.20	58	42.10	48, 58	20.5	45
13.23	161	44–51	201	20.9	68
14.19	52, 53	45.4	48, 58	20.13	52
17.8	48	46.20-21	206	20.14	68
18.7-8	215	46.27-28	66	20.22	68
18.11	208	48.17	202, 206	20.33-44	63
23.1-6	57	48.27	204	20.39	45
23.33	54	49.20	57	21.7	291
23.39	54	50–51	202	21.31	262
24.6	48, 58	50.5	63, 69	22.30	262
25.5	208	50.11	66	23	47, 137
25.34-37	58	50.15	66	24.26-27	291
27.6	206	50.17-19	66	25–32	201
30.5-6	33	50.17	204	25.3-5	66
30.19	57	50.33-37	66	25.3	204
31.1-3	47	50.45	57	25.6	204
31.1	46	51.35-36	66	25.8	65, 204
31.9	47	51.49	66	25.12-14	66
31.14	213	52.12-27	28	25.12	204
31.28	58			25.15	204

26.1-4	66	2.23	56	4.2	51
26.2	204	2.25	54, 55	4.5	46, 51
27.3-25	206	3.1	47	4.11	212
28.2	204	3.5	51	5.3	51
28.24-25	66	4.6	46	6.8	51
29.6-9	66	4.8	46	7.8	46
29.16	66	4.12	46	8.1	51
30.21-22	291	5.3	45	8.2	46
31.3-9	206	7.10	51	8.3	51
32.16	202	8.1	49	8.9	51
33	291	8.2	45, 49	8.10	213
33.22	291	9.13	48	8.11	51
33.23-24	95, 181	9.16-17	59	9.7	65, 66, 69
33.24	98	9.17	52	9.14	46
33.27-28	95	11.1	47	9.15	48, 51, 58
34.1-34	58	11.3	47		
34.1-23	57	11.7	46	*Obadiah*	
34.4	292	12.9	51	1-2	51
34.30	51	13.4-5	55	9-10	66
36.20-23	68	13.4	49, 51	15	66
36.36	48	13.5	45		
37	290	13.12-13	47	*Jonah*	
37.22	47	14.1	47, 51	1.2	203, 207
38.22	292	14.4	47	1.3	209
40.4	290			1.8-12	210
47.22	92-95, 102	*Joel*		1.9	210
		1.13-14	51	1.12	210
Daniel		2.11-14	208	1.14	211
1–6	227	2.13-14	51	1.16	211
9.19	68	2.17-19	46	2.1	211
11.22	49	2.17	48	2.3-10	212
11.28	49	2.26-27	46, 51	2.3	212
11.30	49	2.27	51	2.4-6	212
39.7	68	4.2-3	46	2.4	212
		4.2	48	2.5	212
Hosea		4.16	46	2.6	212
1–2	55, 69			2.7	212
1.9	54	*Amos*		2.8	212
2.1-25a	55	1–2	201	2.9	212
2.1	54	1.6	204	2.10	212
2.16-25	34, 47	1.9	204	3.2-4	207
2.16-23	56	1.11	204	3.2	203
2.16	34	3.1-2	47	3.4	203, 212
2.17	55	3.1	46	3.5	208
2.19	34	3.2	45, 46	3.7	208
2.20	45	3.7-8	51	3.9	208
2.21	40	3.11	51	3.10–4.3	213

Jonah (cont.)

4.1-9	213
4.1	213
4.2-3	213
4.6-8	213
4.6	211, 213
4.7	211
4.8	211, 213
4.9	214
4.10	214
4.11	207, 214

Micah

1.9	46
2.3	47
2.8-9	46
2.12	48
3.3	46
3.5	46
3.11	51
4.1-5	66
4.1-3	205
4.5	51
4.6-8	3
4.9-10	33
5.6	66
7.10	51
7.14	46, 48
7.17	51
7.18	48

Habakkuk

1.12	51
3.13	46
3.19	51

Zephaniah

2.1	47
2.5-10	66
2.7	51
2.9-10	46
2.9	47, 51
2.15	209
3.1-2	209
3.15	51
3.17	51

Haggai

1.12	51
2.4	97
2.14	46, 47

Zechariah

1–8	289
1.4	289
2.8	207
2.11	65, 66, 69
2.14	51
2.15	217
4.10	289
6.5	289
6.8	217
6.25	51
7	289
7.2	191
7.5	97
7.7-13	289
7.9-14	289
8.7-8	46
8.9	289
8.13	3
8.20-22	217
8.22-23	66
9.9	36
9.11-16	63
9.11	49
9.14	51
9.16	51
10.6	51
11.4	51
11.10	65, 66, 69
11.17	57
12.1-9	3
13.7	56
13.9	46, 51
14.5	51
14.16-19	66

Malachi

1.6–2.17	67
1.11	68
1.14	68
2.10	47
2.16	51

3.1	49
3.9	47
3.17	46, 47
3.22	49

APOCRYPHA/DEUTERO-
CANONICAL BOOKS

1 Esdras

1.26	29
2.8	271
9.36	245

Tobit

| 11.16 | 129 |

Judith

| 8.33 | 129 |
| 13.6-11 | 131 |

Ecclesiasticus

7.6	262
7.29	262
7.31	262
8.2	262
8.4	262
11.1	262
13.9	262
20.27	262
38.3	262
44–50	259
44.1	259
44.10	259
44.18	260
44.23	260
45	258
45.4	262
45.5	263
45.6-7	265
45.6	262, 263
45.7	260, 262, 266
45.12-15	262
45.13	265
45.15	260, 262
45.16-25	263
45.16	265, 266

45.17	262, 263, 265	*1 Maccabees*		PSEUDEPIGRAPHA		
		1.15	267, 268	*Jubilees*		
45.18-19	262, 263	1.15 LXX	267	31.11-20	263	
45.18	263, 265	1.30	267	45.16	263	
45.19	261	1.43	267			
45.21-22	261	1.63	267	*T. Levi*		
45.23-26	265	1.64	267	2	263	
45.23-25	259, 264	2.24-27	266	4	263	
45.23-24	266	2.24	266	5	263	
45.23	261, 262, 265	2.54	266-68	8–9	263	
		2.65	267, 268			
45.24	260-62, 265, 270, 271	2.66	268	QUMRAN AND RELATED		
		3.8	267	*1QM*		
		5.62	268	7.3-8	309-11	
45.25-26	259	7.14	269, 273	7.3	310	
45.25	260, 261, 263, 265	9.30	268	7.4	311	
		10.20	268	7.5	311	
45.26	265	10.65	268	7.6	310	
46.7	259	13.6	268	33 14.4	49	
46.13	262	13.41	268			
47.11	260, 262	13.42	268	*1QS*		
49.3	259	14	268	3.23-24	301	
50	190, 264, 265, 269-71	14.20	268	5.11	49	
		14.41	268	5.18	49	
		14.47	268, 270, 271, 274	*1QSa*		
50.1	262, 265			1.1-5	299	
50.4	266	15.1	268	1.6–2.11	299	
50.5-20	264	15.2	268	1.25–2.11	299	
50.5	266	15.21	268	1.25-27	300	
50.6-7	264	45.24 LXX	268	2.3-9	300, 304	
50.9	266			2.5-7	302	
50.12	262	*2 Maccabees*		2.8-11	301	
50.14	266	3.4	271, 273	2.8-9	302	
50.16	262	3.10	273	2.9-11	300, 302, 306	
50.17	266	4.7	273			
50.19	266	4.23-24	273	2.9-10	316	
50.22-24	264	5.22	273	2.11-22	299	
50.22-23	259	6.10	129			
50.22	266	14.3	273	*4Q266*		
50.23	265	14.7	273	f. 5ii1-4	314	
50.24	259, 261, 262, 265, 266, 275, 276	NEW TESTAMENT		*4Q267*		
		Romans		f. 5iii.1-6	314	
		1.26	124			
50.25-26	266					
51.12	264					

4Q273

f. 2.1-2	314
f. 4i2	314
f. 4i5-11	314

4Q491

fl-3.6-10	311

4QMMT

B 49-54	313
B 50-51	313
B 54	313

11QTa

35.2-9	308
45.7-10	307
45.11-12	307
45.12-14	307, 308
45.15-17	307
45.17-18	307
45.17	307

ALD (Aramaic Levi Document)

11.5-6	263

CD

6.21	306
13.6	304
14.12-17	306, 316
14.14-16	304
15.5–16.6	304-306
15.5-15	305
15.5	304
15.15-17	304-306, 314
15.17	304
16.2-6	304

TALMUDS

y. Sukkah

5.1	28
22b	28

MIDRASH

Genesis Rabbah

98.11	28

Ruth Rabbah

1.5	172
2.9	170

Seder Elihu Rabba

18 siman 19	28

JOSEPHUS

Antiquities

11.111	271
12.161	272
12.167	272
12.219	273, 274
12.237	273
12.239	273
12.285	274
12.385	273
12.414	273
13.201	274
13.212	274
14.196	274
14.434	273
20.158	274
20.237	273
20.238	274
20.244	274
20.251	274
8.318	28
8.320	28
8.324	28
8.371	28

INDEX OF AUTHORS

Abrams, J.Z. 277
Achenbach, R. 22, 260, 263, 271, 276
Aharoni, Y. 191
Albertz, R. 22, 23, 90, 187, 276
Alster, B. 23
Alter, R. 171
Anderson, B. 77, 188, 189
Anderson, F.I. 55
Aschkenasy, N. 177, 180
Ashcroft, B. 182
Austin, J.L. 150
Avalos, H. 277, 282, 284

Bach, A. 110, 111, 125
Baden, J. 279
Bae, H.-S. 183
Bakhtin, M.M. 177
Bal, M. 8, 13, 168, 175
Barbour, J. 30
Bardtke, H. 226
Barrera, J.T. 303
Barrick, W.B. 192, 193
Barth, F. 123, 147, 233
Barthèlemy, D. 298, 309
Bauks, M. 100
Baumann, G. 21, 34, 38, 233
Baumgarten, J.M. 314, 315
Beauvoir, S. de 125, 126, 139, 140
Beckman, G. 62
Beentjes, P.C. 259-61, 263
Begg, C.T. 263
Bellis, A.O. 125
Ben Zvi, E. 26, 27, 29, 35-37, 39, 41, 47,
    71, 133, 145, 163, 183, 189, 201, 207, 209,
    215, 217, 225, 231, 233
Bendor, S. 157
Berge, K. 21, 74, 75, 82
Berjelung, A. 270, 274
Berlin, A. 31, 220, 221
Berlinerblau, J. 5
Berquist, J.L. 231, 232
Berthelot, K. 313
Bhabha, H.K. 22, 126

Blenkinsopp, J. 17, 67
Bloch-Smith, E. 97, 193, 194
Boccaccini, G. 264
Bolin, T. 207, 208
Bolin, T.M. 44
Borger, R. 61, 210
Bourdieu, P. 11
Braudel, F. 185
Brenner, A. 8, 11, 12, 17, 145, 157
Brett, M.G. 99, 101, 103, 104
Brueggemann, B.J. 277
Brutti, M. 269
Bultmann, C. 93, 94, 96
Burns, L. 11, 12, 14
Burroughs, W.J. 146, 150
Bush, F.W. 146, 155, 225
Butting, K. 157
Byrne, R. 185

Calhoun, C. 79, 81, 82
Camp, C.V. 107, 108, 114, 125, 267
Carr, D.M. 44, 257
Carruthers, J. 225
Cataldo, J.W. 3, 6, 13
Cazelles, H. 94
Certeau, M. de 132, 142
Cha, J.-H. 42
Chandra, U. 1, 2
Chapman, C.R. 33
Chapman, S. 90
Charlesworth, J.H. 298
Christian, M.A. 23
Clark, G.R. 155
Clifford, J. 79, 80
Clines, D.J.A. 227
Cody, A. 83
Cohen, A. 57
Cohen, M.E. 61
Cohen, S.J.D. 232, 236, 256
Cohn, R.L. 26, 72, 74, 75, 133, 145, 171
Colebrook, C. 3-5, 7
Coleman, J.A. 7
Conczorowski, B.J. 99, 247

Cook, S.L. 50
Cooper, A. 90
Corley, J. 259
Cornell, S.E. 147
Cover, R. 87, 88
Crawford, S.W. 307
Cross, F.M. 56
Crüsemann, F. 89, 96, 194
Cruse, A. 90

d'Alfonzo, L. 62
Davidson, M.J. 304
Davies, P.R. 44, 61
Davis, L.J. 277, 278
Day, L.M. 222, 227
Deissler, A. 45
Delcor, M. 45
Deleuze, G. 4-8
DiLella, A.A. 264
Dijk-Hemmes, F. van 157
Dimant, D. 301
Dion, P.E. 62
Donaldson, L.E. 145, 160
Dor, Y. 234
Dorman, J. 299, 302-305, 307, 309-13
Douglas, M. 135
Duhaime, J. 309
Dumbrell, W. 49
Dyck, J.E. 237, 238, 249, 251, 254

Edelman, D. 40, 91, 187, 188, 190, 191,
    205, 231, 272
Ego, B. 86, 87
Eriksen, T.H. 102
Eskenazi, T.C. 179, 234, 235, 239, 240, 243,
    247
Exum, J.C. 165
Eynikel, E. 186

Fabian, J. 197
Fabry, H.-J. 258, 260, 264, 265, 270, 275
Faust, A. 187, 231
Fensham, F.C. 47
Ferna'ndez, M.P. 312
Fewell, D.N. 2
Finkelstein, I. 96, 191
Finsterbusch, K. 74
Fiorenza, E. 125
Fisch, H. 174, 175
Fischer, C. 204

Fischer, I. 157, 169-71
Fischer, M.M.J. 78
Fishane, M. 175
Fleishman, J. 222
Foreman, D.M. 44
Forkman, G. 303
Forty, A. 195, 196
Foucault, M. 8, 9
Fox, M.V. 220, 222
Fraade, S.D. 312
Frankena, R. 62
Freedman, D.N. 55
Frei, P. 237
Frevel, C. 99, 247
Fried, L. 98
Frymer-Kensky, T. 111, 179, 246
Fuchs, E. 2, 6
Funke, T. 257, 267, 275, 276

García Martínez, F. 297, 303, 306, 312
Garland-Thompson, R. 277, 278
Geertz, C. 146
Gennep, A. van 178
Gera, D. 272
Gerhards, M. 201, 207, 208, 210, 211, 215,
    216
Gerleman, G. 144
Gerstenberger, E.S. 161
Giddens, A. 76
Gillmayr-Bucher, S. 39, 66, 209
Gilman, S. 74
Glover, N. 89, 145, 161, 233
Glueck, N. 154, 155
Goff, J. le 195
Goff, m. 266
Goldstein, B. 90, 269
Goldstein, J.A. 266
Goody, J. 86
Goshen-Gottstein, A. 264
Grabbe, L.L. 186, 270-72, 283, 296
Grad, H. 20
Green, B. 216
Greenberg, M. 290, 291
Grelot, P. 94
Griffiths, G. 182
Groot, C. de 10
Grosby, S. 78
Grossmann, M.L. 312
Gruen, E.S. 200, 219
Guattari, F. 4, 7, 8

Guillaume, P. 100, 101
Gullestad, M. 70

Haarmann, V. 211
Habel, N. 97
Haberman, B.D. 111
Hall, S. 164, 230
Hallo, W.W. 23, 24
Hamborg, G.R. 205
Hamidović, D. 303
Handelman, S. 2, 18, 19
Hardmeier, C. 186
Harlow, D.C. 74
Harrington, H.K. 297
Harris, D. 41
Hartmann, D. 147
Hayes, C.E. 245
Hayward, R.C.T. 262, 270
Hempel, C. 299, 303, 304, 312
Hendel, R. 181
Hengel, M. 261, 271-74
Henten, J.W. van 76
Hentschel, G. 205
Herzog, Z. 190
Hillers, D.R. 47
Hjelm, I. 269, 270
Höffken, P. 263
Hobsbawm, E. 184
Hofstede, G. 42
Honig, B. 176
Hooker, P.K. 29
Horst, P. W. van der 266
Hossfeld, F.-L. 217
Houten, C. van 23, 95
Houtepen, A. 76
Huang, Y. 90
Huffmon, H. 46
Huggan, G. 12
Hutchinson, J. 146, 148
Hyman, T.E. 255

Ikas, K. 22
Isherwood, L. 41

James, P. 77, 83-86
Japhet, S. 92, 285
Jobes, K.H. 227
Jonker, L.C. 183
Joosten, J. 93, 98, 102, 103

Kahana, H. 227
Kaiser, B.M. 11, 12, 14
Kalluveettil, P. 48
Kalmanofsky, A. 108
Kampen, J. 312
Kapera, Z.J. 311
Kartveit, M. 266
Keck, L.E. 17
Keel, O. 192, 267, 269, 270, 272, 273
Kegler, J. 202
Kennedy, E.R. 159
Kessler, J. 95
Kessler, R. 217
Kidd, J.E. 103
Klein, M. 12-14
Klein, R.W. 29, 285, 286
Knohl, I. 96
Knoppers, G.N. 102, 233, 250-53, 263
Köckert, M. 100
Koch, C. 62
Koenen, K. 191
Koltun-Fromm, N. 247, 248
Kooij, A. van der 260, 261
Koole, J.L. 67
Korpel, M.C.A. 145
Kratz, R.G. 72
Krupp, M. 274
Kugel, J.L. 263, 264
Kugler, R.A. 264
Kvam, K.E. 125

LaCocque, A. 32, 219
Labahn, A. 275
Lang, B. 49
Lange, A. 217
Lapsley, J.E. 125
Lévi-Strauss, C. 174
Lévinas, E. 18, 19, 124, 131
Lee, E. 166, 168
Lefebvre, J.-F. 103
Lemos, T.M. 24, 33
Leveen, A. 105, 108, 112, 114-16, 119-21
Levenson, J. 31, 220, 221
Levin, C. 210
Levine, E. 166
Levinson, B.M. 62, 180
Levinson, S.C. 90
Limburg, J. 45
Lipschits, O. 184, 190, 191, 194
Luckenbill, D.D. 58, 59

Luther, M. 226
Lux, R. 213, 216, 217
Lyke, L.L. 172, 173

Macchi, J.-D. 31, 219, 220, 223, 227
Machinist, P. 73
Macintosh, A.A. 55
Magen, Y. 275
Maier, J. 307
Malul, M. 46
Marböck, J. 259, 260, 265, 270
Marx, T.C. 277
Mathys, H.-P. 220
Mayes, A.D.H. 49
Mays, J.L. 56
Mayshar, J. 103
McCarthy, D.J. 48
McConville, J.G. 73, 94
McKinlay, J.E. 145
Melcher, S.J. 277
Meyer, I. 217
Meyers, C. 7, 57, 157, 158
Meyers, E.C. 57
Middendorp, T. 272-74
Miedema, S. 255
Milgrom, J. 23, 25, 96, 98, 103, 108, 112,
    245, 281
Milik, J.T. 56, 298, 303, 309
Millar, J.G. 73
Miller, G.D. 257
Mills, C.W. 9
Misgav, H. 275
Mitchell, C. 29
Mitchell, D.T. 278
Mitchell, H.G. 57
Mittmann-Richert, U. 269
Moore, S. 8
Moran, W.L. 47
Morrow, W.S. 62
Moss, C.R. 277
Müllner, I. 210
Mulder, O. 258, 261-65, 273

Na'aman, N. 184, 191
Newsom, C. 204
Newsom, C.A. 125, 206, 216
Newton, M. 303
Nicholson, E. 185
Nicholson, E.W. 49
Niditch, S. 34, 198

Nihan, C. 91, 93, 96, 97, 99, 103, 276
Nodet, E. 270

O'Connor, K.M. 219
Olyan, S. 91, 196, 199, 244, 245, 261-63,
    274, 277, 279-82, 286, 293, 313
Otto, E. 62, 84
Ozick, C. 176

Pakkala, J. 91, 99, 183-86, 234
Pardes, I. 125
Perdue, L.G. 199
Person, R. 57
Plaskow, J. 123, 125
Polaski, D. 255
Pomykala, K.E. 258, 260-62, 264, 265, 267,
    274
Popović, M. 297, 301
Priest, J. 261
Prinsloo, G.T. 212
Pruin, D. 28
Puech, E. 312

Qimron, E. 311

Raabe, P. 205
Radner, K. 62
Raphael, R. 277-82, 285, 288, 290, 293, 297
Rashkow, I.N. 153
Reiterer, F.V. 260, 262-65
Renan, E. 77
Rendtorff, R. 49, 92
Ringe, S.H. 125
Rojo, L.M. 20
Rooke, D.W. 269, 272
Rosenberg, S. G. 274
Rost, L. 190
Roth, M. 208, 210, 211, 213, 216
Routledge, B.E. 78
Rüterswörten, U. 62
Rudolph, W. 45

Sæbø, M. 57
Said, E. 1, 76, 140
Sakenfeld, K.D. 155
Salters, R.B. 49
Samuel, H. 263, 276
Sasson, J.M. 166
Sauer, G. 270
Saysell, C. 246, 248

Schäfer, P. 32
Schaper, J. 269, 270, 275
Schart, A. 217
Schearing, L.S. 125
Scheff, T. 77
Schenker, A. 188
Schiffman, L.H. 298, 304
Schipper, J. 277, 279, 280, 286, 288, 294
Schmid, K. 97, 287, 296
Schmidt, B.B. 193, 196
Schmitt, C. 237
Schreiner, J. 264
Schubert, F. 275
Schunck, K.-D. 267, 270, 271, 273
Schwartz, B.J. 101
Schwartz, D.R. 268
Schwartz, R.M. 24, 127, 141
Sedgwick, E.K. 8
Seltzer, L.F. 44
Shakespeare, T. 279
Sharp, C.J. 219
Sievers, J. 266, 267
Silberstein, L.J. 73-76
Simon, M. 10
Singer-Avitz, L. 191
Sinha, D. 43
Sinha, J.B.P. 43
Skehan, P.W. 264
Smelik, K.A.D. 28
Smith, A.D. 76, 146, 148, 198, 199
Smith, D.L. 187
Smith, J.Z. 141, 164
Snyder, S.L. 277, 278
Sommer, B.D. 296
Southwood, K. 102
Sparks, K.L. 72, 73, 75, 82, 167
Speiser, E.A. 83
Spickard, P. 146, 150
Spina, F.A. 151
Stadelmann, H. 258, 260, 261, 265, 275
Stavrakopoulou, F. 159
Steenkamp, Y. 212
Stegemann, H. 299
Stern, E. 193
Steudel, A. 299
Steymans, H.U. 62
Stordalen, T. 49, 52, 185, 198
Strawn, B.A. 211
Strugnell, J. 311
Stuart, D. 45

Stuckenbruck, L.T. 298
Sugirtharajah, R.S. 2, 10, 133

Tan, N. 27
Tappy, R. 191
Taylor, C. 189
Taylor, S. 80
Tcherikover, V. 271
Tiffin, H. 182
Tigchelaar, E.J.C. 298, 306
Touraine, A. 1, 11, 14
Tov, E. 186
Triandis, H.C. 42, 43
Tripathi, R.C. 43
Tsfania, L. 275
Turner, V. 178

Uehlinger, C. 185

Valkama, K. 190, 193, 194, 196
VanderKam, J.C. 270
Vialle, C. 227
Vink, J.G. 94
Volf, M. 18

Wagner, G. 22, 193
Wagner, V. 190
Wahl, H.-M. 220
Walsh, C. 26, 145, 163
Walzer, M. 234
Wardekker, W.L. 255
Washington, H. 8
Wassen, C. 301, 303-305, 310
Watts, J.D.W. 67
Wénin, A. 222
Weeks, G.R. 44
Weeks, N. 48, 60
Weimar, P. 201, 208, 209
Weinfeld, M. 61
Weissenberg, H. Von 312
Wells, R.D. 67
Westermann, C. 67
Wetter, A.-M. 26, 133, 162, 163
Whybray, R.N. 67
Willi, T. 148
Williamson, H.G.M. 91
Wills, L.M. 122, 126, 141, 233-35, 237, 240, 243, 245
Wilson, I.D. 185
Wiseman, D.J. 61

Witte, M. 62
Wöhrle, J. 22, 23, 91, 97
Wodak, R. 149
Wright, B.G. 259-61, 264, 274
Wright, D.P. 246, 253
Wright, J. 91
Wright, J.L. 234

Yadin, Y. 307, 309

Zehnder, M. 70, 72, 75
Zelkowicz, T.H. 255
Ziegler, V.H. 125
Žižzek, S. 1, 15-17
Zornberg, A. 167
Zvi, R. 170

CPSIA information can be obtained
at www.ICGtesting.com
Printed in the USA
FFOW01n1515140316
22332FF

9 780567 667526